Professional DotNetNuke™ ASP.NET Portals

Shaun Walker, Patrick J. Santry, Joe Brinkman, Daniel Caron,
Scott McCulloch, Scott Willhite, and Bruce Hopkins

WILEY

Wiley Publishing, Inc.

Professional DotNetNuke™ ASP.NET Portals

Published by
Wiley Publishing, Inc.
10475 Crosspoint Boulevard
Indianapolis, IN 46256
www.wiley.com

Published by Wiley Publishing, Inc., Indianapolis, Indiana

Published simultaneously in Canada

ISBN 13: 978-0-7645-9563-9
ISBN 10: 0-7645-9563-6

Manufactured in the United States of America

10 9 8 7 6 5 4 3 2

1B/SV/QV/QV/IN

Library of Congress Cataloging-in-Publication Data:

Professional DotNetNuke ASP.Net portals / Shaun Walker ... [et al.].
    p. cm.
  Includes index.
  ISBN 0-7645-9563-6 (paper/website)
  1. Active server pages. 2. Web portals—Design. 3. Microsoft
.NET.   I. Walker, Shaun, 1971- .
  TK5105.8885.A26P78953 2005
  005.2'76—dc22

                        2005006846

For general information on our other products and services please contact our Customer Care Department within the United States at (800) 762-2974, outside the United States at (317) 572-3993 or fax (317) 572-4002.

Credits

Acquisitions Editor
Jim Minatel

Development Editor
Kenyon Brown

Technical Editor
Bruce Hopkins

Production Editor
Angela Smith

Copy Editor
Kim Cofer

Editorial Manager
Mary Beth Wakefield

Vice President & Executive Group Publisher
Richard Swadley

Vice President and Publisher
Joseph B. Wikert

Graphics and Production Specialists
Karl Brandt
Carrie A. Foster

Quality Control Technician
David Faust

Permissions Editor
Laura Moss

Proofreading and Indexing
TECHBOOKS Production Services

About the Authors

Shaun Walker is founder and president of Perpetual Motion Interactive Systems Inc., a solutions company specializing in Microsoft enterprise technologies. Shaun has 15 years professional experience in architecting and implementing large scale IT solutions for private and public organizations. Shaun is responsible for the creation and management of DotNetNuke, an open source content management system written for the Microsoft ASP.NET platform. Based on his significant community contributions he was recently recognized as a Microsoft Most Valuable Professional (MVP) in 2004. In addition, he was recently added as a featured speaker to the MSDN Canada Speakers Bureau, which allows him to evangelize DotNetNuke to User Groups across Canada. Shaun resides in British Columbia, Canada with his wife and two children.

Patrick Santry, Microsoft MVP (ASP/ASP.NET) holds MCSE, MCSA, MCP+SB, i-Net+, A+, and Certified Internet Webmaster certifications. He has authored and co-authored several books and magazine articles on Microsoft and Internet technologies. Patrick is frequent presenter on web technologies, having presented at several events including the Exchange 2000 launch, DevDays 2004 in Pittsburgh, Pennsylvania, and to area .NET SIGs on DotNetNuke module development. In addition, Patrick owns and maintains `http://www.WWWCoder.com`, a popular site for news, tutorials, and information for the web development community. Patrick resides in Girard, Pennsylvania, USA with his wife Karyn, and their four children, Katie, Karleigh, P.J., and Danny.

Joe Brinkman, formerly the founder and President of TAG Software Inc, is the Chief Technology Officer for DataSource Inc. (`http://www.datasourceinc.com`), a J2EE development company focused on simplifying and automating development of N-Tier applications with Java. With more than 22 years of IT experience and a Computer Science degree from the United States Naval Academy, he brings a broad range of experience and expertise in a variety of software and hardware architectures. Having worked with DotNetNuke since February 2003, and a founding Core Team member, Joe currently serves as a member of the DotNetNuke Board of Directors, a Lead Architect and Security Specialist.

Dan Caron is a Lead Application Designer & Developer with MassMutual Financial Group, a Fortune 500 global, diversified financial services organization. With MassMutual, Dan designs technical solutions for financial web applications using Microsoft and Java technologies. For more than 10 years, Dan has been designing and developing applications with various programming technologies including Microsoft ASP.NET, XML/XSL, SQL, Java, and JSP. He has been a major contributor to the DotNetNuke open-source portal project since the Core Team was founded in 2003. Some of Dan's noteworthy contributions include the exception handling framework, event Logging Provider and the Scheduler. Dan continues to contribute his talent to the project as a Lead Architect, Core Developer, and member of the Board of Directors. Dan lives in Connecticut, USA with his wife and two children.

Scott McCulloch works as an Application Developer for the Computer Science Corporation, Australia. At 26 years of age, Scott holds a Bachelor and Masters Degree in Computer Science, as well as the three major Microsoft Certifications (MCSD, MCDBA, MCSE). Scott has been part of the DotNetNuke community since the project began (late December, 2002). Today, his role within the DotNetNuke team is contributing as an Architect and Core Developer. He currently resides in Wollongong, Australia with his fiancée, Lenise.

Scott Willhite is an accomplished business and technology professional turned family man. He happily spends his days working closely with his wife on their personal and community oriented business pursuits. Scott's technology pedigree is distinguished, including Bachelor of Science in Computer Science and MBA in Information Systems Management degrees from Baylor University. Scott has worked as Senior Manager and Technical Architect for Andersen Consulting (now Accenture), Associate Director for EnForm Ventures, acting CTO and VP of Technology for 10x Labs, and Program Director for Safeco's Office of the CIO. He's architected, developed, and managed systems built on technologies ranging from COBOL to Java and .NET, solving all kinds of real-world business problems without a certification of any kind. Ever the "Don Quixote" type, Scott's currently tilting at the windmills of open-source and committed to building DotNetNuke (both the software and the community) into something truly extraordinary. His favorite mantra is the core values developed with his partners for their former startup company, 10x Labs: "Speak the truth. Share the wealth. Change the world!" Scott currently lives in West Seattle with his lovely wife Allison, his young son Kyle, a whiny German Shepherd dog, two very weird house cats, and a cast of wonderful friends and neighbors that he wouldn't trade for gold.

Bruce Hopkins, Microsoft MVP (ASP.NET), holds a BSCIS from DeVry University and holds certifications as an MCSE and several flavors of Linux. Bruce is currently the IT Director for Chattahoochee Technical College in Marietta, Georgia and has held a wide variety of positions in technology throughout his career ranging from programming and web design to network administration and management. Bruce remarks that this varied experience is crucial to determining the correct tool for the task at hand. This is shown by the many varied technologies he uses every day. These include Windows, Unix, SQL Server, Oracle, MySQL, and many different Linux-based applications that are an integral part of maintaining the college's infrastructure. Bruce makes his home in Marietta, Georgia with his wife and son.

Contents

Contents

Contents

Contents

Contents

Contents

Preface

This book is aimed at people with development knowledge and for those who are just interested in learning more about how DotNetNuke works.

Who This Book Is For

Experienced developers of ASP.NET and those who are knowledgeable about DotNetNuke may want to skip Chapters 1–6. These chapters provide an overview of DotNetNuke and its operations. Chapters 7–14 get right into DotNetNuke architecture and development. However, we think you'll gain valuable insight into how DotNetNuke works by reading the entire book from front to back.

What This Book Covers

We split this book into two primary sections. The first half provides you with insight into how to perform an installation and the basic operations of a DotNetNuke portal. In addition, you'll gain insight into the history of this open source project brought to you by the individuals who developed it from its beginnings.

The second half of the book provides you with information on how the application is architected, as well as how you can extend it by developing modules and skins.

How This Book Is Structured

This book is broken down into two parts: The first part is aimed at the non-developer or administrator type. We provide you with a history of the project, move on to installing DotNetNuke on the server, and then show how to manage and administer a DotNetNuke portal.

The second part is for developers. Starting with Chapter 7, we discuss the DotNetNuke application architecture and how the application works. We then move on to extending the portal framework by developing modules that plug into a DotNetNuke portal. Finally, we cover the flexible skinning capabilities of DotNetNuke and how you can create your own unique look for your portal.

What You Need to Use This Book

In order to install DotNetNuke and a supporting database you will need either Windows 2003 Server or Windows XP (development only). This book covers a basic install of DotNetNuke using a SQL Server database as the Data Provider. You will need to have access to either SQL Server 2000 or MSDE (development only) on the same machine or a remote machine.

To participate in the development chapters, you will need Visual Studio .NET 2003.

Contributors

In addition to the authors, the DotNetNuke development team is comprised of many individuals working together from around the world. We would like to acknowledge these people and their contribution in this section of the book. We've listed the DotNetNuke contributors and their role within the community.

Board of Directors

The Board of Directors is responsible for managing the long-term strategic vision of the project. They are

Dan Caron, see *About the Authors*.

Joe Brinkman, see *About the Authors*.

Patrick Santry, see *About the Authors*.

Scott Willhite, see *About the Authors*.

Shaun Walker, see *About the Authors*.

Core Team

The Core Team is divided into two levels of participation — an Inner Team and an Outer Team. The two levels represent different levels of trust and responsibility within the DotNetNuke organization.

Inner Core Team

Comprised of individuals who have demonstrated their long-term commitment to the project. They have acted professionally, accepted responsibility, delivered assigned tasks successfully, and are actively engaged with the community. They act as Managers in key functional areas and manage communication with sub-teams of Outer Team members.

Bruce Hopkins, see *About the Authors*.

Charles Nurse has been developing for the World Wide Web using Microsoft Technologies since 1996. While now a Canadian citizen, Charles was born in the UK and has a Bachelor of Arts in Chemistry from Oxford University. In 1978 he moved to Canada and obtained a Ph.D in Chemistry from the University of British Columbia. During his undergraduate and graduate studies he became interested in computer programming and helped develop a molecular modeling application using Fortran, as well as a number of smaller projects in Algol 60. After spending more than 15 years in Chemistry Research and in Scientific Instrumentation Sales, he started his own contract software development business — KeyDance Computer Services. He lives in Langley, BC, Canada with his wife Eileen and two teenage children.

Christopher Paterra is a member of the Bugs & Enhancements Specialist, Core Developer & Lead Release Manager Core Team roles. Chris has had involvement in many areas of DotNetNuke and his more well known enhancement includes the Enhanced Survey to use Personalization for vote tracking and added ability to keep results private. Chris has written several procedure documents for the Core Team and helped organize and manage the skinning contest. Former NT MCSE and now studying MSCAD, Chris has VB.NET, C#, Microsoft SQL Server 2000, C, C++, VB 6 experience.

Chris has implemented DNN with custom modules for use in a school as their lunch inventory/cash control system using swipe card technology. He has also implemented DotNetNuke it in a Call Center with custom modules as its intranet. Another exciting project was one of the first releases of the power of DotNetNuke skinning with the launch of a web site promoting Christina Aguilera.

Dan Caron, see *About the Authors*.

Joe Brinkman, see *About the Authors*.

Patrick Santry, see *About the Authors*.

Philip Beadle (MCAD, MVP) of Byte Information Technology in 2004 (www.byte.com.au). Philip is a foundation member of the DotNetNuke Core Team, a Microsoft Certified Application Developer and is experienced in the development and commercial application of the DotNetNuke Framework based on Microsoft's .NET technology. He has successfully developed and implemented sites for clients in Australia and overseas and was recently awarded the Microsoft Most Valuable Professional (MVP) award in ASP/ASP.NET.

Scott McCulloch, see *About the Authors*.

Scott Willhite, see *About the Authors*.

Shane Colley is a founding DotNetNuke Core Team member who serves the DNN community as an Inner Core Team member, Core Developer, and Security Specialist. Shane's contributions to DNN include development of the Provider Model for rich text editing and multiple security enhancements. He is also active in the DNN forums, providing help and interaction with the community.

Shane is a graduate of Computer Science at Iowa State University and over his nine-year career as an IT professional he has honed his expertise with a wide variety of programming languages, with specific emphasis on web-based .NET development. Shane lives in Chicagoland with his girlfriend Erin and dog Monk.

Shaun Walker, see *About the Authors*.

Vicenç Masanas works as a Developer and Analyst at the Universitat de Girona, Spain. He has been developing web sites with Microsoft technologies, including ASP, VB, ASP.NET, Access, and SQL Server, since 1998. Vicenç joined the DotNetNuke community in summer 2003 coming from IBS portal. Today, his role within the DotNetNuke team is contributing as a Core Developer, Bugs & Enhancement Specialist, and DotNetNuke Evangelist for the Spanish area. Currently, Vicenç is working on a number of projects based on the DotNetNuke platform. Specializing on this platform as a framework for future works, Vicenç has also written VS.NET tools and tutorials for DNN developers, which have been highly acclaimed (available at `http://dnnjungle.vmasanas.net`). He provides online support and training for DotNetNuke and custom module development and consultancy for DotNetNuke projects.

Geert Veenstra, a member of the DotNetNuke Inner Core team, is currently working for Schmit (`http://www.schmit.nl`), a company that specializes in Parking solutions as a technical support specialist. In his daily job he works with a multitude of operating systems (both Windows and Unix variants) and databases (such as Oracle, SQL, and MySql Server). He has created the company's intranet and a customer bug-reporting web site (now both using DotNetNuke of course). He joined the DotNetNuke team in mid 2003 and has been working mainly on Localization and Bug Fixing. The first third-party dotnetnuke dataprovider (for MySql) was created by him as well as a DNN installer.

Jeremy White is founder and president of Webstone Technologies, LLC, and a Founding member of the DNN Core Team. He holds a MCSE, MCP+I, and MCT certifications and has many years of experience in programming, networking, WiFi, VoIP, and CMS technology implementations for a multinational company. Jeremy has been actively involved in designing and developing web solutions with various Microsoft Internet technologies including ASP and ASP.NET. He is the author of the popular "Shadow" module for DNN 1.x and 2.x and has been a frequent DNN forums contributor since February 2003. Jeremy resides on Long Island, New York, with his wife and two dogs.

Outer Core Team

The Outer Core Team is comprised of individuals who have achieved recognition within the DotNetNuke community — sometimes based on technical prowess but most often based upon their unselfish actions assisting other community members. Outer Team members work closely with Inner Team members to help manage various aspects of the project. Once an Outer Team member gains a unanimous vote of respect and trust in the DotNetNuke Core, they will be offered a promotion to the Inner Team.

Bert Corderman is a Senior Database administrator for Symantec's Managed Security Services. Bert is relatively new to programming but has more than seven years of experience in technology. He holds the following certifications: MCSE + Internet (NT 4.0), MCSE(2000), MCDBA, CCNA, and CCDA. He has been involved with the DotNetNuke open-source portal project since May of 2003. He is currently active in the following: Quality Assurance Testers, Bugs & Enhancement Specialists, and Database Developers.

Bo Nørgaard holds a Bachelor degree in Electronic Engineering, is a certified Psion developer and engineer, and is a certified Internet Security Systems security engineer. Bo Nørgaard has been programming since 1979 and been through Comal 80, Pascal, ANSI C, ADA, PLM, ASM (Intel), OO Pascal, Delphi, C++, Perl, PHP, Visual Basic, Java, and now C#. He started teaching in 1991 at the Copenhagen University College of Engineering, and later at the National Theatre School of Denmark. Bo has presented at several events including detailed security practices at CA-World in New Orleans. Bo Nørgaard is CEO of Bonosoft and operates the DotNetNuke developer community site (`www.dotnetnuke.dk`), which has numerous resources for both Visual Basic and Visual C# programmers writing plug-in modules for DotNetNuke.

Bryan Andrews has been developing web applications since Netscape 1.0 and has worked in many different capacities in the past 10 years from infrastructure architecture and management, to the development of collaborative and knowledge management tools. He is one of the Founders and CTO of an Atlanta headquartered marketing agency (Trend Influence) and an associated development company (ApplicationTheory) that produces marketing and communication tools. DotNetNuke has become the platform of choice for many of their clients and as such they have developed a complete suite of tools and agency-specific modules to support these clients.

Cathal Connolly works as a Senior Developer and Consultant with EG Information Consulting (http://www.eg-consulting.com/), based in Belfast, Northern Ireland. Cathal has previously worked for IT companies in the UK, U.S., and Austria, developing both web and Client/Server applications using Microsoft technologies. His current focus is the development of secure Banking applications and bespoke Smart Client .net products. Cathal is an MCSD and holds a BSc in Computer Science.

Chris Hammond, a web application developer for a small software development company in St. Louis, Missouri and is an active speaker on DotNetNuke topics around the Midwest. On the side, he specializes in portal development and search engine optimization through Christoc.com (http://www.christoc.com). Chris has multiple DotNetNuke endeavors including DnnCart.com (http://www.dnncart.com/) where he provides DNN Support and Module development services. He also runs multiple community portals focusing around the Sports Car Club of America, (http://www.solo2.org, http://www.sccaforums.com). You can read more about him on his weblog at http://www.chrishammond.com/.

Clem Messerli, with a vision for using DotNetNuke to train persons who are equipped to use new technologies in the service of the Church, Clem's expertise in web administration and strong background in web development help to provide debugging support and unique insight into future enhancements.

Driven by the Great Commission, Clem has founded CTC Ministries, which is dedicated to building low-cost Cooperative Ministries in the Central Iowa Region where he is currently employed by Rockwell Collins as a Sr. Web Administrator.

David Haggard is an ordained minister, founder of NewCovenant Evangelistic Ministries, an international ministry of the Christian Gospel and an outreach to widows. He also founded NewCovenant Consulting for support of the ministry. The consulting arm specializes in Internet services to churches and non-profits, but provides services to all businesses and individuals that are not counter to the ministry. David's IT background started with Microsoft in Windows 95 support, and grew into web development, ASP, and finally .NET. David lives and works out of his rural home near Thurman, Iowa, USA, with his wife Cheryl.

John Mitchell is the Founder and President of Snapsis Software, Inc. (http://www.snapsis.com). John has more than 20 years of development experience and has been working on the leading edge of Internet technologies for the past seven years, specializing in the architecture, design, development, and implementation of portal/e-commerce applications.

John has led teams in the development of several web sites including http://SamsClub.com and http://www.Maytag.com. John has been using and enhancing DotNetNuke since May 2003 and is also a founding member of the Tulsa .Net Users Group (http://www.TulsaDnug.org).

Jon Henning is senior consultant with Solution Partners Inc., www.solpart.com, a Chicago-based consulting company specializing in Microsoft technologies. He is an MCSD who has been working with Visual Studio .NET since the PDC release. While he has written several articles dealing with all aspects of programming, his current love has been found in the development of rich client-side functionality. Most notably is the Solution Partners ASP.NET Hierarchical Menu, which is the default menu that is used within DotNetNuke. Recently for version 3, Jon initiated the development of the DotNetNuke ClientAPI, which enables developers to write rich client-side cross-browser logic against a simple API.

Jim Duffy is a Microsoft MVP, self-proclaimed DotNetNuke Evangelist, and the president of TakeNote Technologies. TakeNote, a Developer's Choice Award winner for hands-on training, specializes in training and creating business solutions with Microsoft enterprise technologies. In response to his desire to spread the DotNetNuke word to others, Jim authored two DotNetNuke training classes. One focuses on creating and administrating a DNN portal and the other focuses on developing custom DNN modules. He has also presented DotNetNuke topics at a number of regional and international developer conferences including DevTeach 2004 and DevEssentials. Jim is a popular speaker due to his knowledge, humor, and quick-witted approach. He is an exceptional trainer, skilled developer, and has been published in a number of leading publications including CoDe Magazine (www.code-magazine.com). Jim's background also includes a Bachelor of Science degree in Computer and Information Systems and more than 20 years of programming and training experience. Jim is also co-host of Computers 2K4, a weekly call-in radio show (AM 850 The Buzz) in Raleigh, NC. Jim's passion for teaching and presenting, coupled with his desire to help people meet their professional and personal goals, make him a welcome addition to the DNN Core Team.

Leigh Pointer is an accomplished professional with 17 years experience in the IT sector. He is highly experienced in user interaction design, web design, software engineering, problem solving, and user relations. He demonstrates leadership in resource and project management and has an in-depth understanding of Microsoft development tools. Leigh is results-oriented and thrives in an innovative, creative, challenging, fast-paced workplace. He is also the founder of the Netherlands (http://netherlands .dnn-usergroup.net) and European DNN user groups and worked closely with Microsoft to achieve this. Leigh maintains his own modules for DNN at http://www.subzero-solutions.net along with other interesting topics.

Lorraine Young is a Business Analyst for Byte Information Technology based in Melbourne, Australia (http:/www.byte.com.au). Lorraine is a founding member of the DotNetNuke Core Team who provides assistance in the user experience and documentation areas of the DotNetNuke Project.

Lorraine holds a Bachelor of Arts degree in Professional Writing and Literature and a Post Graduate degree in Orientation and Mobility for vision impaired adults and children.

Mark Hoskins is the Founder of KodHedZ Software Development (www.KodHedZ.net) based out of Victoria, BC, Canada where he has been developing ASP.NET Business Management, eCommerce and Dynamic Internet Applications for more than three years, primarily using DotNetNuke as the development platform since its conception in December 2002.

In addition to web applications, Mark has authored many articles and tutorials for developers on implementing and developing solutions using DotNetNuke and provides a wealth of resources at his flagship domain, www.KodHedZ.net.

Matt Fraser has been developing for the World Wide Web since 1996. He is the owner of Liquid Platinum Technologies, specializing in custom Internet applications for small businesses using Microsoft products and technologies. Previously, Matt has worked as a web developer for Chalk Media and the

Bank of Montreal, creating online learning solutions. He also had a key role in designing and building the eyeReturn Voken engine for online advertising and loyalty programs. Matt holds a Bachelor of Computer Science specializing in Software Engineering from 1999. He is currently residing in Los Angeles, CA.

Nina Meiers is a self-employed DotNetNuke web site skinner whose Core Team roles include User Experience Specialist, DotNetNuke Evangelist, and Technical Writing & Marketing Specialist. Nina's experience in graphics and eye for technical perfection as well as an ability to work well with developers and clients alike has helped find her niche in the DotNetNuke community with over 12,500 downloads of many quality free skins available from `http://www.xd.com.au`. Nina also has an extensive portfolio of projects from small business to Fortune 500 companies on her web site.

Nina is married with children and enjoys renovations, reading, writing, and driving her muscle sports car.

Pete Garyga, systems engineer and developer, holds an MSCE, MCSA, MCP, CCNA, and CNA. Pete is employed by Derbyshire Fire & Rescue Service in the UK (`http://www.derbys-fire.gov.uk`) as the Systems Support and Development Officer. Pete's personal web site is `http://www.garyga.com`; he has also recently set up `http://www.dnnresources.com` for the DotNetNuke community.

Phil Guerra is a member of the Bugs & Enhancements Core Team. Phil writes technical articles on various DNN topics, which are posted on his web site, `www.hgworks.com/handcoded`, and have been translated to several languages for posting on a number of sites worldwide. His targeted audience is ASP.NET developers that employ hand-coded methods to build .NET projects. He is a frequent poster on the ASP.NET DNN forums and offers users advice on enhancing their DNN portals and assists in troubleshooting reported DNN issues. His areas of interests include RSS/XML, Graphics, Localization and Globalization, and general VB.NET topics.

Phil has implemented DNN with custom modules for use in various intranet applications, mostly healthcare related. He has worked in the healthcare industry for more than 18 years in various positions as programmer, analyst, support supervisor, and IT Director. He offers services as a private consultant and developer through his consulting company, HGWorks. Phil currently resides in Mission, Kansas, but looks forward to returning to the Phoenix, Arizona metro area.

Robert Collins is the Founder and President of WillowTree Software, Inc. (`http://www.willowtree software.com/`). Robert is a veteran developer with more than seven years of web development experience. Specializing in the design, development, and implementation of e-commerce applications, corporate Intranet tools, and high availability data-driven web applications, Robert has established himself as a leading force in the web development community. Robert founded the successful "Boise .Net Developers User Group" (`http://www.netdug.com/`), a user group dedicated to promotion of the Microsoft .NET Framework and Services. While with the Microsoft Corporation, Rob was responsible for providing high availability web and database application solutions for Microsoft internal services and Microsoft partners.

In addition to web application development, Robert is also an established desktop/client server applications developer, network systems engineer, and cluster services specialist with more than four years of experience working as a systems integrator (MCP, MCP+I, MCSE, MCSE+I).

Salar Golestanian specializes in skinning and UI, working solely in the DotNetNuke environment. He is currently targeting clients wanting content management solutions, and has years of creative design experience. Salar is working on a number of projects based on the DotNetNuke platform. The links to various projects and showcases are available on salaro.com.

Salar's background is in Internet technology using Microsoft tools. He has a Bachelor of Science and MPhil in Physics. He lives with his fiancée and daughter near London UK.

Shawn Mehaffie holds an MCP (ASP.NET) certification and is working on his MCSD certification. Shawn has 14 years of programming experience in VB.NET, ASP.NET, and C# and has worked with .NET since its release. He was on a team that wrote a Payment Engine web service as part of the Microsoft .Net Blaze program. As a side job, Shawn owns his own company, PC Resources, LLC (http://www.pcrresourcesllc.com). Shawn has been a part of the DotNetNuke community since v1.0 and currently uses DotNetNuke to create web sites for his customers. Shawn is the QA Team Leader and a member of the Bug & Enhancement Team. Shawn is excited about being on the DoteNetNuke Core Team and the positive contributions his team can have on future releases of DotNetNuke. Shawn lives in Blue Springs, Missouri with his wife and two sons (Austin and Tyler).

Steve Fabian (Gooddogs.com), has been designing and developing software solutions for 19 years. In addition to programming in more then a dozen different languages, Steve is proficient in graphics and web design and for the past few years has focused on user interface design, .NET development, both client and browser based, and most recently, DotNetNuke. Gooddogs.com provides both free and custom skins for the DotNetNuke community as well as the free Gooddogs Repository Module for DotNetNuke. Steve lives in New Jersey with his wife and his five dogs, Kahlua, Amaretto, Sambucca, Daiquiri, and Whiskey. In his extremely limited free time, Steve and his wife do volunteer work for BARKS, an animal rescue shelter in Byram, New Jersey.

Tam Tran Minh holds an architect degree from HCMC-Vietnam University of Architecture. He is currently Chairman and CIO of TTT Corporation in Vietnam (http://www.tttcompany.com). Since 2003, DotNetNuke is the main content management portal for his company. Tam has developed and contributed several DotNetNuke modules to the community.

Tam is currently developing a management and collaboration system for TTT with Visual Basic, Exchange/Outlook, and now VB.NET. He is author of several articles in PC-World Vietnam and has published a book titled *Architectural Space - Virtual and Reality* (winner of the National Architectural Awards 2002 in Vietnam) based on projects of TTT using computer graphic technologies. Tam speaks both Vietnamese and English.

Todd Mitchell is a Senior Analyst Programmer at Byte Information Technology (http://www.byte .com.au). Prior to joining Byte, Todd ran his own consulting business specializing in IT infrastructure and portal applications for small to medium enterprises, undertaking a range of projects including the customization of DotNetNuke for a major portal application in the telecommunications industry.

Todd is an accomplished IT professional who is expert in driving projects and technologies that support and enhance business growth and has extensive IT infrastructure experience gained in a number of industries. Todd is a founding member of the DotNetNuke Core Team. Todd holds an MCAD and is a proficient programmer in a number of languages including HTML, Java Script, VB Script, ASP, Visual Basic VBA, and SQL.

Yarko Tymciurak has been reading code since 1968, and writing software since 1976. He has worked on control systems, compilers, operating systems, and communication systems. He has lead teams of Software Architects and trained engineering, business, and sales teams in communication skills. Currently he is a System Architect of mobile devices. Yarko holds a BSEE in Computer Engineering from the University of Arizona.

Nik Kalyani is the Founder and CEO of Speerio, Inc., an enterprise software components company. Nik is a successful entrepreneur committed to the business of technology. Speerio is built upon the valuable experience he gained developing and growing his prior two software companies. Nik is proficient in many areas of software development and strives to create the highest quality software using C#, his favorite development language. Nik is a marketing leader, user experience specialist and evangelist on the DotNetNuke Core Team. Nik and his wife live in Washington, D.C., where he continues to learn more about the political process in preparation for a future run for Congress.

Other Members of the Outer Core Team

Jason Graves

Josh Weinstein

Richard Cox

Richard Ferguson

Russ Johnson

Conventions

To help you get the most from the text and keep track of what's happening, we've used a number of conventions throughout the book.

> **Boxes like this one hold important, not-to-be forgotten information that is directly relevant to the surrounding text.**

Tips, hints, tricks, and asides to the current discussion are offset and placed in italics like this.

As for styles in the text:

- ❑ We *italicize* important words when we introduce them
- ❑ We show keyboard strokes like this: Ctrl+A
- ❑ We show URLs within the text like so: http://www.dotnetnuke.com
- ❑ We present code in two different ways:

In code examples we highlight new and important code with a gray background.

The gray highlighting is not used for code that's less important in the present context, or has been shown before.

Source Code

To download DotNetNuke to work with as you make your way through this book you can surf directly to www.dotnetnuke.com, or you can link to the DotNetNuke site through the Wrox site at www.wrox.com. Once at the Wrox site, simply locate the book's title (either by using the Search box or by using one of the title lists) and follow the provided link to www.dotnetnuke.com.

Because many books have similar titles, you may find it easiest to search by ISBN; for this book the 10-digit ISBN is 0-7645-9563-6 and the 13-digit ISBN is 978-0-7645-9563-9.

Errata

We make every effort to ensure that there are no errors in the text or in the code. However, no one is perfect, and mistakes do occur. If you find an error in one of our books, like a spelling mistake or faulty piece of code, we would be very grateful for your feedback. By sending in errata you may save another reader hours of frustration and at the same time you will be helping us provide even higher quality information.

To find the errata page for this book, go to http://www.wrox.com and locate the title using the Search box or one of the title lists. Then, on the book details page, click the Book Errata link. On this page you can view all errata that has been submitted for this book and posted by Wrox editors. A complete book list including links to each book's errata is also available at www.wrox.com/misc-pages/booklist.shtml.

If you don't spot "your" error on the Book Errata page, go to www.wrox.com/contact/techsupport.shtml and complete the form there to send us the error you have found. We'll check the information and, if appropriate, post a message to the book's errata page and fix the problem in subsequent editions of the book.

p2p.wrox.com

For author and peer discussion, join the P2P forums at p2p.wrox.com. The forums are a web-based system for you to post messages relating to Wrox books and related technologies and interact with other readers and technology users. The forums offer a subscription feature to e-mail you topics of interest of your choosing when new posts are made to the forums. Wrox authors, editors, other industry experts, and your fellow readers are present on these forums.

At http://p2p.wrox.com you will find a number of different forums that will help you not only as you read this book, but also as you develop your own applications. To join the forums, just follow these steps:

1. Go to p2p.wrox.com and click the Register link.

2. Read the terms of use and click Agree.

3. Complete the required information to join as well as any optional information you wish to provide and click Submit.

4. You will receive an e-mail with information describing how to verify your account and complete the joining process.

You can read messages in the forums without joining P2P but in order to post your own messages, you must join.

Once you join, you can post new messages and respond to messages other users post. You can read messages at any time on the Web. If you would like to have new messages from a particular forum e-mailed to you, click the Subscribe to this Forum icon by the forum name in the forum listing.

For more information about how to use the Wrox P2P, be sure to read the P2P FAQs for answers to questions about how the forum software works as well as many common questions specific to P2P and Wrox books. To read the FAQs, click the FAQ link on any P2P page.

Professional DotNetNuke™ ASP.NET Portals

Shaun Walker, Patrick J. Santry, Joe Brinkman, Daniel Caron,
Scott McCulloch, Scott Willhite, and Bruce Hopkins

Wiley Publishing, Inc.

An Inside Look at the Evolution of DotNetNuke

As much as I would like people to believe that DotNetNuke was intentionally created as a premier open source project for the Microsoft platform, it is unfortunately not the case. As is true with many open source projects, the software was created with commercial intentions in mind, and only when it was discovered that its true purpose would not be realized was it reconsidered as an open source project.

In 2001–2002 I was working for a medium-sized software consulting company that was providing outsourced software development services to a variety of large U.S. clients specializing primarily in e-Learning initiatives. The internal push was to achieve CMM 3.0 on a fairly aggressive schedule so that we could compete with the emerging outsourcing powerhouses from India and China. As a result there was an incredible amount of focus on process and procedure and somewhat less focus on the technical aspects of software engineering. Because the majority of the client base was interested in the J2EE platform, the company had primarily hired resources with Java skills — leaving myself with my legacy Microsoft background to assume more of an internal development and project management role. The process improvement exercise consumed a lot of time and energy for the company; attempting to better define roles and responsibilities and ensuring proper documentation throughout the project life cycle. Delving into CMM and the PMBOK were great educational benefits for me — skills that would prove to be invaluable in future endeavors. Ultimately the large U.S. clients decided to test the overseas outsourcing options anyway, which resulted in severe downsizing for the company. It was during these tumultuous times that I recognized the potential of the newly released .NET Framework (beta) and decided that I would need to take my own initiative to learn this exciting new platform in order to preserve my long-term employment outlook.

For a number of years I had been maintaining an amateur hockey statistics application as a sideline hobby business. The client application was written in Visual Basic 6.0 with a Microsoft Access backend, and I had augmented it with a simplistic web publishing service using Active Server Pages 3.0 and SQL Server 7.0. However, better integration with the World Wide Web was quickly becoming the most highly requested enhancement and I concluded that an exploration into

ASP.NET was the best way to enhance the application, while at the same time acquire the skills necessary to adapt to the changing landscape. My preferred approach to learning new technologies is to experience them firsthand rather than through theory or traditional education. It was during a Microsoft Developer Days conference in Vancouver, British Columbia in 2001 that I became aware of a reference application known as the IBuySpy Portal.

IBuySpy Portal

Realizing the educational value of sample applications, Microsoft had built a number Source Projects, which were released with the .NET Framework 1.0 Beta to encourage developers to cut their teeth on the new platform. These projects included full source code and a very liberal End User License Agreement (EULA) that provided nearly unrestricted usage. Microsoft co-developed the IBuySpy Portal with Vertigo Software and promoted it as a "best practice" example for building applications in the new ASP.NET environment. Despite its obvious shortcomings, the IBuySpy Portal had some very strong similarities to both Microsoft Sharepoint as well as other open source portal applications on the Linux/Apache/mySQL/PHP (LAMP) platform. The portal allowed you to create a completely dynamic web site consisting of an unlimited number of virtual "tabs" (pages). Each page had a standard header and three content panes — a left pane, a middle pane, and a right pane (a standard layout for most portal sites). Within these panes the administrator could dynamically inject "modules" — essentially mini-applications for managing specific types of web content. The IBuySpy Portal application shipped with six modules designed to cover the most common content types — (announcements, links, images, discussions, html/text, XML) as well as a number of modules for administrating the portal site. As an application framework the IBuySpy Portal (see Figure 1-1) provided a mechanism for managing users, roles, permissions, tabs, and modules. With these basic services, the portal offered just enough to whet the appetite of many aspiring ASP.NET developers.

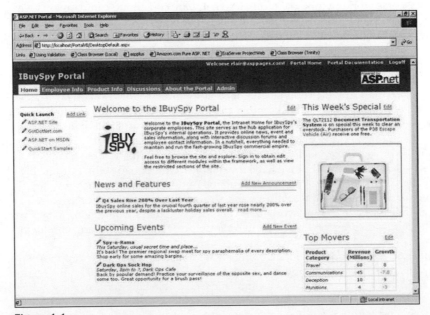

Figure 1-1

ASP.NET

The second critical item that Microsoft delivered at this point in time was a community Forums page on the www.asp.net web site (see Figure 1-2). This Forum provided a focal point for Microsoft developers to meet and collaborate on common issues in an open, moderated environment. Prior to the release of the Forums on www.asp.net there was a real void in terms of Microsoft community participation in the online or global sphere, especially when compared to the excellent community environments on other platforms.

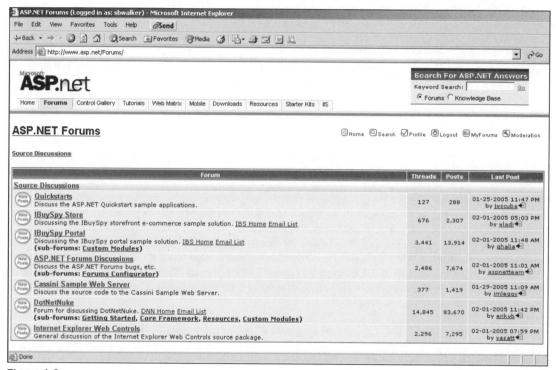

Figure 1-2

One discussion forum on the www.asp.net site was dedicated to the discussion of the IBuySpy Portal application, and it soon became a hotbed for developers to discuss their enhancements, share source code enhancements, and debate IT politics. I became involved in this Forum early on and gradually increased my community participation as my confidence in ASP.NET and the IBuySpy Portal application grew.

In order to appeal to the maximum number of community stakeholders, the IBuySpy Portal was available in a number of different source code release packages. There were VB.NET and C#.NET language versions, each containing their own VS.NET and SDK variants. Although Microsoft was aggressively pushing the newly released C# language, I did not feel a compelling urge to abandon my familiar Visual Basic roots. In addition, my experience with classic ASP 3.0 allowed me to conclude that the new code-behind model in VS.NET was far superior to the inline model of the SDK. As luck would have it, I was able to get access to Visual Studio .NET through my employer. So as a result, I moved forward with the

VB.NET/VS.NET version as my baseline framework. This decision would ultimately prove to be extremely important in terms of community acceptance, as I will explain later.

When I first started experimenting with the IBuySpy Portal application I had some very specific objectives in mind. In order to support amateur sports organizations, I had collected a comprehensive set of end user requirements based on actual client feedback. However after evaluating the IBuySpy Portal functionality, it quickly became apparent that some very significant enhancements were necessary if I hoped to achieve my goals. My early development efforts, although certainly not elegant or perfectly architected, proved that the IBuySpy Portal framework was highly adaptable for building custom applications and could be successfully used as the foundation for my amateur sports hosting application.

The most significant enhancement I made to the IBuySpy Portal application during these early stages was a feature that is now referred to as " multi-portal " or "site virtualization." Effectively, this was a fundamental requirement for my amateur sports hosting model. Organizations wanted to have a self-maintained web site but they also wanted to retain their individual identity. A number of vendors had emerged with semi-self-maintained web applications but nearly all of them forced the organization to adopt the vendor's identity (that is, `www.vendor.com/clientname` rather than `www.clientname.com`). Although this may seem like a trivial distinction for some, it has some major effects in terms of brand recognition, site discovery, search engine ranking, and so on. The IBuySpy Portal application already partitioned its data by portal (site) and it had a field in the Portals database table named PortalAlias, which was a perfect candidate for mapping a specific domain name to a portal. It was as if the original creators (Microsoft/Vertigo) had considered this use case during development but had not had enough time to complete the implementation, so they had simply left the "hook" exposed for future development. I immediately saw the potential of this concept and implemented some logic that allowed the application to serve up custom content based on domain name. Essentially, when a web request was received by the application, it would parse the domain name from the URL and perform a lookup on the PortalAlias field to determine the content that should be displayed. This site virtualization capability would ultimately become the "killer" feature that would allow the application to achieve immediate popularity as an open source project.

Over the next 8 to 10 months, I continued to enhance and refactor the IBuySpy Portal application as I created my own custom implementation (now codenamed SportsManager.Net). I added numerous features to improve the somewhat limited portal administration and content management aspects. At one point I enlisted the help of another developer, John Lucarino, and together we steadily improved the framework using whatever spare time we were able to invest. Unfortunately, since all of this was going on outside of regular work hours, there was very little time to focus on building a viable commercial venture. So at the end of 2002, it soon became apparent that we did not have enough financial backing or a business model to take the amateur sports venture to the next level. This brought the very commercial nature of the endeavor under scrutiny. If the commercial intentions were not going to succeed, I at least wanted to feel that my efforts had not been in vain. This forced me to evaluate alternative non-commercial uses of the application. Coincidentally, I had released the source code for a number of minor application enhancements to the `www.asp.net` community Forum during the year and I began to hypothesize that if I abandoned the amateur sports venture altogether, it was still possible that my efforts could benefit the larger ASP.NET community.

The fundamental problem with the IBuySpy Portal community was the fact that there was no central authority in charge of managing its growth. Although Microsoft and Vertigo had developed the initial code base, there was no public commitment to maintain or enhance the product in any way. Basically the product was a static implementation, frozen in time, an evolutionary dead-end. However, the IBuySpy Portal EULA was extremely liberal, which meant that developers were free to enhance, license, and redistribute the source code in an unrestricted manner. This led to many developers creating their own customized versions of the application, sometimes sharing discrete patches with the general community, but more often keeping their enhancements private; revealing only their public-facing web sites for community recognition (one of the most popular threads at this time was titled "Show me your Portal"). In hindsight, I really don't understand what each developer was hoping to achieve by keeping their enhancements private. Most probably thought there was a commercial opportunity in building a portal application with a richer feature set than their competitor. Or perhaps individuals were hoping to establish an expert reputation based on their public-facing efforts. Either way, the problem was that this mindset was really not conducive to building a community but rather to fragmenting it — a standard trap that tends to consume many things on the Microsoft platform. The concept of sharing source code in an unrestricted manner was really a foreign concept, which is obviously why nobody thought to step forward with an organized open source plan.

I have to admit I had a very limited knowledge of the open source philosophy at this point since all of my previous experience had been in the Microsoft community — an area where "open source" was simply equated to the Linux operating system movement. However, there had been chatter in the Forums at various times regarding the organized sharing of source code, and there was obviously some interest in this area. Coincidentally, a few open source projects had recently emerged on the Microsoft platform to imitate some of the more successful open source projects in the LAMP community. In evaluating my amateur sports application, I soon realized that nearly all of my enhancements were generic enough that they could be applied to nearly any web site — they were not sports related whatsoever. I concluded that I should release my full application source code to the ASP.NET community as a new open source project. So, as I mentioned earlier, the initial decision to open source what would eventually become DotNetNuke happened more out of frustration of not achieving my commercial goals rather than predicated philanthropic intentions.

IBuySpy Portal Forum

On December 24, 2002, I released the full open source application by creating a simple web site with a zip file for download. The lack of foresight of what this would become was extremely evident when you consider the casual nature of this original release. However, as luck would have it, I did do three things right. First, I thought I should leverage the "IBuySpy" brand in my own open source implementation so that it would be immediately obvious that the code base was a hybrid of the original IBuySpy Portal application, an application with widespread recognition in the Microsoft community. The name I chose was IBuySpy Workshop because it seemed to summarize the evolution of the original application — not to mention the fact that the "IBSW" abbreviation preferred by the community contained an abstract personal reference ("SW" are my initials). Ironically, I did not even have the domain name resolution properly configured for www.ibuyspyworkshop.com when I released (the initial download links were based on an IP address, http://65.174.86.217/ibuyspyworkshop). The second thing I did right was require people to register on my web site before they were able to download the source code. This allowed me to track the actual interest in the application at a more granular level than simply by the total number of downloads. Third, I publicized the availability of the application in the IBuySpy Portal Forum on www.asp.net (see Figure 1-3). This particular forum was extremely popular at this time; and as far as I know, nobody had ever released anything other than small code snippet enhancements for general consumption. The original post was made on Christmas Eve, December 24, 2002, which had excellent symbolism in terms of the application being a gift to the community.

5

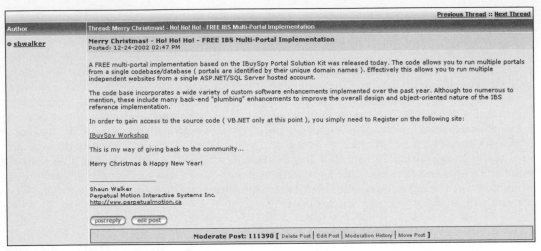

Previous Thread :: Next Thread

Thread: Merry Christmas! - Ho! Ho! Ho! - FREE IBS Multi-Portal Implementation

Author

● **sbwalker**

Merry Christmas! - Ho! Ho! Ho! - FREE IBS Multi-Portal Implementation
Posted: 12-24-2002 02:47 PM

A FREE multi-portal implementation based on the IBuySpy Portal Solution Kit was released today. The code allows you to run multiple portals from a single codebase/database (portals are identified by their unique domain names). Effectively this allows you to run multiple independent websites from a single ASP.NET/SQL Server hosted account.

The code base incorporates a wide variety of custom software enhancements implemented over the past year. Although too numerous to mention, these include many back-end "plumbing" enhancements to improve the overall design and object-oriented nature of the IBS reference implementation.

In order to gain access to the source code (VB.NET only at this point), you simply need to Register on the following site:

IBuySpy Workshop

This is my way of giving back to the community...

Merry Christmas & Happy New Year!

Shaun Walker
Perpetual Motion Interactive Systems Inc.
http://www.perpetualmotion.ca

(post reply)   (edit post)

Moderate Post: 111390 [Delete Post | Edit Post | Moderation History | Move Post]

Figure 1-3

IBuySpy Workshop

The public release of the IBuySpy Workshop (see Figure 1-4) created such a surge in Forum activity that it was all I could do to keep up with the feedback, especially since this all occurred during the Christmas holidays. I had a family vacation booked for the first two weeks of January, and I left for Mexico on January 2, 2003 (one week after the initial IBuySpy Workshop release). At the time, the timing of this family vacation seemed very poor as the groundswell of interest in the IBuySpy Workshop seemed like it could really use my dedicated focus. However in hindsight, the timing could not have been better, because it proved that the community could support itself — a critical element in any open source project. When I returned home from vacation I was amazed at the massive response the release had achieved. The IBuySpy Portal Forum became dominated with posts about the IBuySpy Workshop and my Inbox was full of messages thanking me for my efforts and requesting me for support and enhancements. This certainly validated my decision to release the application as an open source project, but also emphasized the fact that I had started a locomotive down the tracks and it was going to take some significant engineering to keep it on the rails.

Over the coming months I frantically attempted to incorporate all community suggestions into the application while at the same time keep up with the plethora of community support questions. Because I was working a day job that prevented effort on the open source project, most of my evenings were consumed with work on the IBuySpy Workshop, which definitely caused some strain on my marriage and family life. Four hours of sleep per night is not conducive to a healthy lifestyle but, like I said, the train was rolling and I had a feeling the project was destined for bigger things.

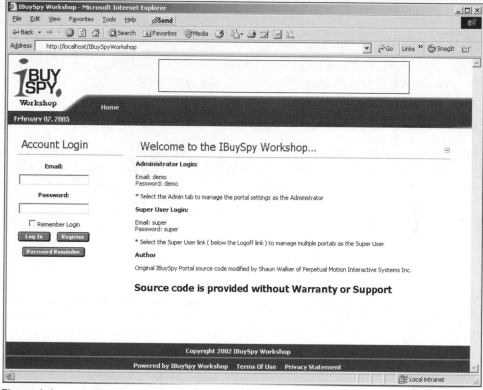

Figure 1-4

Supporting a user base through upgrades is fundamental in any software product. This is especially true in open source projects where the application can evolve very quickly based on community feedback and technical advancements. The popular open source expression is that "no user should be left on an evolutionary dead-end." As luck would have it, I had designed a very reliable upgrade mechanism in the original sports management application, which I included in the IBuySpy Workshop code base. This feature allowed users of the application to easily migrate from one release version to the next — a critical factor in keeping the community engaged and committed to the evolution of the product.

In February 2003, the IBuySpy Portal Forum had become so congested with IBuySpy Workshop threads that it started to become difficult for the two communities to co-exist peacefully. At this point, I sent an e-mail to the anonymous alias posted at the bottom of the Forums page on the www.asp.net site with a request to create a dedicated forum for the IBuySpy Workshop. Because the product functionality and source code of the two applications had diverged so significantly, my intent was to try and keep the

Forum posts for the two applications separate; providing both communities the means to support their membership. I certainly did not have high hopes that my e-mail request was even going to be read — let alone granted. But to my surprise, I received a positive response from none other than Rob Howard (an ASP.NET icon), which proved to be a great introduction to a long-term partnership with Microsoft. Rob created the forum and even went a step further to add a link to the Source Download page of the www.asp.net site, an event that would ultimately drive a huge amount of traffic to the emerging IBuySpy Workshop community.

There are a number of reasons why the IBuySpy Workshop became so immediately popular when it was released in early 2003. The obvious reason is because the base application contained a huge number of enhancements over the IBuySpy Portal application that people could immediately leverage to build more powerful web sites. From a community perspective, the open source project provided a central management authority, which was dedicated to the ongoing growth and support of the application framework; a factor that was definitely lacking in the original IBuySpy Portal community. This concept of open source on the Microsoft platform attracted many developers; some with pure philosophical intentions, and others who viewed the application as a vehicle to further their own revenue-generating interests. Yet another factor, which I think is often overlooked, relates to the programming language on which the project was based. With the release of the .NET Framework 1.0, Microsoft had spent a lot of energy promoting the benefits of the new C# programming language. The C# language was intended to provide a migration path for C++ developers as well as a means to entice Java developers working on other platforms to switch. This left the Visual Basic and ASP 3.0 developer communities feeling neglected and somewhat unappreciated. The IBuySpy Workshop, with its core framework in VB.NET, provided an essential community ecosystem where legacy VB developers could interact, learn, and share.

In late February 2003, the lack of sleep, family priorities, and community demands finally came to a head and I decided that I should reach out for help. I contacted a former employer and mentor, Kent Alstad, with my dilemma and we spent a few lengthy telephone calls brainstorming possible outcomes. However, my personal stress level at the time and my urgency to change direction on the project ulti-mately caused me to move too fast and with more aggression than I should have. I announced that the IBuySpy Workshop would immediately become a subscription service where developers would need to pay a monthly fee in order to get access to the latest source code. From a personal perspective the intent was to generate enough revenue that I could leave my day job and focus my full energy on the manage-ment of the open source project. And with 2000 registered users, a subscription service seemed like a viable model (see Figure 1-5).

However, the true philosophy of the open source model immediately came to light and I had to face the wrath of a scorned community. Among other things I was accused of misleading the community, lying about the open source nature of the project, and letting my personal greed cloud my vision. For every one supporter of my decision there were 10 more who publicly crucified me as the evil incarnate. Luckily for me Kent had a trusted work associate named Andy Baron, a senior consultant at MCW Technologies and a Microsoft Most Valuable Professional since 1995, who has incredible wisdom when it comes to the Microsoft development community. Andy helped me craft a public apology message (see Figure 1-6), which managed to appease the community while at the same time restore the IBuySpy Workshop to full open source status.

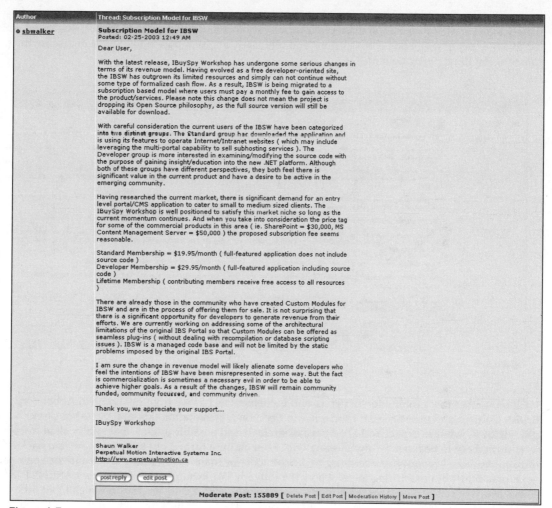

Figure 1-5

Coincidentally, the political nightmare I created in the IBuySpy Workshop Forum with my subscription announcement resulted in some direct attention from the Microsoft ASP.NET product team (the maintainers of the www.asp.net site). Still trying to recover from the damage I had incurred, I received an e-mail from none other than Scott Guthrie (co-founder of the Microsoft ASP.NET Team), asking me to reexamine my decision on the subscription model and making suggestions on how the project could continue as a free, open source venture. It seemed that Microsoft was protective of its evolving community and did not want to see the progress in this area splinter and dissolve just as it seemed to be gaining momentum. Scott Guthrie made no promises at this point but he did open a direct dialogue that ultimately led to some fundamental discussions on sponsorship and collaboration. In fact, this initial e-mail led to a number of telephone conversations and ultimately an invitation to Redmond to discuss the future of the IBuySpy Workshop.

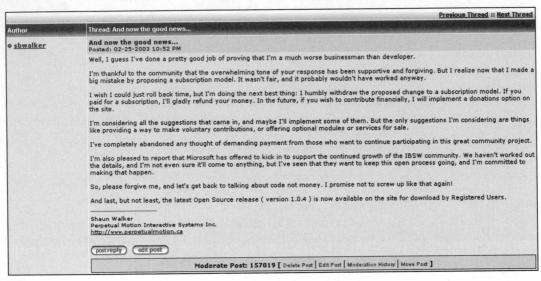

Figure 1-6

I still remember the combination of nerves and excitement as I drove from my home in Abbotsford, British Columbia to the Microsoft head office in Redmond, Washington (about a three-hour trek). I really did not know what to expect and I had tried to strategize all possible angles. Essentially all of my planning turned out to be moot — my meeting with Scott Guthrie turned out to be far more laid back and transparent than I could have ever imagined. Scott took me to his unassuming office and we spent the next three hours brainstorming ideas of how the IBuySpy Workshop fit into the current ASP.NET landscape. Much of this centered on the evolving vision of ASP.NET 2.0 — an area in which I had little or no knowledge prior to the meeting (the Whidbey Alpha had not even been released at this point).

At the beginning of the meeting, Scott had me demo the current version of the IBuySpy Workshop, explaining its key features and benefits. We also discussed the long-term goals of the project as well as my proposed roadmap for future enhancements. Scott's knowledge of both the technical and community aspects of the ASP.NET platform really amazed me — I guess that's why he is the undisputed Father of ASP.NET. In hindsight I can hardly believe my good fortune to have received three dedicated hours of his time to discuss the project — it really changed my "ivory tower" perception of Microsoft and forged a strong relationship for future collaboration.

Upon leaving Redmond, I had to stifle my excitement as I realized that, regardless of the direct interaction with Microsoft, I personally was still in the exact same situation as before the subscription model announcement. Since the subscription model had failed to generate the much-needed revenue that would have allowed me to devote 100% of my time to the project, I was forced to examine other possible alternatives. There had been a number of suggestions from the community and the concept that seemed to have the most potential was related to web hosting.

In these early stages, there were very few economical Microsoft Windows hosting options available that offered a SQL Server database — a fundamental requirement for running the IBuySpy Workshop application. Coincidentally, I had recently struck up a relationship with an individual from New Jersey who was very active in the IBuySpy Workshop forums on www.asp.net. This individual had a solid background in web hosting and proposed a partnership whereby he would manage the web hosting infrastructure and I would continue to enhance the application and drive traffic to the business. Initially, a lot of community members signed up for this service; some because of the low-cost hosting option, others because they were looking for a way to support the open source project. It soon became obvious that the costs to build and support the infrastructure were consuming the majority of the revenue generated. And over time the amount of effort to support the growing client base became more intense. Eventually it came to a point where it was intimated that my contributions to the web hosting business were not substantial enough to justify the current partnership structure. I was informed that the partnership should be dissolved. This is where things got complicated because there had never been any formal agreement signed by either party to initiate the partnership. Without documentation, it made the negotiation for a fair settlement difficult and resulted in some bad feelings on both sides. This was unfortunate because I think the relationship was formed with the best intentions, but the demands of the business had resulted in a poor outcome. In any case, this ordeal was an important lesson I needed to learn; regardless of the open source nature of the project, it was imperative to have all contractually binding items properly documented.

One of the topics that Scott Guthrie and I discussed in our early conversations was the issue of product branding. IBuySpy Workshop had achieved its early goals of providing a public reference to the IBuySpy Portal community. This had resulted in an influx of ASP.NET developers who were familiar with the IBuySpy Portal application and were interested in this new open source concept. But as the code bases diverged there was a need for a new project identity — a unique brand that would differentiate the community and provide the mechanism for building an internationally recognized ecosystem. Research of competing portal applications on other platforms revealed a very strong tendency toward the "nuke" slogan.

The "nuke" slogan had originally been coined by Francisco Burzi of PHP-Nuke fame (the oft-disputed pioneer of open source portal applications). Over the years, a variety of other projects had adopted the slogan as well; so many that the term had obtained industry recognition in the portal application genre. To my surprise a WHOIS search revealed that dotnetnuke.com, .net, and .org had not been registered and, in my opinion, seemed to be the perfect identity for the project. Again emphasizing the bare bones resources under which the project was initiated, my credit card transaction to register the three domain names was denied and I was only able to register dotnetnuke.com (in the long run an embarrassing and contentious issue, as the .net and .org domain names were immediately registered by other individuals). Equally as spontaneous, I did an Internet search for images containing the word "nuke" and located a three-dimensional graphic of a circular gear with a nuclear symbol embossed on it. Contacting the owner of the site, I was given permission to use the image (it was in fact, simply one of many public domain images they were using for a fictitious store front demonstration). A new project identity was born — Version 1.0.5 of the IBuySpy Workshop was rebranded as DotNetNuke, which the community immediately abbreviated to DNN for simplicity (see Figure 1-7).

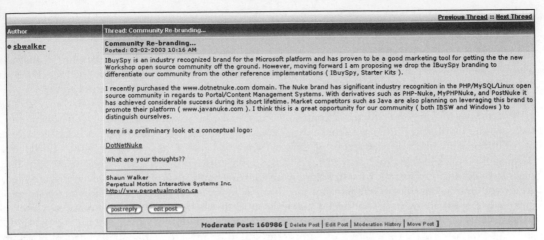

Figure 1-7

A secondary issue that had not been addressed during the early stages of the project was licensing. The original IBuySpy Portal had been released under a very liberal Microsoft EULA license, which allowed for unrestricted usage, modification, and distribution. However, the code base had undergone such a major transformation, it could hardly be compared with its predecessor. Therefore, when the IBuySpy Workshop application was released I had not included the original Microsoft EULA; nor had I included any copyright or license of my own. Essentially this meant that the application was in the public domain. This is certainly not the most accepted approach to an open source project and eventually some of the more legal-savvy community members brought the issue to a head. I was forced to take a hard look at open source licensing models to determine which license was most appropriate to the project.

In stark contrast to the spontaneous approach taken to finding a project identity, the licensing issue had much deeper ramifications. Had I not performed extensive research on this subject, I would have likely chosen a GPL license because it seemed to dominate the vast majority of open source projects in existence. However, digging beneath the surface, I quickly realized that the GPL did not seem to be a good candidate for my objectives of allowing DotNetNuke to be used in both commercial and non-commercial environments. Ultimately, the selection of a license for an open source project is largely dependent upon your business model, your product architecture, and understanding who owns the intellectual property in your application. The combination of these factors prompted me to take a hard look at the open source licensing options available.

If you have not researched open source software, you would be surprised at the major differences between the most popular open source licensing models. It is true that these licenses all meet the standards of the Open Source Definition, a set of guidelines managed by the Open Source Initiative (OSI) at www.open-source.org. These principles include the right to use open source software for any purpose, the right to make and distribute copies, the right to create and distribute derivative works, the right to access and use source code, and the right to combine open source and other software. With such fundamental rights shared between all open source licenses it probably makes you wonder why there is need for more than one license at all. Well, the reason is because each license has the ability to impose additional rights or restrictions on top of these base principles. The additional rights and restrictions have the effect of altering the license so that it meets the specific objectives of each project. Because it is generally bad practice to create brand new licenses (based on the fact that the existing licenses have gained industry acceptance as well as a proven track record), people generally gravitate toward either a GPL or BSD license.

The GPL (or GNU Public License) was created in 1989 by Richard Stallman, founder of the Free Software Foundation. The GPL is what is now known as a "copyleft" license, a term coined based on its controversial reciprocity clause. Essentially this clause stipulates that you are allowed to use the software on condition that any derivative works that you create from it and distribute must be licensed to all under the same license. This is intended to ensure that the software and any enhancements to it remain in the public domain for everyone to share. While this is a great humanitarian goal, it seriously restricts the use of the software in a commercial environment.

The BSD (or Berkeley Software Distribution) was created by the University of California and was designed to permit the free use, modification, and distribution of software without any return obligation whatsoever on the part of the community. The BSD is essentially a "copyright" license, meaning that you are free to use the software on condition that you retain the copyright notice in all copies or derivative works. The BSD is also known as an "academic" license because it provides the highest degree of intellectual property sharing.

Ultimately I settled on a standard BSD license for DotNetNuke; a license that allows the maximum licensing freedom in both commercial and non-commercial environments — with only minimal restrictions to preserve the copyright of the project. The change in license went widely unnoticed by the community because it did not impose any additional restrictions on usage or distribution. However, it was a fundamental milestone in establishing DotNetNuke as a true open source project.

```
DotNetNuke - http://www.dotnetnuke.com
Copyright (c) 2002-2005
by Shaun Walker (sales@perpetualmotion.ca) of Perpetual Motion Interactive Systems
Inc. (http://www.perpetualmotion.ca)

Permission is hereby granted, free of charge, to any person obtaining a copy of
this software and associated documentation files (the "Software"), to deal in the
Software without restriction, including without limitation the rights to use, copy,
modify, merge, publish, distribute, sublicense, and/or sell copies of the Software,
and to permit persons to whom the Software is furnished to do so, subject to the
following conditions:

The above copyright notice and this permission notice shall be included in all
copies or substantial portions of the Software.

THE SOFTWARE IS PROVIDED "AS IS", WITHOUT WARRANTY OF ANY KIND, EXPRESS OR IMPLIED,
INCLUDING BUT NOT LIMITED TO THE WARRANTIES OF MERCHANTABILITY, FITNESS FOR A
PARTICULAR PURPOSE AND NONINFRINGEMENT. IN NO EVENT SHALL THE AUTHORS OR COPYRIGHT
HOLDERS BE LIABLE FOR ANY CLAIM, DAMAGES OR OTHER LIABILITY, WHETHER IN AN ACTION
OF CONTRACT, TORT OR OTHERWISE, ARISING FROM, OUT OF OR IN CONNECTION WITH THE
SOFTWARE OR THE USE OR OTHER DEALINGS IN THE SOFTWARE.
```

The next major milestone in the project's open source evolution occurred in the summer of 2002. Up until this point I had been acting as the sole maintainer of the DotNetNuke code base; a task that was consuming 110% of my free time as I feverishly fixed bugs and enhanced the framework based on community feedback. Yet still I felt more like a bottleneck than a provider, in spite of the fact I was churning out at least one significant release every month leading up to this point. The more active community members were becoming restless due to a lack of direct input into the progress of the project. In fact, a small faction of these members even went so far as to create their own hybrid or "fork" of the DotNetNuke code base, which attempted to forge ahead and add features at a more aggressive pace than I was capable of on my own. These were very challenging times from a political standpoint because I was eventually forced to confront all of these issues in a direct and public manner — flexing my "Benevolent Dictator" muscles for the first time; an act I was not the least bit comfortable performing. Luckily for me, I had a number of very loyal and trustworthy community members who supported my position and ultimately provided the backing to form a very strong and committed Core Team.

As a result of the single-threaded issues I mentioned earlier, most successful open source projects are comprised of a number of community volunteers who earn their positions of authority within the community based on their specific expertise or community support activities. This is known as a meritocracy; a term which means that an individual's influence is directly proportional to the ability that the individual demonstrates within the project. It's a well-observed fact that individuals with more experience and skills will have less time to devote to volunteer activities; however, their minimal contributions prove to be incredibly valuable. Similarly, individuals with less experience may be able to invest more time but may only be capable of performing the more repetitive, menial tasks. Building a healthy balance of these two roles is exactly what is required in every successful open source project; and in fact, is one of the more challenging items to achieve from a management perspective.

The original DotNetNuke Core Team was selected based on their participation and dedication to the DotNetNuke project in the months leading up to the team's formation. In most cases this was solely based on an individual's public image and reputation that had been established in the DotNetNuke Forum on the www.asp.net web site. And in fact, in these early stages, the online persona of each individual proved to be a good indicator of the specific skills they could bring to the project. Some members were highly skilled architects, others were seasoned developers, yet others were better at discussing functionality from an end-user perspective and providing quality support to their community peers.

In order to establish some basic structure for the newly formed Core Team, I attempted to summarize some basic project guidelines. My initial efforts combined some of the best Extreme Programming (XP) rules with the principles of other successful open source projects. This became the basis of the DotNetNuke Manifest document:

❑   Development is a Team Effort: The whole is exponentially greater than the sum of its parts. Large-scale open source projects are only viable if a large enough community of highly skilled developers can be amassed to attack a problem. Treating your users as co-developers is your most effective option for rapid code improvement and effective debugging.

❑   Build the right product before you build the product right: Focus should be directed at understanding and implementing the high-level business requirements before attempting to construct the perfect technical architecture. Listen to your customers.

❑   Incremental Development: Every software product has infinite growth potential if managed correctly. Functionality should be added in incremental units rather than attempting a monolithic implementation. Release often but with a level of quality that instills confidence.

❑   Law of Diminishing Return: The majority of the effort should be invested in implementing features that have the most benefit and widest general usage by the community.

DotNetNuke version 1.0.10 was the proving grounds for the original Core Team. The idea was to establish the infrastructure to support disconnected team development by working on a stabilization release of the current product. A lot of debate went into the selection of the appropriate source control system because, ironically enough, many of the Core Team had never worked with a formal source control process in the past (a fact that certainly emphasized the varied professional background of the Core Team members). The debate centered on whether to use a CVS or VSS model.

CVS is a source control system that is very popular in the open source world that allows developers to work in an unrestricted manner on their local project files and handles any conflicts between versions when you attempt to commit your changes to the central repository. Visual SourceSafe (VSS) is a Microsoft source control system that is supported by the Microsoft development tool suite, which requires developers to explicitly lock project files before making modifications to prevent version conflicts. Ultimately, the familiarity with the Microsoft model won out and we decided to use the free WorkSpaces service on the GotDotNet web site (a new developer community site supported by Microsoft). GotDotNet also provided a simplistic Bug Tracker application that provided us with a means to manage the tracking of issues and enhancement requests. With these infrastructure components in place we were able to focus on the stabilization of the application; correcting known defects and adding some minor usability enhancements. It was during this time that Scott Willhite stepped forward to assume a greater role of responsibility in the project; assisting in management activities, communication, prioritization, and scheduling.

A significant enhancement that was introduced in this stabilization release came from a third party that had contacted me with some very specific enhancements they had implemented and wished to contribute. The University of Texas at El Paso had done extensive work making the DotNetNuke application compliant with the guidelines of the American Disabilities Association (ADA) and Section 508 of the United States Rehabilitation Act. The United States government had made compliancy mandatory for most public organizations; therefore, this was a great enhancement for DotNetNuke because it allowed the application to be used in government, educational, and military scenarios. Bruce Hopkins became the Core Team owner of this item in these early stages; a role that required a great deal of patience as the rest of the team came to grips with the new concept.

Establishing and managing a team was no small challenge. On one hand there were the technical challenges of allowing multiple team members, all in different geographic regions, to communicate and collaborate in a cost-effective, secure environment. Certainly this would have never been possible without the Internet and its vast array of online tools. On the other hand there was the challenge of identifying different personality types and channeling them into areas where they would be most effective. Because there are limited financial motivators in the open source model, people must rely on more basic incentives to justify their volunteer efforts. Generally this leads to a paradigm where contributions to the project become the de facto channel for building a reputation within the community — a primary motivator in any meritocracy. As a result of working with the team, it soon became obvious that there were two extremes in this area — those who would selflessly sacrifice all of their free time (often to their own detriment) to the open source project, and those who would invest the minimal effort and expect the maximum reward. As the creator and maintainer of the project it was my duty to remain objective and put the interests of the community first. This often caused me to become frustrated with the behavior of specific individuals, but in nearly all cases these issues could be resolved without introducing any hard feelings on either side. This was true in all cases except one.

Early in the project history I had been approached by an individual from Germany with a request to maintain a localized DotNetNuke site for the German community. I was certainly not naïve to the dangers of forking at this point and I told him that it would be fine so long as the site stayed consistent with the official source code base, which was under my jurisdiction. This was agreed upon and in the coming months I would have periodic communication with this individual regarding his localization efforts. However, as time wore on, he became critical of the manner in which the project was being managed; in particular the sole maintainer aspect, and began to voice his disapproval in the public Forum. There was a group who believed that there should be greater degree of transparency in the project; that developers should be able to get access to the latest development source code at anytime, and that the maintenance of the application should be conducted by a team rather than an individual. He was able to convince a number of community members to collaborate with him on a modified version of DotNetNuke; a version that integrated a number of the more popular community enhancements available, and called it DotNetNuke XXL.

Now I have to admit that much of this occurred due to my own inability to respond quickly and form a Core Team. In addition, I was not providing adequate feedback to the community regarding my goals and objectives for the future of the project. The reality is, the background management tasks of creating the DotNetNuke Core Team and managing the myriad other issues had undermined my ability to deliver source code enhancements and support to the. The combination of these factors resulted in an unpleasant situation; one that I should have mitigated sooner but was afraid to act upon due to the fragility of the newly formed community. And you also need to remember that the creator of the XXL variant had broken no license agreement by creating a fork; it was completely legal based on the freedom of the BSD open source license.

Eventually the issue came to a head when members of the XXL group began promoting their full source code hybrid in the DotNetNuke Forum. Essentially piggy-backing on the primary promotion channel for the DotNetNuke project, they were able to convince many people to switch to the XXL code base. This had some very bad consequences for the DotNetNuke community. Mainly it threatened to splinter the emerging community on territorial boundaries; an event I wanted to avoid at all costs. This situation was the closest attempt of project hijacking that I can realistically imagine. The DotNetNuke XXL fork seemed to be fixated on becoming the official version of DotNetNuke and assuming control of the future project roadmap. The only saving grace was that I personally managed the DotNetNuke infrastructure and therefore had some influence over key aspects of the open source environment.

In searching for an effective mechanism to protect the integrity of the community and prevent the XXL fork from gaining momentum, some basic business fundamentals came into play. Any product or service is only as successful as its promotion or marketing channel. The DotNetNuke Forum on the www.asp.net web site was the primary communication hub to the DotNetNuke community. Therefore it was not difficult to realize that restricting discussion on XXL in the Forum was the simplest method to mitigate its growth. In probably the most aggressive political move I have ever been forced to make, I introduced some bold changes to the DotNetNuke project. I established some guidelines for Core Team conduct that included, among other things, restrictions on promoting competing open source hybrids of the DotNetNuke application. I also posted some policies on the DotNetNuke Forum that emphasized that the Forum was dedicated solely to the discussion of the official DotNetNuke application and that discussion of third-party commercial or open source products was strictly forbidden. This was an especially difficult decision to make from a moral standpoint because I was well aware that the DotNetNuke application had been introduced to the community via the IBuySpy Portal Forum. Nonetheless, the combination of these two announcements resulted in both the resignation of the XXL project leader from the Core Team as well as the end of discussion of the XXL fork in the DotNetNuke Forum.

The unfortunate side effect, about which I had been cautioning members of the community for weeks, was that users who had upgraded to the XXL fork were effectively left on an evolutionary dead-end — a product version with no support mechanism or promise of future upgrades. This is because many of the XXL enhancements were never going to be integrated into the official DotNetNuke code base (either due to design limitations or inapplicability to the general public). This situation, as unpleasant as it may have been for those caught on the dead-end side of the equation, was a real educational experience for the community in general as they began to understand the longer term and deeper implications of open source project philosophy. In general, the community feedback was positive to the project changes, with only occasional flare ups in the weeks following. In addition, the Core Team seemed to gel more as a result of these decisions because it provided some much-needed policies on conduct, loyalty, and dedication, as well a concrete example of how inappropriate behavior would be penalized.

Emerging from the XXL dilemma, I realized that I needed to establish some legal protection for the long-term preservation of the project. Because standard copyright and the BSD license offered no real insurance from third-party threats, I began to explore intellectual property law in greater detail. After much research and legal advice, I decided that the best option was to apply for a trademark for the DotNetNuke brand name. Registering a trademark protects a project's name or logo, which is often a project's most valuable asset. Once the trademark was approved it would mean that although an individual or company could still create a fork of the application, they legally could not refer to it by the DotNetNuke trademark name. This appeared to be an important distinction so I proceeded with trademark registration in Canada (since this is the country in which Perpetual Motion Interactive Systems Inc. is incorporated).

I must admit the entire trademark approval process was quite an educational experience. Before you can register your trademark you need to define a category and description of your wares and/or services. This can be challenging, although most trademark agencies now provide public access to their database where you can browse for similar items that have been approved in the past. You pay your processing fee when you submit the initial application, but the trademark agency has the right to reject your application for any number of reasons; whereby, you need to modify your application and submit it again. Each iteration can take a couple of months, so patience is indeed a requirement. Once the trademark is accepted it must be published in a public trademark journal for a specified amount of time, providing third parties the opportunity to contest the trademark before it is approved. If it makes it through this final stage, you can pay your registration fee for the trademark to become official. To emphasize the lengthy process involved, the DotNetNuke trademark was initially submitted on October 9, 2003 and was finally approved on November 15, 2004 (TMA625,364).

In August 2003, I finally came to terms on an agreement with Microsoft regarding a sponsorship proposal for the DotNetNuke project. In a nutshell, Microsoft wanted DotNetNuke to be enhanced in a number of key areas; the intent being to use the open source project as a means of demonstrating the strengths of the ASP.NET platform. Because these enhancements were completely congruent with the future goals of the project, there was little negative consequence from a technical perspective. In return for implementing the enhancements, Microsoft would provide a number of sponsorship benefits to the project including web hosting for the www.dotnetnuke.com web site, weekly meetings with an ASP.NET Team representative (Rob Howard), continued promotion via the www.asp.net web site, and more direct access to Microsoft resources for mentoring and guidance. Please note that it took five months for this sponsorship proposal to come together, which demonstrates the patience and perseverance required to collaborate with such an influential partner as Microsoft. Nonetheless, this was potentially a one-time offer and at such a critical stage in the project evolution, it seemed too important to ignore.

An interesting perception that most people have in the IT industry is that Microsoft is morally against the entire open source phenomenon. In my opinion, this is far from the actual truth — and the reality is so much more simplistic. Like any other business that is trying to enhance its market position, Microsoft is merely concerned about competition. This is nothing new. In the past, Microsoft faced competitive challenges from many other sources: companies, individuals, and governments. However, the current environment makes it much more emotional and newsworthy to suggest that Microsoft is pitted against a grass roots community movement rather than a business or legal concern. So in my opinion, it is merely a coincidence that the only real competition facing Microsoft at this point in time is coming from the open source development community. And there is no doubt it will take some time and effort for Microsoft to adapt to the changing landscape. But the chances are probably high that Microsoft will eventually embrace open source to some degree in order to remain competitive.

When it comes to DotNetNuke, many people probably question why Microsoft would be interested in assisting an open source project for which they receive no direct benefit. And it may be perplexing why they would sponsor a product that competes to some degree with several of their own commercial applications. But you do not have to look much further than the obvious indirect benefits to see why this relationship has tremendous value. First and foremost, at this point in time the DotNetNuke application is only designed for use on the Microsoft platform. This means that in order to use DotNetNuke you must have valid licenses for a number of Microsoft infrastructure components (Windows operating system, database server, and so on). So this provides the financial value. In addition, DotNetNuke promotes the benefits of the .NET Framework and encourages developers to migrate to this new development platform. This provides the educational value. Finally, it cultivates an active and passionate community — a network of loyal supporters who are motivated to leverage and promote Microsoft technology on an international scale. This provides the marketing value.

So in September 2003, with the assistance of the newly formed Core Team, we embarked on an ambitious mission to implement the enhancements suggested by Microsoft. The problem at this point was that in addition to the Microsoft enhancements, there were some critical community enhancements, which I ultimately perceived as an even higher priority if the project should hope to grow to the next level. So the scope of the enhancement project began to snowball, and estimated release dates began to slip. The quality of the release code was also considered to be so crucial a factor that early beta packages were not deemed worthy of distribution. Ultimately the code base evolved so much that there was little question the next release would need to be labeled version 2.0. During this phase of internal development, some members of the Core Team did an outstanding job of supporting the 1.x community and generating excitement about the next major release. This was critical in keeping the DotNetNuke community engaged and committed to the evolving project.

A number of excellent community enhancements for the DotNetNuke 1.0 platform also emerged during this stage. This sparked a very active third-party reseller and support community; establishing yet another essential factor in any largely successful open source project. Unfortunately at this point the underlying architecture of the DotNetNuke application was not particularly extensible, which made the third-party enhancements susceptible to upgrade complications and somewhat challenging to integrate for end users. As a Core Team we recognized this limitation and focused on full modularity as a guiding principle for all future enhancements.

Modularity is an architecture principle that basically involves the creation of well-defined interfaces for the purpose of extending an application. The goal of any framework should be to provide interfaces in all areas that are likely to require customization based on business requirements or personalization based on individuality. DotNetNuke provides extensibility in the area of modules, skins, templates, data providers, and localization. And DotNetNuke typically goes one step beyond defining the basic interface; it actually provides the full spectrum of related resource services including creation, packaging, distribution, and installation. With all of these services available, it makes it extremely easy for developers to build and share application extensions with other members of the community.

One of the benefits of working on an open source project is the fact that there is a very high priority placed on creating the optimal solution or architecture. I think it was Bill Gates who promoted the concept of "magical software" and it is certainly a key aspiration in many open source projects. This goal often results in more preliminary analysis and design, which tends to elongate the schedule but also results in a more extensible and adaptable architecture. This differs from traditional application development, which often suffers from time and budget constraints, resulting in shortcuts, poor design decisions, and delivery of functionality before it is has been validated. Another related benefit is that the developers of open source software also represent a portion of its overall user community, meaning they actually "eat their own dog food," so to speak. This is really critical when it comes to understanding the business requirements under which the application needs to operate. Far too often you will find commercial vendors that build their software in a virtual vacuum; never experiencing the fundamental application use cases in a real-world environment.

One of the challenges in allowing the Core Team to work together on the DotNetNuke application was the lack of high-quality infrastructure tools. Probably the most fundamental elements from a software development standpoint were the need for a reliable source code control system and issue management system. Because the project had little to no financial resources to draw upon, we were forced to use whatever free services were available in the open source community. And although some of these services are leveraged successfully by other open source projects, the performance, management, and disaster recovery aspects are sorely lacking. This led to a decision to approach some of the more successful commercial vendors in these areas with requests for pro-bono software licenses. Surprisingly, these vendors were more than happy to assist the DotNetNuke open source project — in exchange for some minimal sponsorship recognition. This model has ultimately been carried on in other project areas to acquire the professional infrastructure, development tools, and services necessary to support our growing organization.

As we worked through the enhancements for the DotNetNuke 2.0 project, a number of Core Team members gained considerable respect within the project based on their high level of commitment, unselfish behavior, and expert development skills. Joe Brinkman, Dan Caron, Scott McCulloch, and Geert Veenstra sacrificed a heap of personal time and energy to improve the DotNetNuke open source project. And the important thing to realize is that they did so because they wanted to help others and make a difference, not because of self-serving agendas or premeditated expectations. The satisfaction of working with other highly talented individuals in an open, collaborative environment is reward enough for some developers. And it is this particular aspect of open source development that continues to confound and amaze people as time goes on.

In October 2003, there was a Microsoft Professional Developers Conference (PDC) in Los Angeles, California. The PDC is the premier software development spectacle for the Microsoft platform; an event that only occurs every two years. About a month prior to the event, I was contacted by Cory Isakson, a developer on the Rainbow Portal open source project, who informed me that "Open Source Portals" had been nominated as a category for a "Birds of Feather" session at the event. I posted the details in the DotNetNuke Forum and soon the item had collected enough community votes that it was approved as an official BOF session. This provided a great opportunity to meet with DotNetNuke enthusiasts and critics from all over the globe. It also provided a great networking opportunity to chat with the most influential commercial software vendors in the .NET development space (contacts made with SourceGear and MaximumASP at this event proved to be very important to DotNetNuke as time would tell).

In January 2004 another interesting dilemma presented itself. I received an e-mail from an external party, a Web Application Security Specialist, who claimed to have discovered a severe vulnerability in the DotNetNuke application (version 1.0). Upon further research I confirmed that the security hole was indeed valid and immediately called an emergency meeting of the more trusted Core Team members to determine the most appropriate course of action. At this point we were fully focused on the DotNetNuke 2.0 development project but also realized that it was our responsibility to serve and protect the growing DotNetNuke 1.0 community. From a technical perspective, the patch for the vulnerability proved to be a simple code modification. The more challenging problem was related to communicating the details of the security issue to the community. On the one hand we needed the community to understand the severity of the issue so that they would be motivated to patch their applications. On the other hand, we did not want to cause widespread alarm that could lead to a public perception that DotNetNuke was an insecure platform. Exposing too many details of the vulnerability would be an open invitation for hackers to try and exploit DotNetNuke web sites; but revealing too few details would downplay the severity. And the fact that the project is open source meant that the magnitude of the problem was amplified. Traditional software products have the benefit of tracking and identifying users through restrictive licensing policies. Open source projects have licenses that allow for free redistribution; which means the maintainer of the project has no way to track the actual usage of the application and no way to directly contact all community members who are affected. The whole situation really put security issues into perspective for me. It's one thing to be an outsider, expressing your opinions on how a software vendor should or should not react to critical security issues in their products. It's quite another thing to be an insider, stuck in the vicious dilemma between divulging too much or too little information, knowing full well that both options have the potential to put your customers at even greater risk. Ultimately, we created a new release version and issued a general security alert that was sent directly to all registered users of the DotNetNuke application by e-mail and posted in the DotNetNuke Forum on www.asp.net.

```
Subject: DotNetNuke Security Alert

Yesterday we became aware of a security vulnerability in DotNetNuke.

It is the immediate recommendation of the DotNetNuke Core Team that all
users of DotNetNuke based systems download and install this security patch
as soon as possible. As part of our standard security policy, no further
detailed information regarding the nature of the exploit will be provided to
the general public.

This email provides the steps to immediately fix existing sites and mitigate
the potential for a malicious attack.

Who is vulnerable?

-- Any version of DotNetNuke from version 1.0.6 to 1.0.10d

What is the vulnerability?

A malicious user can anonymously download files from the server. This is not
the same download security issue which has been well documented in the past
whereby an anonymous user can gain access to files in the /Portals directory
if they know the exact URL. This particular exploit bypasses the file
security machanism of the IIS server completely and allows a malicious user
to download files with protected mappings (ie. *.aspx).
```

```
The vulnerability specifically *does not* enable the following actions:

-- A hacker *cannot* take over the server (e.g. it does not allow hacker
code to be executed on the server)

How to fix the vulnerability?

For Users:

{ Instructions on where to download the latest release and how to install }

For Developers:

{ Instructions with actual source code snippets for developers who had diverged
from the official DotNetNuke code base and were therefore unable to apply a general
release patch }

Please note that this public service announcement demonstrates the
professional responsibility of the Core Team to treat all possible security
exploits as serious and respond in a timely and decisive manner.

We sincerely apologize for the inconvenience that this has caused.

Thank you, we appreciate your support...

DotNetNuke - The Web of the Future
```

The security dilemma brings to light another often misunderstood paradigm when it comes to open source projects. Most open source projects have a license that explicitly states that there is no support or warranty of any kind for users of the application. And while this may be true from a purely legal standpoint, it does not mean that the maintainer of the open source application can ignore the needs of the community when issues arise. The fact is, if the maintainer did not accept responsibility for the application, the users would quickly lose trust and the community would dissolve. This implicit trust relationship is what all successful open source communities are based upon. So in reality, the open source license acts as little more than a waiver of direct liability for the maintainer. The DotNetNuke project certainly conforms to this model because we take on the responsibility to ensure that all users of the application are never left on an evolutionary dead-end and security issues are always dealt with in a professional and expedient manner.

After six months of development, including a full month of public beta releases and community feedback, DotNetNuke 2.0 was released on March 23, 2004. This release was significant because it occurred at VS Live! in San Francisco, California — a large-scale software development event sponsored by Microsoft and Fawcette publications. Due to our strong working relationship with Microsoft, I was invited to attend official press briefings conducted by the ASP.NET Team. Essentially this involved 6–8 private sessions with the leading press agencies (Fawcette, PC Magazine, Computer Wire, Ziff Davis, and others) where I was able to summarize the DotNetNuke project, show them a short demonstration, and answer their specific questions. The event proved to be spectacularly successful and resulted in a surge of new traffic to the community (now totaling more than 40,000 registered users).

DotNetNuke 2.0 was a hit. We had successfully delivered a high quality release that encapsulated the majority of the most requested product enhancements from the community. And we had done so in a manner that allowed for clean customization and extensibility. In particular the skinning solution in DotNetNuke 2.0 achieved widespread critical acclaim.

In DotNetNuke 1.x the user interface of the application allowed for very little personalization; essentially all DNN sites looked very much the same, a very negative restriction considering the highly creative environment of the World Wide Web. DotNetNuke 2.0 removed this restriction and opened up the application to a whole new group of stakeholders — web designers. As the popularity of portal applications had increased in recent years, the ability for web designers to create rich, graphical user interfaces had diminished significantly. This is because the majority of portal applications were based on platforms that did not allow for clear separation between form and function, or were architected by developers who had very little understanding of the creative needs of web designers. DotNetNuke 2.0 focused on this problem and implemented a solution where the portal environment and creative design process could be developed independently and then combined to produce a stunningly harmonious end-user experience. The process was not complicated and did not require the use of custom tools or methodologies. It did not take very long before we began to see DotNetNuke sites with richly creative and highly graphical layouts emerge — proving the effectiveness of the solution and creating a "can you top this" community mentality for innovative portal designs.

DotNetNuke (DNN) Web Site

To demonstrate the effectiveness of the skinning solution, I commissioned a local web design company, Circle Graphics, to create a compelling design for the www.dotnetnuke.com web site (see Figure 1-8). As an open source project, I felt that I could get away with an unorthodox, somewhat aggressive site design and I had been impressed by some of Circle Graphics' futuristic, industrial concepts I had viewed in the past. It turned out that the designer who had created these visuals had since moved on but was willing to take on a small contract as a personal favor to the owner. He created a skin that included some stunning 3-D imagery including the now infamous "nuke-gear" logo, circuit board, and plenty of twisted metallic pipes and containers. The integration with the application worked flawlessly and the community was wildly impressed with the stunning result. Coincidentally, the designer of the DotNetNuke skin, Anson Vogt, has since gone on to bigger and better things, working with rapper Eminem as Art Director — 3-D Animation on the critically acclaimed Mosh video.

One of the large-scale enhancements that Microsoft had insisted upon for DotNetNuke 2.0 also proved to be very popular. The data access layer in DotNetNuke had been re-architected using an abstract factory model, which effectively allowed it to interface with any number of relational databases. Microsoft had coined the term "provider model" and emphasized it as a key component in the future ASP.NET 2.0 framework. Therefore, getting a reference implementation of this pattern in use in ASP.NET 1.x had plenty of positive educational benefits for Microsoft and DotNetNuke developers. DotNetNuke 2.0 included both a fully functional SQL Server and MS Access version, and the community soon stepped forward with mySQL and Oracle implementations as well. Again the extensibility benefits of good architecture were extremely obvious and demonstrated the direction we planned to pursue in all future product development.

Upon review of the DotNetNuke 2.0 code base it was very obvious that the application bore very little resemblance to the original IBuySpy Portal application. This was a good thing because it raised the bar significantly in terms of n-tiered, object-oriented, enterprise-level software development. However, it was also bad in some ways because it alienated some of the early DotNetNuke enthusiasts who were in fact "hobby programmers," using the application more as a learning tool than a professional product. This is an interesting paradigm to observe in many open source projects. In the early stages, the developer community drives the feature set and extensibility requirements which, in turn, results in a much higher level of sophistication in terms of system architecture and design. However, as time goes on, this can sometimes result in the application surpassing the technical capabilities of some of its early adopters. DotNetNuke had ballooned from 15,000 lines of managed code to 46,000 lines of managed code in a little over six months. The project was getting large enough that it required some serious effort to understand its organizational structure, its dependencies, and its development patterns.

When researching the open source phenomenon, I found that there are a few fundamental details are often ignored in favor of positive marketing rhetoric. I would like to take the opportunity to bring some of these to the surface because they provide some additional insight into some of the issues we face in the DotNetNuke project.

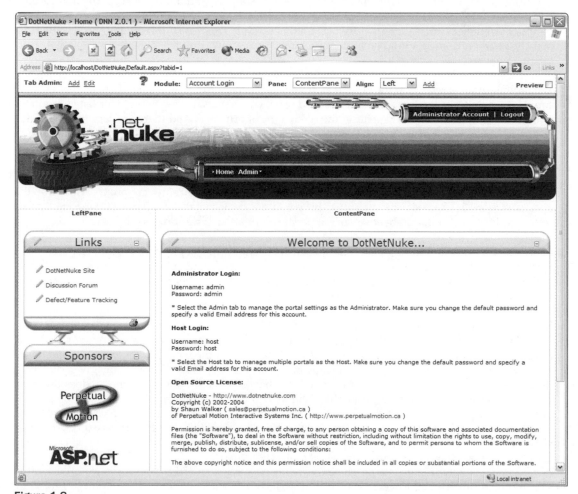

Figure 1-8

The first myth surrounds the belief that open source projects basically have an unlimited resource pool at their immediate disposal. While this may be true from a purely theoretical perspective, the reality is you still require a dedicated management structure to ensure all of the resources are channeled in an efficient and productive manner. An army of developers without some type of central management authority will never consistently produce a cohesive application; and more likely, their efforts will result in total chaos. As much as the concept is often despised by hard core programmers, dedicated management is absolutely necessary to set expectations and goals, ensure product quality, mitigate risk, recognize critical dependencies, manage scope, and assume ultimate responsibility. You will find no successful open source project that does not have an efficient and highly respected management team.

Further to the unlimited resourcing myth, there are in fact very few resources who become involved in an open source project that possess the level of competency and communication skills required to earn a highly trusted position in the meritocracy. More often, the resources who get involved are capable of handling more consumer-oriented tasks such as testing, support, and minor defect corrections. And this is not to say that these resources do not play a critical role in the success of the project; every focused ounce of volunteer effort certainly helps sustain the health of the project. But my point is that there is usually a relatively small group on most open source projects who are responsible for the larger scale architectural enhancements.

Yet another myth is related to the belief that anyone can make a direct and immediate impact on an open source project. While this may be true to some degree, you generally need to build a trusted reputation within the community before you are granted any type of privilege. And there are very few individuals who are ever awarded direct write access to the source code repository. Anyone has the ability to submit a patch or enhancement suggestion; however, this does not mean it is guaranteed to be added to the open source project code base. In fact, all submissions are rigorously peer reviewed by trusted resources, and only when they have passed all validation criteria are they introduced to the source code repository. From a control standpoint, this is not much different than a traditional software project. However, the open source model does significantly alter this paradigm in the fact that everyone is able to review the source code. As a result, the sheer volume of patches submitted to this process can be massive.

There are also some interesting interpretations of open source philosophy that occasionally result in differences of opinion and, in the worst cases, all-out community revolts. This generally occurs because the guidelines for open source are quite non-explicit and subjective. One particularly hot topic that relates to DotNetNuke is related to source code access.

Some open source projects provide anonymous read-only access to the development source code base at all times. This full transparency is appreciated by developers who want to stay abreast of the latest development efforts — even if they are not trusted members of the inner project team. These developers accept the fact that the development code may be in various stages of stability on any given day; yet they appreciate the direct access to critical fixes or enhancements. Although this model does promote more active external peer review it can often lead to a number of serious problems. If a developer decides to use pre-release code in a production environment, they may find themselves maintaining an insecure or unstable application. This can lead to a situation where the community is expected to support many hybrid variants rather than a consistent baseline application. Another issue that can happen is that a developer who succumbs to personal motivations may be inclined to incorporate some of the development enhancements into the current production version and release it as a new application version. While the open source license may allow this, it seriously affects the ability for official project maintainer to support the community. It is the responsibility of the project maintainer to always ensure a managed migration path from one version to the next. This model can only be supported if people are forced to use the official baseline releases offered by the project maintainer. Without these constants to build from, upgrades become a manual effort and many users are left on evolutionary dead-ends. For these reasons, DotNetNuke chooses to restrict anonymous read access to the development source code repository. Instead we choose to issue periodic point releases that allow us to provide a consistent upgrade mechanism as the project evolves.

Following the success of DotNetNuke 2.0 we focused on improving the stability and quality of the application. Many production issues had been discovered after the release that we would have never anticipated during internal testing. As an application becomes more extensible, people find new ingenious ways to apply it, which can often lead to unexpected results. We also integrated some key Roadmap enhancements, which had already been developed in isolation by Core Team members. These enhancements were actually quite advanced as they added a whole new level of professional features to the DotNetNuke code base, transforming it into a viable enterprise portal application.

It was during this time that Dan Caron single-handedly made a significant impact on the project. Based on his experience with other enterprise portals, he proceeded to add integrated exception handling and event logging to the application. This added stability and "auditability"; two major factors in most professional software products. He also added a complex, multithreaded scheduler to the application. The Scheduler was not just a simple hard-coded implementation like I had seen in other ASP.NET projects, but rather it was fully configurable via an administration user interface. This powerful new feature could be used to run background housekeeping jobs as well as long-running tasks. With this in place, the extensibility of the application improved yet again.

An interesting concern that came to our attention at this time was related to our dependence on external components. In order to provide the most powerful application, we had leveraged a number of rich third-party controls for their expert functionality. Because each of these controls was available under their own open source license, they seemed to be a good fit for the DotNetNuke project. But the fact is, there are some major risks to consider. Some open source licenses are viral in nature and have the potential to alter the license of the application they are combined with. In addition, there is nothing that prevents a third party from changing their licensing policy at any time. If this situation occurred, then it is possible that all users of the application who reference the control could be in violation of the new license terms. This is a fairly significant issue and certainly not something that can be taken lightly. Based on this knowledge, we quickly came up with a strategy that was aimed at minimizing our dependency on third-party components. We constructed a policy whereby we would always focus on building the functionality ourselves before considering an external control. And in the cases where a component was too elaborate to replicate, we would use a provider model, much like we had in the database layer, to abstract the application from the control in such a way that it would allow for a plug-in replacement. This strategy protects the community from external license changes and also provides some additional extensibility for the application.

With the great publicity on the www.asp.net web site following VS Live! and the consistent release of powerful new enhancements, the spring of 2004 brought a lot of traffic to the dotnetnuke.com community web site. At this point, the site was very poorly organized and sparse on content due to a lack of dedicated effort. Patrick Santry had been on the Core Team since its inception and his experience with building web sites for the ASP.NET community became very valuable at this time. We managed to make some fairly major changes to improve the site, but I soon realized that a dedicated resource would be required to accomplish all of our goals. But without the funding to secure such a resource, many of the plans had to unfortunately be shelved.

The summer of 2004 was a restructuring period for DotNetNuke. Thirty new community members were nominated for Core Team inclusion and the Core Team itself underwent a reorganization of sorts. The team was divided into an Inner Team and an Outer Team. The Inner Team designation was reserved for those original Core Team individuals who had demonstrated the most loyalty, commitment, and value to the project over the past year. The Outer Team represented individuals who had earned recognition for their community efforts and were given the opportunity to work toward Inner Team status. Among other privileges, write access to the source code repository is the pinnacle of achievement in any source code project, and members of both teams were awarded this distinction to varying degrees.

In addition to the restructuring, a set of Core Team guidelines was established that helped formulize the expectations for team members. Prior to the creation of these guidelines it was difficult to penalize non–performers because there were not objective criteria by which they could be judged. In addition to the new recruits, a number of inactive members from the original team were retired; mostly to demonstrate that Core Team inclusion was a privilege — not a right. The restructuring process also brought to light several deficiencies in the management of intellectual property and confidentiality among team members. As a result, all team members were required to sign a retroactive nondisclosure agreement as well as an intellectual property contribution agreement. All of the items exemplified the fact that the project had graduated from its "hobby" roots to a professional open source project.

During these formative stages, I was once again approached by Microsoft with an opportunity to showcase some specific ASP.NET features. Specifically, a Membership API had been developed by Microsoft for Whidbey (ASP.NET 2.0), and they were planning on creating a backported version for ASP.NET 1.1, which we could leverage in DotNetNuke. This time the benefits were not so immediately obvious and required some thorough analysis. This is because DotNetNuke already had more functionality in these areas than the new Microsoft API could deliver. So in order to integrate the Microsoft components without losing any features, we would need to wrap the Microsoft API and augment it with our own business logic. Before embarking on such an invasive enhancement, we needed to understand the clear business benefit provided.

Well, you can never discount Microsoft's potential to impact the industry. Therefore, being one of the first to integrate and support the new Whidbey APIs would certainly be a positive move. In recent months there had been numerous community questions regarding the applicability of DotNetNuke with the early Whidbey Beta releases now in active circulation. Early integration of such a core component from Whidbey would surely appease this group of critics. From a technology perspective, the Microsoft industry had long been awaiting an API to converge upon in this particular area; making application interoperability possible and providing best practice due diligence in the area of user and security information. Integrating the Microsoft API would allow DotNetNuke to "play nicely" with other ASP.NET applications; a key factor in some of the larger scale extensibility we were hoping to achieve. Last, but not least, it would further our positive relationship with Microsoft; a factor that was not lost on most as the key contributor to the DotNetNuke project's growth and success.

The reorganization of the Core Team also resulted in the formation of a small group of highly trusted project resources which, for lack of a better term, we named the Board of Directors. The members of this group included Scott Willhite, Dan Caron, Joe Brinkman, Patrick Santry, and myself. The purpose of this group was to oversee the long-term strategic direction of the project. This included discussion on confidential issues pertaining to partners, competitors, and revenue. In August 2004, we scheduled our first general meeting for Philadelphia, Pennsylvania. With all members in attendance, we made some excellent progress on defining action items for the coming months. This was also a great opportunity to finally meet in person some of the individuals whom we had only experienced Internet contact with in the past. With the first day of meetings behind us, the second day was dedicated to sightseeing in the historic city of Philadelphia. The parallels between the freedom symbolized by the Liberty Bell and the software freedom of open source were not lost on any of us that day.

Returning from Philadelphia, I knew that I had some significant deliverables on my plate. We began the Microsoft Membership API integration project with high expectations of completion within three months. But as before there were a number of high-priority community enhancements that had been promised prior to the Microsoft initiative, and as a result the scope snowballed. Scope management is an extremely difficult task to manage when you have such an active and vocal community.

The snowball effect soon revealed that the next major release would need to be labeled version 3.0. This is mostly because of "breaking" changes; modifications to the DotNetNuke core application that changed the primary interfaces to the point that plug-ins from the previous version 2.0 release would not integrate without at least some minimal changes. The catalyst for this was due to changes in the Membership API from Microsoft, but this only led to a decision of "if you are forced to back compatibility then introduce all of your breaking changes in one breaking release." The fact is, there had been a lot of baggage that had been preserved from the IBuySpy Portal, which we had been restricted from removing due to legacy support considerations. DotNetNuke 3.0 provided the opportunity to reexamine the entire project from a higher level and make some of the fundamental changes we had been delaying for, in some cases, years. This included the removal of a lot of dead code and deprecated methods as well as a full namespace reorganization, which finally accurately broke the project API into logical components.

DotNetNuke 3.0 also demonstrated another technical concept that would both enrich the functionality of the portal framework as well as improve the extensibility without the threat of breaking binary compatibility. Up until version 3.0 the service architecture for DotNetNuke was completely uni-directional. Custom modules could consume the resources and services offered by the core DotNetNuke framework but not vice versa. So although the application managed the secure presentation of custom modules within the portal environment, it could not get access to the custom module content information. Optional interfaces allow custom modules to provide plug-in implementations for defined core portal functions. They also provide a simple mechanism for the core framework to call into third-party modules, providing a bi-directional communication channel so that modules can finally offer resources and services to the core (see Figure 1-9).

Along with its many technological advances, DotNetNuke 3.0 was also being groomed for use by an entirely new stakeholder, Web Hosters. For a number of years the popularity of Linux hosting has been growing at a far greater pace than Windows hosting. The instability arguments of early Microsoft web servers were beginning to lose their weight as Microsoft released more resilient and higher quality server operating systems. Windows Server 2003 had finally shed its clunky Windows NT 4.0 roots and was a true force to be reckoned with. So aside from the obvious economic licensing reasons, there was another clear reason why Hosters were still favoring Linux over Windows for their clients — the availability of end-user applications.

The Linux platform had long been blessed with a plethora of open source applications running on the Apache web server, built with languages such as PHP, Perl, and Python and leveraging open source databases such as mySQL. The Windows platform was really lacking in this area and was desperately in need of applications to fill this void.

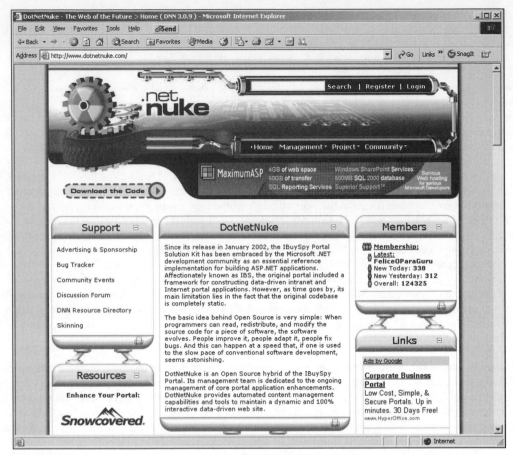

Figure 1-9

In order for DotNetNuke to take advantage of this opportunity, it needed a usability overhaul to transform it from a niche developer–oriented framework to a polished end-user product. This included a usability enhancement from both the portal administration as well as the web host perspectives. Since Rob Howard had left Microsoft in June 2004, my primary Microsoft contact had become Shawn Nandi. Shawn did a great job of drawing upon his usability background at Microsoft to come up with suggestions to improve the DotNetNuke end-user experience. Portal administrators received a multi-lingual user interface with both field-level and module-level help. Enhanced management functions were added in key locations to improve the intuitive nature of the application. Web Hosters received a customizable installation mechanism. In addition, the application underwent a security review to allow it to run in a Medium Trust—Code Access Security (CAS) environment. The end result is a powerful open source portal framework that can compete with the open source products on other platforms and offer Web Hosters a viable Windows alternative for their clients.

DotNetNuke is an evolving open source platform, with new enhancements being added constantly based on user feedback. The organic community ecosystem that has grown up around DotNetNuke is vibrant and dynamic, establishing the essential support infrastructure for long-term growth and prosperity. You will always be able to get the latest high-quality release including full source code from www.dotnetnuke.com.

2

Installing DotNetNuke

In the last chapter you were introduced to DotNetNuke, the concept of portals, and you formed a project plan for a DotNetNuke implementation. You also looked at architectural considerations such as web farms, databases, and web servers.

This chapter examines how to install DotNetNuke. Although the actual process of installing DotNetNuke isn't very difficult, it does consist of a large number of steps. During the installation process you will make critical decisions that affect your application, and undoing any mistakes can be quite time-consuming later. To avoid costly mistakes, you must understand issues such as hardware, software, and hosting prerequisites so that you can choose the best environment for DotNetNuke.

The chapter is divided into four major areas:

- ❑ **Preparation** discusses the goals of your installation based on your earlier project plan. Hardware, software, and hosting prerequisites are also explained.

- ❑ **Implementation** walks you step by step through the installation process.

- ❑ **Explanation** explores what actually happens during an installation and introduces the concept of upgrades.

- ❑ **Installation Templates** introduces a new method of customizing an installation.

Preparation

"Failure to prepare is preparing to fail." –John Wooden

Objectives

The objectives of this chapter are straightforward. You will install DotNetNuke so you can create portals and utilize the application's abilities.

The DotNetNuke application will be installed as a virtual directory with a URL formatted as

```
http:// <server name>/DotNetNuke/
```

The *<server name>* section of the URL could represent your local machine (localhost), a web server on your local network (intranet), or a web server external to your network (Internet).

Because many Internet web hosts offer a variety of different tools to manage the server environment, it is virtually impossible to cover all of these tools within the confines of this book. For that reason, we will only be discussing an installation where you have administrative control over a server and can access it either physically or remotely (remote desktop access).

Hardware Prerequisites

DotNetNuke does not require any hardware prerequisites per se, but it does require a list of software prerequisites, which do require a minimum level of hardware specification.

The following table lists SQL Server's minimum requirements (`www.microsoft.com/sql/evaluation/sysreqs/2000/default.asp`).

Processor	Intel Pentium or compatible 166-megahertz (MHz) or higher processor
Memory (RAM)	• Enterprise Edition: 64 megabytes (MB) of RAM; 128 MB recommended • Standard Edition: 64 MB • Evaluation Edition: 64 MB; 128 MB recommended • Developer Edition: 64 MB • Personal Edition: 128 MB for Windows XP; 64 MB for Windows 2000; 32 MB for other operating systems • MSDE: 128 MB for Windows XP; 64 MB for Windows 2000; 32 MB for other operating systems
Hard Disk	Enterprise, Standard, Evaluation, Developer, and Personal Editions require • 95–270 MB of available hard disk space for the server; 250 MB for a typical installation. • 50 MB of available hard disk space for a minimum installation of Analysis Services; 130 MB for a typical installation. • 80 MB of available hard disk space for English Query. MSDE requires 44 MB of available hard disk space.

Because DotNetNuke is a web application, it is preferable for your server to have a large amount of RAM (1 GB or greater) to avoid disk paging.

Software Prerequisites

Chapter 1 introduced a number of keywords such as web server and database. Both of these items are software prerequisites for DotNetNuke.

Web Server	Microsoft Internet Information Server 5 or greater (contained in Windows 2000 Server, Windows XP Professional, Windows 2003 Server)
Microsoft .NET Runtime	ASP.NET 1.1 or later (**Note:** At the time of writing this book, DotNetNuke will not run under the beta version of ASP.NET 2.0, although we are working toward compatibility as it nears release.)
Database	Microsoft SQL Server 2000 or greater (**Note:** DotNetNuke does run under a number of other databases provided by third parties; see www.dotnetnuke.com for more information.)

Hosting Prerequisites

Although we have already discussed the hardware and software prerequisites required by DotNetNuke, it is important to list the additional prerequisites that you should look for in third-party hosts. You should ask a prospective host if they support the following items:

File Permissions	DotNetNuke requires the account that the ASP.NET process runs under (see the following note) to have the file permission of FULL CONTROL over the root installation folder. (**Note:** The account ASP.NET runs under by default in Windows 2000 is the <MachineName>\ASPNET account; in Windows 2003 it is NT AUTHORITY\NETWORK SERVICE.)

Implementation

This section guides you step by step through the installation process. The steps illustrate an installation to a standalone server as discussed in our objectives. Later in this chapter, we discuss installation to a group of web servers (known as a web farm).

Downloading DotNetNuke

The first step in the installation process is to obtain the DotNetNuke software. The latest version of the software can be downloaded at the official DotNetNuke web site (www.dotnetnuke.com/).

Note: you must be a registered user to reach the download page.

Extracting the Installation File

The DotNetNuke distribution arrives as a single zip file. The zip file contains the source code, documentation, and database scripts necessary for the application to operate. Extract the entire contents of the zip file to your chosen installation directory (for example, c:\websites\dotnetnuke\).

To extract a zip file you can either use the built-in zip functionality of Windows XP or a third-party compression tool such as WinZip, which you can obtain from www.winzip.com/.

Creating the Database

The next step is to create the database that will contain your data for the DotNetNuke application.

To perform this, you should have the Microsoft Sql Server Client Tools installed, and in particular Enterprise Manager. If you do not have these, they can be installed from the CD that Microsoft SQL Server was installed from.

Note: If you do not have access to Enterprise Manager, for example, if you are using MSDE, you can try a third-party tool such as ASP.NET Enterprise Manager, a web-based interface for Microsoft SQL Server and MSDE. It is designed to perform many SQL Server and MSDE administration tasks from any computer with a web browser. You can get this tool at www.aspenterprisemanager.com/.

Once you have opened Enterprise Manager, you can expand the database server you want to create your database. If it's not listed, you will have to register your SQL Server instance with Enterprise Manager. To do this, please refer to the Enterprise Manager help.

Now that you have found your database server — in our case, it is our local machine known as (local) — you can create your database by right-clicking the Databases node under your database and selecting New Database, as shown in Figure 2-1.

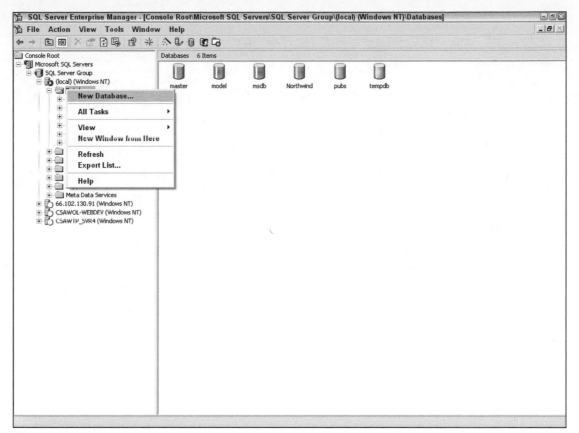

Figure 2-1

A dialog box appears asking for a database name; you can put in any name. For our example, we'll put in DotNetNuke, as shown in Figure 2-2. Once you are happy with the name, click OK.

Further configuration options are listed on the dialog (Data Files and Transaction Log), but we will accept the defaults for the purposes of a quick installation. For further information about these options, please see the help file that comes with Enterprise Manager.

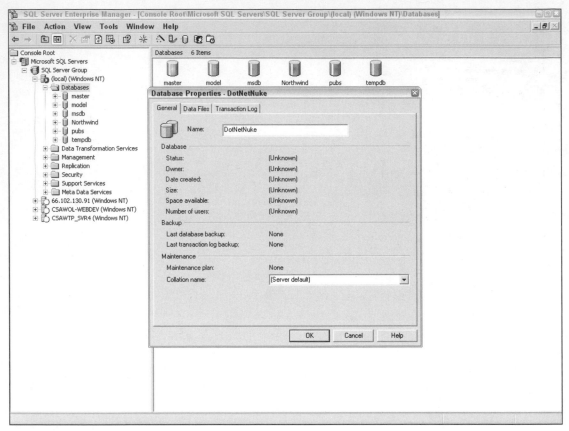

Figure 2-2

Creating the Database User

The next step is the creation of a user account to access the database.

Strictly speaking, you have two options:

❑   **Windows Security** uses the account that your application is running under to access the database. This is the more secure option, but it is not supported in all environments, particularly in shared hosting.

❑   **SQL Server Security** uses a username and password combination to access the database. This is supported in most environments, and is most similar to other database servers.

For the purposes of this book, we'll use SQL Server Security, but we encourage you to explore Windows Security, especially in environments where you control the infrastructure.

To create a user account for the database, you first need to navigate to the Security node located at the top level of the server you are connecting to (in Enterprise Manager). Expand it, select the Logins node, and you should see the list of users who already have access to your database server in the right-hand pane.

Now that you are at the login section, right-click the Logins node and select New Login, as shown in Figure 2-3.

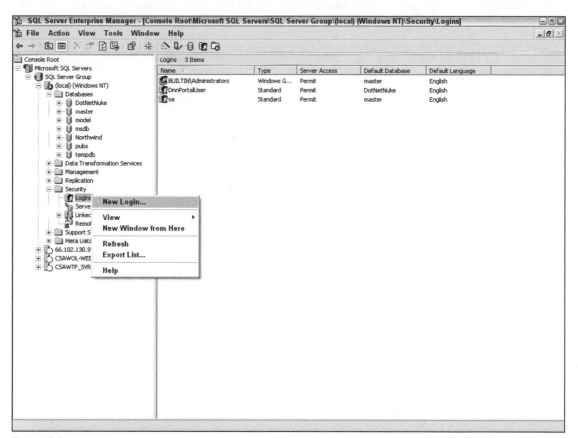

Figure 2-3

You should see a dialog box appear prompting for details about the account. In this case, create a user called DotNetNukeUser as both the username and password. Make sure you select the Sql Server Authentication radio option; otherwise it will create an account for Windows Authentication. Figure 2-4 shows a sample dialog with the details filled in.

You should also select the default database from the drop-down list; in our case it is the name of our database (DotNetNuke). The default database allows that database to be selected by default when connecting as that user.

Before you click OK, there is one more step you need to perform. Even though we have selected DotNetNuke as our default database, we still need to grant our user access to Read/Write from it. To do this, select the Database Access tab and check the Permit check box next to the DotNetNuke database.

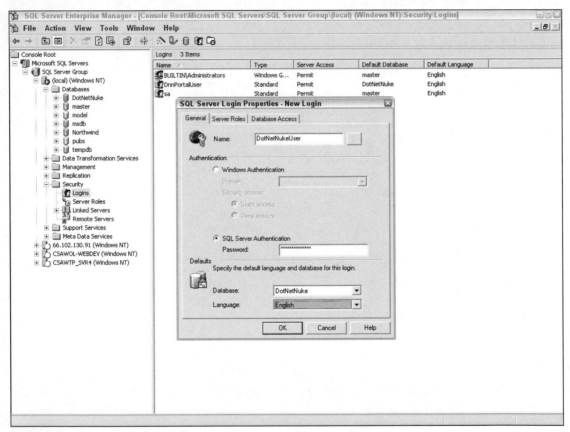

Figure 2-4

You should also grant the account db_owner privileges by checking that check box in the bottom of the dialog. The account needs db_owner privileges because it will be creating and dropping many database objects.

Figure 2-5 shows the correct settings. Once you have them set, click OK, confirm the password as prompted, and click OK again.

Now that you have created the account, it should appear in the right task pane whenever you select the Logins node, and you can come back here anytime to change details about this account.

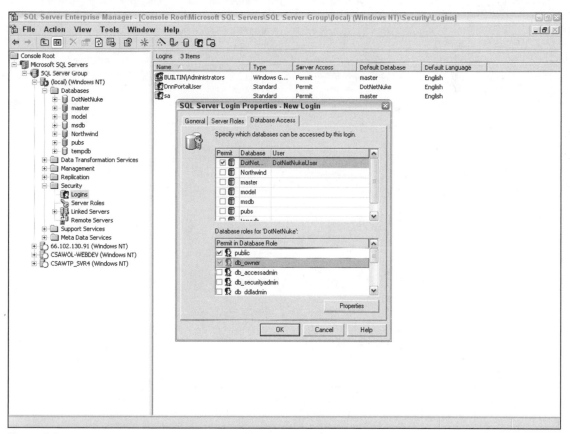

Figure 2-5

Setting Permissions

The next step in the process is to set the file permissions required by the software. DotNetNuke has the capability to create many portals in the one installation, in effect becoming a small host itself. To perform this task, it needs to create, delete, and modify directories and files. It is these operations that require the application to have extra permissions over files within the application.

To assign these permissions, navigate through File Manager to your installation folder (for example, c:\websites\DotNetNuke\). Right-click the root folder and select the "sharing and security" option. When the dialog appears, select the Security tab. The dialog that appears is shown in Figure 2-6.

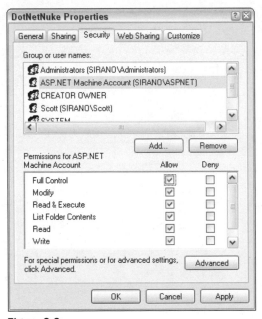

Figure 2-6

You should add either the aspnet user account (Windows 2000, Windows XP), the Network Service user account (Windows 2003), or if you have changed the account your site runs under (for advanced users), then that is the account to specify. The chosen account should be granted Full Control.

Before clicking OK, click the Advanced button and another dialog will appear allowing extra configuration. Ensure that the chosen account listed has a rule of "This folder, subfolders and files." You can see the list of rules in the Permission entries section. Figure 2-7 shows the advanced dialog.

Once confirmed, click OK to close the advanced dialog, and click OK again to close the properties dialog.

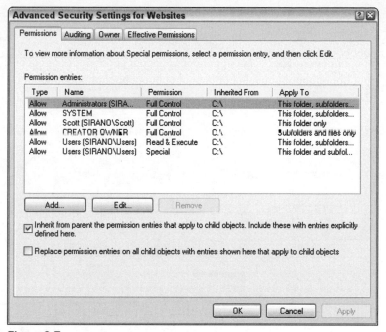

Figure 2-7

Creating the Web Site

So far you've only extracted the files and created a database to store your application's data. It's now time to register your application with your chosen web server. Registering your files with the web server allows you to view the site from `http://<server name>/DotNetNuke/`.

To administer IIS, click the Start Menu; select the Run Command, type in **inetmgr**, and click OK. Alternatively, you can access it from the Control Panel ⇨ Administrative Tools ⇨ Internet Information Services.

The administration console for IIS should appear, showing a node with the local computer's name; expand this item to reveal the list of web sites on the local computer. Figure 2-8 shows the default configuration for IIS.

> *If your IIS is not hosted on the local computer, you can remotely administer IIS by right-clicking the Internet Information Services node, selecting Connect, and following on the on-screen prompts to connect to the remote computer.*

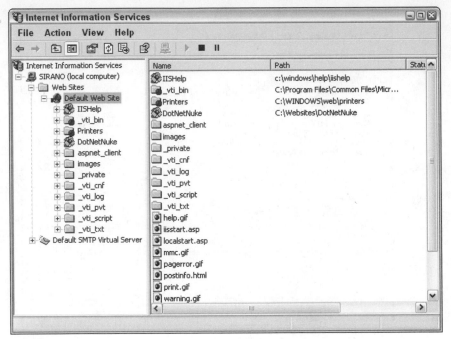

Figure 2-8

Once you have done this, you should see a list of web sites for that IIS instance. Figure 2-8 shows the default web site that is automatically configured when IIS is installed, and serves as a default "catch all" for requests on port 80.

For the purposes of this chapter, we'll be using the default web site. IIS does support multiple web sites, just not under Windows XP. If you want to learn more about configuring multiple web sites (to possibly host many different domain names) see the IIS help.

Before walking through the steps, we'll explain a few key IIS terms and how IIS works from an administrator's perspective.

When developing locally, or on your internal network, you may want to use two features in IIS called Virtual Directories and IIS Applications.

A Virtual Directory refers to a directory underneath a web site that does not actually physically reside in that location. The web site contains a pointer to elsewhere on the file system. This is handy if you do not want to put all of your web sites under the default c:\inetpub\wwwroot\ location. You may instead want to put them under a location such as c:\websites\DotNetNuke.

An IIS Application refers to an entry point of a web application. It allows the ASP.NET runtime to determine where such things as configuration files and assemblies reside for a given application.

So, keeping in mind that you want your URL to look like this:

```
http:// <server name>/DotNetNuke/
```

you'll need to set up a virtual directory that points to your folder where you extracted the DotNetNuke source code files and then set it as an IIS Application.

To do this, right-click the Default Web Site and select New ⇨ Virtual Directory. The Virtual Directory Creation Wizard appears as shown in Figure 2-9.

Figure 2-9

Click Next to proceed to the next step in the wizard, which is specifying the Portal Alias.

The Virtual Directory Alias refers to the virtual name assigned to IIS that will map to your chosen installation directory.

Remember, you want your URL to look like `http://<server name>/DotNetNuke`, so your virtual directory name would be DotNetNuke. Enter this term in the dialog, as shown in Figure 2-10, and click Next.

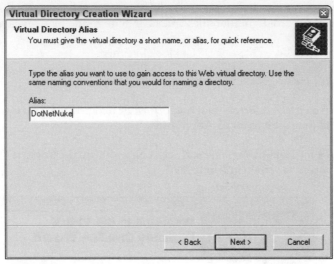

Figure 2-10

The next step is to select the physical file location for the Virtual Directory. This should point to the location from which you extracted your .NET Nuke source files. For our example, this is our installation directory (for example, c:\websites\DotNetNuke\). Figure 2-11 shows the completed step. Once you have selected the location, click Next.

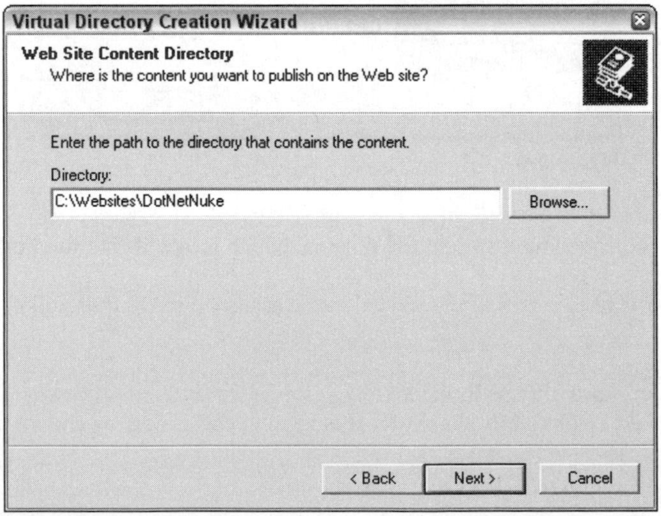

Figure 2-11

The last step is to specify the permissions applicable for the Virtual Directory. You should just keep the defaults of Read and Run Scripts. Once you have ensured that these are selected, click Next and then click Finish. Figure 2-12 shows the correct options.

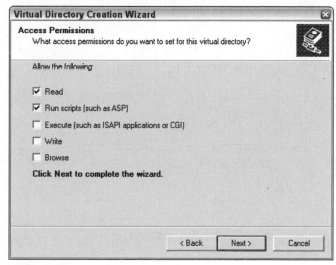

Figure 2-12

If you are installing to a development server, such as your local machine, you may want to check Directory Browsing. This allows you to connect to your web site in Visual Studio .NET via File ⇨ Open ⇨ Project from Web. For production sites, it is not recommended that you check Directory Browsing.

Now that you have set up a Virtual Directory (DotNetNuke) pointing at your unzipped location (c:\websites\DotNetNuke\ or equivalent), there is an additional step in IIS you must perform.

Earlier in this chapter we discussed the concept of an IIS Application as a term that represents the entry point of an application. ASP.NET needs this established to determine at what level to look for configuration files, binary files, and so on.

When you create a Virtual Directory it will automatically be set as an IIS Application. To confirm that your virtual directory is set as an IIS Application, right-click the node DotNetNuke and then click Properties. You should see a screen similar to the one shown in Figure 2-13.

If you look under the Application Settings section of the dialog box, you'll notice that it has an application name, and the button to the right has the name "Remove." If it was not set as an application, it would have the word "Create" to make a new Virtual Directory. You can also tell whether a Virtual Directory is set up as an IIS Application by the type of icon. IIS Applications have icons that look like open boxes.

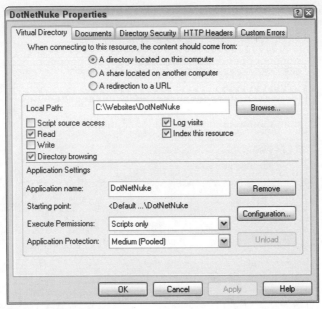

Figure 2-13

You can also change the properties you set during the wizard at any time by returning to this dialog box. For more information about the choices you have available, please consult the IIS help system.

Configuring .NET Nuke

The next step is to tell DotNetNuke how to communicate with the database.

To do this, navigate to your folder (for example, `c:\websites\DotNetNuke\`) and open up the Web.config found in this directory. You can use your favorite text editor to do this, including Visual Studio .NET.

The Web.config is the central administration file for ASP.NET; it is designed to store configuration settings such as connection strings and site-specific settings.

DotNetNuke's web.config file is used to store the database connection string, as well as a variety of other settings relating to how DotNetNuke works, and the various application hooks that are designed in the application.

For the purposes of the installation, you want to set a connection string that will tell DotNetNuke how to connect to your chosen database (Sql Server).

Locate the AppSettings section in the configuration file and then locate the SiteSqlServer element. Change the value attribute to specify the location of your database, the username, and the password. Listing 2-1 shows a sample connection string for a server residing on the localhost.

Once you have made the changes, save the web.config file.

Listing 2-1: Changing the Connection String

```
<appSettings>
<add key="SiteSqlServer"
value="Server=(local);Database=dnnportalbook;uid=dnnportaluser;pwd=dnnportaluser;"
/>
 <add key="MachineValidationKey" value="F9D1A2D3E1D3E2F7B3D9F90FF3965ABDAC304902"
/>
 <add key="MachineDecryptionKey"
value="F9D1A2D3E1D3E2F7B3D9F90FF3965ABDAC304902F8D923AC" />
 <add key="MachineValidationMode" value="SHA1" />
 <add key="InstallTemplate" value="DotNetNuke.install" />
</appSettings>
```

Testing the Installation

Here's a recap of what you have done during the implementation section of this chapter. You should verify that you have performed these steps:

1. Downloaded and extracted the .NET Nuke source to a directory.
2. Created a database (DotNetNuke) and a database user (DotNetNukeUser).
3. Set the necessary ASP.NET permissions on the extracted folder.
4. Created a Virtual Directory in IIS, and made sure it was set as an IIS Application.
5. Changed the connection string in the Web.Config.

If you have completed all these steps, you should be able to open up your web browser and navigate to

```
http://<server name>/DotNetNuke/
```

This request will take some time, so be patient and do not hit Refresh. Here are two reasons why this takes some time:

❑ ASP.NET will be Just-In-Time compiling the assemblies.

❑ DotNetNuke will be building the database to the latest version. (See the following "Explanation" section.)

As it is upgrading, you should see some messages appear on the screen as shown in Figure 2-14. These messages are designed to provide immediate feedback about the installation progress to the administrator.

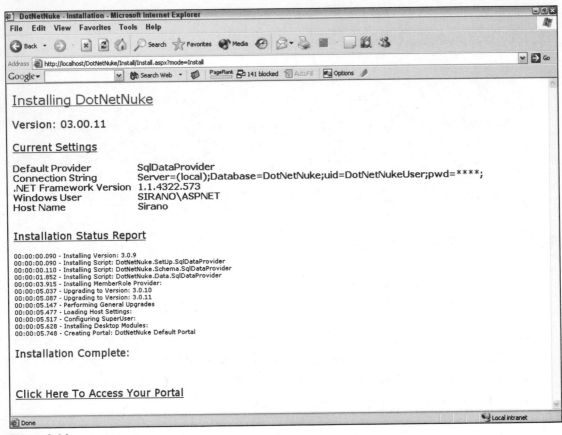

Figure 2-14

If everything is successful, you should now have a link to visit the first page on your site. Click that link and you should be presented with a screen similar to that in Figure 2-15.

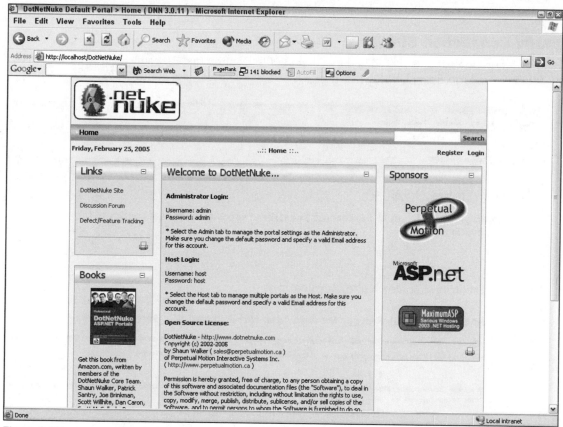

Figure 2-15

Common Installation Issues

Some people may have problems when trying to run the application. We have tried to provide screens to assist in diagnosing an issue associated with an installation. This section describes some common issues.

Invalid Connection String

Your connection string is invalid in the web.config file. Confirm that the connection string is correct, the database has been created, and the user has access to the database (see Figure 2-16).

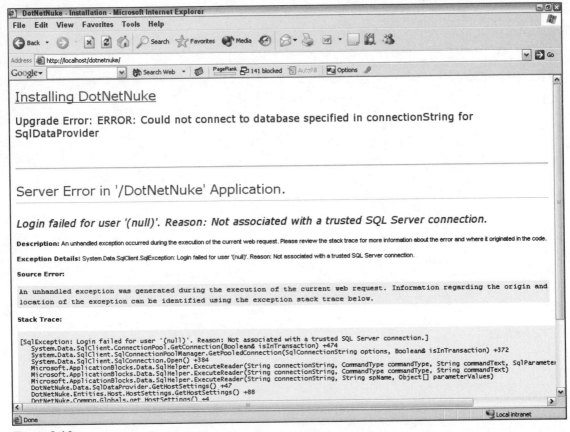

Figure 2-16

Insufficient File Permissions

You have not correctly set the file permissions. This could be because you have not granted access to the root of the folder, or you have specified a different account than the account currently running the ASP.NET request, as shown in Figure 2-17. See the "Setting Permissions" section earlier in this chapter for more information.

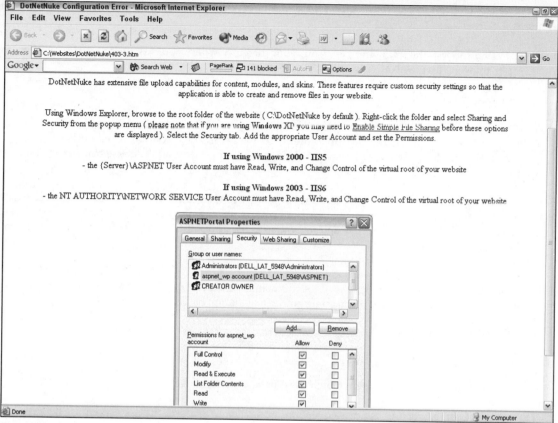

Figure 2-17

Explanation

This section takes a step away from the actual installation and discusses the process DotNetNuke goes through at installation time.

When you download DotNetNuke, you are essentially getting two types of files.

The first group of files is the source code, binary assemblies, and the associated resource files that belong to any web site. These typically have extensions like .aspx, .ascx, .gif, .jpg, and so on, and you should see these scattered throughout the folder you unzipped in the preceding section.

The second group is a collection of SQL scripts; these scripts are versioned and correspond to certain releases issued by the core team.

Because we have already selected Sql Server as our target database (default choice), let's take a look at the SQL Server–specific scripts.

You can find them in the following path from your directory where you extracted your files earlier (for example, c:\websites\DotNetNuke\):

```
\Providers\DataProviders\SqlDataProvider
```

You should see a collection of scripts, ordered in version, from 00.00.00.SqlDataProvider to 01.00.00.SqlDataProvider all the way up to the current version. These scripts are actually Structured Query Language (SQL) scripts, which when executed will upgrade your database from one version to another.

In other applications, these files are executed manually by an administrator. DotNetNuke saves you the time and executes these files during an installation or an upgrade. In a sense, DotNetNuke is responsible for keeping your database up to date and in sync with the application code. Following is a look at how it actually works.

As mentioned in the introduction, DotNetNuke is versioned in two places, at the binary level (code) and at the schema level (database). So what does this actually mean? It means at runtime you can ask questions about the versions, and perform an upgrade/installation based on the answers.

The questions essentially are

❑   What assembly version am I?

❑   Does that assembly version match the database version?

The next decision is when to ask these questions and when to perform the corresponding actions; ideally you would like to ask them when the application first starts, for example when the first person requests a page. ASP.NET provides a number of hooks into the pipeline of a request. One hook is an event that occurs during the initialization of an application (application_start). The questions (and actions) just mentioned are placed in this event.

To better explain the process, the following sections look at the only two scenarios: a brand new installation and an upgrade from an earlier version.

Scenario 1: The Clean Install

This scenario examines the process of installing a new install of DotNetNuke on a site that does not currently exist.

When the initial request is sent to DotNetNuke, it checks the version of the assembly. At the time of this writing, that version number is 3.0.11. It then checks the version held in the database. This essentially would be version 0.0 on a clean install because none of the tables have actually been created.

So, given that the version is 0.0, it will run the SQL scripts in order to build the database. Each version ever released has its own SQL script. Once the database has been upgraded, DotNetNuke will render the Installation Complete page.

Scenario 2: The Upgrade

The next scenario is very common; the core team has released a new version of DotNetNuke and it has great new features that you want to take advantage of.

You've backed up your file structure and your database, and you are ready to upgrade. Once you copy the new files to your site, and the first request is received, DotNetNuke checks the assembly version, which would be the new value (say, 3.0.11), and then it checks the database version (say, 2.1.2). It then proceeds to execute the scripts between these two values until they match.

Your site will retain the content, skins, and modules it already had, and you have effectively upgraded your site and can now take advantage of the new features that version offers.

Installation Templates

One of the exciting new features in DotNetNuke version 3 is the introduction of installation templates. These are designed to give administrators more control over the installation process and the default content/configuration that is created. This is specifically targeted at web hosts or administrators offering a packaged solution.

These templates allow you to customize aspects of an installation such as the following:

❑ SQL scripts to build the database

❑ User accounts to create

❑ Default settings inside DotNetNuke such as Mail Server, Proxy Server, Friendly Urls, and so on

❑ Portals to create

❑ Modules installed

The DotNetNuke installation source contains a file (dotnetnuke.install.resources), which is an xml file containing the various settings discussed above. Figure 2-18 shows an example file.

You can find it in the following path:

```
"/Portals/_default"
```

The template itself is broken up into a number of sections, as described next.

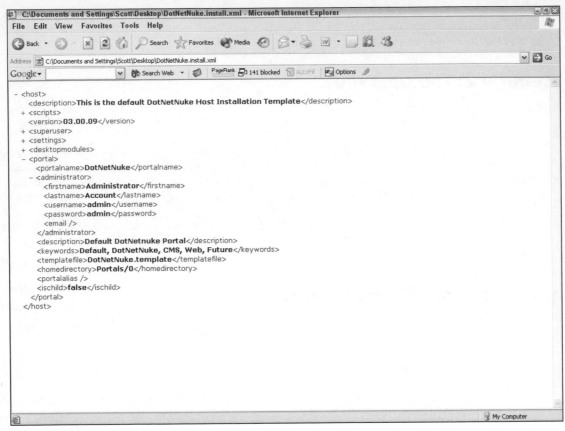

Figure 2-18

The <host> node is the root node of the template. All other nodes are the children of <host>. There are eight immediate children:

- ❑ **<description>:** Provides a description of the template.

- ❑ **<schemascript>:** Name of the Script file that builds the Database Schema (this file must be located in the folder indicated by the providerPath attribute of the default Data provider in web.config).

- ❑ **<datascript>:** Name of the Script file that builds the required Database Data (this file must be located in the folder indicated by the providerPath attribute of the default Data provider in web.config).

- ❑ **<version>:** The database version that the <schemascript>, <datascript> files build. This is usually the current version, but if the version is less than the current version the appropriate upgrade scripts are run to make the database version equal app version.

- ❑ **<superuser>:** Information about the superuser (Host Account). This node allows you to specify a default superuser other than the default (Host/Host).

❑ **<settings>:** The default host settings for the application — the child nodes of this node correspond to the HostSettings table in the database, and are managed under the Host/Host Settings menu (after installation).

❑ **<desktopmodules>:** The desktop modules to install for this installation. This can be very useful when you want to reduce the default number of modules a user can see within a portal.

❑ **<portal>:** The default portal configuration.

If you want to make a new file so you can change the settings, you can point to a new file via the web.config file using the following element:

```
<add key="InstallTemplate" value="DotNetNuke.install" />
```

Summary

This chapter covered a typical DotNetNuke installation. It provided a step-by-step guide to installing your own DotNetNuke application, as well as introduced the new method of customizing an installation.

Hopefully by following the steps in this chapter you can perform a successful installation. We hope to make DotNetNuke a piece of software that requires very little administration by technical people and becomes more about site administration by end users.

Portal Overview

This chapter looks at the various sections of the DotNetNuke application from an administrator and user's view. The application offers 15 content modules natively, which allow a broad range of content to be presented to your visitors, and a wide range of modules that provide an interface for administering your installation. The base installation of DotNetNuke allows you to set up a fully functional web site that will provide the presentation of information most web sites will need. You can also find a wide range of third-party modules that will easily plug into the application and allow you to extend the functionality of DotNetNuke further. Let's look at some of the features available to you from a base installation of the application.

What Is a Portal?

DotNetNuke uses the term *portal* to describe a separation between each web site one instance of the application may contain. So you might ask, what is a portal? Webster defines a web application portal as "a website considered as an entry point to other websites, often by being or providing access to a search engine." This can be true of DotNetNuke, but it is really more than just a doorway to other applications or search engines. It can, in essence, perform these functions as well as a host of others associated with displaying information to your users.

For the purposes of this discussion we can define a portal as the related data for one web site hosted within your DotNetNuke installation. The application natively provides the ability to host multiple web sites from the same code base, all containing different information and presented to the user at runtime based on the URL the user uses to access the code base. Exactly how the application accomplishes this task is covered in another chapter. For our discussion we can refer to two types of portals, parent or child portals, which are discussed in detail later in this chapter. As the portal administrator you can set up hundreds of various web sites on the same portal. These can be a combination of parent and child portals, and at runtime the application will determine the proper content to display to the user based on the PortalID of the portal that is accessed. This is one of the most powerful features of this application and probably accounts for the rapid growth of the application since its inception. You define the difference between whether a portal becomes a child or parent portal when you create the portal.

Portal Organizational Elements

This section examines the organizational elements of a portal.

Parent/Child Portals

Let's look at the differences in the format of the URL between the two types of portals. A parent portal's URL takes the format of http://www.YourDomain.com and a child portal takes the format of http://www.YourDomain.com/YourChildPortal. The application installation may contain any combination of parent or child portals. The only real difference between how you set up the various types of portals is how you define the portal. Figure 3-1 shows the options available in the Portal administration module.

The Portal module gives you several options when setting up a new portal. Notice the radio buttons for selecting a parent or child portal. Selecting the child portal requires no further configuration outside of the application. To set up a parent portal you must perform some additional steps. You first need to set up an additional web site in your IIS Manager with host headers for your domain name and create a DNS record to point to the IP address of your web server. Information on how to perform these tasks is outside of the scope of this book, so please refer to your IIS and DNS help files for the steps. You can find specific details on how to use each of the functions for setting up a new portal in Chapter 5, which covers the host functions of DotNetNuke.

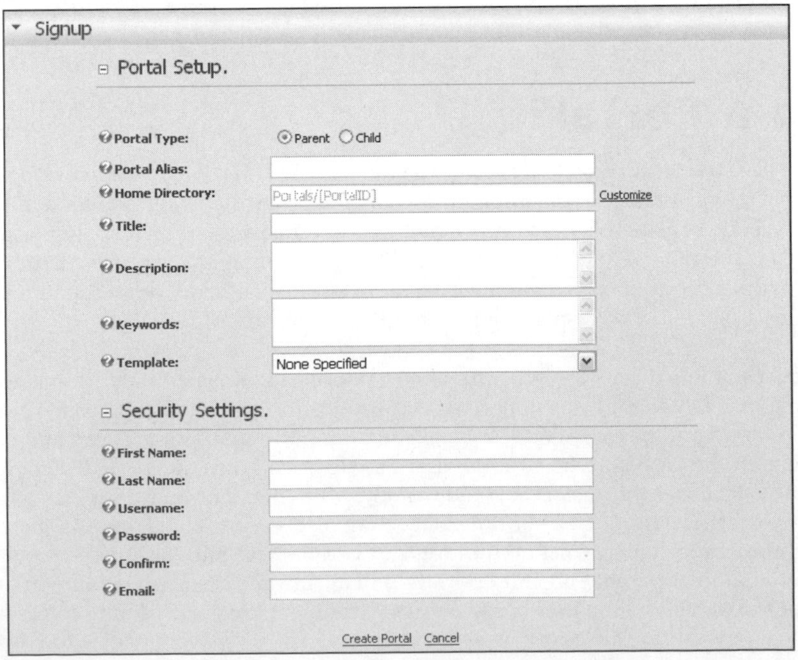

Figure 3-1

Pages

Pages are a relatively new concept in DotNetNuke. Prior to version 3.x these were referred to as tabs. This change was made to allow for a more user-friendly experience for the novice who may not be a programmer by trade. You can think of a page in the same way you think of a static html page. The difference is that the application loads the content based on the parameters passed to it at runtime.

In reality there is really only one page in the application that displays all the content to your users. Exactly how this works is explained in detail in the architecture and API chapters. Figure 3-2 shows the options for administering your portal pages.

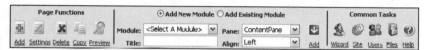

Figure 3-2

In the left corner you will notice the Page Functions menu. These functions allow you to manage your pages. These are fairly self-documenting and you can deduce the purpose of each function by its name. Table 3-1 describes each of the available functions.

Table 3-1: Page Functions

Function	Description
Add	This is where you add a new page to the portal. After you select this menu option you are presented with the Page Management control, where you can define your page properties such as Page Name, Title, Keywords, Security, and so on.
Settings	The Settings menu allows you to modify a page created earlier. You will be taken to the edit page for the current page and you will be able to modify all the properties of the page.
Delete	Delete allows you to remove the current page from your portal.
Copy	Copy defaults to allow copying of the modules located on the current page. You also have the option of duplicating the content in the modules of the current page. This is a real time-saver when setting up your portal.
Preview	Preview allows you to view your page in the same manner your users will view it. This helps you ensure that your users see your content as you intended. This function also produces more questions than any other function for novices with DotNetNuke. If you are administering your portal and suddenly notice you can no longer edit the individual items of your modules, ensure this Preview mode is turned off because it is likely your problem.

As you can see, the name adequately describes each option's function. DotNetNuke attempts to follow this same structure throughout the application. Figure 3-3 illustrates the options available in the Page Management page, which you use to add new pages to your portal.

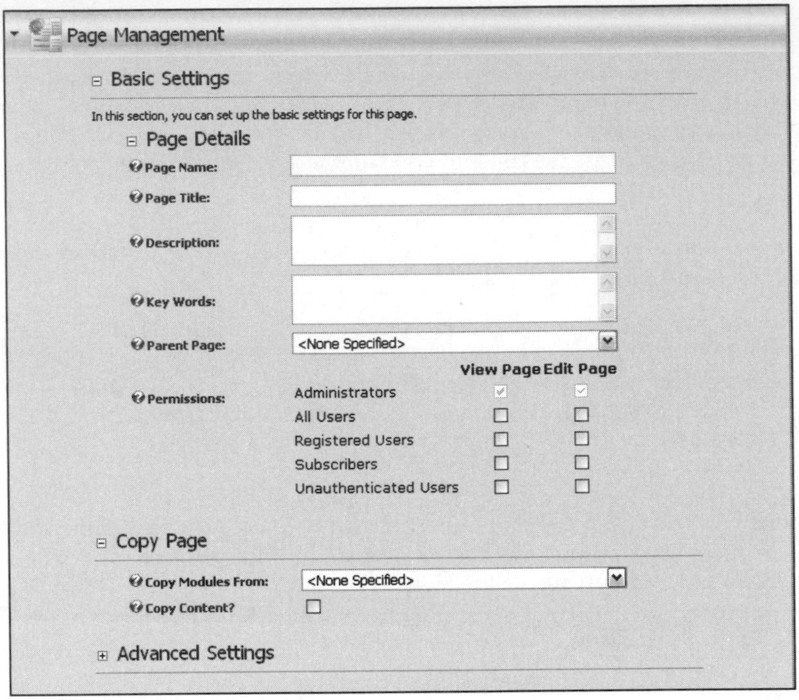

Figure 3-3

As you will see in later chapters, DotNetNuke utilizes an object-oriented approach in all functions where feasible. This allows the application to reuse various components of the application, which creates a common user interface for most of the functions. You will see many of the same options available throughout the administration screens. The application utilizes the same user controls in numerous areas, which accomplishes two main functions: it allows a consistent look and feel to the application and it simplifies the amount of code required to perform these functions. One thing new to DNN 3.X is the addition of field-level help. Notice the question mark images in Figure 3-3. These images expand when clicked, offering some additional descriptions on the type of information the field expects. This helps reduce the learning curve associated with managing your content.

Panes

Panes are the areas of your skin that hold the various content modules you will drop on each page. These allow you to organize your content in a manner that makes the best use of your site real estate. The number of panes is controlled by your skin design. For a full discussion on creating skins, see Chapter 13. Panes are dynamically populated at runtime with the modules assigned to the page. The types of modules you can use to display your content are discussed in the "Modules" section later in this chapter.

One thing to be aware of when you are changing skins in your portal is that the pane names must match the ones in your current skin. Otherwise, you will need to reposition your modules to the proper pane because a skin change may cause your modules to all become defined in the ContentPane. The

ContentPane is strict requirement for skins and a skin will not function without this pane. DotNetNuke ships with several prebuilt skins to help you get started launching your new site.

Containers

Containers allow you to enhance the look of your portal without any design changes to your skin. A container's purpose is to surround the content of a module with some design element, which allows you to bring more attention to the content of the module. You have two options for applying containers to your portal: You can apply a default container to your entire portal or set a container for each individual module. Let's add a module to a page and set up a container for a visual reference.

Now, modify the container of the Links module to change the look of the default page. First select the Settings option from the module actions menu as shown in Figure 3-4.

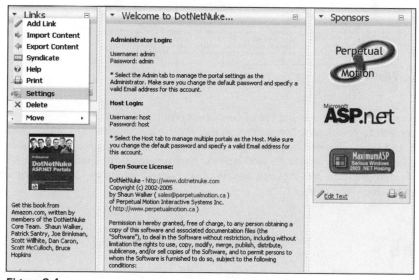

Figure 3-4

Selecting the Settings tab navigates you to the Module Settings page for the Links module. You will notice the Module Settings page contains many of the same options as the Portal Settings page; this is an example of maintaining a consistent interface throughout the application through the use of the object-oriented programming we've used in DotNetNuke. Scroll down to the Page Settings ➪ Basic Settings Panel in the Module Setting control (you may need to expand the panels by clicking the + sign for each panel and selecting a new container for this module). Currently this module is using one of the default containers that ship with the application. Select the DNN - Blue - Text Header - White Background container and update your module. You are then taken back to your original page and you will immediately see the difference this one change makes. Go ahead and update all the modules on this page so you can really see the difference. As you can see in Figure 3-5, the entire look of this page changes with only a few mouse clicks.

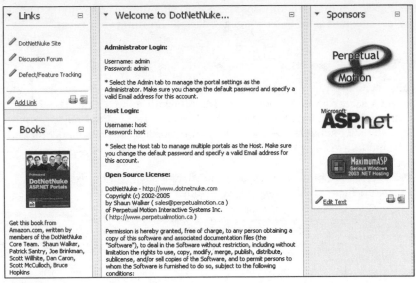

Figure 3-5

You can see by this example that the use of containers offers you a lot of flexibility with controlling the display of content to your users. Normally you will want your containers to match the colors and design of your site, and most skins provide these complements as part of the package. Many commercial and free versions of skins are available for DotNetNuke that you can download or purchase. Refer to the DotNetNuke web site for links to a wide variety of skins and containers. Creating skins and containers is covered extensively in Chapter 13.

Modules

Modules are the meat and potatoes of the DotNetNuke application. Modules are the components that allow DotNetNuke to finally serve its intended purpose of displaying relative, easy-to-update content to your visitors. The applications for these modules and how to use them to add your content is covered in Chapter 6. Hundreds of free and commercial modules are available that you can obtain to extend the functionality offered by the application. Just perform a web search for "DotNetNuke Modules" with your favorite search engine and you will be able to find a module to meet almost any need you may have for managing content. This section of the chapter provides an overview of each module and prepares you for the detailed information in Chapter 6, which shows you how easy it is to use the modules to present content to your users. With version 3 of DotNetNuke, all the content modules have been divided into separate projects, which allows you to pick and choose the modules you need for your installation. So, if your specific business requirement does not need an RSS module, you can remove it from your installation without any adverse effects or any modifications of the core code. This is an important enhancement from a business perspective because it allows you to easily modify the application to accommodate your unique business rules and needs.

Account Login

The Account Login module provides the login interface as a module. In can be useful in two scenarios:

❑ The first scenario is when you would like the login dialog to appear on the home page (without the user clicking the login link).

❑ The second scenario is to be used on a login page, which could contain additional modules. You can specify any page within your portal as the login page via the administration screens located at Admin ➪ Site Settings ➪ Advanced Setting ➪ Page Management.

Announcements

As its name suggests, the Announcements module is used to present a list of announcements. Each announcement includes a title, text, and a "read more" link. Optionally, the announcement can be set to expire after a specified date.

Banners

DotNetNuke provides a rich set of vendor management tools. One of the tools provided is the Banners module. This module is used to display the advertising banners of vendors created within the portal. Management of these vendors and creation of banners is performed in the administration area located at Admin ➪ Vendors. The module itself provides facilities to select the number of banners to display and the banner type.

Contacts

The Contacts module renders contact information for a group of people; some example groups are a project team, a sporting team, or personnel within your department. The module provides an edit page, which allows authorized users to edit and add contacts.

Discussions

The Discussions module is a threaded discussion board; it provides groups of messages threaded on a single topic. Each message includes a Read/Reply Message page, which allows authorized users to reply to existing messages or add a new message thread. Although this is not a full-fledged forum module, it offers some functionality that you can use to enable light forum activities on your site.

Documents

The Documents module renders a list of documents, including links to browse or download the document. The module includes an edit page, which allows authorized users to edit or add the information about a document (for example, a friendly title).

Events

The Events module renders a list of upcoming events, including time and location. Individual events can be set to automatically expire from the list after a particular date. The module includes an edit page, which allows authorized users to edit or add an event.

FAQ

The FAQ module allows an authorized user to manage a list of Frequently Asked Questions and their corresponding answers. This is a great module for reducing support calls to your customer service center because you can compile a list of the questions you receive about your business or services and present this data to your users.

Feedback

The Feedback module allows visitors to send messages to the administrator of the portal. With version 3 of the portal software you have the ability to customize this module to send e-mails to various individuals within your organization depending on the message content. This was not available in previous versions because all e-mails sent from the module were sent to the portal administrator. This is just one more example of how DotNetNuke allows you to assign different tasks to the correct individuals in your organization.

IFrame

The IFrame module is an Internet Explorer browser feature that allows you to display content from another web site within a frame on your site.

Image

The Image module renders an image using an HTML IMG tag. This module includes an edit page that allows an authorized user to specify the location of the image that can reside internal or external to the portal. The authorized user can also specify height and width attributes, which permits you to scale the image.

Links

The Links module renders a list of hyperlinks. This module includes an edit page, which allows authorized users to edit and add new links. Each link can be customized to launch new windows or capture information such as how many times that link has been clicked.

News Feeds (RSS)

The News Feed module allows you to consume syndicated news feeds in Rich Site Summary (RSS) format. This module includes an edit page that allows you to specify the location of the news feed and the style sheet (XSL) used to transform the news feed.

Search Input

The Search Input module provides the ability to submit a search to a given search results module.

Search Results

The Search Results module provides the ability to display search results.

Text/HTML

The Text/HTML module renders a snippet of HTML or text. This module includes an edit page, which allows authorized users to edit the HTML or text snippets directly (using the configured rich text editor).

User Accounts

The User Accounts module allows users to register and manage their account.

User Defined Table

The User Defined Table module allows you to create a custom data table for managing tabular information.

XML/XSL

The XML/XSL module renders the result of an XML/XSL transform. This module includes an edit page, which allows authorized users to specify a location for the XML document and the XSL style sheet used for transformation.

Remember, this is not a definitive list of the modules available within DotNetNuke; you have the option of installing modules provided by third parties, or to even author your own module. For complete instructions on how to use each of these modules, refer to Chapter 6, which covers the administration of the DotNetNuke base modules. Chapters 9 through 12 cover the aspects associated with authoring your own modules to solve a unique business need for your organization.

Additional Modules

DotNetNuke also provides some additional modules that are available in the download but not installed by default in the application:

- **User's Online:** This module allows you to display information about the current number of visitors accessing your portal at any given time.
- **Survey:** This module allows you to conduct online surveys with your portal.

At the time of this writing, several other modules are under development that will enhance the usability of the application even further. Several members of the DotNetNuke Core Team are developing a full-fledged forum module and a photo gallery module, which will be included in later releases of the application.

User Roles

DotNetNuke offers a fairly robust method for dealing with the permissions and controlling the tasks a particular user is allow to perform. It does this with a roles-based security module, where every page and module in the application is assigned roles that determine what the user is allowed to do within the context of the application. As you saw earlier in the chapter, you have the option of setting permissions at several levels within the portal. A user may be allowed access to edit certain modules, or be given access to edit the entire page as you deem necessary. These functions also apply to actual viewing of a module's content or a specific page. Basically, all you need to do is create the necessary security roles and assign the permissions you want that role to perform to the module or page. Once you have the roles and permissions defined you can then place your users in the appropriate role, which will allow or restrict their access based on those permissions. This allows very granular control over the actions of users in your portal.

Summary

This chapter introduced the concepts of DotNetNuke terms and basic application functionality. The chapters that follow dive deeper into these items and introduce the details on how each DotNetNuke function can be implemented in your unique installation. As you can see from this chapter, the application offers a lot of functionality from a base installation and will allow you to quickly move your web site from conception to production. The next chapter looks at the host functions required to set up the application to host your various child and parent portals.

Portal Administration

Chapter 3 introduced basic concepts that define a portal in DotNetNuke. This chapter details the rich features and functions available to customize the look, feel, and function of your DotNetNuke portal and maintain it throughout its life.

To make this information more practical, examples in this chapter illustrate a real-world scenario of building a site for a pee-wee soccer team called The Gators. Where applicable, you'll not only learn how to do things, but also when and why to do them. As the administrator of a DotNetNuke portal, you now hold the keys to a powerful resource and you'll want to know how to manage it well.

In Chapter 3 you learned about the concept of hosting multiple portals on a single installation of DotNetNuke. This chapter assumes no knowledge of any portal in the installation other than the one you are currently administering. As far as the Portal Administrator is concerned, their portal exists alone in its own corner of cyberspace separate from any other.

Who Is the Portal Administrator?

When the Host creates your portal, a new user is created as well (see Chapter 5). This user is automatically associated with the portal in the Administrator security role and so becomes the default Portal Administrator. The features discussed in this chapter are available to users who belong to the Administrator security role (and SuperUsers such as the Host).

There is only one Portal Administrator — you! However, you have the authority to delegate privilege to other users to perform administrative tasks. Later in this chapter you'll learn how to give Administrator access to another user. But regardless of how many users have administrative privilege, it is the user information of the one Portal Administrator that is used by DotNetNuke. For example, it is the Portal Administrator's e-mail address that will appear as the "from" address for all e-mail sent by the portal and as the default to address for the Feedback module.

Ideally, a Host will not associate the Portal Administrator user with an individual, but rather with an account. In this way, the user information can be maintained separately and changed for the specific purpose of managing the portal (like specifying an appropriate e-mail address). The Portal Administrator account can be used to create additional users with administrative privileges that are associated with real people.

Where Do I Begin?

Begin at the beginning and go on until you come to the end; then stop. This little piece of advice is as wise today as it was when the King of Hearts delivered it to the White Rabbit. So we'll take a cue from Lewis Carroll and start at the beginning — logging in. Follow these steps:

1. Navigate to your web site. Our example is located at `http://soccer.dotnetnuke.com`, although your location will vary.

2. Click the Login link in the upper right-hand corner of the page.

3. Log in to your portal using the Portal Administrator User Name and Password assigned by your Host. Enter your User Name and Password and click Login (see Figure 4-1).

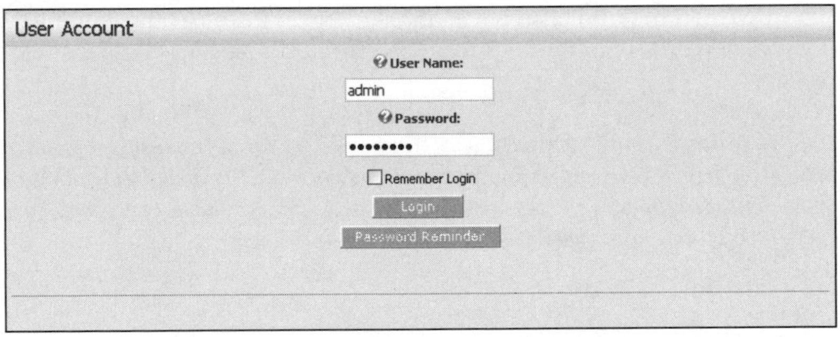

Figure 4-1

If you've entered your User Name and Password correctly, the first thing you will notice upon logging in is that the screen looks a little bit different than it did before (see Figure 4-2).

Three main differences are immediately visible. The first is the addition of the Control Panel, which spans the top of the browser window. The second is the layout of the skin panes, and the third is the addition of the Admin menu. You'll learn more about panes and skinning in Chapter 13. For now we'll focus on the Control Panel.

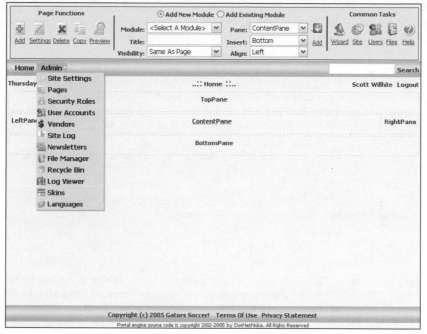

Figure 4-2

The Control Panel

The Control Panel is primarily a palette of shortcuts to frequently used tasks, most of which are accessible from elsewhere on the Admin menu. In DotNetNuke version 3.0 it is divided into three main sections for Page Functions, Adding Modules to the current page, and Common Tasks (see Figure 4-3).

Figure 4-3

In DotNetNuke version 2.1, the Control Panel had far fewer functions and a much thinner profile (see Figure 4-4). That version of the Control Panel is still an option in version 3.0 at the discretion of the Host. We'll discuss it briefly before covering the enhanced version in more detail.

Figure 4-4

You'll note that the main differences between the Classic (version 2.1) and ICONBAR (version 3.0) Control Panels are the addition of extra Page Functions, extra Module Options, and Common Tasks. These differences are pretty straightforward and will become more obvious as you move along. The remaining difference is the deprecation of the Content check box.

In version 2.1, ill behavior of a poorly written module could result in a rather nasty error message that would keep a module from being displayed. In this case, it was virtually impossible for a Portal Administrator to remove the offending module. The Content check box provided a way to instruct modules not to display their content, which preempted the nasty error message and gave the Portal Administrator access to the modules settings where it could be deleted from the page. This condition no longer exists under version 3.0 and so the Content check box does not appear on the ICONBAR version of the Control Panel. It is no longer necessary.

The only functions on the Control Panel that can't be accessed through other navigation are the Site Wizard, Help, and Preview.

The Site Wizard

A slick addition to version 3.0, the Site Wizard is the quickest way to make the most common customizations for someone new to managing their own web site. It takes you through a short conversational process, step by step, with extensive help and the ability to cancel at any time without saving changes. Standard navigational controls appear on each page of the wizard for Back, Next, Finish, Cancel (without saving changes), and Help.

Clicking the Wizard button in the Control Panel brings you to Step 1 (see Figure 4-5).

Step 1: Choose a Template for Your Site

This optional step gives you the choice of applying a template to your portal. The purpose of a template is to add predefined functionality and content (pages, modules, and so on) to your site. For example, a Host might provide a variety of commonly used templates to jumpstart your club web site, family web site, small business web site, and so on.

> **For advanced users and developers, templates provide a very powerful mechanism for sharing predefined portal functionality. Templates can carry rich information including portal settings, security roles, pages, modules, permissions, and so on. Template creation is a function available to Host Administrators (see Chapter 5).**

Clicking the check box for Build your site from a template (below) enables the list of available templates just below it (see Figure 4-6). You select a template from the list by clicking on it. If you do not want to apply a template to your site, simply leave the check box empty.

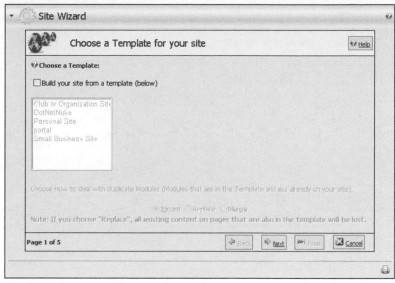

Figure 4-5

A group of radio buttons at the bottom of the page tell the wizard how to handle any conflicts that might be encountered during application of a template. A conflict is encountered when an existing component in your site matches a component that is also specified in the template (for example, when a module's title matches that of a module specified in the template). Table 4-1 summarizes the effects of each choice.

Site templates are additive. This means that when you apply a template, it will incorporate those elements specified in the template into your existing web site. A template will not remove existing pages, modules, or content except as part of resolving a conflict.

Table 4-1: How to Deal with Duplicate Modules	
Ignore	If a module of the same name and type as the one in the template already exists, the template definition is ignored.
Replace	If a module of the same name and type as the one in the template already exists, it is replaced by the definition in the template.
Merge	If a module of the same name and type as the one in the template already exists, the content is appended to the existing module content.

Select the option that best suits your needs. If you are beginning with a new (or empty) portal, the Replace option would be most appropriate. Remember that you can click the Help button at any time for assistance.

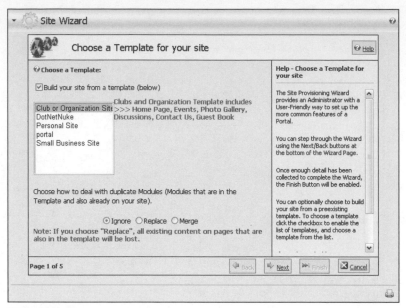

Figure 4-6

Step 2: Select a Skin for Your Site

This step is where the fun begins! DotNetNuke has powerful skinning capabilities that enable administrators to choose how their site should look. You can scroll though a list of the skins that are available and select the look you want applied to your site. If the author of the skin has provided an image for preview, it will be displayed in a thumbnail format (see Figure 4-7). You can click the thumbnail to view a larger image.

The skin you select will be applied by default to any page that you add to your site. You'll be able to override that choice if you want and we'll explore that capability a bit later in this chapter. For now just know that you'll be able to customize the look of other pages if you want to, even though you have chosen a default for all new pages here.

DotNetNuke comes preinstalled with several variations on its default skin (new for version 3.0). You can choose a version with vertical or horizontal menus, which display in fixed width or variable (browser) width and in any of five available colors (Blue, Gray, Green, Red, or Yellow). If your Host has enabled the option for your portal, you can upload additional skins that you can obtain from a variety of sources or that you can create yourself.

When you have selected the default skin for your site, click Next.

If you are an advanced user or developer, you can find detailed information on how to create and package your own skins in Chapter 13.

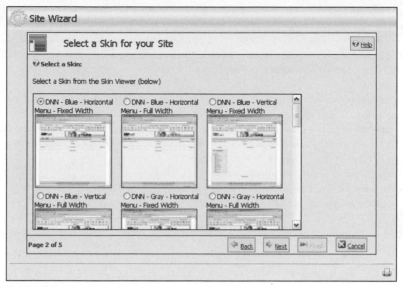

Figure 4-7

Step 3: Choose a Default Container for Your Site

In this step, you are asked to choose a default container (see Figure 4-8). The default container is auto-matically applied to every new module that you add to your pages. Just like with your default skin, you'll be able to override that choice if you want.

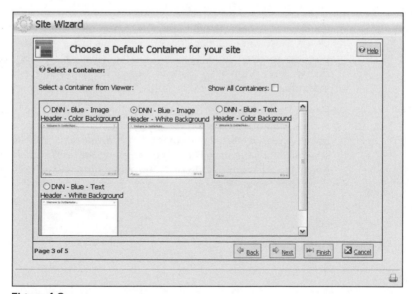

Figure 4-8

The container choices displayed in the wizard represent those that have been specifically packaged for the skin you chose in the previous step. Because we chose a DNN - Blue skin for our example, the container choices are DNN - Blue also. However, clicking the check box for Show All Containers displays all available containers for every skin that is available to you, so if you want to apply a yellow container as the default with the blue skin, you are free to do so.

DotNetNuke comes preinstalled with several variations on its default containers for each skin (new for version 3.0). You can choose a version with complementary background shading or white shading for the content area and image or text headers. Image headers provide a gradient fill image as the background for the module title, whereas text headers leave the background alone, matching the content area shading.

When you have selected the default container for your site, click Next. At this point the wizard has enough information to display your site if you want to stop, so you could also click Finish.

If you are an advanced user or developer, you can find detailed information on how to create and package your own containers in Chapter 13.

Step 4: Add Site Details

Table 4-2 lists each field and describes how its value affects your portal.

Table 4-2: Site Wizard, Site Details	
Name/Title	Name/Title is used in a number of places in the operation of your portal. Most notably it is displayed in the title bar of the user's browser window. It is also used to refer to your portal in outgoing mail for user registration, password reminders, and so on.
Description	Description is used as a default value to populate the HTML META tag for DESCRIPTION in each page of your site. This tag is important because it provides search engines (such as Google, Yahoo, and MSN) with an informative description of your site (or page). The value can be set for each page individually; however, if it is omitted this default description will be used.
KeyWords	Keywords are also used as a default value to populate the HTML META tag for KEYWORDS in each page of your site. This tag can be useful to help improve search engine placement. Key words and or phrases should be separated by a comma. The value can be set for each page individually; however, if it is omitted these default keywords will be used.

When you have finished adding details for your site, click Next or Finish (See Figure 4-9).

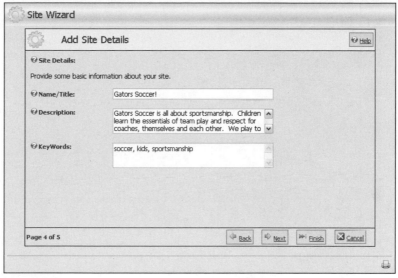

Figure 4-9

Step 5: Choose a Logo

In this optional step you are invited to select or upload an image for your logo (see Figure 4-10). For the default skins provided with DotNetNuke, the logo will appear in the upper left-hand corner of the browser window. For this example, leave the logo as unspecified.

Custom skins may place your logo in another location or ignore it altogether (that's a skin designer's choice). You'll want to make sure your logo looks good on any new skin that you choose.

The File Location and File Name drop-downs provide a simple way to locate the available files in your portal's root directory. Changing File Location changes the list of files available (note that only web-friendly image files will be listed). If your logo file is on your local computer and not your site, you can choose to upload it by clicking the Upload New File button. The page will refresh to reveal a standard upload control (see Figure 4-11). Note that you'll still specify the File Location so the control will know in which subdirectory to store the image file. Click Save Uploaded File to get the file from your local computer to your portal, or click Select An Existing File to return to the previous selector.

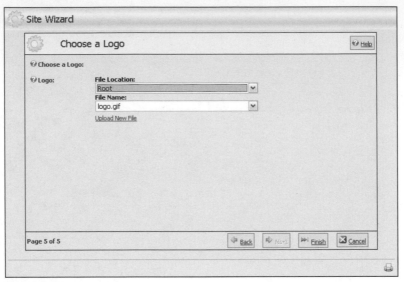

Figure 4-10

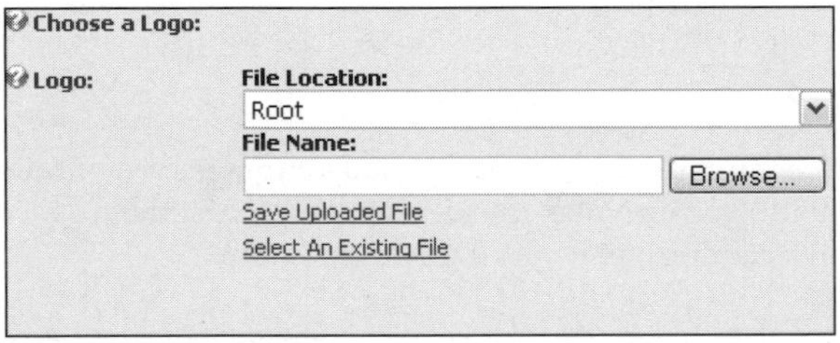

Figure 4-11

When you have finished choosing the logo for your site, click Finish or Cancel.

Having completed the Site Wizard you can now take a look at your newly configured web site by navigating to any page (try clicking the Home menu item). Because you applied the Club or Organization Site template in Step 1, the site will now have some additional pages and example content instead of the empty web site that you began with. You can see the sample Gallery page in preview mode in Figure 4-12.

Figure 4-12

The Help Button

The Help button is a link that is configured by your Host (see Chapter 5). In the default installation this link is configured to open the default help page at dotnetnuke.com. Your Host may opt to direct this link to another site that contains help that is more personalized or relevant to your specific hosting plan.

> *DotNetNuke has plenty of built-in help for its administrative functions. But the Help button gives Hosts some ability to create help completely customized for their (and your) purposes and put it right at your fingertips. For example, a Host-provided help site might have specific information related to their customized templates available through the Site Wizard.*

The Preview Button

The Administrator's view of the site differs from a regular user's view because of the need to see skin panes, edit icons, module actions, and so on. But sometimes you just need to know how things are going to look to a non-administrative user; this is what the Preview button on the Control Panel is for.

When you click the Preview button, you will notice two things. First, your view of the portal (below the Control Panel) changes; the pane definitions and the edit options all vanish. Second, the Preview button icon changes (a plus becomes visible under the magnifying glass) to indicate that you are in Preview mode.

It can be easy to forget that you are in Preview mode, so don't forget to toggle this setting back off when you no longer need it.

Configuring Your Portal

Now that your site has basic navigation, sample content, and a chosen look, you'll want to begin configuring other features to make your site special. The Portal Administrator has access to a wealth of configuration options for customization of the look, content, and behavior of the site. This section discusses many of the set-it-and-forget-it types of configuration options. These are things that, for the most part, you'll want to include in your initial planning, set, and then leave alone until your next improvement project. This section also exposes you to a few tools that serve a purpose in both configuration and maintenance of your site (which will be covered later in this chapter).

Site Settings

You can reach your site settings in one of two ways, either by clicking the Settings button in the Common Tasks area of the toolbar or by selecting Site Settings in the Admin menu. There you will be presented with a page that contains expandable/collapsible categories of configuration options.

There are two important text buttons at the very bottom of the Site Settings page. Because a number of controls on the Site Settings page generate postbacks, you might occasionally be tempted to think that your changes have been saved — but no changes are saved until the Update button is clicked. The Submit Site To Google button formats and submits a request for Google to add your site to its search index.

Search engine ranking is based on a number of factors. In order to improve your site's ranking you should add appropriate Title, Description, and Keyword text to each page before submitting your site to Google or any other search engine.

In working with the Site Wizard you already learned about all of the options available under Basic Settings, Details. So we'll skip those settings here and move on to the rest.

Basic Settings: Appearance

These settings control the configuration choices that affect the appearance of your site to visitors. Several of these settings involve the use of a similar selector (see Figure 4-13).

Figure 4-13

This selector utilizes a radio button to specify the source for populating the associated drop-down list box. The Host may provide skins/containers to all Portal Administrators and/or additional selections available only to your site (see Table 4-3). If the Host has enabled the Portal Administrator to upload skins, you'll be able to add your own and they will be available under the Sites option.

The Preview link button provides a convenient way to see what a skin or container will look like in real life. Clicking Preview launches another browser window, which opens to the front page of the site using the option selected. This window should be closed when you have finished previewing.

Table 4-3: Site Settings, Appearance

Logo	See the previous section on the Setup Wizard.
Body Background	This value is used in the HTML body tag of every page to render a tiled background image. If the selected skin hides background images, this setting may appear to have no effect. You should leave this field clear if you don't intend to use a background image because it does add unnecessary weight to the rendered page.
Portal Skin	This setting specifies the skin for all non-administrator (and non-host) pages within the site. The skin is applied to all pages in the site where another skin has not been specifically chosen on those pages' individual settings. It also applies by default to all new pages.
Portal Container	Similarly, this setting specifies the standard module container for all non-administrator (and non-host) pages within the site. The same rules of application and inheritance apply for containers as well as skins. This choice applies to all modules in the site where another container has not been specifically chosen on those modules' individual settings. It also applies by default to all new modules.
Admin Skin	The Admin Skin is the look seen only on administrator (and host) pages within the site. Typically your choice of Admin Skin should be lightweight to reduce excessive image transfer and emphasize productivity over pizzazz. There are a few pages that are owned by the portal that face the public, and so retain the Admin Skin. These are the default Login page and the Registration/Membership Services pages. You'll learn how you can customize these pages later in this chapter.
Admin Container	The Admin Container is the same as the Portal Container but affects only the administrator (and host) pages.

If the Host has enabled Skin Upload Permissions for Portals, two additional text buttons will appear at the bottom of the Basic Settings category (Upload Skin and Upload Container). These functions are covered in detail in Chapter 13.

Advanced Settings: Security Settings

Portal Registration drives fundamental behavior of your site that should be part of your initial design. Through registration, anonymous site visitors can join (or apply to join) the Registered Users role and be granted access to privileged content or site functionality. Because the Registered Users role requires registration and authorization (either explicit or automatic), these functions combine to provide for different options in the registration process (see Figure 4-14).

Figure 4-14

Your choice of registration type should be based on the functional access requirements for visitors to your site. Table 4-4 summarizes the choices and how they impact site behavior.

Table 4-4: Site Settings, Security, Portal Registration Options

None	Registration is not an available option to site visitors. The Login button remains visible so that administrative access can be gained; however, the Registration button is hidden. Often, sites that select this option will change their skin to move the Login button to a less prominent location than it normally appears on the default skin. This setting is appropriate for sites that do not publish privileged content or that process registration offline.
Private	Registrants apply for privileged access to the site. Until authorization is explicitly granted, access is limited to that of any anonymous user. This setting is appropriate for sites that require approval of registration requests (for example, a private family web site that invites friends and relatives to apply). An e-mail is sent to the registrant advising him or her of the private nature of the site. An additional e-mail is sent upon authorization (if and when performed). It is good practice to explain the process for approval of private registration prominently on your site.
Public	Registration is automatically (and immediately) authorized without validation of the e-mail address. A welcome e-mail is sent to the registrant. This setting is appropriate for sites that want to track usage but do not require validation of contact information.
Verified	Registration generates a verification code, which is included in the welcome e-mail sent to the address supplied by the registrant. Authorization is granted when the user supplies the verification code at the time of first login. This process ensures that all registered users have supplied a valid e-mail address.

You can customize the content of the e-mails generated through the registration process by editing the appropriate language resources. You'll learn explicitly how to do this later in this chapter.

Remember that site registration is only the first step available for managing access to privileged content. Once registered, you can manage a user's access to pages and modules at a very granular level through the application of security roles.

Advanced Settings: Page Management

Earlier you learned that some standard pages are owned by the portal. These settings give you the ability to customize those pages and a few other aspects of your site's general navigation (see Figure 4-15).

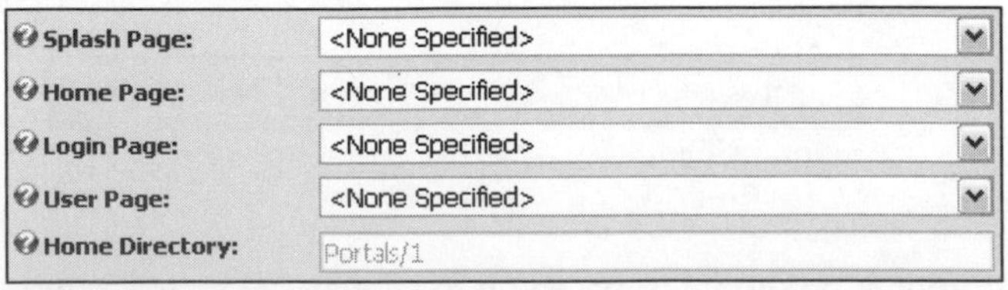

Splash Page:	\<None Specified\>
Home Page:	\<None Specified\>
Login Page:	\<None Specified\>
User Page:	\<None Specified\>
Home Directory:	Portals/1

Figure 4-15

Each of the options consists of a drop-down list box for selecting a custom page within your portal. The None Specified selection for any of these configuration options results in default behavior. Table 4-5 explains the behavioral impact of each setting.

Table 4-5: Site Settings, Page Management

Splash Page	When a visitor reaches your site via its alias (for example, `http://www.dotnetnuke.com`), the default behavior is to display the Home Page. If a Splash Page is specified, it will be displayed to the visitor instead. This affects only the initial landing page for site navigation or invalid links and does not change the location of Home for other purposes. It is left to you to determine the appropriate method and timing of redirection to the Home Page. A typical implementation would be to specify a page that is defined as a link to a Flash introduction (which redirects when finished).
Home Page	The Home Page is the default target for site navigation (in the absence of a Splash Page). It is also used as the destination link for the site logo as well as any other default site behavior that results in redirection to the Home Page. If no Home Page is specified, the first page in the navigation order will be used.
Login Page	The default Login Page is provided for your convenience, however as a system page it lacks the capability for skinning and may not be consistent with the look of your site (it retains the admin skin). If specified, the Login Page will be used as the target for login requests instead of the default page. This allows for full customization and skinning including additional modules and page elements. But don't forget to include the Account Login module on the page and be sure the page and module permissions specify visibility to Unauthenticated Users (or All Users). If you make a mistake and find yourself unable to access your custom login page, you can force display of the system login page. Simply add the following query string value to the address in your browser: `ctl=Login` (for example, `http://www.dotnetnuke.com/default.aspx?ctl=Login`). A simple example of a custom login page would be to include the Account Login module on the Home Page, visible only to the Unauthenticated Users role.
User Page	The User Page displays a user's registration information and preferences, provides for password changes, and lists available membership services. It is most readily seen by clicking the Registration button or by clicking on your username if already logged in (see Figure 4-16). The default User Page is provided for your convenience. As another system page it has the same skinning limitations and customization characteristics as the Login Page (see above). When creating a custom User Page, be sure that the User Account module is visible to the All Users role. It serves the dual purpose of collecting registration information for Unauthenticated Users and displaying account information for Registered Users.

Table continued on following page

Home Directory	This display-only field identifies the path to the directory that holds all the portal's files. The directory is specified by the Host and represents a location relative to the web site root (for example, http://www.dotnetnuke.com/Portals/1)

This is an opportune time to set defaults for what information is required for users to enter upon registration. On the User Page, internal functions require that users enter a first and last name, username, password, and e-mail address. Other contact information fields are optional, but you can choose to require them by clicking the check box next to the field (as seen in Figure 4-16).

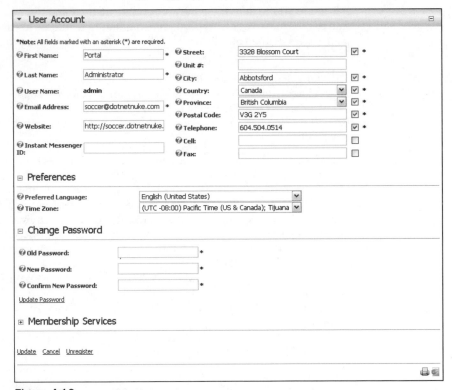

Figure 4-16

Advanced Settings: Payment Settings

These payment settings have been preserved from earlier versions of DotNetNuke for legacy support purposes. Only the PayPal(r) option is supported using the POST method to emulate PayPal's Buy Now button functionality. These settings come into play when public roles are defined with fees or when online portal signup is permitted.

Several eCommerce store and/or payment components are available for DotNetNuke through third-party providers. These payment settings will ultimately be deprecated in a future version in favor of a more robust eCommerce API (see Figure 4-17).

Figure 4-17

Since our Gators will offer at least one premium content area for subscription, you'll sign up for a PayPal account and use it to process payments for these services.

Other Settings

This group of miscellaneous settings (see Figure 4-18) has significant impact on several key display characteristics of your portal. Table 4-6 explains the impacts of each setting.

Figure 4-18

Table 4-6: Site Settings, Other Settings

Copyright	This setting is used to populate the text of the skin object token [COPYRIGHT]. In each of the default skins, the copyright notice appears at the bottom of the page. If your skin does not implement the COPYRIGHT skin object, this setting will have no effect. For more information on skin object tokens, see Chapter 13.
Banner Advertising	This setting controls the behavior of the skin object token [BANNER]. The None option nullifies the token, resulting in no display of banners. The Site and Host options select whether banners are displayed from your portal's Vendor List or from the Host's Vendor List. The Host option provides for leveraging a single Vendor List across all portals. If your skin does not implement the BANNER skin object, this setting will have no effect. If you had applied the DotNetNuke template in the Site Wizard, you would see a banner on the upper-right side of the default skin, which is a default banner that appears if none exist in the Vendors List.
Administrator	Recall that the Portal Administrator's contact information is used for the "from" address in outgoing e-mail, the default-to address in the Feedback module, and so on. You can choose to designate another portal user (who is also in the Administrator role) as the primary Portal Administrator.

Table continued on following page

Default Language	DotNetNuke supports localization of text, dates, and currency within the portal framework. English and German languages are installed by default but additional language packs are available. The default language is displayed to anonymous site visitors and Registered Users that have not selected a default language in their own membership settings.
Portal TimeZone	DotNetNuke supports localization of time zone similarly to languages. The default time zone is used for anonymous site visitors and Registered Users that have not selected a default time zone in their own membership settings. This feature is primarily available for support of modules that may require it. Timestamps visible in the Log or for create and update events for individual records are based on server time, rather than localized time. There are no features in the default installation of DotNetNuke that display localized time.

The footer area of the default skins contains the [COPYRIGHT] skin object token, which displays the copyright notice specified in Other Site Settings (see Figure 4-19).

Copyright 2002-2005 DotNetNuke   Terms Of Use Privacy Statement

Figure 4-19

Changing the default language setting translates all static portal content (labels, admin and host menus, date and currency formats) to the language specified. You can even customize the static labels if desired. Contrast Figure 4-18 and Figure 4-20 to see how the choice of default language affects your portal. Note that dynamic content (like the text of the Copyright notice) is not translated.

It is worth noting that core support for Multilanguage module content (and versioning) is on the development roadmap for a future version of DotNetNuke.

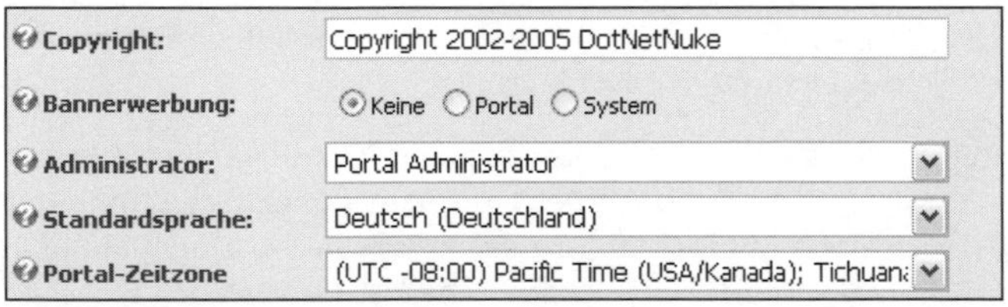

Copyright:	Copyright 2002-2005 DotNetNuke
Bannerwerbung:	⦿ Keine ○ Portal ○ System
Administrator:	Portal Administrator
Standardsprache:	Deutsch (Deutschland)
Portal-Zeitzone:	(UTC -08:00) Pacific Time (USA/Kanada); Tichuan：

Figure 4-20

Stylesheet Editor

DotNetNuke supports cascading style sheets so that skin and container designers, as well as module developers, have a means to customize components they provide. The highest level style sheet is located in the portal's Home Directory, appropriately named portal.css. The Stylesheet Editor gives you a convenient way to quickly update any style supported within the DotNetNuke framework (see Figure 4-21).

```
□ Stylesheet Editor

/* ================================
   CSS STYLES FOR DotNetNuke
   ================================
*/


/* PAGE BACKGROUND */
/* background color for the header at the top of the page  */
.HeadBg {
}

/* background color for the content part of the pages */
Body
{
}

.ControlPanel {
}

/* background/border colors for the selected tab */
```

Save Style Sheet   Restore Default Style Sheet

Figure 4-21

If you should ever need it, there is a button to Restore Default Style Sheet, which returns the template to its original settings. Any customizations you have made will be lost, so it's a good idea to make a backup copy of this file first.

Security Roles

The DotNetNuke architecture allows you to control access to your content both at the page and the module level through the application of user roles. A role can be thought of as a group with a purpose (for example, Newsletter Subscriber, Gallery Administrator, or Team Member). You'll learn to apply roles later in this chapter, but for planning purposes you should consider that roles should address two types of purposes (that is, permissions): View and Edit.

Some very important security roles are predefined and you can define others as necessary. You are already acquainted with (and a member of!) the Administrators role. You've also touched briefly on the Registered Users role, which includes all users that have registered on your site and have been authorized, whether by an Administrator, through public access, or verification at login. Figure 4-22 shows the Security Roles page and predefined roles for a default portal.

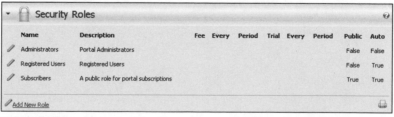

Name	Description	Fee	Every	Period	Trial	Every	Period	Public	Auto
Administrators	Portal Administrators							False	False
Registered Users	Registered Users							False	True
Subscribers	A public role for portal subscriptions							True	True

Add New Role

Figure 4-22

Two additional built-in roles you will find useful are the Unauthenticated Users and All Users roles. The Unauthenticated Users role has no explicit definition because it denotes anonymous users who belong to no real security role at all. Likewise, the All Users role includes both users who are currently logged in as well as those who are not. You'll see how both of these roles are used later when working with page and module permissions.

Your portal may have additional roles based on the template you specified using the Site Wizard earlier in this chapter.

Creating a New Role

In designing The Gators web site, it was determined that a couple of additional roles would be needed. You'll add an opt-out role that all new users are automatically assigned to. The preconfigured Subscribers role is an example of this, but you'll create your own in this exercise. You'll also add a public role for subscription to premium services.

Basic Settings

After you click Add New Role, you'll wind up on the Edit Security Role page looking at the basic settings (see Figure 4-23). Table 4-7 describes the fields in the basic settings.

Table 4-7: Add New Role, Basic Settings	
Role Name and Description	The Role Name and Description are visible to Administrators on the list of Security Roles (see Figure 4-22) and also in the Membership Services area of the Account Profile page if the role is defined as Public (see Figure 4-25).
Public Role	Roles that are defined as Public show up as user-selectable options in the Membership Services area of the Account Profile page (see Figure 4-25). This is useful to enable user selection of optional services.
Auto Assignment	If checked, the role is retroactively applied to all existing users and is automatically assigned to all new users.

You'll define a role that is used to determine who should receive your monthly newsletter. This role is automatically assigned to each new user but, as a public role, can be canceled by the user at any time. Figure 4-23 illustrates the setup of your new role.

Figure 4-23

Alternatively, you might choose not to auto-assign the role in favor of allowing your users to opt-in specifically. This would be a more acceptable option for marketing-oriented communications because the default user registration does not currently include the ability to opt-out at the time of signup.

Advanced Settings

You'll also define an optional role with a fee, which you'll use to expose privileged content to paid subscribers. The Gators site will provide access to a gallery of photos and for a small fee users can download high-quality images for printing. For this you'll need to apply some advanced settings (see Figure 4-24). Table 4-8 describes the fields in the advanced settings area.

Table 4-8: Add New Role, Advanced Settings	
Service Fee	This is the fee associated with the service that is enabled via the role. The fee is applied in the currency specified in your portal settings. If you've specified PayPal as your payment processor, be sure that your account is set up to accept payments in the chosen currency.
Billing Period (Every)	These two fields define how often a user is billed for the service. It may be a one-time or recurring fee.
Trial Fee	You can choose to allow for a trial period for services at a different rate than the full service amount. Free trial services are often offered for a limited time.
Trial Period	These two fields define the duration of the trial period. When a trial role is granted, it is given an expiration date that is based on this time period.

You'll apply a small monthly fee to this role. When users subscribe to it they'll be taken to the PayPal web site where they can authorize a payment to your account. Upon completion of the process they will be transferred back to the home page of your web site. The update to the user's account is processed asynchronously.

Figure 4-24

Remove the preconfigured Subscriber role since you've just created your own.

Public Roles and Membership Services

Public roles, such as those you defined in the previous section, are made available to users via the Membership Services area of their User Account page (see Figure 4-25).

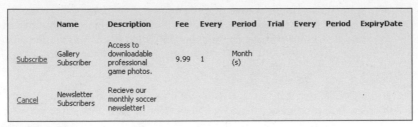

	Name	Description	Fee	Every	Period	Trial	Every	Period	ExpiryDate
Subscribe	Gallery Subscriber	Access to downloadable professional game photos.	9.99	1	Month (s)				
Cancel	Newsletter Subscribers	Recieve our monthly soccer newsletter!							

Figure 4-25

Delegating Authority and/or Assigning Privileges

Roles that are not public typically define privileged access for users or areas of responsibility for maintenance purposes. We'll assume you've already defined such a role for the person(s) that will maintain the file download area called Gallery Maintenance. You'll navigate there by clicking the text button Manage Users In This Role from the Edit Security Roles page (see Figure 4-26).

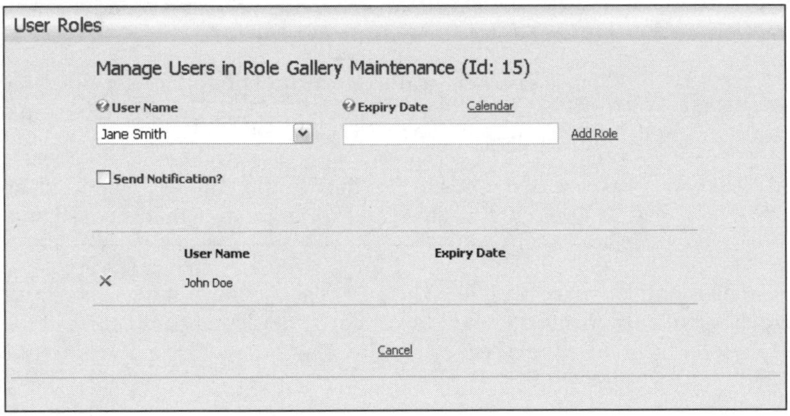

Figure 4-26

To add a user to the role, simply select the user in the User Name drop-down and click Add Role. If appropriate, an expiry date may be specified, after which the role has no effect. The Send Notification check box (if checked) will result in an e-mail being sent from the Portal Administrator to the user advising them of their addition to the role.

All users currently assigned to the role appear in the list. Clicking the red x next to any user's name will remove them from the role.

Now that you can create roles and assign users to them you're ready to put those roles to use. In the next section you'll create a page that your Gallery Subscriber role can access but a normal registered user cannot. Likewise, your Gallery Maintenance role should be able to edit the page while others (except Administrators) cannot.

Pages

Pages are the building blocks of your DotNetNuke portal. They are the real estate where you deposit content to create an interesting site. You can see them represented in menu items, bread crumbs, and site links. You've already dealt with a number of system pages, but in this section you learn all about creating and managing pages of your own.

Creating New Pages

The quickest way to create a new page is by clicking the Add button in the Page Functions area of the Control Panel. You can also create a page by first navigating to the Page List via the Pages item on the Admin menu and clicking the Add New Page button. Table 4-9 explains the basic settings.

Table 4-9: Add New Page, Basic Settings

Page Name	This value appears as the text in the menu item, Recycle Bin, and anywhere that pages are listed (for example, drop-down selection lists).
Page Title	The page title is displayed in the title bar of the user's browser. It is also typically used by search engines as a key indicator of relevance. So be sure to make your page titles fully descriptive of the page content (for example, Soccer Team Photos for Download).
Page Description	You already added a default description back when you imported your portal template (see Table 4-2). However, it is recommended that you add a relevant description for each page within your site.
Key Words	You already added default keywords as well (see Table 4-2). But again, unique keywords can improve your ranking for search engines.
Parent Page	This property drives the navigation hierarchy of your site*. Any page that does not have a parent specified will appear as a top-level menu item. Any page that has a parent specified will appear as submenu item to the parent page. Although a page can only have one parent, it is also possible to create a page that is really just a reference to another (existing) page. So you can reference the same page from more than one place in the menu structure (see Link URL in Table 4-10).
Permissions	Each role in your portal can be explicitly assigned permissions to view or edit the page. Edit permissions are the same as those available to the Portal Administrator (for page-level actions only). View permissions determine whether the page is displayed to the role (see Figure 4-28).

---

* You can take this hierarchy as deep as you like, but conventional wisdom tells us that going more than about two levels deep becomes difficult to navigate. Not every page needs to be accessible from the main menu.

When creating a new page, you will also have the option to copy the structure and/or content of an existing page (see Figure 4-27).

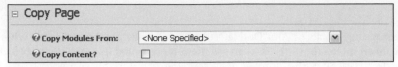

Figure 4-27

If you have created a page that employs a layout of modules that will be common in your site, it may be useful to begin development of new pages using that same layout. You can specify which page to copy and whether or not the module content should be the same. If Copy Content is selected, the modules on the new page will be shadows of existing modules on the Copy Modules From page. All of the shadow copies are linked so that changes to any one will update every instance on each copied page. This can be particularly helpful for things like links modules used for navigation, banner modules displayed on selected pages, and so on. If unselected, new empty modules will be placed on the page in the same layout and with the same permissions as the page specified to copy from.

Table 4-10 explains the fields in the advanced settings area.

Table 4-10: Add New Page, Advanced Settings

Icon	Identifies an image that will be displayed beside the page name in the menu. Menu text bottom aligns with the images, so 16x16 icons tend to look best.
Page Skin	This optional setting will associate a skin specifically to this page. This is useful if you have a skin with special formatting or a functional need to appear different than the rest of your site. If this option is <Not Specified>, the page inherits the default skin as specified in the Site Settings (see Figure 4-13).
Page Container	Likewise, this setting will associate a default container specifically to this page.
Hidden	This option has nothing to do with the visibility of your page (recall that visibility is a function of roles that you were introduced to earlier). You select this option to keep a page from being added to the menu. You may have many pages that are not part of your top-level navigation but that are linked in other ways throughout your site.
Disabled	If a page is disabled, it is not accessible to any user of the site who is not a member of the Administrator role. This feature is useful for suppressing content without manipulating roles (for example, universally hiding a page until it is updated).
Start Date	Specify a date that the page (and menu item) becomes visible. Before the start date the page will function as if it were disabled.
End Date	Specify a date after which the page (and menu item) is no longer visible. The page will function as if it were disabled.

Link Url	This option allows you to change the target of your page. The default is a URL with no specified location, which is interpreted as an internal page. URL: Your menu item will act as a direct link to the target URL specified. Page: Your menu item will act as a link to an existing page in your site. This option enables you to create multiple navigational items that point to the same place (for example, a descriptive page that applies to multiple products). File: Your menu item will act as a link to a file in your portal root (for example, a link to a PDF document or image).

Securing Privileged Content

Earlier in this chapter you learned to create security roles to logically group users. Page (and module) permissions allow you to give privileges to those groups of users. You'll note that the built-in Administrator role always has both View and Edit permissions on every page.

Figure 4-28 illustrates the permissions that you'll apply to The Gators Gallery page. By giving All Users View Page permissions, even anonymous users browsing the site will have access to the menu item and the page. And you'll give edit access to the Gallery Maintenance role, which will have responsibility for keeping this page current (for example, adding new photos).

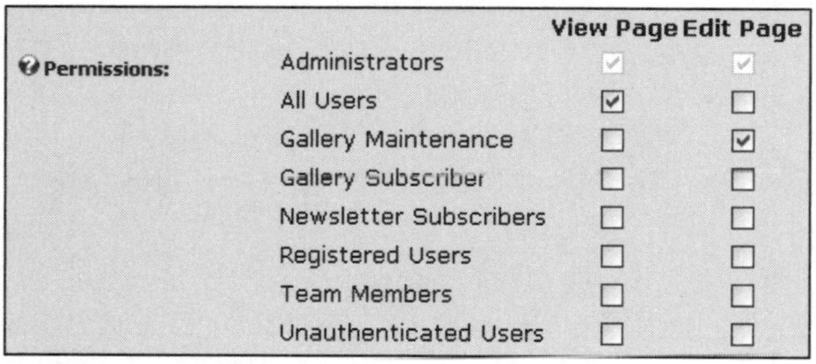

Permissions:		View Page	Edit Page
	Administrators	☑	☑
	All Users	☑	☐
	Gallery Maintenance	☐	☑
	Gallery Subscriber	☐	☐
	Newsletter Subscribers	☐	☐
	Registered Users	☐	☐
	Team Members	☐	☐
	Unauthenticated Users	☐	☐

Figure 4-28

The permissions specified in Figure 4-28 only secure the edit privilege of the page. You'll recall that The Gators also have a paid role for Gallery Subscribers, which should give them access to premium content. When those pages are created, you'll uncheck All Users and give View Page permissions to the Gallery Maintenance and Gallery Subscriber roles.

Now You See It, Now You Don't

The Unauthenticated Users role can be quite useful. It allows you to present a completely different view of your site to an anonymous user than to your registered users. If View Page permissions are assigned only to the Unauthenticated Users role, they will essentially disappear from view once a user is logged in.

One way of applying this concept is to define a splash page (shown previously in Figure 4-15) such that its View permissions are set only for Unauthenticated Users. This creates a landing page that is no longer visible once a user is logged in, but preserves the behavior of the home page after login. Further, if the specified home page is set only for Registered Users, its information remains private and the splash page functions as a home page for the anonymous user.

Take care when planning your site's navigation using the Unauthenticated User role. You wouldn't want to hide a menu item if it had submenu items that you wanted to keep visible!

Changing Navigational Structure

You've used the Parent Page setting to specify navigational structure. But if that was the only mechanism you had to reorganize your site it would be a little challenging. So the other method involves the Pages list, which you can reach by selecting Pages from the Admin menu (see Figure 4-29).

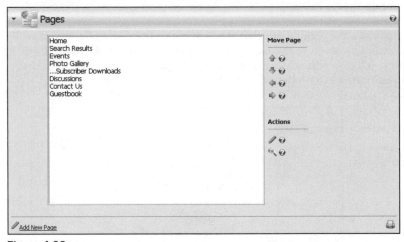

Figure 4-29

This list displays all the pages in your site in an organization that closely matches your menu structure. Items at the top of this list are leftmost in your menu, moving right along the menu as you move down in the list. Items that are indented (for example, . . . Subscriber Downloads) is an indication of submenu items. The buttons available on the right provide a means to change the defined parent of a selected page, moving it (and all its children) up or down within the menu hierarchy or changing its (and all its children's) position in the parent/child relationship. You can also choose to Edit or View a page as well.

Regardless of the visibility settings of the page (whether by start/end dates, enable/disable, hidden/unhidden), it will appear in this list. And so the menu hierarchy can become more difficult to see if you have a large number of pages on your site. For this reason, it may be advantageous to define a few phantom pages for organizational purposes. For example, you might define a hidden page called Orphans and assign it as the parent to pages that are suppressed from the menu.

Skins

The Skins page, accessible from the Admin menu, gives you the ability to browse and apply skins and containers to customize the look of your site (see Figure 4-30). You'll recall learning a bit about this functionality within the context of the Site Wizard, but you can access this functionality directly through this page.

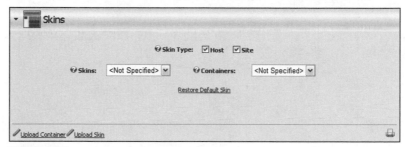

Figure 4-30

You can specify whether the drop-down containers will list Host and/or Site–supplied skins. If your Host has enabled the option, you may also see buttons to Upload Container and Upload Skin (otherwise these buttons will not be visible to you). Clicking the Restore Default Skin button changes your site's default settings to those originally specified by your Host.

Selecting a skin or container from their respective drop-downs displays the available selections in a gallery format (see Figure 4-31). If provided by the designer, the galleries will include thumbnail previews and the skin gallery will include associated containers.

If you'd like to know more about development of custom skins and containers, this topic is covered extensively in Chapter 13.

From the gallery you can click a thumbnail image to see a larger image (if provided by the designer). You can also see how a skin or container would look on your home page by clicking Preview, or go ahead and set it as the default for the portal by clicking Apply. You'll have the option to specify whether this should be applied to Admin and/or Portal pages in a check box below the gallery. If you selected a Site skin from the drop-down, you'll have the option to delete individual skins and containers as well.

If the skin designer included an `about.htm` file in their package, you'll also see an About <skin name> button below the gallery. Clicking this button opens the designer-supplied file.

If you have pages with modules placed just the way you like them, be careful about changing your skin. If you specify a skin that has a different pane layout than the one you are currently using, DotNetNuke won't know where to put some of those modules and will put them in the ContentPane by default. Changing back to the old skin will not restore the original position because the damage will have already been done. If you're experimenting with skins on a page with lots of content, make a copy of your existing page first and experiment on that. Or just stick with the Preview option in the gallery.

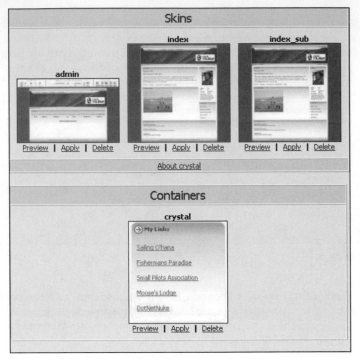

Figure 4-31

File Manager

File management is an area that is radically improved in version 3.0. Prior to introduction of the File Manager, all files were maintained in a flat structure in the portal root directory, which could easily become unwieldy. Now files can be managed in subdirectories and those directories can be protected through role-based permissions.

Figure 4-32 shows the basic features of the File Manager. Most operations are intuitive and the interface is pretty forgiving, providing feedback if you do something incorrectly. Group file and folder operations require that you select either a group of files or a folder first.

Folder Permissions

In Figure 4-32 you can see that there are multiple folders within the portal root. By default, only the Administrator role has permission to either view or write files in all of these folders. So if you want your Gallery Administrator to be able to upload photos, you'll want to grant that role appropriate permissions (see Figure 4-33).

These security settings are applied everywhere that the DotNetNuke file management controls are used. You've seen these controls in the Portal Administrators interface in a number of places, including the logo file selector in the Site Wizard (shown previously in Figure 4-11). These same controls are used in many modules (for example, the Documents module), which you will learn more about in Chapter 6.

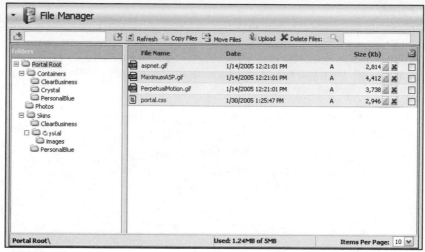

Figure 4-32

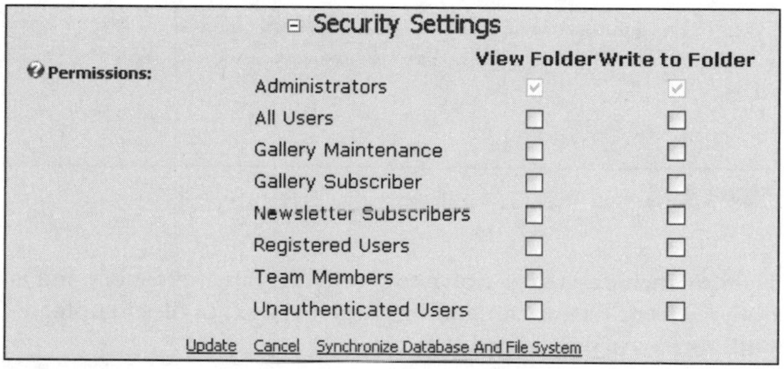

Security Settings

Permissions:		View Folder	Write to Folder
	Administrators	☑	☑
	All Users	☐	☐
	Gallery Maintenance	☐	☐
	Gallery Subscriber	☐	☐
	Newsletter Subscribers	☐	☐
	Registered Users	☐	☐
	Team Members	☐	☐
	Unauthenticated Users	☐	☐

Update Cancel Synchronize Database And File System

Figure 4-33

The Gallery Administrator will need permission to select files from the drop-down in order to add pictures to the gallery, and will also need to be able to write to the folder to upload new photos. So be sure to grant both View and Write permissions to the Gallery Maintenance role for the Photo folder.

Note that in Figure 4-34, both the Root and Photo folders are available to the file upload control. Access to the portal root directory is provided by default to preserve functionality for users upgrading from version 2.x to version 3.0. It is recommended that upgraded sites review their file and folder management policies.

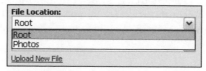

Figure 4-34

Uploading Files

If you click the Upload button in the File Manager, you'll find yourself looking at the original DotNetNuke file upload page. This upload control provides a lot of rich functionality and is used in many places within DotNetNuke for uploading various component packages like modules, skins, language packs, and so on. Here you're looking at the control in its plain vanilla state, waiting for you to specify generic files to upload (see Figure 4-35).

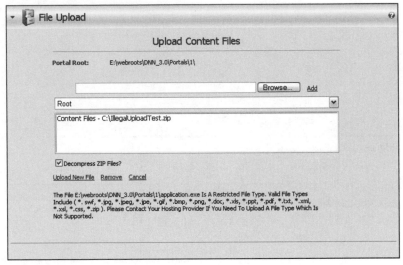

Figure 4-35

The File Upload control includes a drop-down to specify the target directory and an Add button that captures input from the basic file selector and includes it in a list of files to upload. This feature enables you to upload multiple files in one upload step.

The check box for Decompress ZIP Files allows you to upload a zipped file (preserving bandwidth) that is unzipped for you into the target directory. Note in Figure 4-35 that an invalid file type was stopped from unpacking in this upload. Both individual files and the content of zip files are matched against an allowable file types list, which is configurable by the Host.

Using FTP with File Manager

The File Manager provides a convenient way to move files through the interface. However, for bulk operations you may prefer to utilize FTP to transfer files (if permitted by your Host). If files are added to your site through any means other than the file upload interface, you'll need to click the Synchronize Database And File System button. This command instructs DotNetNuke to iterate through the portal root and resolve for any files and folders that may be added or missing. Your Host may have enabled a scheduled job to perform this synchronization for you on a periodic basis, but if you do it yourself you'll see those files in your drop-down lists immediately.

Languages

Languages and localization features are primarily controlled by the Host account; however, the Portal Administrator does have limited control to override localization strings and to define the default language for your portal. These settings are specific to your portal and therefore no mechanism is provided to export or import these changes.

Changing Your Default Language

Recall that you set the default language for your site earlier in this chapter. The default language is used in cases where the user has not been authenticated, and therefore does not have a preferred language of their own. Also, the default language will be used as the default choice for the preferred language when a new user registers on the portal. The default language is controlled from the Site Settings page, as shown previously in Figure 4-18. Once users log on to the site (this includes the Portal Administrator and Host accounts as well), their preferred language will be used instead of the default language.

The Language Editor

To create custom localization strings for the portal, select Languages from the Admin menu. The Custom Portal Locale screen (see Figure 4-36) provides the ability for Administrators to customize resource strings for any of the installed locales.

Figure 4-36

The tree on the left-hand side of the screen allows you to easily navigate to any resource file. Each resource file corresponds to the various controls or shared resources in the portal. The first time you attempt to edit a resource file, you are asked to verify that you want to create a custom resource file (see Figure 4-37). The resource file will be saved in the directory alongside the other resources.

Resource files are named using a standard pattern based on the associated file: [FileName].resx for English resources, [FileName].[Culture].resx for non-English resources. When portal-specific resource files are created, the system prepends the .resx extension with Portal-[PortalID]. In the example from Figure 4-37, the local portal copy of the English resource file would be named SkinControl.ascx.Portal-0.resx. The German (Deutsch) version would be named SkinControl.ascx.de-DE.Portal-0.resx.

When the portal-specific localized file is created, all resource strings are included. Once the portal resource file is created, any changes in the comparable host file are overridden by the portal file, even if the portal file strings were not changed. In Figure 4-38 the values for Host.Text, Preview.Text, and Site.Text are written to the resource file when the portal file is created.

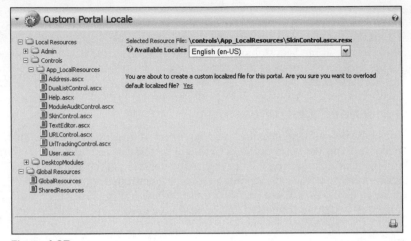

Figure 4-37

Each resource displays the Resource Name, Default Value, and Localized Value. The Resource Name corresponds to the key used by the portal for looking up the localized value. The default System Locale for DotNetNuke is English (en-US). The English language resources are used for all default values.

Localized values correspond to the locale selected in the Available Locales drop-down list box. Localized values can be edited directly using the associated textarea boxes. Once you have completed editing the localized values, click the Update link button to save your changes.

This works well for simple strings and allows you to edit multiple strings without requiring multiple postbacks to the server. Long strings, or resource strings that contain HTML are more difficult to edit using the textarea boxes. To edit these resources, click the arrow button to the right of the textarea.

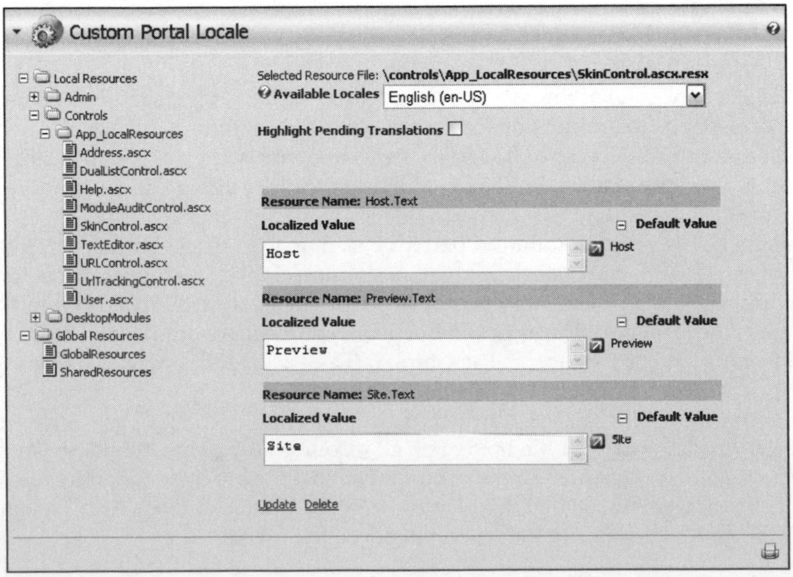

Figure 4-38

Because the button will cause a postback to the server, and we are not yet ready to save changes for the associated localized value, you may lose any data that has been changed but not updated. To prevent data loss, DotNetNuke will display a dialog (see Figure 4-39) asking you to confirm that you want to proceed.

Figure 4-39

Click Cancel to return to the main editing screen in order to save any pending changes. Click OK to proceed to the Language Editor screen (see Figure 4-40).

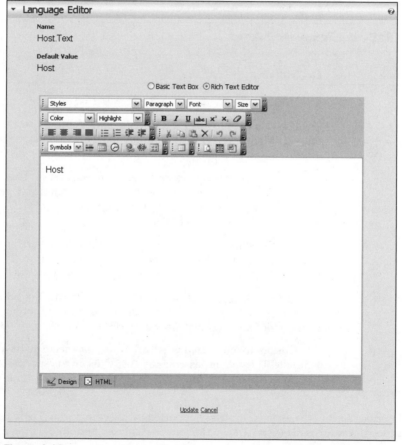

Figure 4-40

The Language Editor uses the HtmlEditorProvider defined in the `web.config` file. The editor provides advanced text and HTML editing functionality. (See Chapter 8 for more information about using the HTML Editor.) Once you have completed making changes to the resource string, select Update to save your changes and return to the Custom Portal Locale screen, or select Cancel to discard your changes and return.

Customizing Your E-mail Templates

Most Portal Administrators will choose to keep almost all of the default resource strings for their web site. However, you should at least review the standard system messages used for generating e-mails to your web site users. Previous versions of DotNetNuke provided a central location for managing the e-mail templates used by the system. In DotNetNuke 3.0, these templates were incorporated into the resource files so that they could be localized like other static elements of the portal.

Because static e-mail templates would not be very useful, DotNetNuke supports the use of special tokens, which will be replaced at runtime with the specified property value. DotNetNuke currently recognizes six different tokens (see Table 4-11) that follow the pattern [TokenName:Property]. Valid properties for each of these tokens are defined in Appendix C.

Table 4-11: E-mail Template Tokens

Token Name	Description
Host	The Host token provides access to a limited set of HostSettings properties.
Portal	The Portal token provides access to the PortalSettings properties. This token also supports the URL property that corresponds to the HTTP Alias for the current portal.
User	The User token provides access to UserInfo properties. This token also supports the VerificationCode property, which is dynamically generated based on the Portal ID and User ID in the form [*PortalID*]-[*UserID*]. The user token is not valid for all templates.
Membership	The Membership token provides access to UserMembership properties. This information is specific to the currently selected user. The Membership token can only be used for templates that also support the User token.
Profile	The Profile token provides access to the UserProfile properties. This information is specific to the currently selected user. The Profile token can only be used for templates that also support the User token.
Custom	The Custom token is used when arbitrary data needs to be included in the template. The data is passed as an ArrayList and is specific to each e-mail template. Not all templates support the use of custom values.

Table 4-12 describes each of the e-mail templates supported by the core portal. These templates can all be found in the global resources file (`\App_GlobalResources\GlobalResources.resx`).

Table 4-12: Site-Generated E-mail Templates

Resource	User Token	Custom Token
EMAIL_USER_REGISTRATION_PUBLIC_SUBJECT EMAIL_USER_REGISTRATION_PUBLIC_BODY Sent to users when they register on a site that is not set to Private Registration. This e-mail is also sent when a registration is manually authorized.	Yes	None
EMAIL_USER_UNREGISTER_SUBJECT EMAIL_USER_UNREGISTER_BODY Sent to the Portal Administrator when a user is unregistered whether by user self-service or through deletion.	Yes	None
EMAIL_SMTP_TEST_SUBJECT Sent to the Host when testing SMTP configuration.	No	None
EMAIL_PORTAL_SIGNUP_SUBJECT EMAIL_PORTAL_SIGNUP_BODY Sent to the new Portal Administrator whenever a portal iscreated, whether by the Host or by a user when they sign up for a portal as a free trial (Host option).	Yes	None
EMAIL_USER_REGISTRATION_PRIVATE_SUBJECT EMAIL_USER_REGISTRATION_PRIVATE_BODY Sent to the user at the time of registration, only on sites where Private Registration is set. This is the e-mail that should explain your approval policy.	Yes	None
EMAIL_USER_REGISTRATION_ADMINISTRATOR_SUBJECT EMAIL_USER_REGISTRATION_ADMINISTRATOR_BODY Sent to the Portal Administrator on every registration.	Yes	None
EMAIL_PASSWORD_REMINDER_SUBJECT EMAIL_PASSWORD_REMINDER_BODY Sent to the user when a reminder is requested.	Yes	None
EMAIL_ROLE_ASSIGNMENT_SUBJECT EMAIL_ROLE_ASSIGNMENT_BODY Sent to the user when a role is assigned by the Administrator and the Send Notification option is checked.	Yes Yes	None 0: RoleName 1: Description
EMAIL_ROLE_UNASSIGNMENT_SUBJECT EMAIL_ROLE_UNASSIGNMENT_BODY Sent to the user when a role is removed by the Administrator and the Send Notification option is checked.	Yes Yes	None 0: RoleName 1: Description

Table continued on following page

EMAIL_AFFILIATE_NOTIFICATION_SUBJECT	No	None
EMAIL_AFFILIATE_NOTIFICATION_BODY	No	0: VendorName 1: AffiliateID

Sent to the affiliate when the Send Notification button is
clicked on the Edit Vendor page.

The Privacy Statement and Terms of Use

Like e-mail templates, the Terms of Use and Privacy Statement resources are also another set of resources
that you are likely to need to customize (see Table 4-13). Because these two resources are generic to the
entire web site, the User, Membership, Profile, and Custom tokens are not usable. Links to the terms and
privacy statement are included in the default skins (see Figure 4-19).

Table 4-13: Terms of Use and Privacy Statement Resources

Resource	User Token	Custom Token
MESSAGE_PORTAL_TERMS	No	None
MESSAGE_PORTAL_PRIVACY	No	None

Maintaining Your Portal

Once you have your portal set up and working just the way you want it, you'll start finding good reasons to enhance or change things. You'll delegate maintenance work to others; you'll pick up some site advertising or want to track affiliate referrals; you'll want to communicate with your registered users; you'll want to recover work that you've previously discarded; and you'll want to know what kind of traffic your site is getting.

You've already experienced a very feature-rich environment for configuration of your portal's look, feel, and function. DotNetNuke provides an equally rich suite of tools for maintenance tasks as well.

User Accounts

Figure 4-18 introduced you to the User Details page, which provides for user self-management. The Portal Administrator is also able to manage users from the User Accounts page on the Admin menu. Figure 4-41 shows the list of users as seen on the User Accounts page.

The page supports several methods of finding a user, which is helpful when your number of registered users becomes large. Clicking a letter filters the list by username, displaying a maximum of the number of records specified in the drop-down in the upper-right corner of the page. Standard buttons will appear for First, Previous, Next, and Last if there are enough users in the list to require paging. If you need to find a specific user, the search box can accept either a username or an e-mail address.

Figure 4-41

Depending on the type of Portal Registration Options you selected (see Table 4-4), you may have particular interest in finding unauthorized users. Private registration requires the Portal Administrator to manually approve users so the button to list them, the check box to indicate them, and the button to delete them are handy features. Once you've listed the unauthorized users and approved the ones you'd like to permit access, you can click Delete Unauthorized Users to remove the remaining registrations you've deemed inappropriate for your site.

When you click the pencil icon next to a user's name you'll find yourself on the Edit User Accounts page (see Figure 4-42). This page is similar to the User Account page in Figure 4-16, but it differs in a couple of key ways. There is a check box to flag the user as Approved or not and the Membership Services control is missing in favor of a link button to Manage Roles for This User.

> In previous versions of DotNetNuke it was possible to change the name of a user, but this feature is not present in version 3.0. The default Membership Provider used by DotNetNuke incorporates an ASP.NET 2.0 component (MemberRole) with lots of sophisticated security features. One of the security tenets of this component prohibits changing of a user's identity once it is set.

In support of the Private Registration option, checking Authorized causes an e-mail to be sent to users providing them with their login credentials and a welcome message.

The Preferred Language and Time Zone settings work exactly as they do for the Site Settings (see Table 4-6). These settings will override the default site settings when the user is logged in.

Managing Security Roles

Earlier in this chapter you were introduced to managing security roles within the context of the list of roles (see Figure 4-26). When approaching this task from the list of users, the Manage Roles For This User button brings you to a similar page (see Figure 4-43).

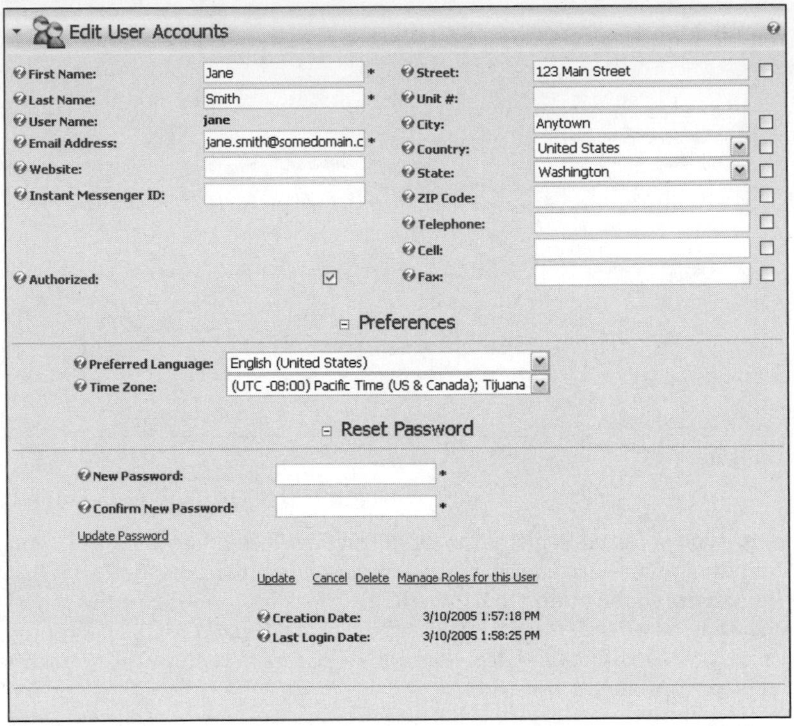

Figure 4-42

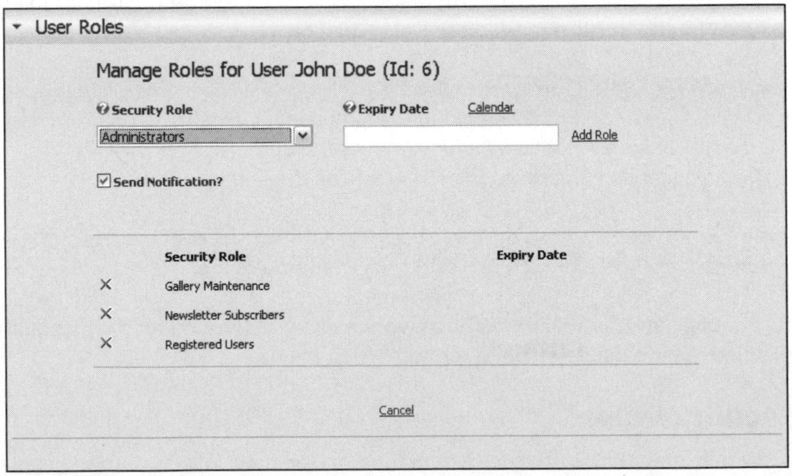

Figure 4-43

You can assign a role to your user along with an expiration date (if desired), or remove existing roles. You can also choose whether or not you'd like the user to receive e-mail notification of the change.

Vendors

At some point, you may want to develop partnerships with others in promoting your web site and/or complimentary products and services. DotNetNuke provides a number of built-in features to get you started in developing these relationships.

The Vendor management features provide a lot of basic functionality, but for enterprising developers there is also a lot of room to build on this foundation to provide additional services.

Creating a New Vendor

Open the Vendor List page by selecting Vendors from the Admin menu (see Figure 4-44). You can select Add New Vendor from the bottom of the page or from the action menu.

On the Edit Vendors page (not pictured), you'll add basic contact information for the vendor as you would for any user. You'll also have the option to specify a vendor's web site, logo, key search words, and classification.

At the time of this writing, most of these optional fields are unused. However, they are reserved for future use as DotNetNuke architecture/services continue to develop in this area.

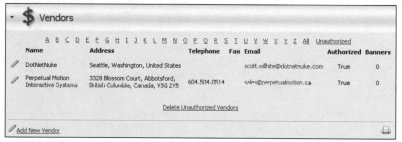

Figure 4-44

Banner Advertising

Once a vendor has been added, you can create banners for them that can be displayed on your site. Navigate to the Edit Vendor page for your vendor, expand the Banner Advertising section, and click Add New Banner. Table 4-14 explains the settings.

Table 4-14: Edit Banner Settings

Banner Name	This value identifies the banner in lists, but it is also used as the ALT text for graphic banners and as hyperlinked text on text banners.
Banner Type	Of the available banner types, only two really impact how the banner fields are used. When you place banners on your site with the Banner module, you'll select which type of banner it should display. Choosing Banner, MicroButton, Button, Block, and Skyscraper just provides logical groupings

Table continued on following page

of banners that fall into common width and height formats. There are no actual rules, but these groupings help to organize banners so that you don't wind up displaying wide banners in button-sized locations in your skin. Text and Script types are special cases. If you choose a Text banner you can mimic the look of Google AdSense (see Figure 4-45). Choosing a Script banner allows for freeform HTML in the text box, which is helpful for a number of generated links for things like Amazon products.

Banner Group	This value serves to further aid in the ad-hoc grouping of banners. For example, DotNetNuke.com displays rotating button banners for its sponsors. To keep sponsor buttons separate from other banners, they each have Sponsor in their Banner Group field. Likewise, the Banner Options for the module specifies Sponsor in its Banner Group.
	Since this field is ad-hoc, there is no real way to track how or where it is used. You'll have to keep up with that on your own. But it does provide for all the logical separation you should ever need.
	Be on the lookout for continued enhancements to these features!
Image	Specify whether your image (if applicable) is to be rendered from a file on your site or from a remote URL.
Text/Script	The text in this field is handled differently depending on the Banner Type selected above. For most banner types you'll just leave this field blank. For type Text, this value will appear as simple text (unlinked) below the hyperlinked Banner Name field (see Figure 4-45). For type Script, this field can contain raw HTML, supporting a variety of link types and formats.
	Field length is limited to 1000 characters.
URL	If this value is populated, it will be used instead of the URL associated with the vendor. So you can use this URL to point to specific pages in a vendor's site or to configure extra query string parameters. This field is also displayed as hyperlinked text on banners of type Text (see Figure 4-45).
CPM/Cost	At the time of this writing, the CPM value is not used for any calculation. However, it does provide a convenient place to record this information in the context of the banner.
Impressions	If specified, this value is one of the criteria used to determine whether a banner should or should not be shown. If you want to limit a banner's display based on the number of impressions, this field will remove it from rotation once this value has been reached.
Start Date	Use this field to set up banners in advance to begin displaying at a future date.
End Date	Together with Start Date, you can create banners to run for specific date durations for events, special deals, holidays, and so on.

Criteria	This choice specifies how the Impressions and Date constraints should be enforced. If enforced independently of one another (OR), a banner will cease to display outside of its date constraint or even within its date constraint if the number of impressions has been reached. If enforced jointly (AND), all criteria must be true for the banner to cease display.
	The AND option helps to address a lack of throttling control. On a busy site with few banners in rotation, a given number of impressions can be chewed up very quickly and so displayed over only a brief time period. By jointly evaluating the criteria, a more equitable rotation is achieved by providing for additional banner impressions during the time period.

Figure 4-45

You can advise vendors of the status a banner by clicking the Email Status to Vendor button at the bottom of the Edit Banner page. This sends an e-mail to the address specified in the Vendor details, which relays the banner field information (text, costs, and constraints) and performance (view and click-through counts).

Vendors as Affiliates

Just as your site links to vendors through the use of banners, your vendors may also link to you. If you would like to be able to track your vendors' click-through performance to your site, you can click Add New Affiliate. Define a tracking period and associated cost per click (CPC) and cost per acquisition (CPA) and e-mail the vendor their link information by clicking Send Notification (see Figure 4-46).

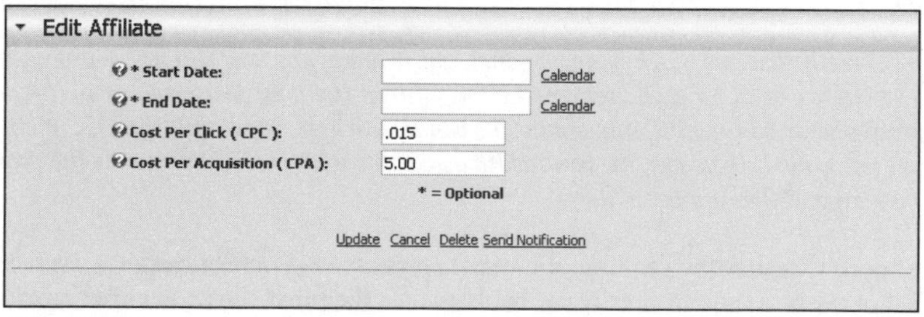

Figure 4-46

The CPC information for affiliate referrals will be summarized in the Edit Vendor list, just as click-through is for banners. However the CPA information is currently unused. You can specify multiple affiliate relationships under a single vendor to provide for tracking during discrete time periods.

> *At the time of this writing, it is possible to create affiliate referrals with overlapping date ranges. This will produce double counts of vendor performance during the period of overlap. So be sure to end one affiliate period before starting another.*

Newsletters

Periodically, you'll want to communicate with your users. The Newsletter page provides a very convenient way for you to do this by allowing you to send e-mail to users in specified roles (see Figure 4-47). Remember when you set up the Newsletter Subscribers role? Here's where you put that to use.

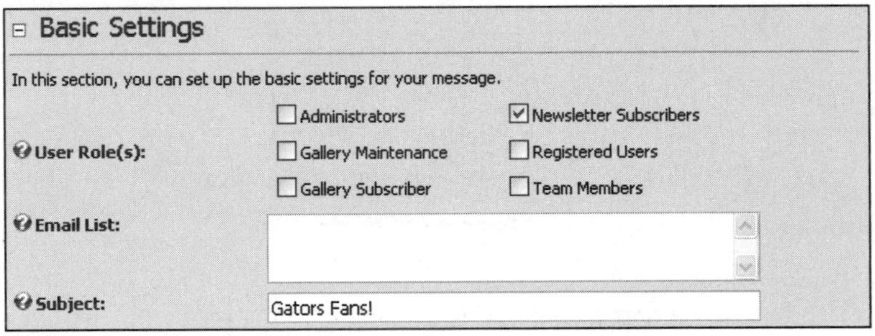

Figure 4-47

Just select the role(s) that you want to be included in the distribution. If a user belongs to more than one role, they'll still only get one e-mail. You can also specify additional recipients separated by semicolons in the Email List field. And you can format your e-mail as either text or HTML.

Figure 4-48 displays the advanced e-mail options, which include sending a file attachment and choosing the priority setting. The Send Method option allows you to specify whether or not your e-mail is personalized. Choosing the BCC method sends just one e-mail, which will be delivered to all users. Choosing the TO method causes your e-mail to be personalized (for example, Dear John Doe).

> *Using the TO method seems much more personal, but it comes at a cost. First, the processing required to create a separate e-mail for each user could be significant (with large user volume). Second, it significantly increases your bandwidth utilization. The bandwidth associated with the BCC method is minimal — just one e-mail. However, the bandwidth associated with the TO version is the product of the size of the e-mail and the number of users.*

You can also choose whether the sending of e-mail is processed synchronously or asynchronously. If you have a large list of users, asynchronously probably makes the most sense. In either case, a summary e-mail is sent to the Portal Administrator reporting on the number of recipients, number of pieces of e-mail actually sent (1 or n), and the start/stop times for processing the job. DotNetNuke batches e-mail addresses into groups in the background so you'll never actually be trying to send an e-mail with thousands of BCC recipients.

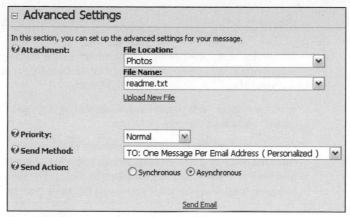

Figure 4-48

Site Log

The Site Log displays text-based reports only, as shown in Figure 4-49.

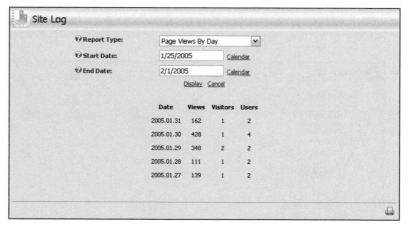

Figure 4-49

Table 4-15 identifies the available report types.

Table 4-15: Site Log Report Types	
Affiliate Referrals	Track referrals from vendors who are defined as affiliates. By using their affiliate ID numbers in links to your site, you'll be able to capture how productive those affiliate links are.
Detailed Site Log	This detailed log of site activity includes all users and displays date and time, user name, referrer, user agent, user host address, and page name.

Table continued on following page

Page Popularity	Display the total number of visits to the pages on your site in the period specified. Date and time of the last page visit is included.
Page Views By	This series of reports provides a summary of the number of visitors (anonymous) and users (logged in) that accessed your site in the intervals specified (Day, Day of Week, Hour, Month).
Site Referrals	Summary list of web pages (including search engines) that users have clicked on to lead them to your site.
User Details	This series of reports provides a summary of the number of page visits recorded according to the characteristic specified (Agents, Frequency, Registrations by Country, and Registrations by Date). The Report by Frequency can be interesting — it identifies your most frequent visitors in any given period.

Logging occurs at the discretion of the Host, who has a number of options for how it is configured. If the Host chooses to generate text-based log files (like IIS logs), these reports will become obsolete because they work only with database logging information (at this time). See Chapter 5 for more information on Host settings that control logging.

Recycle Bin

Have you ever deleted a file on your computer only to experience a panic moment? Portal Administrators might feel that too once in a while, which is why DotNetNuke has a Recycle Bin feature (see Figure 4-50).

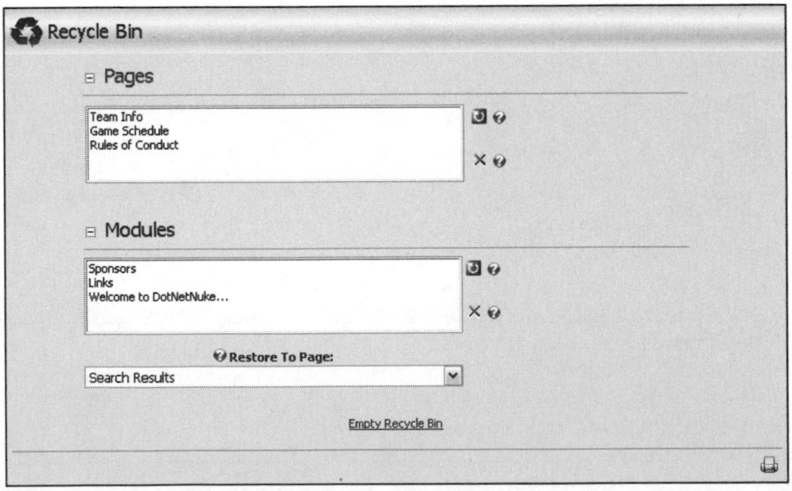

Figure 4-50

The act of deleting a page or module doesn't really delete anything; it merely sets a flag that DotNetNuke understands internally as deleted and so ignores it in the general interface. Items that have this flag set can be found (and restored from) the Recycle Bin.

Developers can see this implementation by looking at the database fields Tab.IsDeleted and Modules.IsDeleted.

Recycling Pages

You can select single or multiple pages to restore or delete. However, when doing either you must follow the hierarchy of the pages in order for it to work. If you think about this, it makes perfect sense, but it is not obvious. In the example in Figure 4-50 the Team Info page was the parent to the others (in the menu structure). If you attempt to restore the Game Schedule page first it would have nowhere to go, so you would receive a warning like that shown in Figure 4-51.

Figure 4-51

Likewise, if you try to permanently delete the top-level page (Team Info) before deleting the child pages, you would receive a warning like the one in Figure 4-52.

Figure 4-52

You'll note that when a page is deleted its modules do not appear listed individually in the Recycle Bin. That's because a page is considered to include all of its content (which is restored along with it).

Recycling Modules

When modules are deleted, they lose their association to a specific page. So when they are restored you must select a target page for them to appear on.

Currently, a restored module will have the same view and edit permissions that it did originally. However, this may not be what you have in mind if you are restoring a module that has been in the Recycle Bin for a while. In fact, since there is no convenient way to look at a module that is in the bin, you might be just restoring one to see what it was! The best way to do this is to restore modules to a page that is not visible to your users (a staging page). Then you can check it out for yourself and change whatever settings are necessary before moving it to its final (visible) home.

Modules are always restored to the ContentPane on the target page (shown previously in Figure 4-12). Because a skin designer can create virtually any number of panes in a skin, DotNetNuke can only rely on the existence of this one required pane. This is one more reason why it's a good practice to restore modules to a staging page before relocating them.

Cleaning Up

As you might have gathered, it's possible to accumulate quite a bit of junk in the Recycle Bin if you do a lot of creating and deleting of pages/modules. It's a good idea to do a little housecleaning here every once in a while so that when you really need it, the Recycle Bin is easier to navigate.

Log Viewer

The Log Viewer gives a Portal Administrator the ability to monitor a variety of events and associated details including (but not limited to) exceptions. Out of the box, DotNetNuke is configured to log exceptions only; however, any of the (approximately) 48 defined events can be logged at the discretion of the Host.

A single set of logs is implemented as a group of XML files that are located in the default portal root directory. Records from these files are filtered to display only those generated by your portal. The Portal Administrator can filter the list by event type, limit the size of the list displayed, and even e-mail list contents to a specified recipient if assistance is needed (as shown in Figure 4-53).

> **To view the full set of default logs, take a look at the following files:**
>
> `\Portals\_default\Logs\Application.xml.resources`
> `\Portals\_default\Logs\Exception.xml.resources`
> `\Portals\_default\Logs\Scheduler.xml.resources`
> `\Portals\_default\Logs\Log.xml.resources`
>
> **For an in-depth review of logging, see Chapter 8.**

When sending log entries, the body of the e-mail message is populated with the XML text exactly as it appears in the log files.

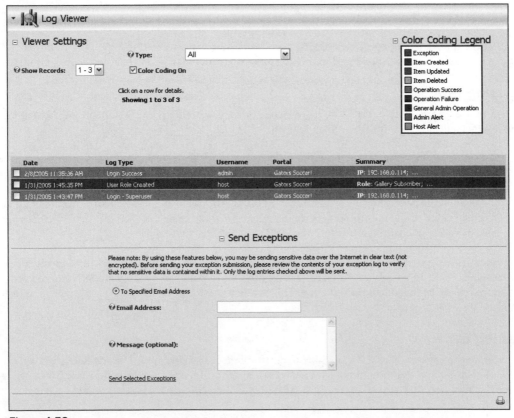

Figure 4-53

Clicking an entry in the Log Viewer expands it to show the full details of the event. Some events contain as little as one or two items of detail, however some contain many more. The event detail for a module load exception is illustrated in Figure 4-54.

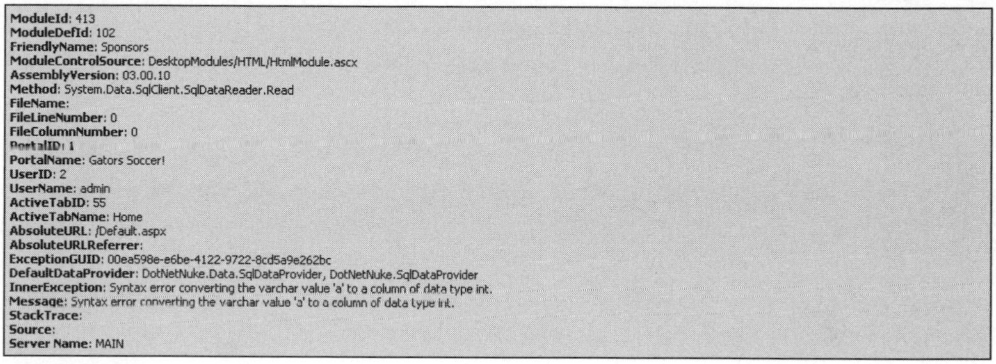

```
ModuleId: 413
ModuleDefId: 102
FriendlyName: Sponsors
ModuleControlSource: DesktopModules/HTML/HtmlModule.ascx
AssemblyVersion: 03.00.10
Method: System.Data.SqlClient.SqlDataReader.Read
FileName:
FileLineNumber: 0
FileColumnNumber: 0
PortalID: 1
PortalName: Gators Soccer!
UserID: 2
UserName: admin
ActiveTabID: 55
ActiveTabName: Home
AbsoluteURL: /Default.aspx
AbsoluteURLReferrer:
ExceptionGUID: 00ea598e-e6be-4122-9722-8cd5a9e262bc
DefaultDataProvider: DotNetNuke.Data.SqlDataProvider, DotNetNuke.SqlDataProvider
InnerException: Syntax error converting the varchar value 'a' to a column of data type int.
Message: Syntax error converting the varchar value 'a' to a column of data type int.
StackTrace:
Source:
Server Name: MAIN
```

Figure 4-54

Summary

In this chapter you learned just about everything there is to know about the Portal Administrator and the features and functions available to you in that role. Key features that you should understand include the following:

- ❑ Control Panel
- ❑ Site Wizard, Preview Mode, and Help
- ❑ Preview Mode

You should be familiar with the tools available to configure your portal, such as the following:

- ❑ Site Settings
- ❑ Security Roles
- ❑ Pages
- ❑ Skins
- ❑ File Manager
- ❑ Languages

And the tools available to maintain your portal over time:

- ❑ User Accounts
- ❑ Vendors
- ❑ Newsletters
- ❑ Site Log
- ❑ Recycle Bin

You should have some understanding of how to do things, and when and why to do them as well.

5

Host Administration

In Chapter 4 you learned just about everything there is to know about administering a DotNetNuke portal. In this chapter you learn everything there is to know about administering a collection of portals, their environment, and runtime features.

As the Host you function essentially as the "creator" of the DotNetNuke universe in which the portals exist. While a lofty sounding role, it is an accurate description because the Host has absolute sway over what portals within their installation can and cannot do. Where each Portal Administrator is subject to the "laws of nature" established by the Host, the Host has complete authority to change those laws at will. Some of those laws apply to all portals in the installation universally, but others will apply discretely to individual portals.

> *Understanding the Host role is very important. While the Portal Administrators consider their portal to be alone in its own corner of the cyber-universe, the Host knows otherwise. Host options provide for differentiation between one installation of DotNetNuke and another. Configuration choices made by the Host can affect function and performance of all portals and must therefore be made wisely and with deliberate intent.*

Upon completion of this chapter, you'll know everything you need to know as a Host to effectively configure and manage an installation of DotNetNuke.

Who Is the Host?

Continuing with the Host as "creator" analogy could get you in trouble in some circles (not to mention with your editor!). Since DotNetNuke is an "equal opportunity application," we'll find another way to describe the Host that is less prone to cause this particular brand of excitement. DotNetNuke generates plenty of excitement in business and technology circles and we're quite content with that.

To clearly identify the Host requires us to first review a defining characteristic of DotNetNuke. You'll recall from Chapter 3 that DotNetNuke is defined as supporting "multiple web sites from the same codebase." With one installation of DotNetNuke you can create as many unique portals as you like, each with its own URL(s), identity, features, users, data, and so on. You learned in Chapter 4 that each portal has its own administrator, but this begs the question, "Who administers the creation of portals?" So this is how the scope of the role first comes into focus. The Host is the user who creates portals. But the Host does a lot more too. So much more that we've devoted an entire chapter to the role.

Prior to version 3.0, the Host was alone in his sovereignty, carrying all the responsibility that went along with being the only user in that role; big title, big job. There was only one Host account and that was it. Version 3.0 introduces the role of "SuperUser," so now instead of being forced to play deity a Host can open ranks to allow for a more "Justice League" approach to configuration and maintenance. All SuperUsers have "super powers" in the DotNetNuke universe.

So the first thing you've learned is that "Host" is already a legacy term in version 3.0, carried forward from previous generations of DotNetNuke. Understanding this, you can now feel free to interchange the terms Host and SuperUser anywhere that you see them — in all but one case. The default installation of DotNetNuke has one SuperUser account preinstalled whose username actually is "host."

Where Do I Begin?

If you're going to master a universe, you'll have to manifest your superpowers and take some cues from the most famous "in the beginning" of all! Breathe some life into a new user, or, in keeping with the "Justice League" theme, be a hero and get a "sidekick."

The very first thing you'll want to do is to create another SuperUser account. Once that is done, you'll retire the default host account. It's a prudent security measure in any software installation to retire default administrative accounts to thwart dubious hacking efforts. At a minimum, you'll want to change the password for the default host account, although you can also delete it entirely.

In version 3.0, DotNetNuke utilizes a version of Microsoft's ASP.NET 2.0 MemberRole component in the default Membership Provider. One of the many distinct features of this component is the implementation of user lockout. After a specified number of invalid password attempts a user account will be unable to log in. Although DotNetNuke resets the password lockout after 10 minutes, the nuisance can be avoided entirely by using a different account and username.

Log in by using your new SuperUser account username and password. You'll notice that you have the same view as the Portal Administrator (see Figure 4-2 in Chapter 4) with one small exception: you also have an additional top-level menu "Host" as shown in Figure 5-1. You'll be getting into all the details of all these options in this chapter, but right now just concern yourself with the SuperUsers Accounts menu item.

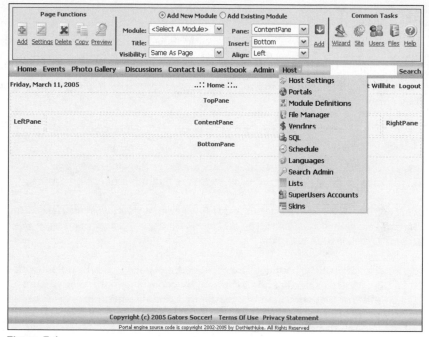

Figure 5-1

SuperUsers Accounts

When you navigate to the SuperUsers Accounts page you'll see a familiar view. The SuperUsers Accounts page (see Figure 5-2) is literally the same control that is used for managing other users' accounts and works in the same way, so if you need a refresher on how this works, consult Chapter 4.

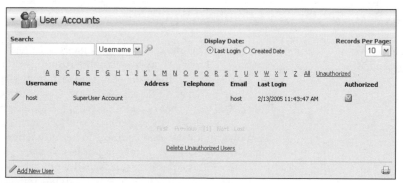

Figure 5-2

To some extent the sorting, searching, and paging functions are unnecessary because you're not likely to have more than a couple of SuperUsers, but it does keep the interface consistent and familiar.

Configuring Your Installation

As you're about to see, the Host has a lot of options and tools for configuring the environment in which portals live. As you learned in Chapter 4 in the context of the Portal Administrator, some capability is specifically appropriate for initial configuration, some for routine operations, and some for ongoing maintenance, reporting, and issue resolution. As we move through each of the Host Settings, we'll consider how they apply to those needs.

Host Settings

Host Settings is broken down into two different categories for the sake of organization. The Basic Settings and Advanced Settings categories each consist of a number of option groups.

As with Site Settings, there is an important text button at the very bottom of the Host Settings page. Despite the fact that a number of controls on the Host Settings page generate postbacks, no changes are saved until the Update button gets clicked.

There is also a final control at the bottom of the Host Settings page that falls outside of any option group, the Upgrade Log For Version selector and Go button. By choosing a particular version and clicking Go, you can view a log file for that version (if one exists) that contains any errors or warnings recorded during the install/upgrade process. The log files are created in the folder of the Data Provider, so in the default install of DotNetNuke those files are located in

```
\Providers\DataProviders\SqlDataProvider\*.log
```

Basic Settings: Site Configuration

Table 5-1 describes each of the read-only fields displayed in the Site Configuration group under Basic Settings. This group is particularly helpful in identifying the context under which your installation of DotNetNuke is running. If you are communicating with an ISP or hosting company, these details may be very helpful in diagnosing any issue you might be investigating.

Table 5-1: Basic Settings, Site Configuration

DotNetNuke Version	Indicates what version of DotNetNuke is currently running. Until version 3.0, the only way to verify the running version was to check a database value or to enable an option to display the version in the browser's title bar (see Show Copyright Credits in Table 5-3). The format of a DotNetNuke version number is `[Major Version].[Minor Version].[Package Version]`. Major and minor versions combine to identify which functional version of DotNetNuke you are using (for example, 3.0). The Package Version indicates a particular package that may be an alpha or beta testing release, a public release, a security patch release, and so on.
Data Provider	Identifies which Data Provider DotNetNuke is currently using.

.NET Framework	Indicates which version of the .NET CLR that DotNetNuke is running under. This can be particularly helpful to ensure proper setup when your server environment supports multiple versions of the ASP.NET framework. For developers this is `System.Environment.Version`.
ASP.NET Identity	Identifies the Windows account name under which DotNetNuke is running (or the name of the account being impersonated). For developers this is `System.Security.Principal.WindowsIdentity.GetCurrent.Name`.
Host Name	Identifies the host name of the system DotNetNuke is running on. For developers this is `Dns.GetHostName`.

Basic Settings: Host Details

The host details establish the identity of the installation for both internal processing and external identity (see Table 5-2). For the most part, the settings of individual portals define their own identity. However, skin object support is available to pass on host information into portal-level skins. This can be useful for portals whose support requirements are met by their host so that they can dynamically inject appropriate title and contact information where needed.

Table 5-2: Basic Settings, Host Details

Host Portal	This drop-down selection identifies which portal in the installation is to be considered the default. The default portal attributes are used where no other portal context can be determined. For example, when an invalid URL is used to reach the installation, the request is answered on the first alias of the specified Host Portal.
Host Title	This value is used to populate the text for the skin token `[HOSTNAME]`. Prior to version 3.0, you could see the `[HOSTNAME]` skin token in action on the bottom of the default skin. It was often imposed by the host as a means of injecting a "powered by" link into each portal's skin.
Host URL	The Host URL is not the same as an alias for the default portal. It specifies the link target for the Help button in the Control Panel and the skin token `[HOSTNAME]`.
Host Email	Most e-mail in DotNetNuke is sent to or from the individual Portal Administrators. However, there are a few specific cases where the Host e-mail address is used (for example, SMTP configuration test, skin token `[HELP]`, and so on). To avoid potential problems with outbound e-mail, ensure that the Host Email is a valid address on the SMTP Server (see Table 5-5).

Basic Settings: Appearance

In Chapter 4 you learned about a number of optional settings for default portal appearance. If those choices are left unmade, these host default choices are applied. Additionally, the host has a couple of other configuration options that will affect the appearance of portals in this installation. Table 5-3 summarizes the effects of each choice.

Table 5-3: Basic Settings, Appearance	
Show Copyright Credits	If checked, this setting inserts the DotNetNuke version number into the browser's title bar and populates the [DOTNETNUKE] skin object. In the default skin this is displayed as a small thin bar across the bottom of the page that displays the DotNetNuke copyright (see bottom of Figure 5-3).
Use Custom Error Messages	This setting specifies whether DotNetNuke will intercept module errors or whether ASP.NET will intercept them. If this option is selected, DotNetNuke will display only basic friendly messages to non-Admin users. However, if the user encountering the error is an Admin (or Host) user, full error information is made available. Figures 5-4 and 5-5 illustrate the difference between the same error messages presented to Users and Administrators/SuperUsers, respectively. Detailed information is also retained in the error log.
Host Skin	If a skin is not specified in the portal Site Settings, this skin will be used as the default for each page where a skin is not explicitly specified in Page Settings. The Host Skin, Host Container, Admin Skin, and Admin Container settings work exactly like their counterparts in the Portal Administrators Site Settings. For more detail, please see Chapter 4.
Host Container	If a container is not specified in the portal Site Settings, this container will be used as the default for each module where a container is not explicitly specified in Module Settings.
Admin Skin	If a skin is not specified in the portal Site Settings, this skin will be used as the default for admin pages.
Admin Container	If a container is not specified in the portal Site Settings, this container will be used as the default for modules on every admin page.
Upload Skin	Uploading a skin from the Host Settings will load it into the Host's default folder, which will make it available to *all* portals. This is in contrast to uploading from Site Settings, where it will load into the Portal Root folder. Skins uploaded from here are located in \Portals_default\Skins.
Upload Container	Uploading a container from the Host Settings will load it into the Host's default folder, which will make it available to *all* portals. This is in contrast to uploading from Site Settings, where it will load into the Portal Root folder. Containers uploaded from here are located in \Portals_default\Containers.

The Show Copyrights setting can be helpful in a development environment for quick reference to the running version (see Figure 5-3). However, in a production environment it can pose a risk of exposure to anyone trolling specifically to locate DotNetNuke web sites. A simple Google search of the copyright statement or "DNN" in the title bar will yield results for sites that have not disabled this option.

Figure 5-3

ASP.NET error messages can be helpful and informative for developers, but the familiar "yellow screen of death" doesn't do much for the confidence of users and clients. DotNetNuke's Custom Error Messages option intercepts errors and encapsulates them within either the offending module's container or, in the case of a non-module error, injects them into the top of the ContentPane (see Figure 5-4).

Figure 5-4

Because the error information is confusing for users but valuable for support personnel, DotNetNuke displays different error information based on the current user (see Figure 5-5). If the current user is an Administrator or SuperUser, full detailed information is provided. Other users are spared the gory details and presented with a friendlier message.

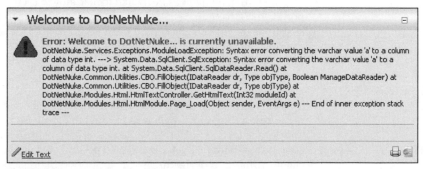

Figure 5-5

Basic Settings: Payment Settings

You learned in Chapter 4 that many of these Payment Settings have been preserved from earlier versions of DotNetNuke for legacy support purposes. For the Host, these settings only come into play as defaults for new portal creation or for portal subscription renewal. These Payment Settings will ultimately be deprecated in a future version in favor of more robust eCommerce APIs (see Table 5-4).

Table 5-4: Basic Settings, Payment Settings

Hosting Fee

Hosting Fee represents a default monthly charge associated with hosting a portal. This value is displayed on the Host's list of portals and is applied to new portals at the time of their creation. The value can also be specified within a portal template, which would override this default value. If subscription renewal is activated, this fee will be used for the monthly renewal rate.

Hosting Currency

Default host currency is used in conjunction with the specified Payment Processor (for example, as a required parameter for PayPal processing). This value is applied to new portals at the time of their creation but can also be overridden within a portal template.

Hosting Space (MB)

This value specifies a default disk space limit for new portals. As with many other portal values, this value can be overridden in a portal template. The value is an enforced limit that is displayed at the base of the File Manager in the Portal Administrators view (see bottom of Figure 5-32).
As Host, you can change this value in the Site Settings for a specific portal.

Demo Period (Days)

If Anonymous Demo Signup is enabled, the Expiry Date for a new portal is set this many days into the future.
As Host, you can change this value in the Site Settings for a specific portal.

Anonymous Demo Signup

If disabled, only the Host Administrator is able to create a new portal. However, if enabled, this feature allows anonymous users to sign up and immediately log in as Portal Administrator to their own child portal. You'll have to create your own link somewhere to reach the signup page, but you can copy it from your browser's address bar after clicking Add New Portal on the Portals page. It should have a form like the following:

`http://soccer.dotnetnuke.com/Default.aspx?ctl=Signup&mid=321`

This page is not illustrated specifically, but it uses the same control as regular portal signup, which is illustrated in Figure 5-12.
This legacy feature of DotNetNuke was originally provided to showcase the ability of DotNetNuke to host private portals for potential clients. Although this feature is still supported in version 3.0, it is not without its share of legacy issues.
Demo signup is enabled throughout the installation, not just on the Host Portal. So a clever anonymous user who locates a DotNetNuke site might try the demo portal signup. The Portal Root ensures file separation and the host File Upload Extensions protects from unsafe files, but a malicious user who finds your site could use you as an anonymous download location for the duration of the demo period (or until you caught them). Further, since the user chooses the child

portal name, you could wind up with unpleasantly named folder paths indexed by search engines that you would rather not have. Since demo signup creates the user as Portal Administrator, a valid e-mail address is not even required.
Use of this legacy feature is highly discouraged.

The Hosting Space option is included with the Payment Settings because it is recognized as a factor that commands premium pricing from a web host, and therefore generally also from a VAR (value added reseller). If a file upload is attempted that causes the hosting space to be exceeded, an error message is displayed (see Figure 5-6).

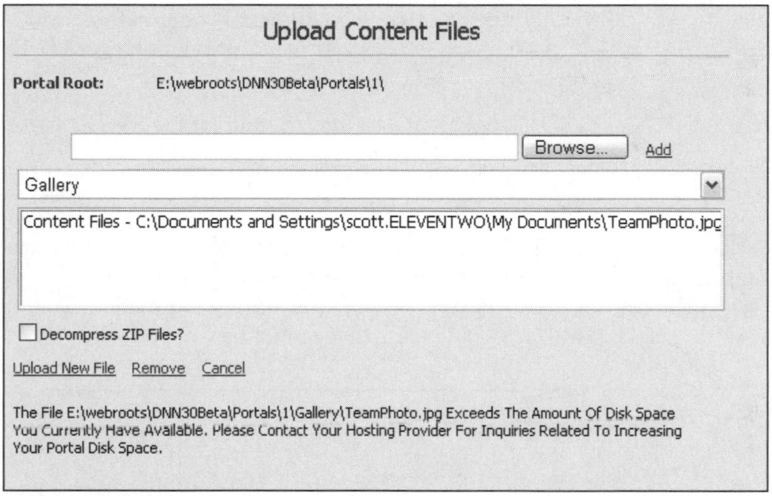

Upload Content Files

Portal Root: E:\webroots\DNN30Beta\Portals\1\

[   ] [Browse...] Add

Gallery   [v]

Content Files - C:\Documents and Settings\scott.ELEVENTWO\My Documents\TeamPhoto.jpg

☐ Decompress ZIP Files?

Upload New File   Remove   Cancel

The File E:\webroots\DNN30Beta\Portals\1\Gallery\TeamPhoto.jpg Exceeds The Amount Of Disk Space You Currently Have Available. Please Contact Your Hosting Provider For Inquiries Related To Increasing Your Portal Disk Space.

Figure 5-6

Enforcing the file upload limit protects you from rampant file uploading by well-meaning clients that don't understand the value of limited disk space. It provides the ability to proactively allocate your available disk space among clients as well as an opportunity to assess charge-back for additional usage.

File upload capabilities through an HTML Provider may be disabled. Unless the control maker has made it possible to intercept and filter file upload requests, DotNetNuke cannot ensure integrity of the portal files based on hosting space, allowable file extensions, or directory security. By default, all file uploads should be performed through the File Manager.

Advanced Settings: Proxy Settings

In general, DotNetNuke should not require specific Proxy Settings. However, some modules may address additional ports for which Proxy Settings are required in your environment (for example, RSS, FTP, NNTP, and so on). Standard settings are configurable for the Proxy Server Name, Port, UserID, Password, and Timeout duration.

Check with your network administrator about appropriate values for these settings in your location.

Advanced Settings: SMTP Server Settings

Outbound e-mail requires that a valid SMTP server is specified. Table 5-5 explains the SMTP Server Settings in more detail.

Table 5-5: Advanced Settings, SMTP Server Settings	
SMTP Server	This value must resolve to a valid SMTP server. You can specify the server by computer name (for example, MYSERVER or Local host), IP address (for example, 127.0.0.1) or URL (for example, smtpauth.earthelink.net).
SMTP Authentication	Unless your SMTP server is an open relay or filtered by IP, you'll need to specify an authentication method. Most SMTP servers will utilize Basic authentication, however MS Exchange servers prefer NTLM.
SMTP Username	Login name for the account on the SMTP Server (optional).
SMTP Password	Password for the account on the SMTP Server (optional).

Once you have configured the SMTP Settings, you can click the Test button to send a message to the Host Email. If the send operation is successful, you'll see a message to this effect at the top of the page. If the operation is unsuccessful, you may receive a CDO error (see Figure 5-7). This error is generally produced as a result of specifying an SMTP server that cannot be reached.

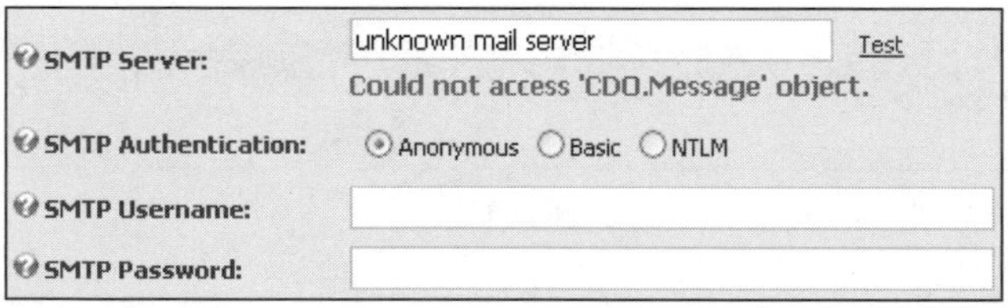

Figure 5-7

In hosting situations, the web server itself often runs a simple SMTP service for handling outbound e-mail generated by web sites. Although this setup does initiate outbound e-mail, that mail is often flagged as SPAM by the target domains (especially domains like Hotmail.com, Yahoo.com, and so on). For best results, the SMTP server you specify should be the one specified in the MX record for your domain. Depending on your SMTP server's configuration, it may be necessary for Portal Administrators' e-mail addresses to be recognized on the server as well.

If you are testing from a home network via a broadband connection you should also be aware of your ISP's policies regarding SMTP servers. Generally speaking, most ISPs will not allow the trafficking of e-mail from other SMTP servers on their networks (as a SPAM control measure). You'll either need to configure DotNetNuke to use the credentials of your ISP account (just as you would in your local e-mail client) or configure a local SMTP server to relay through your ISP and specify that local server in DotNetNuke.

Advanced Settings: Other Settings

This last area covers a lot of ground and includes a number of settings that fall into the category of "superhero" powers. Each setting is described in Table 5-6, but a number of them will be explained in greater detail in later sections of this chapter that cover the functional aspects of the features that these settings control.

Table 5-6: Advanced Settings, Other Settings	
Control Panel	Select the Control Panel that Portal Administrators will use. Chapter 4 contains a full description of the choices (see Figures 4-3 and 4-4). The ability to select the Control Panel exists largely to promote the concept of creating customized Control Panels for the host. If you created your own Control Panel, what would you make it look like?
Site Log Storage	This option allows you to specify whether site log information will be stored in the database or in files. File-based logs are written using the IIS 6 log conventions and are stored in the each portal folder with the following naming convention: `/portals/ <portalid>/logs/ex<yymmdd>.log`.
Site Log Buffer (Items)	This value defines the number of site log entries that are held in memory before storing them. Setting the buffer to 0 turns logging off entirely.
	Changing the buffer value does not affect the actual I/O cost of logging, but it does change where/when the cost is incurred. For example, if the log buffer is set to 1, every page request in every portal will incur the (slight) overhead of the log I/O, whereas if the log buffer is set to 20, only 1 in 20 requests will incur the overhead, but it will incur the overhead of all 20 I/O requests.
	If cache is cleared (whether by app restart, in host settings, or by other means) any uncommitted items in the log buffer are lost. Note that individual buffers are cached for each portal but this setting applies globally to all of them. Setting this value too high could result in data loss for low traffic sites whose cache might expire (and be lost) before reaching the buffer threshold.
Site Log Buffer (Days)	DotNetNuke performs site logging on an individual portal level and retains that information for the number of days specified. This value represents the default duration that will be applied to each new portal created. Changing this value has no effect on current logging configuration.
	As Host, you can change this value in the Site Settings for a specific portal.
	Expiration of site log data is contingent upon execution of a scheduled job, which periodically truncates the buffer to the duration specified. The PurgeSiteLog job must be enabled in the Scheduler for this to occur; otherwise the SiteLog table can grow unchecked. Job scheduling is covered later in this chapter.

Table continued on following page

Disable Users Online	"Users Online" is popular functionality in many online portal applications, tracking and displaying the number of users registered on the site, how many users are currently using the site, and so on. However, this functionality would impose unnecessary processing overhead on each page request for sites that don't need it. By checking this option, logic within DotNetNuke that populates UsersOnline tracking tables and cache objects is bypassed. Setting this option is only half the process required to enable/disable UsersOnline. An essential part of UsersOnline is a corresponding scheduled job that performs periodic cleanup on the associated database tables AnonymousUsers and UsersOnline. If this job is enabled without UsersOnline in use, it is an unnecessary drain on system resources. Conversely, if it is not enabled when UsersOnline is in use, these tables will grow unchecked. Job scheduling is covered later in this chapter.
Users Online Time (Minutes)	UsersOnline tracks the presence of users who have been active on the system within this time period. When the scheduled job runs to clear the tracking tables, it uses this time period as a basis for determining which records to clear. UsersOnline does not track or log personal information and is not a mechanism for "spying" on users. It makes temporary note of who is logged in, what page they are currently visiting (no history), and how many anonymous users are currently viewing the site. The data is deleted after this duration has passed.
File Upload Extensions	This comma-separated list specifies the file extensions that are permissible through the File Manager. It comes prefilled with a variety of common "safe" file extensions and can be fully customized. The file management utilities within the portal are "intelligent" and reference this allowable file list. So, for example, a file that is renamed in the File Manager cannot be renamed with an invalid file extension. Likewise, files with invalid file extensions are ignored when unpacking an uploaded zip file. Note that file upload capability in the default HTML Editor Provider is disabled. This is because DotNetNuke file upload extensions, directory permissions, and disk space limits cannot be enforced through that interface.
Skin Upload Permissions	You can enable Portal Administrators to upload their own skin and container files by selecting Portal. To restrict skin and container uploads, select Host.
Performance Setting	A variety of cache objects in DotNetNuke provide for increased performance. These objects do not all have the same duration; they expire based on their specific functionality (for example, User objects expire more often than Portal objects). But changing this setting applies a common multiplier that affects their relative duration (or lifespan). While this duration is enforced within DotNetNuke, it is still subject to external settings that govern the site (such as recycling of the ASP.NET worker process). Moderate caching is the default setting.

	The No Caching option is primarily a developer/support-oriented selection. Without the benefit of the caching features of ASP.NET, the amount of work performed on each page request renders Dot-NetNuke very slow to run and is not recommended. However, this option can be very useful if necessary to track down a caching-related issue.
Clear Cache	This button enables the Host to manually clear the cache on demand. Generally this is not required; however, as Host you also typically have access to manipulate database tables directly. Table updates applied in this way bypass the application and so are not reflected until the cache is updated. You can force update of cache to reflect your manual changes by clearing it.
	Note that clearing the cache in this way also dumps buffered logs and so should be performed only when necessary.
Scheduler Mode	The Timer Method maintains a separate thread to execute scheduled tasks while the worker process is alive. Alternatively, the Request Method triggers periodic execution of tasks as HTTP Requests are made. You can also disable the Scheduler by selecting Disabled. The Scheduler is examined in detail later in this chapter.
Scheduler Polling Rate	If the Request Method is selected (above), this setting specifies the interval between scheduled task execution cycles. The Scheduler task is not invoked on every request, rather just on the first request within the specified interval.
Enable Event Log Buffer?	Like the site log, the event log can also be buffered for performance to avoid the overhead associated with logging I/O on every request. If checked, this setting will cause event log entries to be buffered into cache and periodically written to the data store. If unchecked, log entries are written immediately.
	Unlike site logging, event log buffering is governed by a scheduled task (PurgeLogBuffer). If this task is not enabled or if the Scheduler is stopped, this setting will have no effect and logging will occur as if this setting were unchecked. Event Logging is covered in more detail later in this chapter.
Use Friendly Urls	If checked, DotNetNuke will invoke the FriendlyUrl Provider. By default, DotNetNuke installs a provider that will produce "machine friendly" URLs that provide for better indexing by search engines. For developers, the default provider behavior is controlled by a rule file (`siteurls.config`) located in the web root.
	The default modules provided with DotNetNuke all work well with this provider. However, you should understand that not every module may work well with any specific implementation of FriendlyUrls. It is advisable to ensure that any module you employ works with your FriendlyUrl Provider. For more information on FriendlyUrls, consult Chapter 8.

Managing Portals as Host

A number of settings defined at the portal level are limited to SuperUser access. Some of these were pointed out in the previous section but there are a few additional ones as well. Since these settings are applicable on a per-portal basis, you'll need to be in the context of the portal in question in order to change them. You can reach the site settings for any portal through the Portals page on the Host menu. Just click the pencil icon next to one of the portal names (see Figure 5-8).

Portals

Navigate to the Portals page on the Host menu as illustrated in Figure 5-8. From this page you'll be able to create and maintain portals as well as generate a portal template for import into another DotNetNuke installation.

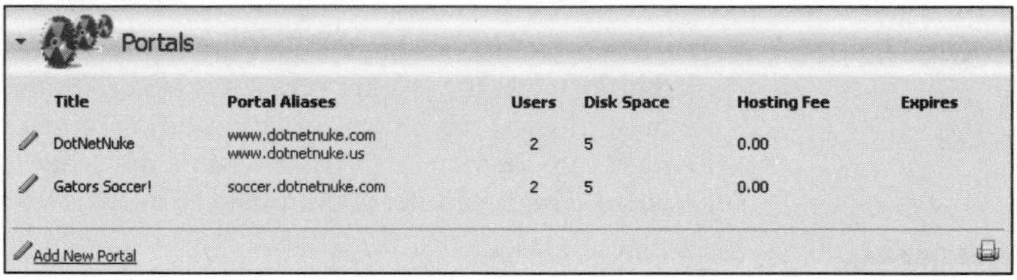

Title	Portal Aliases	Users	Disk Space	Hosting Fee	Expires
DotNetNuke	www.dotnetnuke.com www.dotnetnuke.us	2	5	0.00	
Gators Soccer!	soccer.dotnetnuke.com	2	5	0.00	

Add New Portal

Figure 5-8

At a glance the list enables you to see what portals are configured as well as their portal aliases, number of registered users, disk space threshold, hosting fee, and expiration date (if set). Clicking the pencil icon next to any entry takes you to the Site Settings page for that portal (see Chapter 4). While logged on as the Host you'll have access to additional configuration items that the Portal Administrator cannot see (see Figure 5-9).

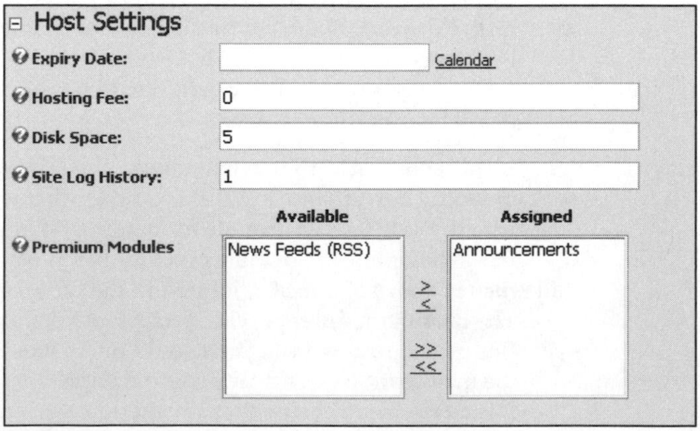

Figure 5-9

Figure 5-10 shows an additional group of configuration items under Advanced Settings. Table 5-7 explains how each of these options affects the portal.

Table 5-7: Host-Only Site Settings

Expiry Date	When the expiry date for a portal is exceeded, a friendly message is displayed in the place of regular content (see Figure 5-10).
Hosting Fee	The default for this value was set in the Host Settings. It is primarily a display field, but indicates the value appropriate for monthly renewal.
Disk Space	The default for this value was set in the Host Settings. It limits the amount of disk space available to a Portal Administrator through the File Manager.
Site Log History	The default for this value was set in the Host Settings. It keeps the site log for this portal truncated to the number of days indicated.
Premium Modules	Modules can be installed for use by any portal or can be limited to use in specific portals by setting them as "premium." This set of controls identifies which premium modules have been applied to this portal. You'll learn more about modules later in this chapter.

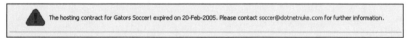

The hosting contract for Gators Soccer! expired on 20-Feb-2005. Please contact soccer@dotnetnuke.com for further information.

Figure 5-10

You'll also see a new control at the bottom of the Site Settings page for maintaining the list of aliases (domain names) for the portal (see Figure 5-11).

Portal Aliases
HTTP Alias
soccer.dotnetnuke.com
Add New HTTP Alias

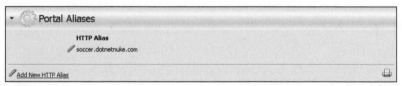

Figure 5-11

Prior to version 3.0, all portal aliases were maintained in a comma-delimited string, which restricted the number of aliases that could be assigned. Additionally, it made processing based on individual aliases more complex and inefficient. In version 3.0 portal aliases are maintained as a list of separate items. To add an additional portal alias, simply click Add New HTTP Alias and enter it in the text box provided. A portal can answer to an unlimited number of portal aliases.

Adding a New Portal

To create a new portal, simply navigate to the Portals page on the Host menu and click Add New Portal on the bottom of the page (or select it from the action menu). From there you'll be taken to the Signup page as illustrated in Figure 5-12.

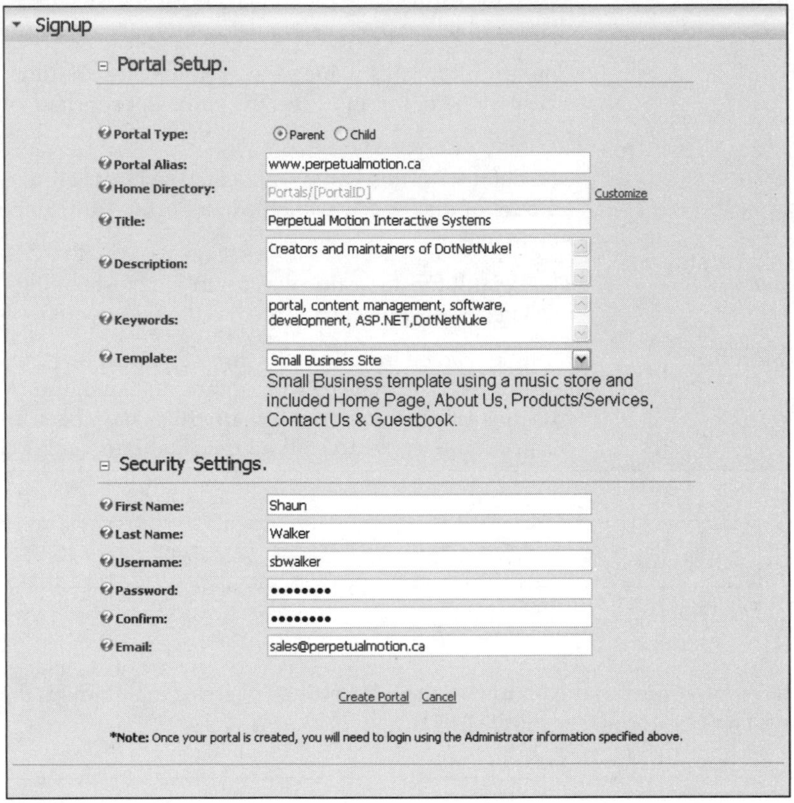

Figure 5-12

The default root directory for the portal can be overridden. But aside from this, there should be only one field on this page that might be unfamiliar to you. You'll learn about Parent and Child portals in the next section.

Parent Portals and Child Portals

In Chapter 3, you were introduced to the concept of Parent and Child portals. Portal setup is where you'll put these concepts into practice by specifying either a Parent or Child portal. The only real distinction between a Parent and a Child portal is that a Parent portal alias has a simple URL attributed to it, whereas a Child portal consists of a URL and subdirectory name. An example of a valid Parent portal name is www.dotnetnuke.com. Alternatively, you can specify an IP address instead of a domain name (for example, 216.26.163.25). An example of a valid Child portal name is www.dotnetnuke.com/soccer, and an IP address can be substituted here as well (for example, 216.26.163.25/soccer). A Child portal can be turned into a Parent portal simply by adding a URL to its list of portal aliases.

When a new Child portal is created, a physical directory is also created in the root of the web site with the Child portal's name. A page called `subhost.aspx` is copied into the directory as `default.aspx`. This is how DotNetNuke is able to implement addressing of the Child portal by the alias name (for example, `www.dotnetnuke.com/soccer`) without making modifications to IIS. Without existence of a physical path and filename (for example, `www.dotnetnuke.com/soccer/default.aspx`) IIS would normally process the request without ever handing it to ASP.NET, rendering an HTTP 404 Error or "page not found." You might be tempted to ask why a simple change to IIS would not be a better solution. It might be, but DotNetNuke is built to provide the functionality in environments where this level of control may not be available (that is, in a shared hosting environment).

So why would you create a Child portal instead of a Parent anyway? With a single registered domain name you can create an infinite number of cname portals (for example, `soccer.dotnetnuke.com`) as long as your ISP will support a DNS wildcard for your domain. The most popular reason for creating a Child portal is the ability to emulate a single sign-on solution where credentials "appear" to be shared between portals. This is a popular implementation in intranets where departmental portals are involved. Because Child portals exist in the same domain as the Parent portal, they share access to a domain cookie, which will preserve their "logged in" status across sub-portals as long as their username and password are synchronized.

Portal Templates

In Chapter 4 you learned about portal templates in the context of importing one through the Site Wizard. As Host, you have the ability to create your own portal templates, which truly qualifies as a "super power." Figure 5-13 illustrates the Export Template function, which is the second component of the Portals page on the Host menu.

This feature allows you to select an existing portal, supply a name and description, and then generate a template that contains all the information necessary to re-create the portal on another installation (see Listing 5-1). Two files are generated in this process (`<name>.template` and `<name>.template.resources`). The `.template` file is a plain-text file that contains a complete XML representation of the portal, its pages, modules, settings, and file structure. The `.resources` file is just a zip file of the portal root that is exported as content (if this option was selected).

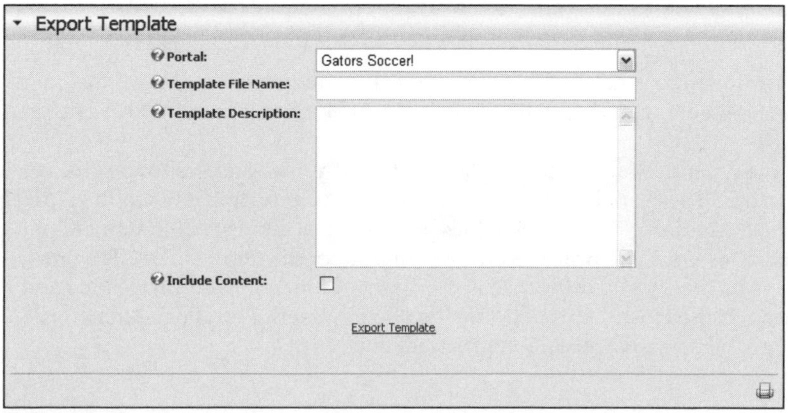

Figure 5-13

Portal templates are a new and powerful capability in DotNetNuke 3.0 — but it is also still "raw." This means that we've yet to provide user interface controls to direct how a template file is exported. At this point, template files contain everything including the kitchen sink! If you are creating templates, it would be wise to actually read through the generated file and make sure that there are no options specified that would be inappropriate for where you intend to apply them. As a standard XML file, this is a pretty simple thing to do and simply removing nodes that you don't want should work fine.

Listing 5-1: Portal Template (Settings Node)

```
<settings>
  <logofile>logo.gif</logofile>
  <footertext>Copyright 2002-2005 DotNetNuke</footertext>
  <expirydate>0001-01-01T00:00:00.0000000+11:00</expirydate>
  <userregistration>2</userregistration>
  <banneradvertising>1</banneradvertising>
  <currency>USD</currency>
  <hostfee>0</hostfee>
  <hostspace>5</hostspace>
  <backgroundfile />
  <paymentprocessor>PayPal</paymentprocessor>
  <siteloghistory>60</siteloghistory>
  <defaultlanguage>en-US</defaultlanguage>
  <timezoneoffset>-480</timezoneoffset>
</settings>
```

For example, a generated template will contain nodes with all the settings for the current portal. As you can see in Listing 5-1, there are a few nodes here that you might not want to override in a portal that imports the template; nodes such as `<userregistration>`, `<hostspace>`, and `<paymentprocessor>`. These settings might be appropriate for a new portal, but templates located in the Host Root (`/Portals/_default`) are available to the Site Wizard and can be applied to existing portals as well.

Templates provide a lot of power and promise for automatic configuration and for sharing of portal information. However, they should be used with care until they're more "fully cooked."

Skins

The Portal Administrator and the Host each have their own version of the Skins page. As Host, both are visible and accessible to you and so it is essential that you understand which one you are working with.

When using the Admin/Skins page, you (as Host) always have access to the Upload Skin and Upload Container buttons. These are only visible to the Portal Administrator when the Skin Upload Permission is set to "Portal" (see Table 5-6). This enables you to upload skins and containers that are private to the specific portal; those files are uploaded to the Portal Root directory (\Portals\<PortalId>). When using the Host/Skins page the only difference is the target of the uploaded files. Skins and containers uploaded through the Host/Skins page are installed in the Default Portal directory (\Portals_default) and so are available to every portal in the installation.

If you want to upload skins for a specific portal only, you'll want to log in to that specific portal as a SuperUser to do that. A quick way to navigate to any given portal is to go to the Portals list on the Host menu and click the portal alias name.

Log Viewer

In Chapter 4 you learned some basic information about the Log Viewer from the Portal Administrator's perspective. As the Host, there are two specific differences in your view of the logs as well as a few additional features. First, your view includes exceptions (and any other events that are hidden from the Portal Administrator). Second, your view can contain log entries from all portals (if selected as an option). You also have access to some additional functions including the ability to select and delete specific log entries, clear the entire log, and edit the log configuration.

To view the full set of logs, take a look at the following files:

```
\Portals\_default\Logs\Application.xml.resources
\Portals\_default\Logs\Exception.xml.resources
\Portals\_default\Logs\Scheduler.xml.resources
\Portals\_default\Logs\Log.xml.resources
```

For an in-depth review of logging, see Chapter 8.

Edit Log Configurations

From the Log Viewer, select Edit Log Configurations from the bottom of the page or from the action menu. You'll find yourself looking at the Edit Log Settings page as illustrated in Figure 5-14.

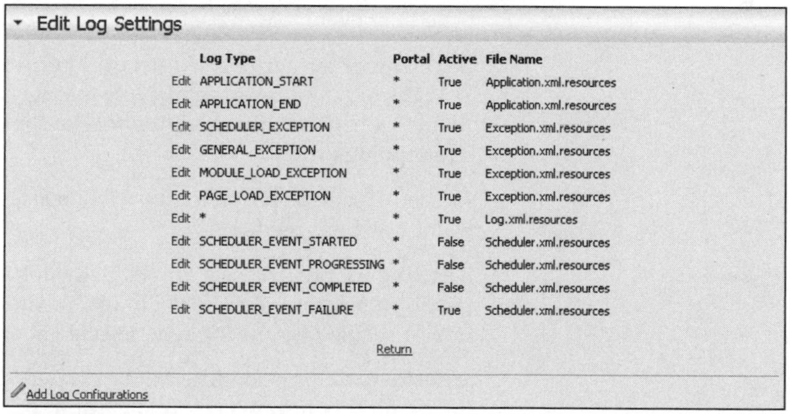

Edit Log Settings

	Log Type	Portal	Active	File Name
Edit	APPLICATION_START	*	True	Application.xml.resources
Edit	APPLICATION_END	*	True	Application.xml.resources
Edit	SCHEDULER_EXCEPTION	*	True	Exception.xml.resources
Edit	GENERAL_EXCEPTION	*	True	Exception.xml.resources
Edit	MODULE_LOAD_EXCEPTION	*	True	Exception.xml.resources
Edit	PAGE_LOAD_EXCEPTION	*	True	Exception.xml.resources
Edit	*	*	True	Log.xml.resources
Edit	SCHEDULER_EVENT_STARTED	*	False	Scheduler.xml.resources
Edit	SCHEDULER_EVENT_PROGRESSING	*	False	Scheduler.xml.resources
Edit	SCHEDULER_EVENT_COMPLETED	*	False	Scheduler.xml.resources
Edit	SCHEDULER_EVENT_FAILURE	*	True	Scheduler.xml.resources

Return

Add Log Configurations

Figure 5-14

You'll notice a number of preconfigured logging events; some enabled and some disabled. For example, because the Scheduler is disabled in the default installation of DotNetNuke, its logging events are also disabled. You can add a new configuration or edit an existing one, as shown in Figure 5-15.

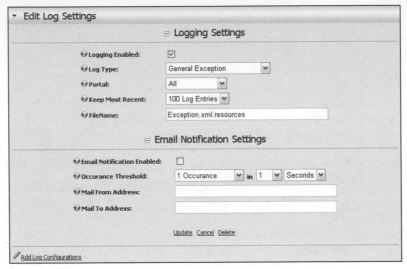

Figure 5-15

Table 5-8 explains each of the log configuration settings.

Table 5-8: Edit Log Settings

Logging Enabled	Turns logging on for the item. Items can be defined in the log settings without being enabled (for example, the default Scheduler event logging settings).
Log Type	Select one of the system-defined event types to log or the All category (as appropriate). Note that it is acceptable to define more than one log setting for the same event or for overlapping events.
Portal	Indicate a specific portal for (or All portals) for which this event is to be logged.
Keep Most Recent	Selecting All preserves all entries in the log. Any other value results in truncation of the log to the maximum number of items specified for the log type selected above.
FileName	If desired, multiple log files can be created. This can be handy for monitoring performance and/or activity related to a given portal or event type.
Email Notification Enabled	If e-mail notification is enabled when the SendLogNotifications scheduled job runs, it will assemble and send e-mail according to the Edit Log Settings.

Occurrence Threshold	Specifies how often an event must occur in order to trigger e-mail notification.
Mail From Address	Sent from address specified on outgoing e-mail.
Mail To Address	To address specified on outgoing e-mail.

Other Host Tools

In addition to the portal-specific settings you've just learned about, SuperUsers have access to many other powerful tools and configuration options. These are not visible to the Portal Administrator and affect your entire DotNetNuke installation and, therefore, all portals. The level of sophistication of these configurable items is quite deep and will challenge you to think about how best to customize your installation to achieve your unique objectives.

Module Definitions

The Module Definitions page serves as the administration area for all of the modules installed in DotNetNuke. This page allows you to edit or delete existing module definitions and to add new modules as well.

DotNetNuke comes preinstalled with a number of basic modules (identified in Chapter 3). Figure 5-16 illustrates the Module Definitions page for a default installation. Each module in the list is shown with a name, description, and a true/false option indicating whether or not it is marked as "premium."

What Is a Premium Module?

A module that has been marked "premium" is not freely available to Portal Administrators. Non-premium modules automatically show up in the selector on the Portal Administrator's Control Panel, but premium modules require Host configuration on a per-portal basis (see Figure 5-17). The premium module setting allows you to hide special-purpose modules installed or developed for one client from those installed or developed for another. It also enables you to segment your product offerings, providing extra functionality at a "premium" rate.

Editing Module Definitions

To edit a module definition (for example, if you want to mark an existing module as premium), click the pencil icon next to the module you want to edit (for example, Announcements).

Each module definition is comprised of three sections: the module description (see Figure 5-16), the module definitions, and the module controls (see Figure 5-17).

The module description settings hold the basic properties of the module. Name is used in the drop-down list of modules available to Portal Administrators on the Control Panel. Description is displayed on pages that describe the modules (for example, Module Definitions page). Version is used by module developers when issuing updates of their modules. And Premium is used to determine if a module is available to all portals or only those specifically given access.

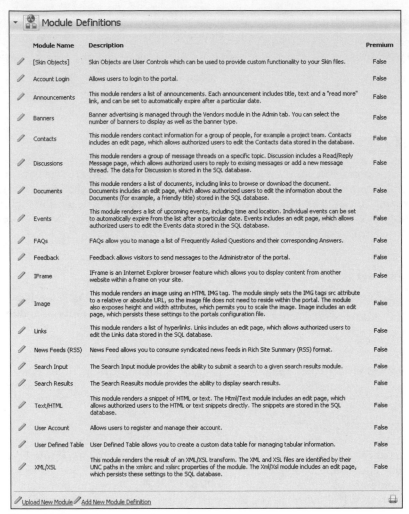

Figure 5-16

Module Name	Description	Premium
[Skin Objects]	Skin Objects are User Controls which can be used to provide custom functionality to your Skin files.	False
Account Login	Allows users to login to the portal.	False
Announcements	This module renders a list of announcements. Each announcement includes title, text and a "read more" link, and can be set to automatically expire after a particular date.	False
Banners	Banner advertising is managed through the Vendors module in the Admin tab. You can select the number of banners to display as well as the banner type.	False
Contacts	This module renders contact information for a group of people, for example a project team. Contacts includes an edit page, which allows authorized users to edit the Contacts data stored in the database.	False
Discussions	This module renders a group of message threads on a specific topic. Discussion includes a Read/Reply Message page, which allows authorized users to reply to exising messages or add a new message thread. The data for Discussion is stored in the SQL database.	False
Documents	This module renders a list of documents, including links to browse or download the document. Documents includes an edit page, which allows authorized users to edit the information about the Documents (for example, a friendly title) stored in the SQL database.	False
Events	This module renders a list of upcoming events, including time and location. Individual events can be set to automatically expire from the list after a particular date. Events includes an edit page, which allows authorized users to edit the Events data stored in the SQL database.	False
FAQs	FAQs allow you to manage a list of Frequently Asked Questions and their corresponding Answers.	False
Feedback	Feedback allows visitors to send messages to the Administrator of the portal.	False
IFrame	IFrame is an Internet Explorer browser feature which allows you to display content from another website within a frame on your site.	False
Image	This module renders an image using an HTML IMG tag. The module simply sets the IMG tags src attribute to a relative or absolute URL, so the image file does not need to reside within the portal. The module also exposes height and width attributes, which permits you to scale the image. Image includes an edit page, which persists these settings to the portals configuration file.	False
Links	This module renders a list of hyperlinks. Links includes an edit page, which allows authorized users to edit the Links data stored in the SQL database.	False
News Feeds (RSS)	News Feed allows you to consume syndicated news feeds in Rich Site Summary (RSS) format.	False
Search Input	The Search Input module provides the ability to submit a search to a given search results module.	False
Search Results	The Search Reasults module provides the ability to display search results.	False
Text/HTML	This module renders a snippet of HTML or text. The Html/Text module includes an edit page, which allows authorized users to the HTML or text snippets directly. The snippets are stored in the SQL database.	False
User Account	Allows users to register and manage their account.	False
User Defined Table	User Defined Table allows you to create a custom data table for managing tabular information.	False
XML/XSL	This module renders the result of an XML/XSL transform. The XML and XSL files are identified by their UNC paths in the xmlsrc and xslsrc properties of the module. The Xml/Xsl module includes an edit page, which persists these settings to the SQL database.	False

Upload New Module   Add New Module Definition

Figure 5-16

Module Name: Announcements

Description: This module renders a list of announcements. Each announcement includes title, text and a "read more" link, and can be set to automatically expire after a particular date.

Version:

Premium?   ☐

Update   Cancel   Delete

Figure 5-17

A module can have any number of definitions. A definition directly matches to a single component of a module. For this reason, most modules usually have only one definition; they only add one component to the page. The Announcements module, for example, has only one component and it is called "Announcements" as shown in Figure 5-18.

Some modules may add many components to a page, each component providing differing functionality but part of a logical group. For example, a blogging module might contain a calendar, a list of blog entries, and a search module. These would be configured as three different definitions, but would still belong under the same Module Name (for example, myblog).

In this section you can add definitions by typing in their name and clicking Add Definition. Alternatively, you can select an existing definition from the drop-down list and click Delete Definition.

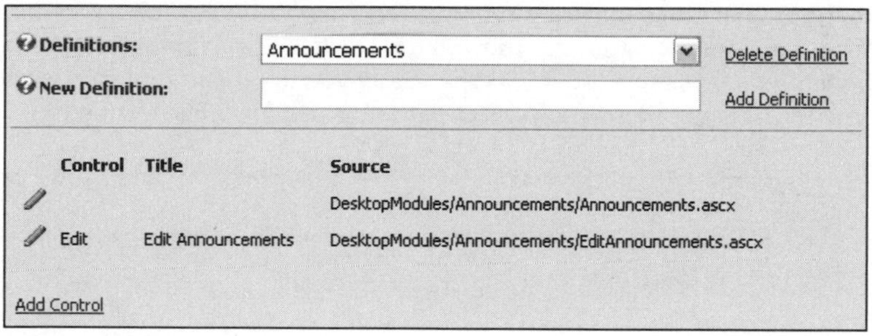

Figure 5-18

Each definition may have a number of a controls associated with it. These controls directly map to ASP.NET user controls and each is marked with a name known as a key. This key allows DotNetNuke to determine which control to load at runtime.

The Announcements module has only two controls, the user control that displays the announcements (`announcements.ascx`) and the edit announcement page (`editannouncements.ascx`). Complex modules may have a dozen or more configured controls.

This section allows you to add new controls by clicking the Add Control link; edit an existing control by clicking the pencil icon; or delete a control by editing it first and then clicking Delete on the Edit page.

Installing a New Module

Two methods exist for installing new modules into your DotNetNuke environment. The first method is an automated install. The second method is by manually adding your definition. Chapter 14 contains a thorough examination of the packaging and installation of modules and other DotNetNuke add-ons, but we'll summarize the module installation processes here for the sake of continuity.

The manual method is popularly used by developers during the process of creating new modules. Hosts that are not involved in module development will probably never use it.

An automated install involves uploading a zip file containing the contents of a module. These zip files are generally available from independent developers and companies that create them.

Many modules and other resources are also available at **www.dotnetnuke.com**.

DotNetNuke is packaged with two sample modules (Survey & Users Online). They are not installed by default because they serve as examples for developers. We'll demonstrate installation of the Survey module now, just to show you how it's done.

Click the Upload New Module button at the bottom of the Module Definitions page or on its action menu (see Figure 5-16). You'll see the familiar file upload page, only with no options for selecting a target directory. This is because a module's install locations are not configurable.

Click the Browse button and locate the `DotNetNuke.Survey.zip` file. At the time of this writing it is packaged with the DotNetNuke application in the /DesktopModules/Survey folder, although for the purposes of this example any module zip file will do. Once the selection has been made, click the Add button. The filename is added to a list of files that allow you to upload multiple modules at once. Once you are happy with the list of files to upload, click the Upload New File button (see Figure 5-19).

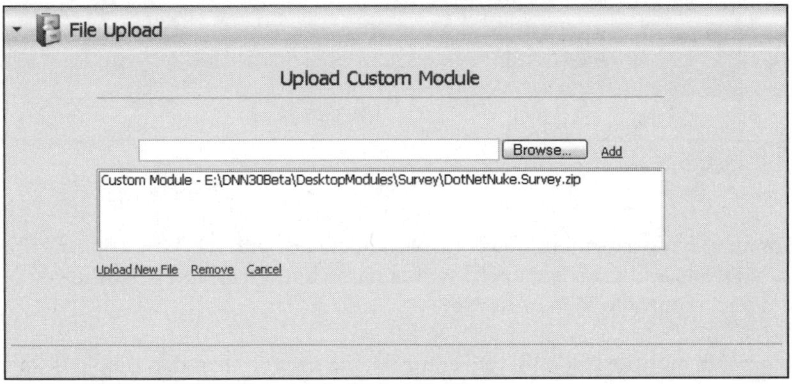

Figure 5-19

When the module is installed (or uploaded), a detailed log is displayed showing what happened during the install (see Figure 5-20). If any portion of the installation process fails, error messages will appear in this log highlighted in red. If your module has a red error message, you should contact the module provider for technical support.

If there are no red error messages in the log, your module has been successfully installed and is now available to use within your installation. Figure 5-20 illustrates a portion of what an installation log would look like for a successful install.

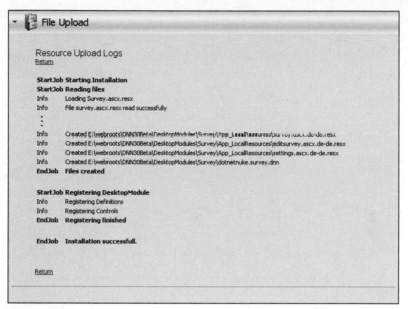

Figure 5-20

Manually Installing a New Module

As previously mentioned, installing a new module in this manner is usually reserved for developers creating new modules. But to install a new module manually, click the Add New Module Definition button at the bottom of the Module Definitions page or on its action menu (shown previously in Figure 5-16).

Once you have arrived at the Add New Module Definition page, you should be able to create your own module definitions using the same method as editing module definitions (described earlier in this chapter).

File Manager

The File Manager works in exactly the same way for SuperUsers as it does for Portal Administrators (with a couple of minor exceptions). If you need a refresher on basic operation, consult Chapter 4 (see Figure 4-32).

You learned previously that the Host has access to provide resources to all portals (for example, templates, skins, and so on) by making them available through the "Host Root" folder (that is, \Portals_default). Where the Admin\FileManager provides access to each Portal Root, the Host\File Manager provides access to the Host Root (see Figure 5-21).

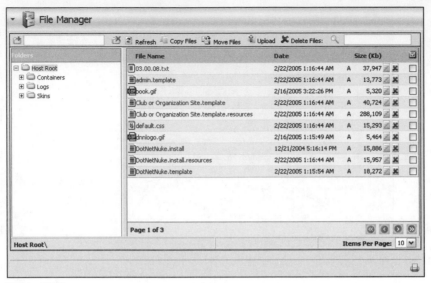

Figure 5-21

You'll also notice that there is no additional control for applying permissions (see Figure 4-33). That's because the Host Root permissions are not configurable; only SuperUsers can add, change, modify, or delete files in the Host Root.

Vendors

Like the File Manager, the Host Vendor page works in exactly the same way for SuperUsers as it does for Portal Administrators. If you need a refresher on basic operation, consult Chapter 4 (see Figure 4-44).

The only difference between the Host Vendor page and the Portal Administrator Vendor page is the underlying vendor list. You maintain a vendor list separate from the individual portals, which is visible by all of them. This is a particularly useful feature for Hosts that maintain multiple portals of their own (rather than belonging to clients). One list of vendors can be maintained and used to serve advertising and/or affiliate relationships with multiple portals. In the Banner module, a Portal Administrator can choose to display banners from either source (Host or Site)

SQL

The Host SQL page is a handy utility for inquiry or remote maintenance (see Figure 5-22). It provides for the processing of simple queries and returns results in a tabular format. It is also capable of executing compound queries and update queries by selecting the Run as Script check box.

Figure 5-22 illustrates a couple of handy queries for managing user accounts locked out by the MemberRole Provider due to invalid password attempts. Although this can be accomplished on a user basis on each portal's User page (or by waiting 10 minutes), this method can unlock all users in all portals with one query (if so desired) and is a convenient example.

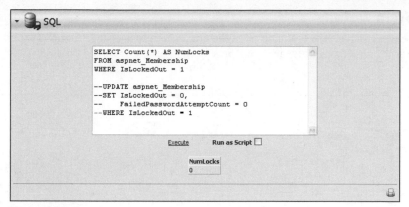

Figure 5-22

Schedule

In DotNetNuke 2.0 two pieces of functionality were introduced that required recurring operations to be processed regularly (Users Online and Site Log), emulating "batch processing." Ultimately, there are many applications for the services of a batch processor and the Scheduler serves that function in DotNetNuke. Figure 5-23 illustrates the list of items available on the Schedule page and their default settings at the time of installation.

You should carefully assess the items in the default schedule list, their settings, and enabled/disabled status to ensure that they meet your specific operating requirements.

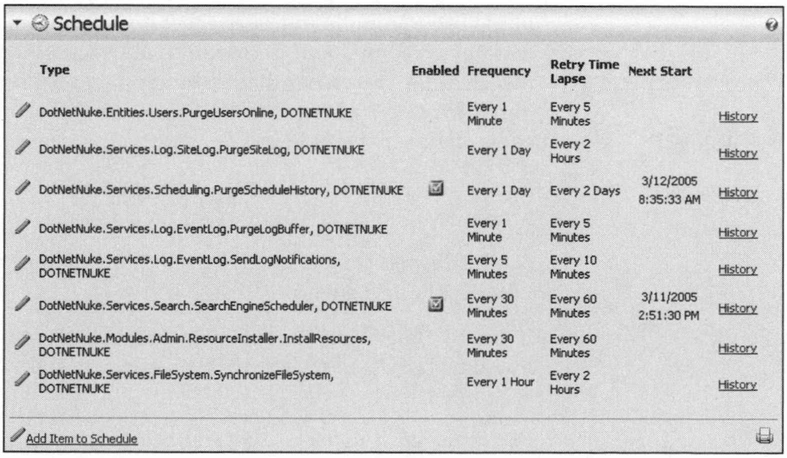

Type	Enabled	Frequency	Retry Time Lapse	Next Start	
DotNetNuke.Entities.Users.PurgeUsersOnline, DOTNETNUKE		Every 1 Minute	Every 5 Minutes		History
DotNetNuke.Services.Log.SiteLog.PurgeSiteLog, DOTNETNUKE		Every 1 Day	Every 2 Hours		History
DotNetNuke.Services.Scheduling.PurgeScheduleHistory, DOTNETNUKE	☑	Every 1 Day	Every 2 Days	3/12/2005 8:35:33 AM	History
DotNetNuke.Services.Log.EventLog.PurgeLogBuffer, DOTNETNUKE		Every 1 Minute	Every 5 Minutes		History
DotNetNuke.Services.Log.EventLog.SendLogNotifications, DOTNETNUKE		Every 5 Minutes	Every 10 Minutes		History
DotNetNuke.Services.Search.SearchEngineScheduler, DOTNETNUKE	☑	Every 30 Minutes	Every 60 Minutes	3/11/2005 2:51:30 PM	History
DotNetNuke.Modules.Admin.ResourceInstaller.InstallResources, DOTNETNUKE		Every 30 Minutes	Every 60 Minutes		History
DotNetNuke.Services.FileSystem.SynchronizeFileSystem, DOTNETNUKE		Every 1 Hour	Every 2 Hours		History

Add Item to Schedule

Figure 5-23

The Schedule page provides access to edit the settings of each item, or to add a new item by clicking the Add Item to Schedule button or selecting the action menu item. It also provides appropriate "at a glance" information such as the enabled/disabled status, recurring frequency, next scheduled execution time, and access to a detailed history report.

Schedule Item Details

Click the pencil icon next to an item to open the Edit Schedule page (see Figure 5-24). Table 5-9 explains each of the schedule item settings in detail. Setting changes made on the Edit Schedule page take effect immediately.

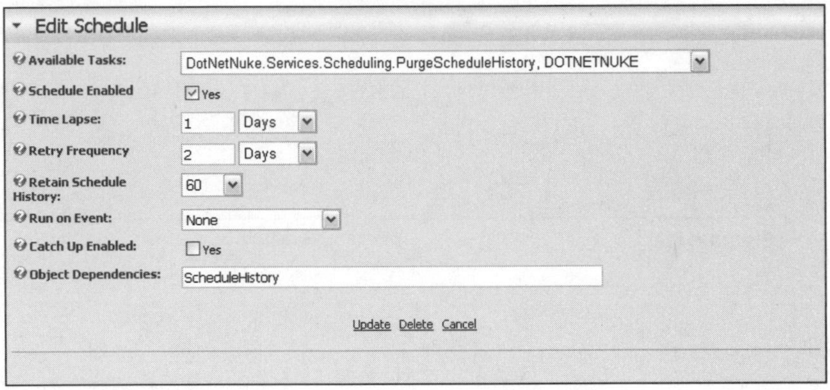

Figure 5-24

Table 5-9: Edit Schedule Settings

Available Tasks	This drop-down list includes all classes in any assemblies in the /bin directory that inherit from DotNetNuke.Scheduling. SchedulerClient. Assemblies may belong to modules, skin objects, or other components you have installed that leverage the Scheduler's programming interface. Installing a component (or module) may actually create a Scheduler item for you rather than relying on you to create it yourself. You'll want to read the instructions carefully for any modules or components that you install.
Schedule Enabled	Enable or disable the schedule item. If disabled (unchecked), the Scheduler ignores this item when processing.
Time Lapse	Set the desired frequency for running this item (that is, every x minutes/hours/days).
Retry Frequency	If the task fails when it runs according to the specified frequency, it will be retried according to this setting until the next regularly scheduled start.
Retain Schedule History	Each time an item, its success/fail status, and a number of other useful information items are logged. This value determines the number of log records that are retained in this history. Older items are truncated from the log.

Run on Event	You can enable a job to run on an event rather than on a schedule. The only event currently supported is APPLICATION_START because events triggered on APPLICATION_END are not guaranteed to run in ASP.NET.
Catch Up Enabled	If the Scheduler is unable to run when the scheduled start time of an item passes, the item will not be run. This condition could be caused by any number of things, including a server reboot or recycling of the ASP.NET worker process. This setting indicates whether, at the next scheduled start time, an item should run only once according to the schedule or play "catch up" and run once for each scheduled start that was missed. Under normal circumstances this setting will not be necessary, but it is available for custom schedule items that require it.
Object Dependencies	When the Scheduler Mode is set to the Timer Method (see Host Settings) it executes as a multithreaded process. This requires some method of protection against possible deadlock conditions for simultaneously running threads. This field provides for the specification of one or more comma-separated string values, which serve as semaphores to avoid deadlock. For example, if one schedule item performs a select on the Users table and another item performs a massive update on the Users table, you might want to prevent these two items from running at the same time. So both items should have an object dependency on the same string value (for example, "LockUsers-Table"). The dependency will suppress start of any other items until the currently running item has finished.

Schedule History

If you click the History link next to an item, you'll see the Schedule History page (Figure 5-25). This page simply displays a log of results from previous runs of the scheduled item. You'll recall that the size of this log (number of items) was set in the Item Settings.

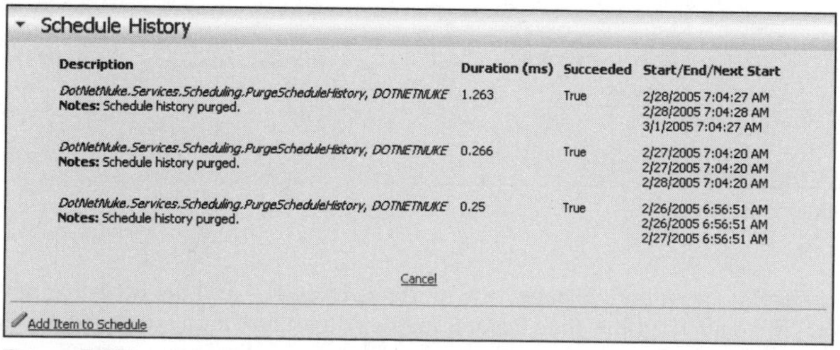

▾ Schedule History

Description	Duration (ms)	Succeeded	Start/End/Next Start
DotNetNuke.Services.Scheduling.PurgeScheduleHistory, DOTNETNUKE **Notes:** Schedule history purged.	1.263	True	2/28/2005 7:04:27 AM 2/28/2005 7:04:28 AM 3/1/2005 7:04:27 AM
DotNetNuke.Services.Scheduling.PurgeScheduleHistory, DOTNETNUKE **Notes:** Schedule history purged.	0.266	True	2/27/2005 7:04:20 AM 2/27/2005 7:04:20 AM 2/28/2005 7:04:20 AM
DotNetNuke.Services.Scheduling.PurgeScheduleHistory, DOTNETNUKE **Notes:** Schedule history purged.	0.25	True	2/26/2005 6:56:51 AM 2/26/2005 6:56:51 AM 2/27/2005 6:56:51 AM

Cancel

Add Item to Schedule

Figure 5-25

Schedule Status

The Schedule Status page is reached by selecting View Schedule Status from the action menu on any of the schedule-related pages (see Figure 5-26).

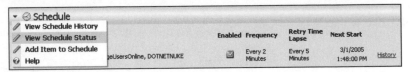

Figure 5-26

The Schedule Status page gives a detailed view of the current state of the Scheduler and running or pending items (see Figure 5-27). Refreshing the page will illustrate quickly that DotNetNuke is busily working in the background to process your scheduled items.

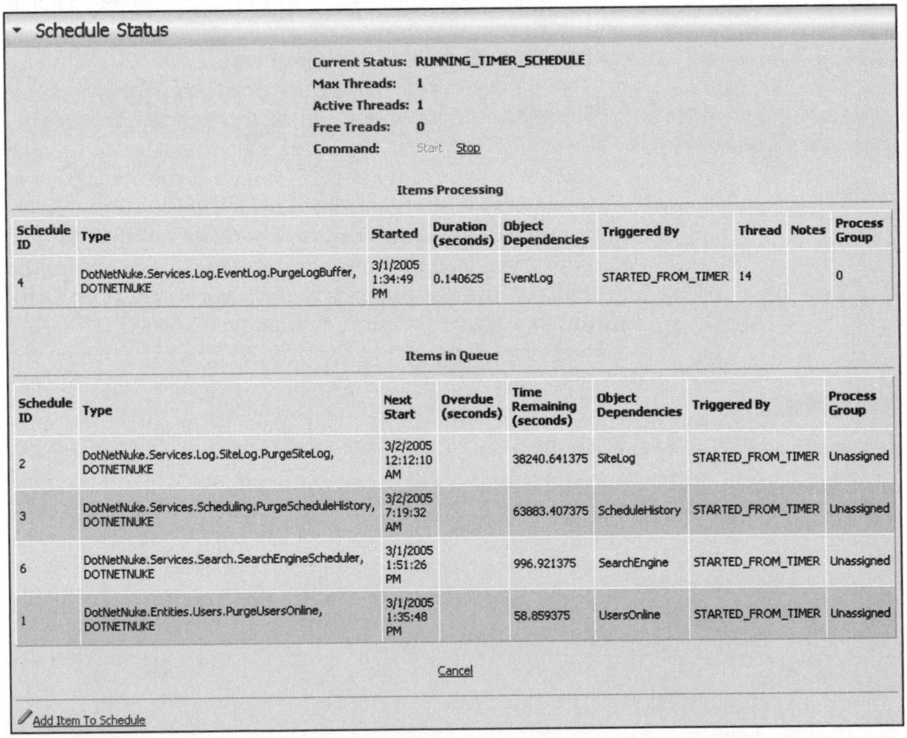

Schedule Status

Current Status: **RUNNING_TIMER_SCHEDULE**
Max Threads: **1**
Active Threads: **1**
Free Treads: **0**
Command: Start Stop

Items Processing

Schedule ID	Type	Started	Duration (seconds)	Object Dependencies	Triggered By	Thread	Notes	Process Group
4	DotNetNuke.Services.Log.EventLog.PurgeLogBuffer, DOTNETNUKE	3/1/2005 1:34:49 PM	0.140625	EventLog	STARTED_FROM_TIMER	14		0

Items in Queue

Schedule ID	Type	Next Start	Overdue (seconds)	Time Remaining (seconds)	Object Dependencies	Triggered By	Process Group
2	DotNetNuke.Services.Log.SiteLog.PurgeSiteLog, DOTNETNUKE	3/2/2005 12:12:10 AM		38240.641375	SiteLog	STARTED_FROM_TIMER	Unassigned
3	DotNetNuke.Services.Scheduling.PurgeScheduleHistory, DOTNETNUKE	3/2/2005 7:19:32 AM		63883.407375	ScheduleHistory	STARTED_FROM_TIMER	Unassigned
6	DotNetNuke.Services.Search.SearchEngineScheduler, DOTNETNUKE	3/1/2005 1:51:26 PM		996.921375	SearchEngine	STARTED_FROM_TIMER	Unassigned
1	DotNetNuke.Entities.Users.PurgeUsersOnline, DOTNETNUKE	3/1/2005 1:35:48 PM		58.859375	UsersOnline	STARTED_FROM_TIMER	Unassigned

Cancel

Add Item To Schedule

Figure 5-27

There are two display areas on this page; one for Items in Queue and the other for Items Processing. If you refresh while watching the Time Remaining run down to 0 for a specific item, you may catch it actually in execution, which is when it will display in the Items Processing area.

Command buttons at the top of this page allow you to stop/start the Scheduler if necessary. This suspends the execution of the jobs though the timers continue to run. Note that these buttons are not enabled if the Scheduler is running under the Request Method (see Table 5-6).

Configuration

The Scheduler has a couple of useful settings that can be manipulated in the application's `web.config` file. To locate these settings, look for the section that resembles Listing 5-2. The effect of these settings is summarized in Table 5-10.

Listing 5-2: Schedule Provider Section of web.config

```
<add name="DNNScheduler"
        type="DotNetNuke.Services.Scheduling.DNNScheduling.DNNScheduler,
             DotNetNuke.DNNScheduler"
        providerPath="~\Providers\SchedulingProviders\DNNScheduler\"
        debug="false"
        maxThreads="-1"/>
```

Table 5-10: Schedule Provider Configuration Settings

Debug	When set to "true," this will cause a lot of log file entries to be generated that help in debugging Scheduler-related development (that is, developing your own Scheduler items). Debugging multithreaded applications is always a challenge. This is one setting that can help you figure out why a task is or isn't getting run.
maxThreads	Specifies the maximum number of threads to use for the Scheduler (when in Timer Method mode). "-1" is the default, which means "leave it up to the Scheduler to figure out." If you specify a value greater than 0, it will use that number as the maximum number of thread pools to use.

Considerations

One limitation of the Scheduler (mode: Timer Method) is that it cannot run 24/7 without help from an external program, the ASP.NET worker process. This is a limitation of ASP.NET, and not DotNetNuke. The worker process used within IIS will periodically recycle according to settings in `machine.config`. Some hosts may have settings that recycle the worker process every 30 minutes (forced), while others may have more complicated settings, such as recycling the worker process after 3000 web site hits, or after 20 minutes of inactivity. It is this recycling of the worker process that will shut down the Scheduler, until the worker process is started again (that is, by someone hitting the web site, which in turn starts up the worker process, starting up the Scheduler as well).

This functionality is actually a major benefit to web applications as a whole, in a hosted environment, because it keeps runaway applications from taking down the server. But it isn't without its drawbacks.

The bottom line is that the Scheduler will run 24/7 (mode: Timer Method) as long as someone is visiting your web site frequently enough to keep the worker process active. It is during periods of dormancy that the worker process could possibly shut down. It is for this reason that you should carefully plan the types of tasks you schedule. Make sure that the tasks you schedule are not "time critical," that is, don't have to run "every night at midnight" and so on. A more suitable task is one that runs "once per day" or "once every few minutes," that doesn't mind if it's not run during periods of inactivity.

The Request Method does not have the same dependency upon the ASP.NET worker process. However, it is entirely dependent upon the timing of visitors to your web site. During periods of inactivity on your web site, scheduled jobs will not run.

Languages

In Chapter 4 you learned that Portal Administrators have some limited control over the supported languages and localized strings in their portal. The Host has access to a number of other features and configuration options. Selecting Languages from the Host menu takes you to the Languages administration page as shown in Figure 5-28.

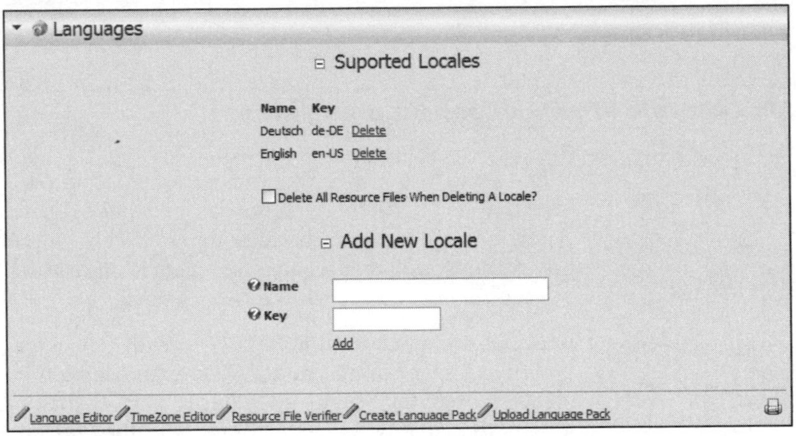

Figure 5-28

Background

Software applications are frequently used in many different countries, each with their own unique language and culture. This is certainly the case with DotNetNuke, which has users from around the globe. In an effort to better support users from other countries and cultures, DotNetNuke implements a localization framework to allow the portal to better handle these users' needs. Not only do other cultures have different languages, but they also may be in different time zones, have different currencies, and express times and dates in a different format. Any localization framework has to take all these factors into account in order to be effective.

In developing the localization framework, the DotNetNuke developers examined many different implementations and ultimately chose a solution that closely followed the ASP.NET 2.0 framework. Although the underlying architecture may differ slightly, DotNetNuke uses the same resource file format and file locations, thereby simplifying the future migration path to ASP.NET 2.0 when it becomes available.

The Languages page is the primary stepping-off point when configuring language support. These settings will determine the languages available to each portal and the default localized strings. Additionally, the Host controls the definitions of time zones within the associated portals.

To define localized strings, you must first create a locale. A locale identifies the culture associated with a group of localized strings. This culture is identified by a friendly name and a key value that corresponds to specific culture. The .NET Framework documentation defines the culture as:

The culture names follow the RFC 1766 standard in the format "<languagecode2>-<country/regioncode2>", where <languagecode2> is a lowercase two-letter code derived from ISO 639-1 and <country/regioncode2> is an uppercase two-letter code derived from ISO 3166. For example, U.S. English is "en-US".

To define a locale, enter the Name and Key and click the Add link. This will create a new entry in the `Locales.xml` file and create a localized copy of the `TimeZones.xml` file as well. Once you have created a new locale definition, you are ready to create localized resource strings.

Select the Language Editor link from the Languages administration screen in Figure 5-28. This will take you to the Language Editor. The Language Editor, as shown in Figure 5-29, is the same editor available to Portal Administrators and was covered in Chapter 4. The only difference is that any localized resources created by the Host will become the default resource strings for all portals.

If the Portal Administrator edits a resource file, it will override all resources loaded from the default resource file. Even if the Host subsequently makes changes to the same set of resource strings, these changes will not be reflected in the portal, which has its own copy of the original resources.

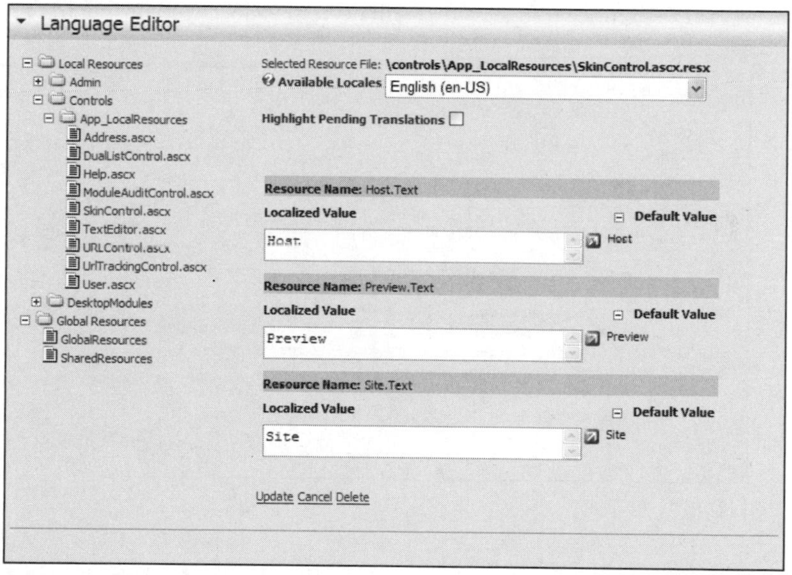

Figure 5-29

The standard portal installation includes more than 115 resource files for each locale. After a new locale is added by the host, DotNetNuke must create corresponding localized resource files for the new locale. The portal only creates the new resource file when using the Language Editor (see Figure 5-29) to edit the localized strings. If the resource for the new locale is not edited, then the default locale (English en-US) will be used when localizing content.

So, with 100 plus files to edit, you must be asking yourself "How do I ensure I have created localized versions of each resource file?" That is where the Resource File Verifier (see Figure 5-30) comes in. You can reach the Verifier from the Language Administration screen.

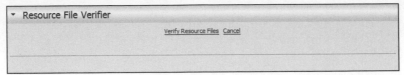

Figure 5-30

Click the Verify Resource Files link to examine the portal for any old or missing resource files. Once the portal has examined the available resource files, you will get a list of missing resource files, resource files with missing entries, files with obsolete entries, and files that have entries created prior to any changes to the default resources (seen previously in Figure 5-4).

The test for determining "Files Older than System Default" is based on file modification dates. Therefore, if you change multiple resources in the system default file and then change just one resource string in the localized file, this check will not be able to detect that other resource strings may still need to be updated.

The Resource File Verifier will examine each locale and report the results as shown in Figure 5-31. You should use this report to identify resources that still need to be localized or that may not be up to date.

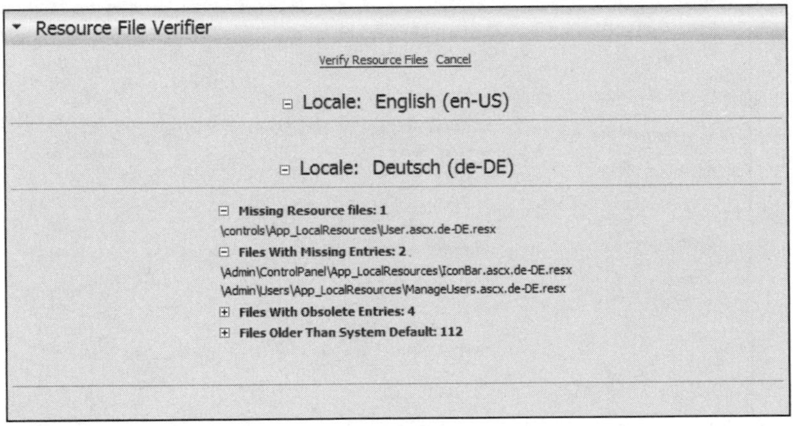

▾ Resource File Verifier

Verify Resource Files Cancel

⊟ Locale: English (en-US)

⊟ Locale: Deutsch (de-DE)

⊟ **Missing Resource files: 1**
\controls\App_LocalResources\User.ascx.de-DE.resx
⊟ **Files With Missing Entries: 2**
\Admin\ControlPanel\App_LocalResources\IconBar.ascx.de-DE.resx
\Admin\Users\App_LocalResources\ManageUsers.ascx.de-DE.resx
⊞ **Files With Obsolete Entries: 4**
⊞ **Files Older Than System Default: 112**

Figure 5-31

Using the Verifier makes managing localized resources much easier, but ultimately it is still up to you to handle localization. If this still seems like too much work, then DotNetNuke provides a shortcut. Instead of localizing resources yourself, you can load resource packs that were created by someone else. See Chapter 14 for more information about how to create and load resource packs.

Globalizing an application requires more than just having content appear in a specific language. Another aspect of globalizing an application requires that the application understand the time zone of the current user. If the server logs show that a critical event happened at 1:00 AM, what does that really mean? If you are in Germany and the web server is in Texas, what time did the event happen? To solve this problem, DotNetNuke stores all time in Universal Time Coordinated (UTC) format. Each user can associate a TimeZone with their profile. This setting is used to localize the time for the current user.

The TimeZone Editor shown in Figure 5-32 is accessible from the Language Administration screen and allows the Host to edit the available TimeZone definitions. Like all other resources, the TimeZone definitions are localized. When creating new locales, remember to edit the TimeZones for the new locale as well!

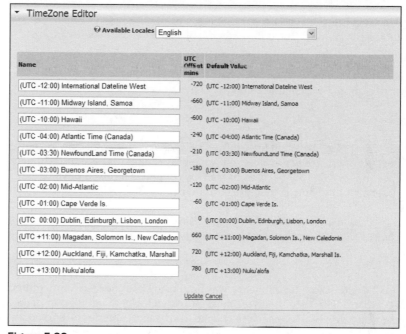

Figure 5-32

Search Admin

The Search Admin page gives you the ability to configure certain aspects of the search engine features. It's important to remember that you are configuring the search for the entire installation, not just for any specific portal. There are just a few options, as shown in Figure 5-33.

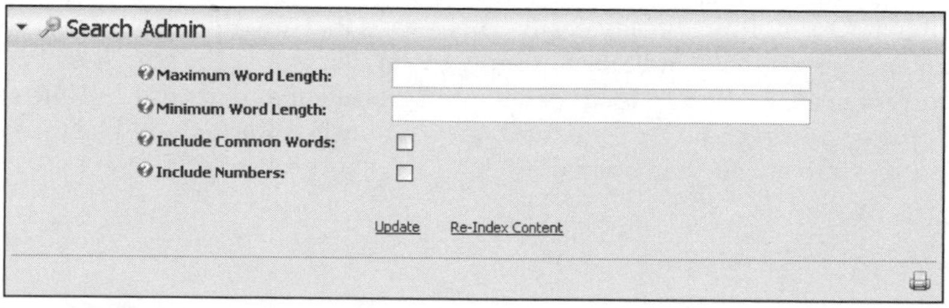

Figure 5-33

Setting the Maximum and Minimum Word Lengths can help you keep from indexing unreasonable terms. The internal default values are currently 50 and 4, respectively. If you deselect Include Common Words, the search engine will not bother indexing words that exist in the SearchCommonWords database table. If you look at this table you'll notice that it has the ability to create common word entries for each locale (for multilanguage customization) although only the English language common words are included by default. Likewise, you can choose to Include Numbers or to ignore them when content is indexed.

Clicking the Update button saves your preferences. Clicking Re-Index Content causes the search engine to empty its tables and re-index the full content of all portals in the installation.

Keeping It Current

When you learned about the Scheduler, you may have noticed a scheduled item for the search engine:

```
DotNetNuke.Services.Search.SearchEngineScheduler
```

If you want for your portal's content to be current, it is essential that this job be configured to run periodically. As Portal Administrators add content to their web sites, it is not immediately available through site search. It will not become available until the new content is indexed the next time this job runs or until a SuperUser clicks the button to re-index content.

It is also important to understand that the engine that drives search also drives RSS syndication. Updated content will not be reflected in syndication until the next time the search index is run.

Background

Prior to version 2.0, site search functionality was built using complex (and convoluted) database queries and was limited to use with the built-in modules provided by DotNetNuke. To make search work with a third-party module, you had to manually change the database queries or find an alternative search implementation. And its usage was fairly crude by today's standards, without any configuration options or advanced search features.

In version 2.0, the previous implementation became totally obsolete with the introduction of the Data Abstraction Layer and Data Providers. And so the design of a new search engine began in earnest. Before this effort progressed much beyond the design stage, the team development target shifted from version 2.2 to version 3.0, so DotNetNuke version 2 never did get a replacement for its lost search functionality.

In DotNetNuke 3.0, the search engine is fully integrated into the core application and modules are able to hook into this powerful functionality easily. This means that any third-party module can participate in full site search and/or content syndication, simply by implementing the search API as documented in Chapter 8. Currently, the core provides a search input module that performs full site search and a default search results page. However, by the time this book is published there should be many enhancements to this first iteration of advanced Search capability!

Lists

DotNetNuke includes a common utility for the management of lists. This allows you to manage the content of those lists (where appropriate) and augment them to customize your installation. If you select Lists from the Host menu you will find yourself of a page that looks like Figure 5-34.

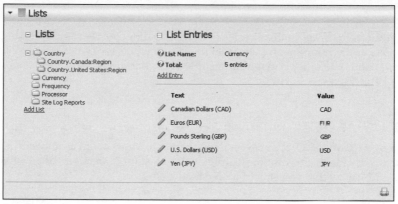

Figure 5-34

The List manager is fairly straightforward, providing an index of the lists it is currently tracking as well as a summary of the entries and the ability to add new entries or edit existing ones.

Not all lists are ones you should edit without an understanding of the potential impacts. For example, if you were to remove an entry from the Site Log reports list, it would prevent Portal Administrators from ever running that report on their portal. You might consider this a good thing if it was necessary to remove a report that was adversely affecting performance! However, adding a new item to that list would result in application errors because the Site Log report would not know how to process them.

One of the first customizations you might make to your installation's Lists would be to add a new Country sublist, as illustrated in Figure 5-35.

In this example we're adding region entries for the British Virgin Islands so that when our users register from there, we can require them to specify their island of residence. DotNetNuke is preconfigured for Canada and the United States, but you are fully capable of customizing your installation for any regional list that you require.

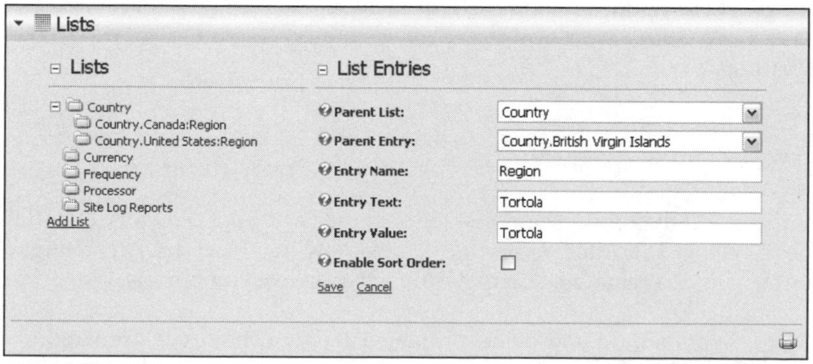

Figure 5-35

Skins

You should recall from earlier in this chapter that the only difference between working with skins from the Admin menu and working with skins from the Host menu is the target location of the upload, which determines availability to other Portal Administrators. For additional information on skins and skinning, see Chapters 4 and 13, respectively.

Summary

In this chapter you learned just about everything there is to know about administering a collection of portals, their environment, and runtime features as the Host (or SuperUser) of a DotNetNuke installation. Key Host functions that you should understand include

- ❑   Host Settings
- ❑   Portals
- ❑   Module Definitions
- ❑   File Managers
- ❑   Vendors
- ❑   SQL
- ❑   Schedule
- ❑   Languages
- ❑   Search Admin
- ❑   Lists
- ❑   SuperUsers Accounts
- ❑   Skins

You should have some understanding of which Portal Administrator–level functions contain Host configurable settings. These Portal Admin functions include

- ❑   Site Settings
- ❑   Skins
- ❑   Log Viewer

You should understand the location and relevance of the Host Root directory (\Portals_default) versus the Portal Root directory (\Portals\<portalid>), and know that Host default settings are used to create individual portals, but that changing them has no effect on existing portals.

Your SuperUser powers should now be fully enabled and you should be prepared to assume leadership of your very own DotNetNuke "Justice League" (cape and super hero sidekick not included).

6

Modules

Now that you are familiar with the Host and Administration capabilities available within DotNetNuke, this chapter looks at a concept familiar to most portals — modules.

A module is a pluggable user interface component that processes requests and generates dynamic content. This definition is similar to that of an ASP.NET page, with the exception that a module can only appear on an ASP.NET page, and that page can contain any number of module "instances."

Modules are also defined by another important characteristic known as its type. The module type governs what functionality it provides. DotNetNuke provides a number of modules out of the box; these modules range from FAQs and Announcements to Documents. You can even author your own modules that provide alternate functionality.

By the end of the chapter, you should have a good understanding of the architecture surrounding modules and how they relate to the DotNetNuke Portal System. This chapter also discusses the practical aspects regarding modules such as management and installation, and provides an introduction to each of the modules included within DotNetNuke.

Module Architecture

This section explains the concepts of a portal, page, module container, and the module itself. A walkthrough of how a page is constructed is also presented.

Portal

As discussed in earlier chapters, a portal can be defined as a web-based application that provides content aggregation from different sources and hosts the presentation layer (modules) of information systems.

Figure 6-1 depicts a portal's basic architecture. To help explain the diagram, DotNetNuke needs to perform a number of steps in order to process a page request. The following steps execute during the initialization of the page. This event occurs at initialization so that modules can handle their own life cycle and process events such as initialization, load, and render.

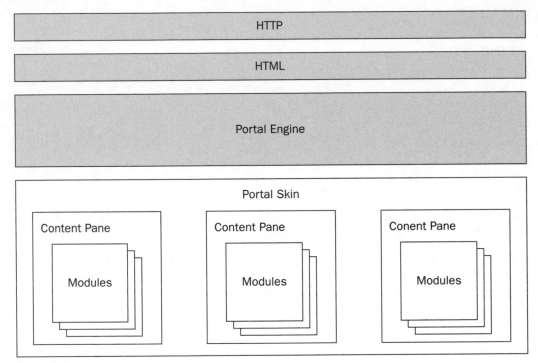

Figure 6-1

First Step

The first step is to retrieve the modules for the requested page. The retrieval step comprises a number of important pieces of information such as the modules that appear on the page, the section of the page on which they will appear (known as content panes), and finally, the security roles associated with each module.

Second Step

The second step is to make some decisions about the security information retrieved in the previous step. By examining the current user roles (whether a registered user or anonymous) and the view roles associated with each module, a list of "authorized" modules is formed for the current page.

Third Step

The third (and final) step is to dynamically inject the "authorized" modules into the corresponding content panes of the page. Once each of the modules has been loaded, each module is then able to execute its own series of events and render content.

Page

Figure 6-2 depicts the basic portal page components. The page itself represents a complete markup document consisting of a number of "content panes," and in each content pane a number of modules. In addition to the modules, a page also consists of navigation areas and site banners. To learn more about how to customize the look of these other areas, see Chapter 13.

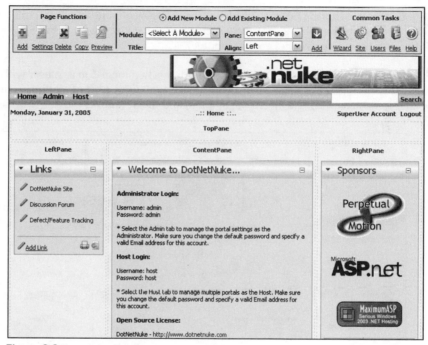

Figure 6-2

Each module consists of a title, decorations, and the content produced by the module. The decorations can include buttons, links, and a hover menu that can change the module's state or perform functionality specific to that module.

Module

As mentioned previously, a portal is a web-based application that processes requests and generates dynamic content. Each module produces its own piece of markup (known as a *fragment*) and together with the skin's markup shows a complete document.

Because each module produces its own markup, they can be viewed as tiny applications within a larger application. Usually, users interact with the content produced by each module by clicking links or submitting forms that are then processed by the portal system, and the actions are passed to the correct module.

Module Container

The decorations surrounding a module is known as the module container. Through this container, a user is able to interact with the module and perform such actions as minimize/maximize or more advanced features (if the user has edit privileges on that module).

Figure 6-3 shows the module container of a "links" module when logged in as a user with edit access. The diagram shows a number of items, such as the hover menu with a list of administration options (discussed later in this chapter), the title of the module, and the minimize/maximize option.

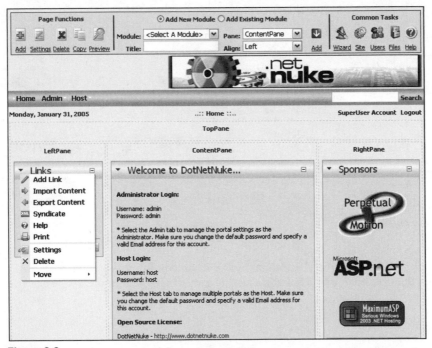

Figure 6-3

Types of Modules

Now that you are familiar with the concepts surrounding modules, this section examines the 15 user content modules that are bundled with DotNetNuke. Another four modules exist that are not really content modules, so we will not discuss the Search or User Account Management modules that you can utilize in your portal pages. We list each module and include a brief description.

Before starting, however, let's discuss the core team's policy surrounding bundled modules. The aim of the core team has not been to include every new module within the core, but to provide an extensible and rich platform. By concentrating on the core platform, third parties have an opportunity to build upon the functionality that is missing within the bundled modules. However, that being said, the bundled modules are designed to meet the majority of needs.

Announcements Module

The Announcements module allows you to create short articles for your visitors and even allows you to expire the older articles as the content becomes obsolete. This module provides an easy-to-use interface for keeping your content fresh and rotated. You can use the module as a method of displaying news releases, a collection of related articles, or merely as a teaser to other content in your portal. You will now add an Announcements module to your base installation and see exactly how this module works. Start by opening your web browser to the application and logging in with the administrator account to add the module to your page. Then you will add some content to your module instance.

We should note here that you do not have to be the administrator in order to accomplish this task. If you wanted, you could set up a role with edit permission to your page and offload this task to another individual in your organization. This is made possible by the roles-based security the application employs to control access to content and administration.

First, add the module on your page. You use the Add Module function as shown in Figure 6-4 to accomplish this task. This process will be the same for every type of module you add. For clarity, we are including the exact steps you will need to take to add the Announcements module, but as we discuss the other modules available we will just cover the specifics related to the particular module. Look at Figure 6-4 to begin this process.

Figure 6-4

When you log in to your portal and navigate to a page where the user has edit privileges, you will see the control panel shown in Figure 6-4. You may remember from earlier in the chapter that we used this interface to add a new page to our portal using the page functions. You are now going to use the module section of this interface to add your Announcements module. This is the interface you will use to add any module to your portal pages. As in the page function section, the titles of the available functions are self-documenting. The Module drop-down control lists all the types of modules you have installed in your DotNetNuke instance and you will be able to select any available module type from the list. One thing new to version 3 is the ability to add an existing module instance with content to a page. If you select the Add Existing Module radio button, the content of the Module DDL will change to reflect instances of other modules you have already added elsewhere in your portal instance. Assume you have a navigation module you need to show only on certain pages to enable navigation to deeper content areas of your site, but you do not want to show on all pages of the portal. This function allows you to easily duplicate your navigation for only the pages for which you need the functionality to be available. The Module control enables you to specify the pane where you want the module to appear and how you need the module aligned inside that pane, with the Pane and Align DDL controls, respectively. Notice that you can also specify the title for the module instance as you add the instance. The preceding directions do not apply only to the Announcements module; they apply to any module you add to a page.

Now that you understand all the functions available, take a look at Figure 6-5, add the Announcements module, and set the settings of your module instance.

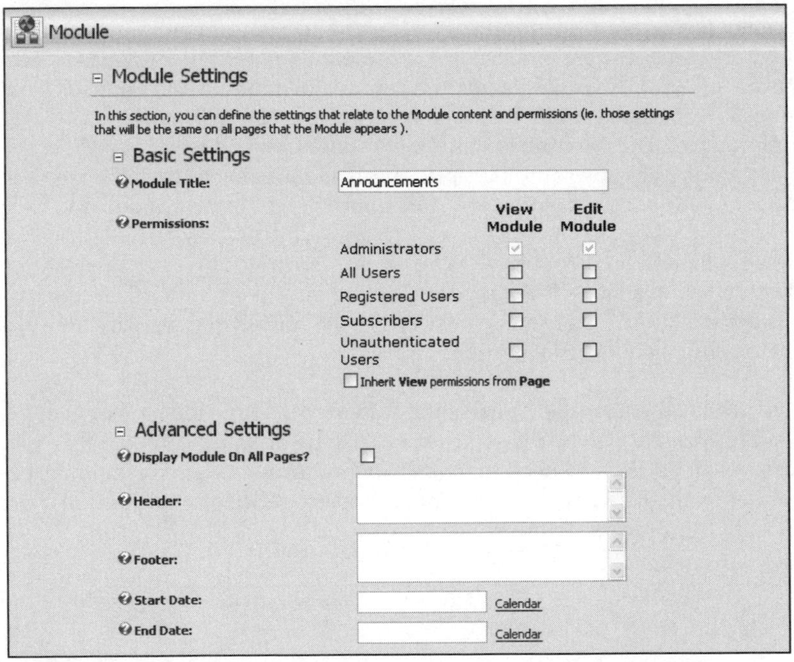

Figure 6-5

You've now added your announcements instance and navigated to the settings for your module. You will notice the Module Settings control looks familiar to the Page Settings control used earlier in the chapter. This is by design because it decreases the learning curve associated with managing the application. Notice that this control utilizes the same type of field-level help available in the Page Settings control, which allows you to get a description of the type of content the application expects for this module instance. Table 6-1 describes these associated settings.

Table 6-1: Announcements: Basic and Advanced Module Settings

Setting	Description
Module Title	As the name suggests, this is the title for your module.
Permissions	This is where you set which roles will have access to edit the content in your module. As you can see, several options are available for controlling the security of the module's content.
Display Module On All Pages	Enabling this check box allows you to define a module that will appear on all pages within your portal. This is very useful when defining advertising or navigation-type modules you need to display to your users regardless of the page they are visiting.
Header	Here you can define content to display above your module's content.
Footer	Here you can define content to display below your module's content.
Start Date	This is the date you want the content to start displaying to your users. This is very useful for planning content that you only need to appear after a certain date.
End Date	This setting allows you to expire content that is no longer current.

These settings options are pretty much concurrent across all instances of the various modules. Notice the Page Settings panel below the Modules Settings panel. This is where we set our container for the Links module earlier in this chapter. Figure 6-6 shows the panel for the Page Settings of our module, and Table 6-2 explains each of these functions for this area. Note that although this may appear exactly like the Page Settings covered in Chapter 3, there are some differences and these settings have some unique settings just for our current module instance. Figure 6-6 illustrates page settings you will see in the base modules throughout the application.

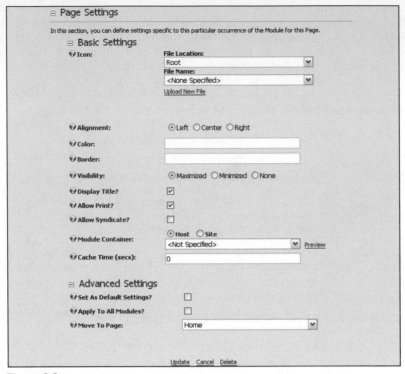

Figure 6-6

Table 6-2 lists each of these settings. You will encounter this section throughout the modules in the application.

Table 6-2: Module Page Settings Panel	
Setting	**Description**
Icon	This is an interesting function that you can use to enhance the display of your module. Setting an icon for your module replaces the title with an image. The file you use for this must reside in one of the areas defined in your file manager area. To set the image you use the File Location and File Name DDLs to specify the file's location.
Alignment	This setting allows you to specify the alignment of your module in the pane.
Color	This setting allows you to specify the background color of the content that appears in this module.
Border	This setting allows you to specify a border width for your content in the module.

Visibility	DotNetNuke exposes methods to allow your users to expand and collapse content to save real estate. These options allow you to define the default visibility behavior of the module and whether you want the users to be able to hide or display the module's content.
Display Title	This check box enables you to display or hide the module's title from the users.
Allow Print	This function allows you to expose the print module action, which displays a print icon your users can select to print the module's content in a print-friendly format.
Allow Syndicate	This function allows you to expose your module's content in an XML format, which allows other web authors to consume and display your content on another web site.
Module Container	Here you can set the container to use for the module's display in the portal.
Cache Time	DotNetNuke utilizes caching to increase the performance of the application. Here you can set the number of seconds you would like for this module to remain cached in memory.
Set As Default Settings	This setting allows you to utilize this module's settings as the default for all the modules you add to your portal.
Apply To All Modules	This is a time-saver if you decide you want the default behavior of all modules to be different than your original settings. You can apply the settings to one module and push those settings out to all instances of modules in the portal.
Move To Page	This setting allows you to move this module instance to another page in the portal.

The settings listed in this section are implemented from the base module settings class, so this information is pertinent to all modules that inherit the classes, and it is a programming requirement that modules inherit the class. This means that you will have the above functionality no matter which module you are working with, whether it's a base module or another third-party module you have obtained from one of the many module developers. Now that you have your module settings updated, you can go ahead and add a couple of announcements for your users. Figure 6-7 illustrates the view the Announcements module will now contain as a result of your changes to the settings.

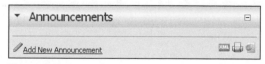

Figure 6-7

Because you set up your module to Allow Print and Allow Syndicate, you will notice the XML and Print icons showing up in the module instance. If you had not enabled these options, those icons would not be available. Click the Add New Announcement command link, which will navigate you to the edit control for your Announcements module. Here, you can define your announcement, as shown in Figure 6-8.

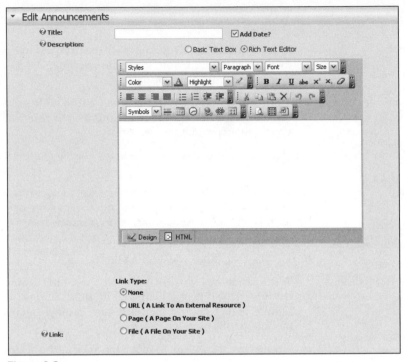

Figure 6-8

Like the other areas of the portal, the names are self-explanatory, but Table 6-3 lists and describes each option.

Table 6-3: Adding Announcements

Option	Description
Title	This is the title that describes the individual announcement. By default the date the announcement is created is appended to the title you define here. If you do not want this date to appear to your users, uncheck the Add Date check box.
Description	Here you type the content for your announcement. This module utilizes the Free Text Box (FTB) control to make it easier for users to format the display of the text. If this particular announcement does not require Rich Text formatting functionality, you can use the text box option, which will dynamically remove the instance of FTB and allow you to only use a text box for this function.

Link	This section allows you to specify a location where the user can obtain more information about the announcement. When you enable this option, a link is created at the end of your announcement, which when clicked by the user will allow navigation to the link you define. You have several options here to define what kind of link you will create. The default is a link to an external site. If you select Page or File, the Location control will change to a DDL, which will allow selecting the page or file where your additional information resides. Auditing information can be defined with the other controls in this section, so you can capture information on your users' actions and behavior for further analysis.
Expires	This allows you to set a date when the content should expire and no longer be viewable by your users.
View Order	By default, announcements are displayed in ascending order according to the date the announcement was created. Setting the view order allows you to define the order you want announcements to appear.

You now have all the knowledge necessary to create and maintain announcements for your portal. The other base portal modules follow similar methods for creating content. Because many of these modules use the same methods for the common functions, we will not cover these methods in detail in the later module descriptions, but we will emphasize the differences. One thing to keep in mind if you have aspirations of creating your own modules to extend DotNetNuke is that the code contained in the Announcements module is a good head start for creating the layout of your own modules. For more on developing your own modules, refer to Chapters 9 through 12, which cover module development.

Banner Module

The Banner module provides a method of offering advertisements in the DotNetNuke application. Administering this module is a little different than any of the other base modules because this module works in conjunction with the Vendors module, which is an administrator-only module. Advertisement can be controlled from the Host level or Portal level and the host or SuperUser account controls this behavior.

Probably the first thing you will notice when you add this module to a page is that you only see a Banner Options action and not Add New Action, like the other modules display. This is because the banners will need to be added from either the Admin Vendors page or from the Host Vendors page. This is one of the functions that makes DotNetNuke a viable host platform, because you can offer free or inexpensive portals for your users and then recuperate your hosting costs from offering advertising on the individual portals in your DotNetNuke installation.

Exactly how to add these is covered in the next two chapters, which discuss the Host and Admin functions. For now, assume you have already added a vendor and are ready to display a banner advertisement for that vendor. After you add the module to a page, click the Banner Options action. You are presented with the Edit Control in Figure 6-9.

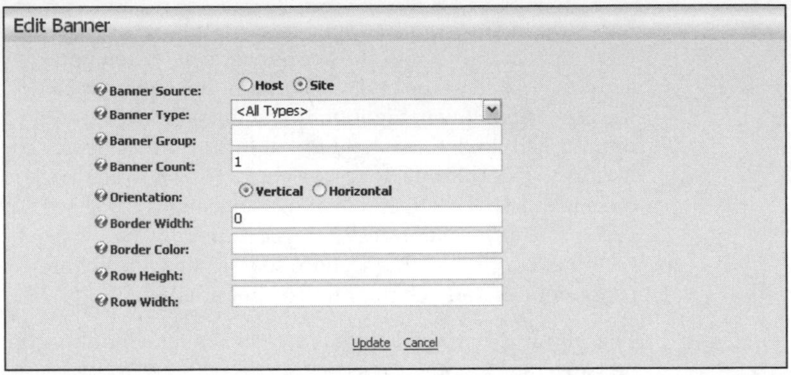

Figure 6-9

As you can see, there is no option to add a banner to this control. Those actions are handled in the respective Vendors module by the Host or Portal Administrator, and this module is the mechanism you will use to display those settings to the user. For a full description of managing the Vendor functions in DotNetNuke, refer to Chapters 4 and 5. A description of each of the Edit Banner functions is shown in Table 6-4.

Table 6-4: Edit Banner Options

Setting	Description
Banner Source	Selecting one of these radio buttons allows you to specify whether the vendor banners shown in this module should originate from the host or from the portal.
Banner Type	This dictates the type of banner that should be shown in this module. Banner types include Banner, MicroButton, Button, Block, Skyscraper, Text, and Script. It should be noted that selecting a specific type means the vendor must have that type assigned to its account or the module will not show that particular vendor's advertisements.
Banner Group	This setting allows you to associate a group of banners together in the administrator vendor's module, such as Site Banner group. Entering the banner group here will allow you to group the same types of banners together.
Banner Count	Here you can define the number of times a banner will display to the users.
Orientation	This defines the orientation of the banner. The type of banner you chose usually dictates what you choose in this setting.
Border Width	This setting allows you to define a border.
Border Color	This setting allows you to set the border color.
Row Height	This setting allows you to set a row height for your banner.
Row Width	This setting allows you to set a row width for your banner.

Once you have set up your vendor accounts on the vendor pages, you will be able to earn revenue from your DotNetNuke installation. As you saw, there is really no direct editing of content from this module. This is a design decision, so you can let other roles in your installation handle these remedial types of tasks while you can control your revenue generation from the higher accounts. You will still need to set up the module settings for this module, but because this module contains the same functions as the Announcements module, we will not cover those settings again.

Contacts Module

Almost every web site, regardless of content area, needs a method to provide information to contact the site's owners and employees. This is the purpose of the Contacts module. You can add your contact information and provide an easy-to-use interface for updating it to maintain current information. You can create an entire company directory from this module or display contact info for only a few individuals. The types of information you can display include the name, employee role, e-mail address, and telephone numbers for the individuals listed. Look at the settings control in Figure 6-10 to add a Contacts module to your test portal.

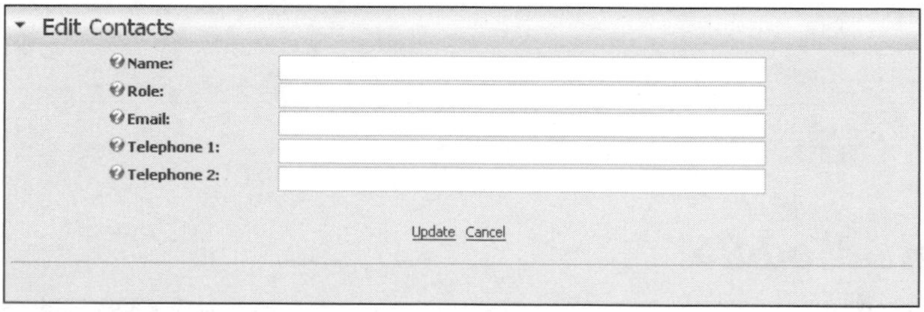

Figure 6-10

Here you can enter in the information for each contact you want to display and the module will display the information to the roles you approve. When the module information is entered, the e-mail will be formatted as a mailto link; your users will be able to use this link to send e-mail to the contact using their default mail client.

Discussions Module

The Discussions module is a lightweight forum module your users can use to share information. This module is not designed to be a full-fledged forum platform, but it will work for light forum activities you may need to offer on your web site. This module uses the same settings as the previous modules have used so we do not need to cover those activities again. Figure 6-11 shows the interface for creating new threads in the module.

As you can see, this is the simplest interface we've encountered so far. This module is very simple to use — you just enter a title and write your message. In order for users to reply to your thread they must click on the thread and click Reply. We suggest you play around with this module because it may meet your needs to provide this functionality to your users. Several other full-fledged forum modules are available for DotNetNuke. Some of these are free and some require a small license fee. Refer to the DotNetNuke web site if you require a more robust forum system for your portal.

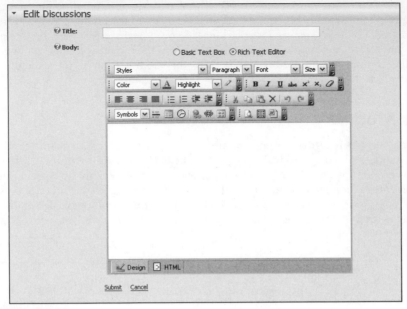

Figure 6-11

Documents Module

The Documents module allows you to offer files that your users can download from your site. This is a fairly useful module because you will likely need to offer examples or additional information in the form of Word documents or other types of files to your users. The types of files you can use with this module is controlled by the file type settings under the Host Settings page. By default, DotNetNuke will allow the following extensions:

- ❑ .jpg
- ❑ .jpeg
- ❑ .jpe
- ❑ .gif
- ❑ .bmp
- ❑ .png
- ❑ .doc
- ❑ .xls
- ❑ .ppt
- ❑ .pdf
- ❑ .txt

- ❑ .xml
- ❑ .xsl
- ❑ .css
- ❑ .zip

If you require additional file types not allowed by default, you will need to add the extension under the Host Settings page in the File Upload Extensions field. If you are going to allow your users to upload files, you should be careful as to the type of files allowed because it's possible users may introduce viruses or other undesirable files into your portal file system. The application offers no default protection in this area, so diligence is needed to protect the integrity of the system.

Figure 6-12 shows the interface you use to add new documents to this module. As in other areas of the application, the files you make available through this module will reside in your portal default file directory.

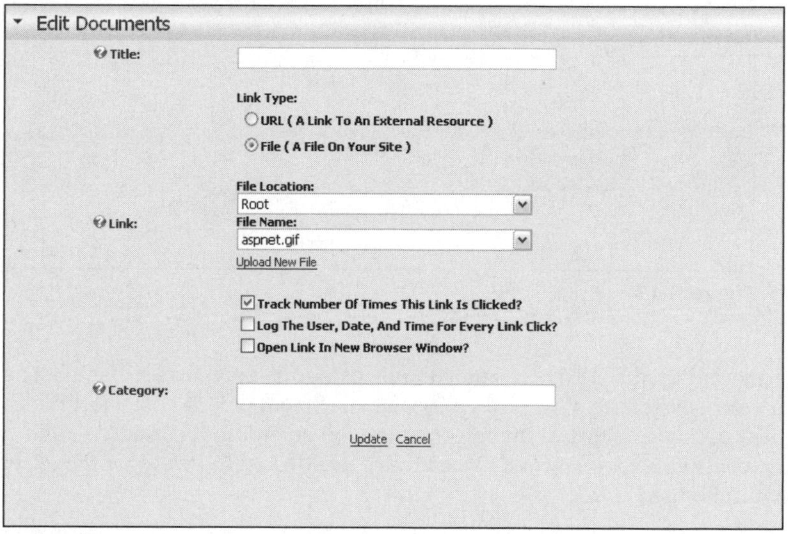

Figure 6-12

Here you will enter the title, link, and category for your module. You may notice the Link section appears almost exactly like the links control in the Announcements module. Here is another example of the object-oriented programming of DotNetNuke at work. We attempt to reuse code wherever possible to enable a simpler user interface for the user and to promote best programming practices when possible. You will notice there are some differences between the links control in the Announcements module and this one in the Documents module. The only difference between the two is that in the Announcements module you have an option to select a page in your portal as one of the links. Because it should never be necessary to offer a page for download, this option is not included in the Documents module. You will also notice that like the Announcements module, the Documents module allows the tracking of your users' actions so you will be able to determine the content that your users are most interested in receiving. The Category field offers you the ability to logically group the files in this module. This category will be displayed as part of the Documents module so your users will understand the type of file they are about to download or view.

Events Module

The Events module allows you to list upcoming events to announce to your users. This module has some additional settings that control the display of the module. The rest of the module settings are the same as the ones we have already covered, so we will only look at the settings that are unique to this module. See Figure 6-13.

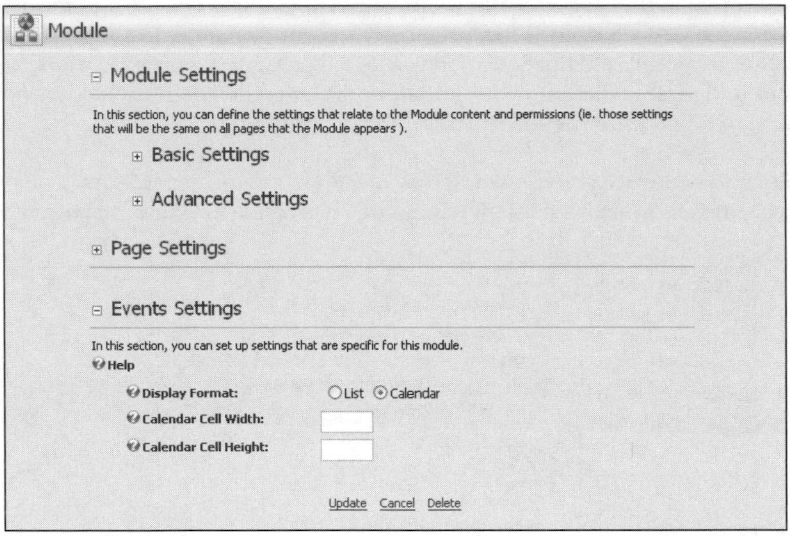

Figure 6-13

As you can see from Figure 6-13, the Events module can be displayed as either a list or a calendar control depending on your needs. The other two options are pertinent only if you select the Calendar option. Selecting the List option will format the information you enter into the module into a sequential list of the upcoming events you have entered. Once you've decided on the view for the events, you can add the event as shown in Figure 6-14.

You will notice you have many of the same functions available in this module as you do in the other modules. It should be noted that if you use the calendar view you will want to limit the amount of text in the description, because there is only limited room in the calendar view for events. If your events need a longer description to convey the meaning to your users, you will need use the list view for the Events module. Table 6-5 explores each of the options available in this module.

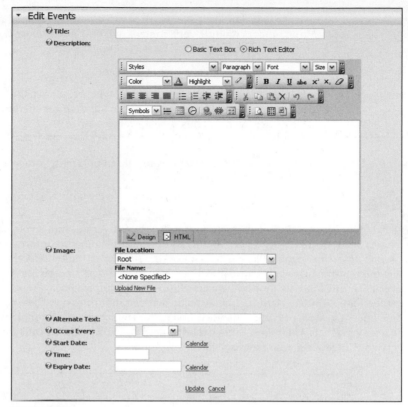

Figure 6-14

Table 6-5: Edit Events Module

Settings	Description
Title	Here you can enter the title of your individual event.
Description	Here you can enter a description for your event that will provide your user with detailed information that is not included elsewhere in the module.
Image	You can select an image to be associated with your event. This is usually used to easily convey more information about your event to your users.
Alternate Text	This is information describing your image. This is important for meeting 508 accessibility for visually challenged users who may access your site using screen readers.
Occurs Every	Here you can define how often this event will occur. Options are to set the event to occur periodically based on day, week, month, or year. This is a time-saver because if you have recurring events to announce, you only need to set the event once and the module will take care of the rest for you.

Table continued on following page

Start Date	This is the first date your event will occur. We should note that unlike the Announcements module your content will be visible before the date you enter here. This date signifies the start of your event.
Time	This is the time of day your event will occur.
Expiry Date	The last day of your event. This is useful when you are using the Occurs Every function and you no longer need to show the event, but would like to keep earlier events of this type for reference.

As you can see, the Events module is very useful, and you are sure to find many other uses for it as well.

FAQs Module

You can use the FAQs or Frequently Asked Questions module to answer questions your users may have about your web site or products. This is a very useful module for disseminating information that you receive questions about on an ongoing basis. This is one of the simpler modules in DotNetNuke, but it is also one of the more powerful ones because it will save you many hours of replying to e-mails if you utilize its functionality. The interface for adding a new FAQ is very simple and warrants little discussion. Basically, you enter a question you want to provide an answer for and then enter the answer for that question. The module offers the ability to utilize the Rich Text editor so that you can format your questions and answers in a way that is easy for your users to understand and to convey the intended message. Figure 6-15 shows the interface for the Edit functions of the module.

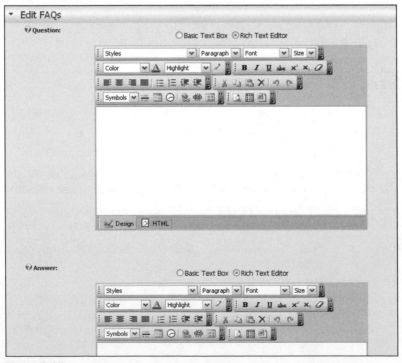

Figure 6-15

Feedback Module

The Feedback module offers you a mechanism for allowing users to contact you without exposing your e-mail address to the many SPAM Bots that regularly scan the Internet. The module does not have an Add function like the other modules we have explored because the purpose of the module does not need this functionality. Basically users are adding feedback when they send you feedback. The module does contain some settings you can use to control the display of the module to users and to specify the e-mail address to which you want the e-mails created from the module to be sent. Prior to version 3 of the portal, the only option to send these requests to was the administrator account. With this version you have the option to change this behavior. One thing to be aware of is that this module relies on the mail server settings on the Host Settings page to function properly. Ensure you have successfully added your mail server and tested the settings before attempting to utilize this module's functionality. You will notice in Figure 6-16 that you also have the option of setting the width and rows of this module, which controls the display of the module to your users.

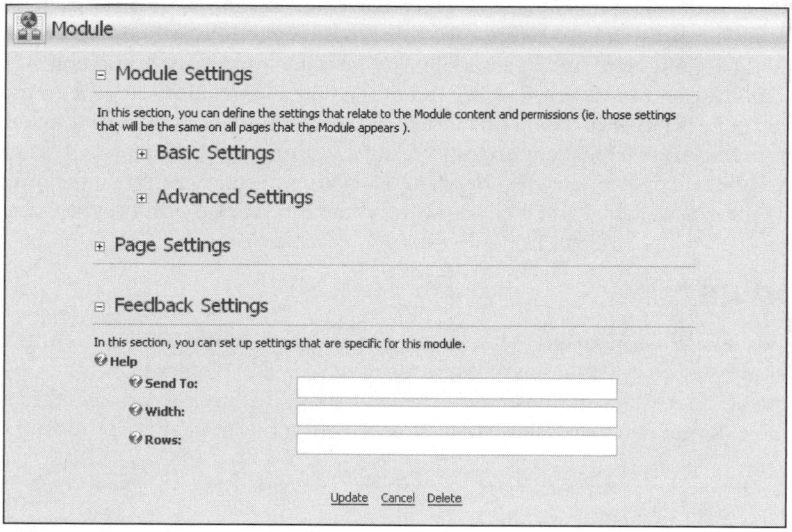

Figure 6-16

IFrame Module

The IFrame module allows you to display web pages from other web sites in your portal. When you set the page, the module should display and add an IFrame tag to your page and load the remote site into the frame. One of the main uses for this module mentioned in the DotNetNuke forums is to utilize legacy applications that were created with ASP or some other dynamic language that must still be used for some functionality. This allows companies to take advantage of the benefits of DotNetNuke while still utilizing other functionality they had in previous applications. This is usually a short-term fix people employ. As they become more familiar with DotNetNuke module development, they can convert their legacy applications to fully compliant DotNetNuke modules to take advantage of full integration with DotNetNuke roles and user control functions. The settings available for the IFrame module are illustrated in Figure 6-17.

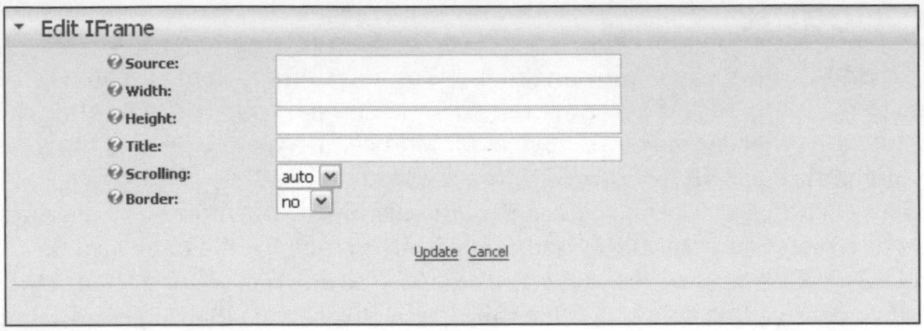

Figure 6-17

The Source of the IFrame module is the location of the web page you would like to add to display in your module. The Width and Height fields determine the size of the IFrame and should be adjusted to fit the page you need to display. These fields can be entered either as pixels or a percent depending on your needs. Title is a little confusing here because the title is not the module title, nor will it be shown to normal users. This title is a requirement for 508 accessibility compliance and you should enter a descriptive value in this field. Scrolling determines whether the IFrame should add scrollbars for the frame. This is important if the target web page is larger than you can show in your portal without impeding the display or omitting certain content of the target page. Your options are auto, yes, and no. Auto is usually the best choice here because the module will determine whether or not the bars are needed based on the target page dimensions. The last option is to define whether you want a border to appear around your target page.

Image Module

The Image module offers you an easy way to add images to your portal. The module allows you to add an image to a page where it would not make sense to have a skin element and you do not require the ability to link to another site from the image. The image you display can reside either in your portal file system or on an external resource. Figure 6-18 shows the options available for adding a link.

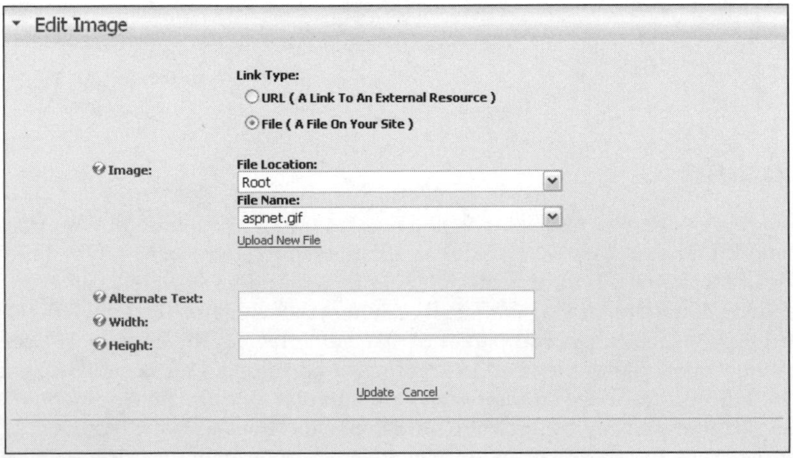

Figure 6-18

You will notice the same familiar file picker interface you have seen in other modules. Selecting the URL option for the link type will produce a post back and present you with a text box to enter in the path to the remote image. If you want to use an image that resides in your portal directories, you can select the image from the drop-down lists. This interface also allows you to enter in the Alternate Text for the image and specify the Width and Height of the image. Leaving the proportion text boxes blank will cause the image to be displayed in its actual size.

Links Module

The Links module is probably one of the most used modules in DotNetNuke installations; it probably is only used less than the HTML/Text and Announcements modules. As its name suggests, this module allows you to add links your users can use to navigate to other areas of your site or to remote web sites. This module has a few unique settings you need to be familiar with. Figure 6-19 shows the Module Settings pane for the Links Settings.

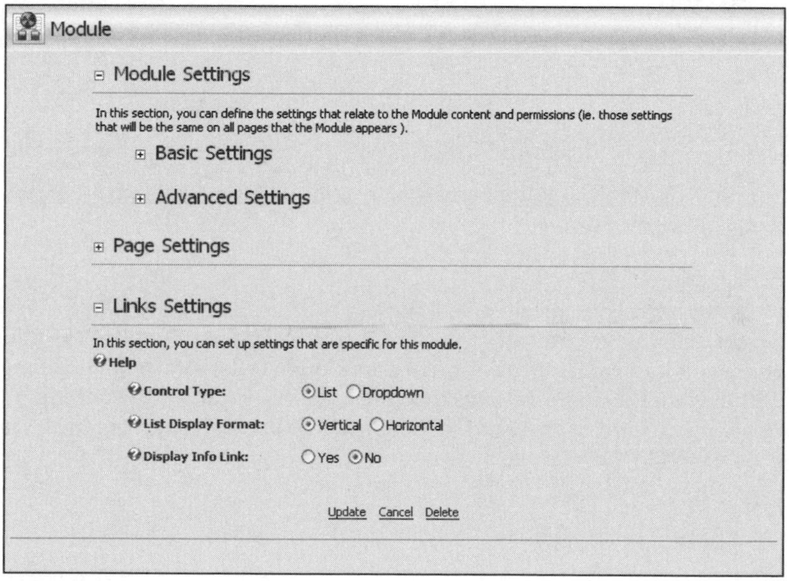

Figure 6-19

As you can see, you have several options for controlling the behavior and view of the Links module. Selecting the Control Type will allow you to define whether the link list will display as a drop-down list or a normal data-bound list. You also have the option of displaying the orientation of the list with the List Display Format option. The last option available is whether you want to show the user a short description of the web page where the link navigates to. This is a useful option to allow some additional keywords to be associated with the link. Figure 6-20 shows your options for adding links to your modules. For this example, just accept the defaults in the Link Settings in Figure 6-19 and move on to adding your link as shown in Figure 6-20.

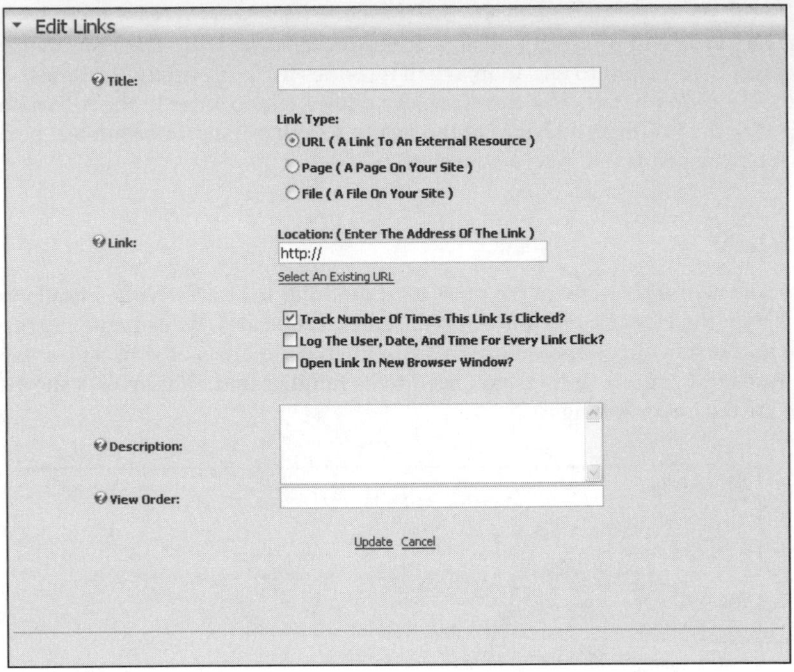

Figure 6-20

The title is what users will see as the link. You also use the file picker control in this module and you have the options of defining an external, page, or internal file in your module. The audit controls on this module let you track your visitors' behavior. The Description is the information we mentioned earlier is where you select the info link in the settings then the user will see an additional link where they can read the information you enter in this field. The View Order allows you to organize the order in which your links are displayed in the module.

News Feed (RSS)

The News Feed module allows you to consume RSS content from another resource and display it to your users. Many web sites offer syndicated feeds that you can consume and display relevant content for your portal. Many of these resources are available on the Internet, some of which are free and some that require a fee to consume. The News Feed module allows you to consume both of these types of feeds and display the information according to your feed style sheet, as shown in Figure 6-21.

The Source is the location of the source you want to consume. You also have the option of specifying the style sheet to use with the feed. Most news feeds provide a style sheet especially for their feed that you can use or you can specify your own style sheet. DotNetNuke offers the flexibility to use the style sheet that meets your business needs. Some feeds require you to present credentials authorizing access to their content before you can consume a feed. The Username and Password text boxes are where you enter this type of authentication information.

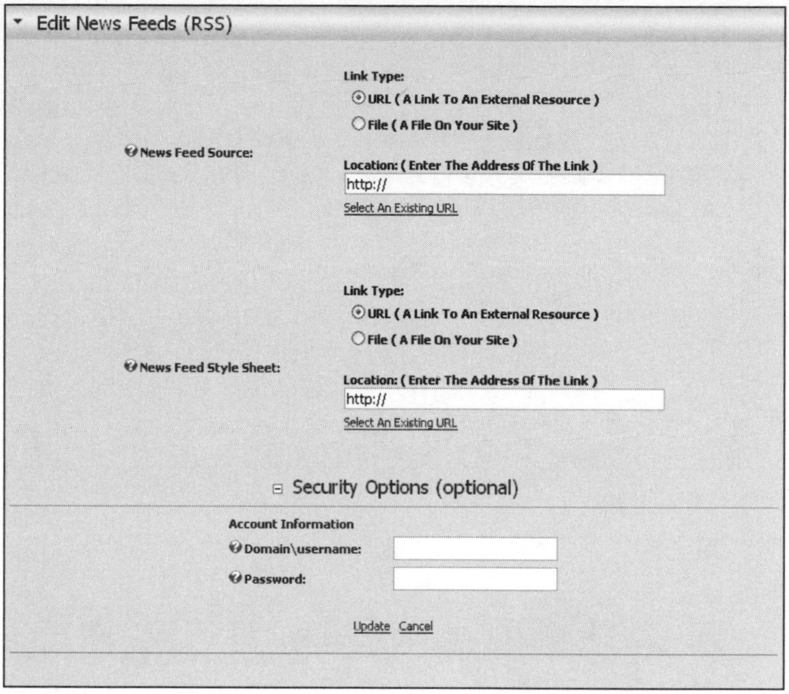

Figure 6-21

HTML/Text Module

The HTML/Text module, or HTML mod for short, is probably one of the most used modules in DotNetNuke portals. It allows you to format your content with the easy-to-use Free Text Box editor and it also allows for a large amount of content to be displayed. This module also fits with what most webmasters need for their content display. You have the option of using the editor or, if you're a hard-core HTML programmer, you can type in your HTML directly with out relying on the controls rendering your markup. The HTML/Text interface is very straightforward and includes only two controls, as shown in Figure 6-22.

The first option is where you will enter your content to be displayed in the module and the second is a search summary. The DotNetNuke 3 search functions have the ability to index all the content in this module. The type of content entered in this module may become quite large, so the core team felt it would be pertinent to allow a mechanism for the module administrator to add a summary of the content for the search engine to utilize. This accomplishes two functions. First, it allows you to provide the gist of the content that will be displayed to users when they search for similar content and, second, it helps with the performance of the search engine because there is no need to index all of the content that may appear in this type of module.

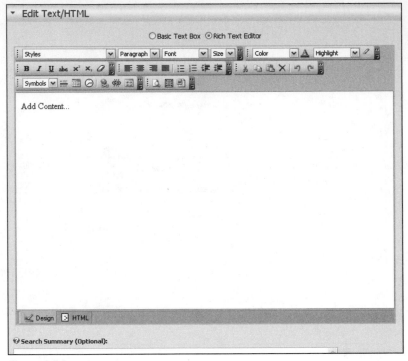

Figure 6-22

User Defined Table Module

The User Defined Table is a catch-all type of module. This module allows you to define your own data type and display this information to your users in an organized manner. The easiest way to understand the use of this module is through an example. Suppose you need an additional field for your portal's contacts. You could open up the Contacts project and modify the code to add your field and then recompile, but you could also use the User Defined module to accomplish the same task. First, add the module to your page and open the Manage User Defined Table action item. Click the Add New Column link. You are presented with the screen shown Figure 6-23.

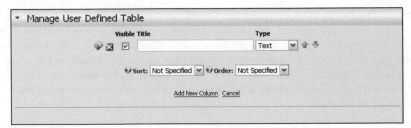

Figure 6-23

As you can see, you have the ability to add your own defined fields in the module. For simplicity, assume you only need to display the person's name, title, and birthday in your Contacts module. So, you add three fields of these types and now have your fields defined as in Figure 6-24.

Figure 6-24

You not only have the ability to add your own unique fields, but you also have the ability to specify the data type. Your data type options for this module include text, integer, decimal, date, and Boolean. These types give you the ability to create some pretty interesting scenarios out of this module. Figure 6-25 shows the finished user defined table. To add a new item to the module you can now select the Add New Row action from the module menu.

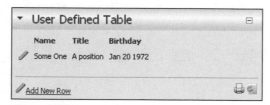

Figure 6-25

As you can see, you can display information in a manner that was previously not available with the portal, and you have accomplished your goals with just a few clicks and without ever opening up an IDE to display your data. We suggest you spend some time exploring the functionality of this module and see what other functions it may allow you to perform.

XML/XSL Module

The XML/XSL module allows you to display XML data from an external data source and display it in your portal according to the accompanying XSL transformation file. This module further increases the type of data you can display in your portal and is only limited by the XML technology and your imagination. Figure 6-26 shows the Edit settings of this module.

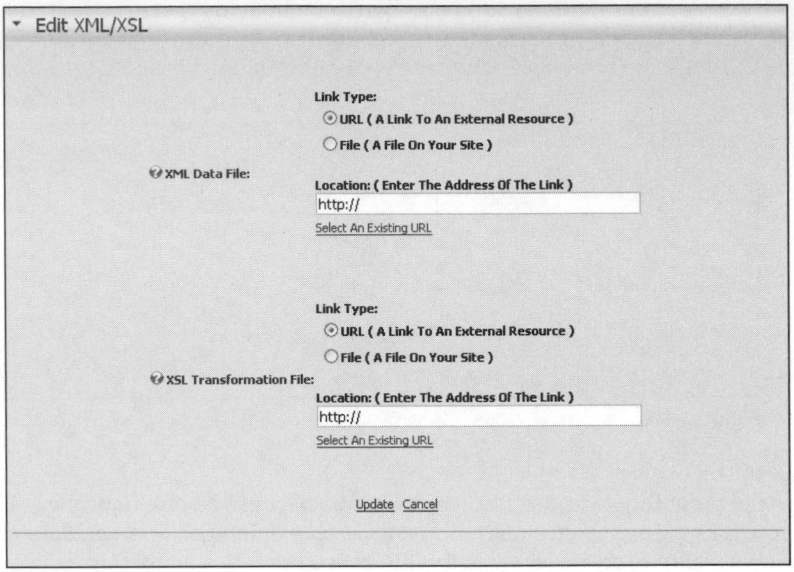

Figure 6-26

You can see from the figure that this module utilizes the file picker controls available in other modules to allow you to select the source of your XML data and the transformation file you will use to describe that data. This module enables DotNetNuke to consume data from a wide variety of sources, because most modern data sources enable a method for exporting its data to XML format.

Management

Now that we have discussed the architecture and explored the modules bundled within DotNetNuke, it's time to examine the management functionality surrounding modules. This section discusses the module options that appear in the top toolbar, such as adding a module to a page, and also discusses the options surrounding a module, such as minimize/maximize, site settings, delete, and so on.

Page Management

Figure 6-27 shows the module section of the administration toolbar that appears for portal administrators or users with sufficient edit permissions.

This toolbar has two modes of operation, depending on the radio option you select. The default mode of operation is Add New Module, as shown in Figure 6-27. This mode allows you to add new modules to the current page. To add a new module, select the desired module from the drop-down list, specify the pane to inject the module into, specify a title for the desired module, and choose the alignment for the text within the module. Click the Add button to inject the module into the current page.

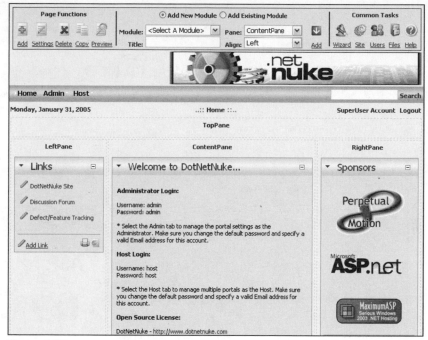

Figure 6-27

The other mode of operation is Add Existing Module, as shown in Figure 6-28. This mode allows you to add the exact same instance of a module that appears on another page. This means that any updates done to the module will automatically appear in both locations no matter which page the update was performed on. To add an existing module, select the desired page from the drop-down list, specify the pane to inject the module into, select the module (populated from the page selected) you want to add to the current page, and choose the alignment for the text within the module. Click the Add button to inject the module into the current page.

Now that you have added a module to a page, you may notice a red border around the module with the keyword "Administrators." The red border dictates that this module is not publicly viewable. The process has been designed so that only the administrators of the current page can see newly added modules. To make it publicly viewable, see "Settings" under "Hover Menu" in the following section.

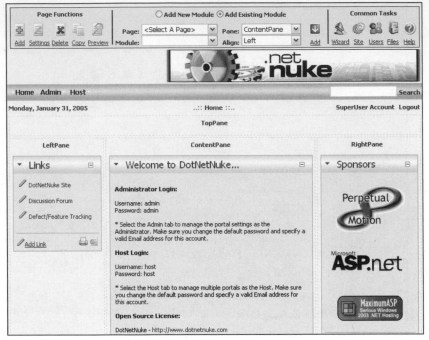

Figure 6-28

Module Management

Now that you are able to add modules to pages, this section discusses the options available to you once a module is on the page. Earlier in this chapter we discussed the concept of a module container:

> "Each module consists of a title, decorations, and the content produced by the module. The decorations can include buttons, links, and a hover menu that can change the module's state, or perform functionality specific to that module."

This section explains the various decorations (buttons, links, and hover menu) that are available in each module (providing the user is an authorized role). The following features are described:

❑ **Drag and Drop:** Allows you to reorganize modules on a single page.

❑ **Hover Menu:** Provides a variety of options.

❑ **Minimize/Maximize:** Allows a user to control the visibility of module's content.

Drag and Drop

Drag and Drop is a relatively new feature in DotNetNuke. It allows an authorized user to select a module for relocation, drag the module to the new location (content pane), and unclick to drop the module into its new location.

To relocate a module, select the title of a module with your left mouse button, hold down the button, and drag the module to the new location, as shown in Figure 6-29. The pane you are dragging the module to should highlight, indicating that it is okay to drop it (unclick the mouse button).

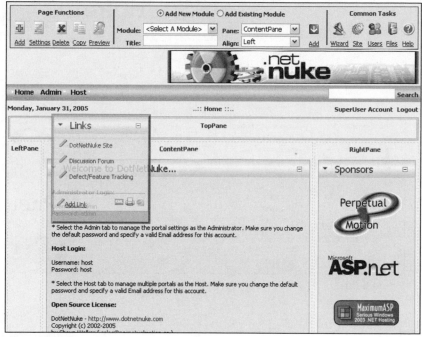

Figure 6-29

Using Drag and Drop provides a time-efficient method of reorganizing content once it is on a page.

Hover Menu

The hover menu contains a variety of options and is ordered in a similar fashion for all modules. The first one or two options available in the menu are module-specific.

Figure 6-30 shows the Announcements module and its hover menu. As you can see, the first option is Add New Announcement, which is specific to the Announcements module. In this section, we won't be discussing options that are specific to a module, but rather the general options available to all modules.

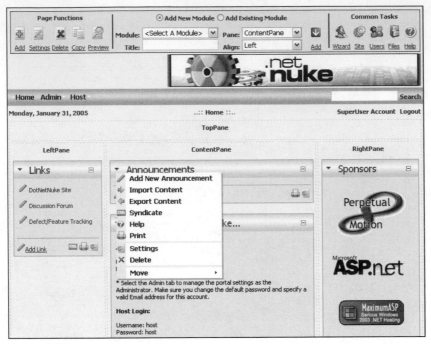

Figure 6-30

Import Content

The Import Content option allows you to import a module's content from another portal. Be aware that not all third-party modules support this option.

Export Content

The Export Content option allows you export a module's content to a single file. Be aware that not all third-party modules support this option.

Syndicate

The Syndicate option links to a Rich Site Summary (RSS) feed for that module.

Help

The Help option links to the configured help for that module. Module authors have a number of mechanisms for providing help, and this option will link to the mechanism they have selected.

Print

The Print option takes you to a screen containing only that module for printing purposes.

Settings

The Settings section is the most important menu option in the hover menu, as discussed earlier in this chapter. It takes you to an edit screen for that module where you can edit various options about the selected module. The Basic Settings options include the title and permissions for the module, as shown in Figure 6-31.

The Advanced Settings options (also shown in Figure 6-31) include the option to provide a header or footer for the module, a start and end date for display purposes, and finally, the option to show the module on all pages.

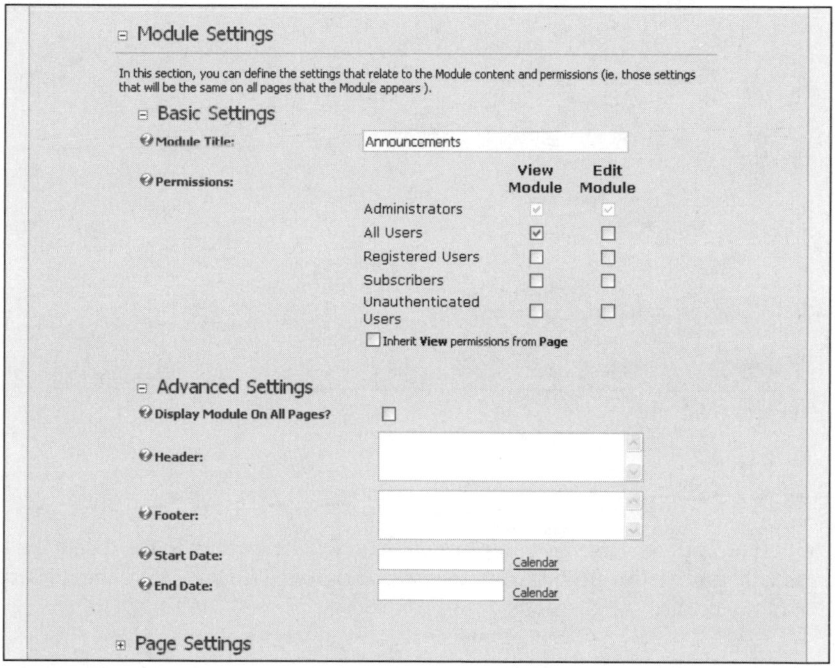

Figure 6-31

The Page Settings options (as shown in Figure 6-32) include options for controlling the look of the module, such as icon, color, border, alignment, and visibility. Other options include Display Title, Allow Print, Allow Syndication, Override Container, and a Cache Time option that allows output caching of the module's content, which is particularly useful on high-traffic sites. The last section of this area allows the authorized user to apply these settings to all modules, or move the module to another page.

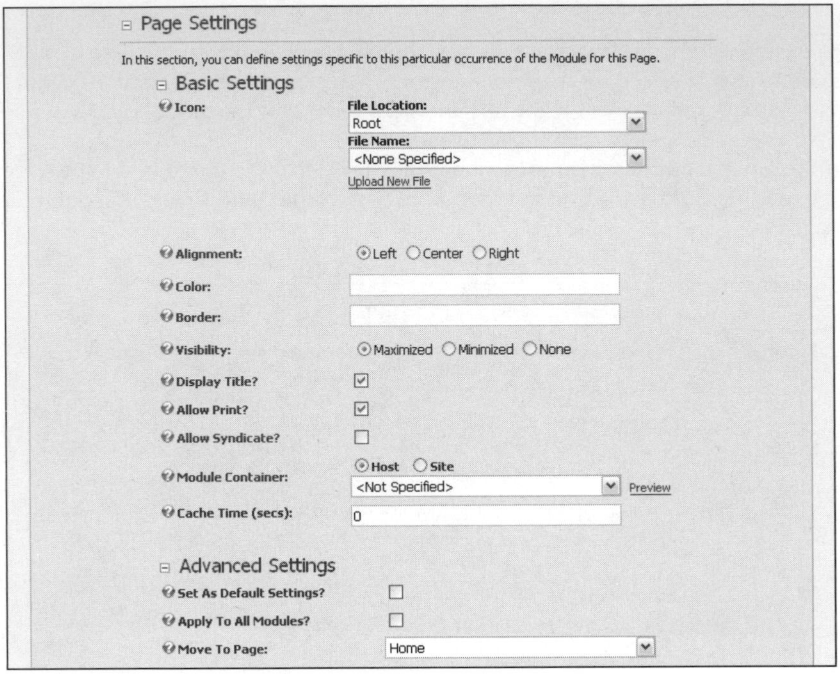

Figure 6-32

Delete

The Delete option prompts the user for a confirmation on whether or not to the delete the selected module. Answering yes will remove the module from the page and place it in the recycle bin located in the administration section of the portal.

Move

The Move option provides optional menus underneath this option. The number of options depends on the portal skin, but it allows you to specify a valid pane to move this module to. This is an alternative method of moving a module to the drag-and-drop method discussed earlier.

Minimize/Maximize

The Minimize/Maximize feature allows a user to control the visibility of a module's content. This feature is personalized on a user-to-user basis, although you can set a default state in the module settings section of a module. Figure 6-33 shows a minimized module.

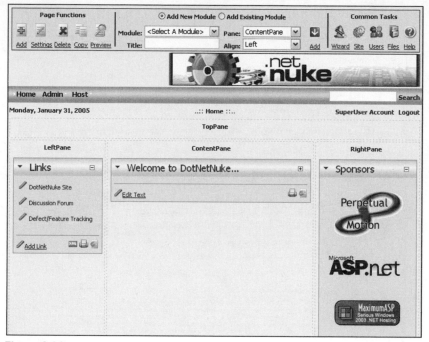

Figure 6-33

Installation

Now that you are familiar with the concept of modules and using the default modules within your portal, you can add new modules to your DotNetNuke installation. As discussed earlier, DotNetNuke is an extensible platform; that is, it allows you to install third-party modules into your portal environment.

This section walks you through the steps of uploading a new module; in particular, it uses the Survey module that comes bundled with DotNetNuke but is not installed by default.

An earlier chapter introduced the Module Definitions page. It is the Module Definitions page that allows you to install new DotNetNuke modules. To find this page, make sure you are logged in as a SuperUser and navigate to Host ➪ Module Definitions. Figure 6-34 shows the Module Definitions page.

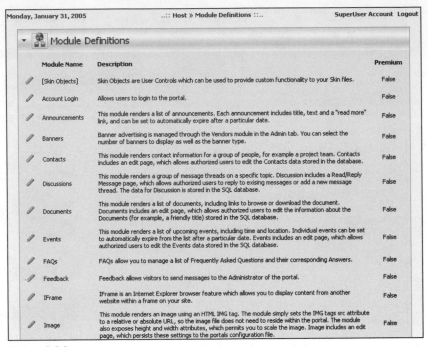

Figure 6-34

To add a new module from the Module Definitions page, move your mouse over the hover menu and select Upload New Module. Once on this screen, you are presented with the screen the shown in Figure 6-35.

To upload the module, click the Browse button and choose your module install file, which should be a zip file. The Survey module zip file is located at the following path:

```
<DotNetNuke Installation Directory>/DesktopModules/Survey/DotNetNuke.Survey.Zip
```

Once the file has been selected, click Add and then Upload New File.

The resulting screen presents a series of log entries showing you what happened during the installation of the module. Once you are happy with the installation (for example, there are no glaring red error messages), click the Return hyperlink or navigate to any page within your portal system. This page hit may take some time since the cache has been flushed by installing a new module.

To confirm that the module has been installed successfully, you should now see it in the drop-down list in the top toolbar. In this particular case, you should see an entry named "CompanyName – Survey" in the module drop-down list.

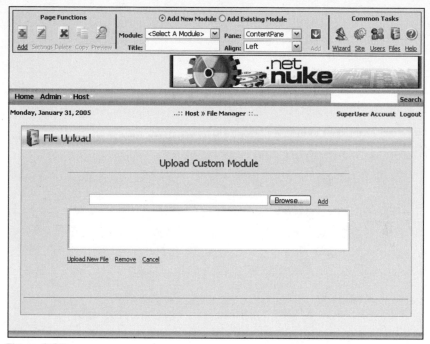

Figure 6-35

Summary

This chapter introduced the concept of modules, and discussed their architecture in a portal context. You should now be familiar with the terms portal, page, module, and module container.

The chapter also discussed the types of modules included with DotNetNuke and the management of those modules from a site administrator's perspective. It also examined management from a page perspective and examined the various controls, such as the hover menu, that are included within a module.

Lastly, it discussed the installation of third-party modules and walked through the installation of the Survey module that is bundled within DotNetNuke.

DotNetNuke Architecture

The architecture of DotNetNuke has evolved from a rewrite of the IBuySpy Portal into a best practice example of design patterns and coding standards. This chapter explains the components of the architecture behind DotNetNuke.

Before diving deep into the architectural overview, you should understand some key technologies that DotNetNuke employs. The following section covers several interesting technologies and design patterns used in the DotNetNuke 3.0 architecture.

Technologies Used

As covered in Chapter 1, DotNetNuke was originally derived from the IBuySpy Portal Solution Kit. IBuySpy was written in VB.NET and showcased some interesting design concepts. If you look under the hood of DotNetNuke 3.0 today, though, it doesn't even resemble IBuySpy. We have taken the best concepts from IBuySpy and applied many best practice design patterns and coding standards that have evolved as the .NET Framework has evolved.

DotNetNuke 3.0 uses several key technologies in its architecture:

❑ Windows 2000 Server, Windows 2003 Server

❑ ASP.NET

❑ Visual Basic .NET

❑ Web Forms

❑ Microsoft Internet Information Services

❑ ADO.NET

❑ Microsoft SQL Server 2000

In addition, DotNetNuke showcases several key design patterns and concepts that differentiate it from many other portal applications. These design patterns and concepts provide a foundation that demonstrates and encourages best practices programming:

❑ Provider Model

❑ Custom Business Objects and Controllers

❑ Centralized Custom Business Object Hydration

❑ Membership/Roles/Profile Providers using ASP.NET 2.0 API

❑ Localization framework that mirrors the ASP.NET 2.0 implementation

The DotNetNuke application has attracted a lot of attention in its use of these key design patterns. An important driver to that attention has been the ability for developers to learn many of the ASP.NET 2.0 features before ASP.NET 2.0 is released. Developers have also learned from DotNetNuke about the extensibility of the Provider Model and how it can help them construct better applications.

Provider Model

The Provider Model is a design pattern that is used in the DotNetNuke architecture to allow core functionality to be replaced without modifying core code. The introduction of the Provider Model started with Microsoft in its need to provide a simple and extensible API in .NET. The Provider Model has been formalized in ASP.NET 2.0 as a best practice design pattern. The purpose of the Provider Model is to provide an easy-to-understand and well-documented API that has the benefits of simplicity and the power of extensibility.

To provide both simplicity and extensibility, the *API* is separated from the *implementation of the API*. A provider is a contract between an API and the business logic that establishes the functionality that the implementation of the API must provide. When a method in the API is called, it is the implementation of the API that fulfills the request. Simply, the API doesn't care "how" the job is done, as long as it is done. If there is one useful concept garnered from this section, let it be this oversimplification of the purpose of the Provider Model:

"Build things so they do not depend on the details of other things."

This fundamental design concept was recognized well before the Provider Model came to fruition, but it truly speaks to what the Provider Model brings to developers. The API in the Provider Model does not depend on the details of the implementation of the API. It is because of this that the implementation of the API can be changed very easily, and the API itself is unaffected due to the abstraction.

Several areas in DotNetNuke use the Provider Model:

❑ Data Provider

❑ Scheduling Provider

❑ Logging Provider

- ❑   HTML Editor Provider
- ❑   Search Provider
- ❑   Friendly URL Provider

The first implementation of the Provider Model in DotNetNuke was the Data Provider. DotNetNuke originally supported only Microsoft SQL Server. The core of the portal was tightly coupled with the data tier. Many requests came from the community to extend DotNetNuke to support other data stores, so we needed a way to support a diverse array of data stores while maintaining a simple data access layer and allowing for extensibility. This is when the concept of the Provider Model was first introduced into DotNetNuke.

Figure 7-1 shows that the Data Provider API is not dependent on a tightly coupled implementation of the API. Instead, the Data Provider API doesn't even know what kind of data store is being used until you configure an XML setting in the web.config file. Other than the settings in web.config, the only other requirement of the Data Provider API is that the implementation of the API must fulfill its contract by providing the necessary functionality defined in the base class. For example, all methods marked with MustOverride in the Data Provider API must be overridden in the implementation of the API.

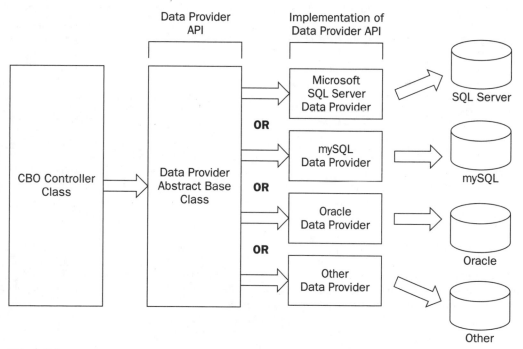

Figure 7-1

Provider Configuration

The Provider API has to be configured to work with the implementation of the API. The API needs to be configured to know which type and assembly to use for the implementation of the API. As mentioned in the previous section, this is configured in the web.config file.

The configuration settings are in XML in the web.config file. There is no standard for naming conventions or the structure of the configuration settings in the Provider Model in general. However, DotNetNuke has followed a consistent pattern in each Provider Model API and the associated configuration settings.

Each API may have different requirements for configuration settings. For instance, the Data Provider API needs a connection string defined in its configuration settings. The XML Logging Provider needs its log configuration file location defined in its configuration settings. So each API will have configuration settings that are specific to that API.

The DotNetNuke core providers store the Provider Model API configuration settings in web.config under the /configuration/dotnetnuke node. When a Provider Model API is first instantiated, it collects these settings, which allows it to use the specified implementation of the API. The configuration settings are then cached so that in subsequent requests the configuration settings are retrieved more quickly. Listing 7-1 shows a section of the web.config file that contains the Data Provider API's configuration settings.

Listing 7-1: Data Provider Configuration Settings

```
<data defaultProvider="SqlDataProvider">
    <providers>
        <clear />
        <add name="SqlDataProvider"
        type="DotNetNuke.Data.SqlDataProvider, DotNetNuke.SqlDataProvider"
        connectionStringName="SiteSqlServer"
        upgradeConnectionString=""
        providerPath="~\Providers\DataProviders\SqlDataProvider\"
        objectQualifier=""
        databaseOwner="dbo" />
    </providers>
</data>
```

The Provider Model has brought great value to DotNetNuke in the way that it allows for functionality to be replaced without modifying the core code. In DotNetNuke, like most open-source applications, the core code should not be modified by its consumers if at all possible. The Provider Model helps to enforce this fundamental standard of open-source application development. It also provides a new level of abstraction between the data access layer and the data store.

Custom Business Objects

Custom Business Objects (CBOs) are essentially a blueprint, or representation, of an object that is important to the application. In DotNetNuke, an example of a CBO is an instance of the DotNetNuke.Services.FileSystem.FileInfo class found in /components/FileSystem/FileInfo.vb. An instance of this class contains information about a single file, as shown in Listing 7-2.

Listing 7-2: The FileInfo CBO Class

```
<XmlRoot("file", IsNullable:=False)> Public Class FileInfo
    Private _FileId As Integer
    Private _PortalId As Integer
    Private _FileName As String
    Private _Extension As String
    Private _Size As Integer
    Private _Width As Integer
    Private _Height As Integer
    Private _ContentType As String
    Private _Folder As String

    <XmlIgnore()> Public Property FileId() As Integer
        Get
            Return _FileId
        End Get
        Set(ByVal Value As Integer)
            _FileId = Value
        End Set
    End Property
    <XmlIgnore()> Public Property PortalId() As Integer
        Get
            Return _PortalId
        End Get
        Set(ByVal Value As Integer)
            _PortalId = Value
        End Set
    End Property
    <XmlElement("filename")> Public Property FileName() As String
        Get
            Return _FileName
        End Get
        Set(ByVal Value As String)
            _FileName = Value
        End Set
    End Property
    <XmlElement("extension")> Public Property Extension() As String
        Get
            Return _Extension
        End Get
        Set(ByVal Value As String)
            _Extension = Value
        End Set
    End Property
    <XmlElement("size")> Public Property Size() As Integer
        Get
            Return _Size
        End Get
        Set(ByVal Value As Integer)
            _Size = Value
        End Set
    End Property
    <XmlElement("width")> Public Property Width() As Integer
```

```
        Get
            Return _Width
        End Get
        Set(ByVal Value As Integer)
            _Width = Value
        End Set
    End Property
    <XmlElement("height")> Public Property Height() As Integer
        Get
            Return _Height
        End Get
        Set(ByVal Value As Integer)
            _Height = Value
        End Set
    End Property
    <XmlElement("contenttype")> Public Property ContentType() As String
        Get
            Return _ContentType
        End Get
        Set(ByVal Value As String)
            _ContentType = Value
        End Set
    End Property
    <XmlElement("folder")> Public Property Folder() As String
        Get
            Return _Folder
        End Get
        Set(ByVal Value As String)
            _Folder = Value
        End Set
    End Property
End Class
```

The FileInfo class has no methods, only properties. This is an important distinction to recognize —
CBOs only have properties. The methods to manage the CBO are in a CBO Controller class specific to
the CBO. A *CBO Controller* class contains the business logic necessary to work with its associated CBO
class. For instance, there is a FileController class found in /components/FileSystem/FileController.vb
that contains business logic for the FileInfo CBO. For the sake of the core File Manager module, the
FileInfo data is stored in the database. Therefore, the FileController class contains the logic necessary to
hydrate the FileInfo object (or a collection of FileInfo objects) with data retrieved from the database.

CBO Hydrator

One very powerful core service is the CBO Hydrator, which can be found in the CBO class in
/components/Shared/CBO.vb. The *CBO Hydrator* is a collection of methods that provide a centralized
means of hydrating a CBO or a collection of CBOs.

Figure 7-2 shows how a CBO Controller class makes a call to the CBO Hydrator by sending in an open
DataReader and the type of object to fill. Depending on the method called within the CBO Hydrator, it
will return either a single hydrated object or a collection of hydrated objects. When the CBO Hydrator

fills an object's properties, it discovers the properties of the CBO using reflection. Then it caches the properties that it has discovered so the next time an object of the same type is hydrated, the properties will not need to be discovered. Instead, they will be pulled from the cache.

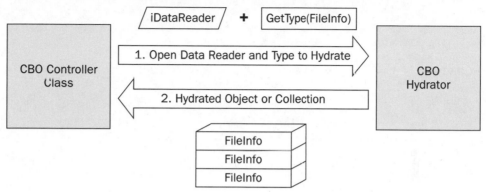

Figure 7-2

To hydrate a collection of CBOs, use the `DotNetNuke.Common.Utilities.CBO.FillCollection` method. The method accepts an IDataReader and a type as input parameters. It returns an ArrayList of objects of the type specified in the `objType` parameter. For example, the code-behind for the Portals module ($AppRoot/admin/Portal/Portals.ascx.vb) needs a collection of `PortalInfo` objects so it can display a list of Portals in the portal module's rendered output. The code-behind calls `DotNetNuke.Entities.Portals.PortalController.GetPortals()` to get an ArrayList of `PortalInfo` objects. That ArrayList is filled by the `DotNetNuke.Common.Utilities.CBO.FillCollection` method, which converts an `iDataReader` object (from a database query) into a collection of hydrated `PortalInfo` objects. The `DotNetNuke.Common.Utilities.CBO.FillCollection` method signature is as follows:

```
Public Shared Function FillCollection(ByVal dr As IDataReader, ByVal objType As _
Type) As ArrayList
```

To hydrate a single CBO rather than a collection, use the `CBO.FillObject` method. This method accepts the same input parameters, but returns a single object. For example, in the code-behind for the Site Settings module ($AppRoot/Admin/Portal/SiteSettings.ascx.vb) needs a `PortalInfo` object to display the portal settings in the module's rendered output. The code-behind gets the `PortalInfo` object from a call to `DotNetNuke.Entities.Portals.PortalController.GetPortal`. The `GetPortal` method uses the `DotNetNuke.Common.Utilities.CBO.FillObject` method to convert an `iDataReader` object (from a database query) into a hydrated `PortalInfo` object. The method signature for `DotNetNuke.Common.Utilities.CBO.FillObject` is as follows:

```
Public Shared Function FillObject(ByVal dr As IDataReader, ByVal _
objType As Type) As Object
```

The FileController shown in Listing 7-3 is an example of a CBO Controller that utilizes the CBO Hydrator.

Listing 7-3: The FileController CBO Controller Class

```
Public Class FolderController
    Public Function GetFoldersByPortal(ByVal PortalID As Integer) As ArrayList
        Return _
        CBO.FillCollection(DataProvider.Instance().GetFoldersByPortal(PortalID), _
        GetType(Services.FileSystem.FolderInfo))
    End Function
    Public Function GetFolder(ByVal PortalID As Integer, ByVal FolderPath As _
    String) As FolderInfo
        Return CType(CBO.FillObject(DataProvider.Instance().GetFolder(PortalID, _
        FolderPath), GetType(Services.FileSystem.FolderInfo)), FolderInfo)
    End Function
    Public Function GetFolder(ByVal PortalID As Integer, ByVal FolderID As Integer)
    As ArrayList
        Return CBO.FillCollection(DataProvider.Instance().GetFolder(PortalID, _
        FolderID), GetType(Services.FileSystem.FolderInfo))
    End Function
    Public Function AddFolder(ByVal objFolderInfo As FolderInfo) As Integer
        Return DataProvider.Instance().AddFolder(objFolderInfo.PortalID, _
        objFolderInfo.FolderPath)
    End Function
    Public Sub UpdateFolder(ByVal objFolderInfo As FolderInfo)
        DataProvider.Instance().UpdateFolder(objFolderInfo.PortalID, _
        objFolderInfo.FolderID, objFolderInfo.FolderPath)
    End Sub
    Public Sub DeleteFolder(ByVal PortalID As Integer, ByVal FolderPath As String)
        DataProvider.Instance().DeleteFolder(PortalID, FolderPath)
    End Sub
End Class
```

Using the CBO Hydrator significantly reduces the amount of code needed to fill an object or collection of objects. Without using the CBO Hydrator, you would have to code at least one line per CBO property in order to fill that object with the contents of a DataReader as shown in Listing 7-4. This is an example of filling a single FileInfo object without using the CBO Hydrator.

Listing 7-4: Traditional Method of Filling an Object

```
Dim dr As IDataReader
Try
    dr = DataProvider.Instance().GetFolder(PortalID, FolderPath)
    Dim f As New FileInfo
    f.ContentType = Convert.ToString(dr("ContentType"))
    f.Extension = Convert.ToString(dr("Extension"))
    f.FileId = Convert.ToInt32(dr("FileId"))
    f.FilcName = Convert.ToString(dr("FileName"))
    f.Folder = Convert.ToString(dr("Folder"))
    f.Height = Convert.ToInt32(dr("Height"))
    f.PortalId = Convert.ToInt32(dr("PortalId"))
    f.Size = Convert.ToInt32(dr("Size"))
    f.Width = Convert.ToInt32(dr("Width"))
    Return f
```

```
Finally
    If Not dr Is Nothing Then
        dr.Close()
    End If
End Try
```

Instead of writing all of that code, the CBO Hydrator can be used to greatly simplify things. The code snippet in Listing 7-5 does the same thing as the code in Listing 7-4, only it uses the CBO Hydrator.

Listing 7-5: Filling an Object Using the CBO Hydrator

```
Return CType(CBO.FillObject(DataProvider.Instance().GetFolder(PortalID, _
        FolderPath), GetType(Services.FileSystem.FolderInfo)), FolderInfo)
```

This section covered how Custom Business Objects are used throughout DotNetNuke to create a truly object-oriented design. The objects provide for type safety and enhance performance by allowing code to work with disconnected collections rather than with DataReaders, DataTables, or DataSets. Use the CBO Hydrator whenever possible to reduce the amount of coding and to enhance the maintainability of the application.

Architectural Overview

The DotNetNuke architecture permits the application tiers to be distributed across two servers: the web server and the database server, as shown in Figure 7-3. The web server contains the presentation, business logic, and data access layers. The database server contains the data layer.

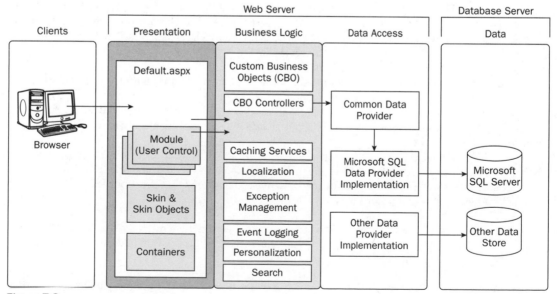

Figure 7-3

195

Presentation Layer

The presentation layer provides an interface for clients to access the portal application. This layer consists of the following elements:

❑ **Web Forms:** The primary web form is the Default.aspx. This page is the entry point to the portal. It is responsible for loading the other elements of the presentation layer. You can find Default.aspx in the root installation directory.

❑ **Skins:** The Default.aspx web form loads the skin for the page based on the settings for each page or portal. You can find the base Skin class in /admin/Skins/Skin.vb.

❑ **Containers:** The Default.aspx web form also loads the containers for the modules based on the settings for each module, page, and portal. You can find the base Container class in /admin/Containers/Container.vb.

❑ **Module User Controls:** Modules will have at least a single user control that is the user interface for the module. These user controls are loaded by Default.aspx and embedded within the containers and skin. You can find the module user controls in .ascx files in /DesktopModules/[module name].

❑ **Client-Side Scripts:** Several client-side JavaScript files are used by the core user-interface framework. For instance, the /DotNetNuke/controls/SolpartMenu/spmenu.js script file is used by the SolPartMenu control. Custom modules can include and reference JavaScript files as well. You can find client-side JavaScript files that are used by the core in the /js folder. Some skins may use client-side JavaScript and in this case you would find the scripts in the skin's installation directory. Any client-side scripts used by modules are located under the module's installation directory.

Rendering the Presentation

When visiting a DotNetNuke portal, the web form that loads the portal page is Default.aspx. The code-behind for this page ($AppRoot/Default.aspx.vb) loads the selected skin for the active page. The Skin is a user control that must inherit from the base class DotNetNuke.UI.Skins.Skin. The Skin class is where most of the action happens for the presentation layer.

First, the Skin class iterates through all of the modules that are associated with the portal page. Each module has a container assigned to it; the container is a visual boundary that separates one module from another. The container can be assigned to affect all modules within the entire portal, all modules within a specific page, or a single module. The Skin class loads the module's container and injects the module control into the container.

Next, the Skin class determines whether the module implements the DotNetNuke.Entities.Modules .iActionable interface. If it does, the Skin class discovers the actions that the module has defined and adds them to the container accordingly.

Next, the Skin class adds references to the module's style sheets to the rendered page. It looks for a file named module.css in the specific module's installation directory. If it exists, it adds an HtmlGenericControl to the page to reference the style sheet for the module.

All of this happens within the Skin class in the Init event as shown in Figure 7-4. The final rendering of the contents of a module is handled within each module's event life cycle.

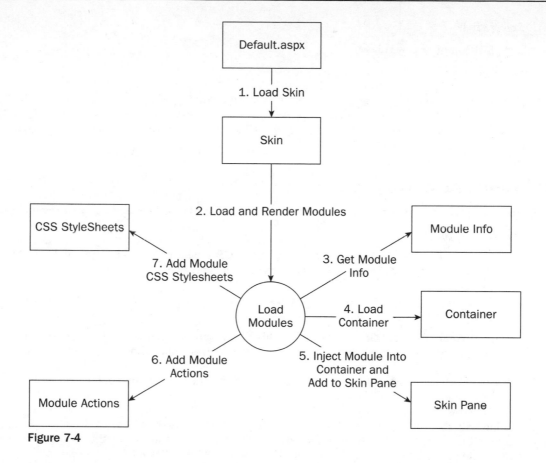

Figure 7-4

Finally, the code-behind ($AppRoot/Default.aspx.vb) renders the appropriate cascading style sheet links based on the configuration of the portal and its skin. See Chapter 13 for more details on style sheets and the order they are loaded in.

Business Logic Layer

The business logic layer provides the business logic for all core portal activity. This layer exposes many services to core and third-party modules. These services include

- ❑ Localization
- ❑ Caching
- ❑ Exception Management
- ❑ Event Logging
- ❑ Personalization

❑ Search

❑ Installation & Upgrades

❑ Security

The business logic layer is also home to *custom business objects* that represent most entities that collectively make up the portal. Custom business objects are discussed in more detail later in this chapter. For now it is important to understand that the fundamental purpose of custom business objects is to store information about an object.

Data Access Layer

The data access layer provides data services to the business logic layer. This layer allows for data to flow to and from a data store.

As described earlier in this chapter, the data access layer uses the Provider Model to allow DotNetNuke to support a wide array of data stores. The data access layer consists of two elements:

❑ **Data Provider API:** This is an abstract base class that establishes the contract that the implementation of the API must fulfill.

❑ **Implementation of Data Provider API:** This class inherits from the Data Provider API class and fulfills the contract by overriding the necessary members and methods.

The core DotNetNuke release provides a Microsoft SQL Server implementation of the Data Provider API.

Beginning with the CBO Controller class, the following code snippets show how the Data Provider API works with the Implementation of the Data Provider API. Listing 7-6 shows how the IDataReader that is sent into CBO.FillObject is a call to DataProvider.Instance().GetFolder(PortalID, FolderPath).

Listing 7-6: The FolderController.GetFolder Method

```
Public Function GetFolder(ByVal PortalID As Integer, ByVal FolderPath As String) As
FolderInfo
    Return CType(CBO.FillObject(DataProvider.Instance().GetFolder(PortalID, _
    FolderPath), GetType(Services.FileSystem.FolderInfo)), FolderInfo)
End Function
```

Figure 7-5 breaks down each of the elements in this method call.

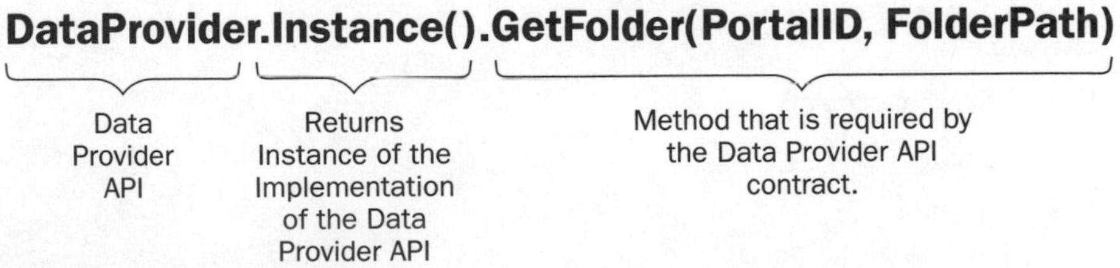

DataProvider.Instance().GetFolder(PortalID, FolderPath)

| Data Provider API | Returns Instance of the Implementation of the Data Provider API | Method that is required by the Data Provider API contract. |

Figure 7-5

The Instance() method is returning an instance of the implementation of the Data Provider API, and is therefore executing the method in the provider itself. The GetFolder method called in Listing 7-6 is an abstract method that is detailed in Listing 7-7.

Listing 7-7: The DataProvider.GetFolder Abstract Method

```
Public MustOverride Function GetFolder(ByVal PortalID As Integer, _
ByVal FolderPath As String) As IDataReader
```

This abstract method is part of the contract between the API and the implementation of the API. It is overridden in the implementation of the API as shown in Listing 7-8.

Listing 7-8: The SQLDataProvider.GetFolder Method

```
Public Overloads Overrides Function GetFolder(ByVal PortalID As Integer, ByVal _
FolderPath As String) As IDataReader
    Return CType(SqlHelper.ExecuteReader(ConnectionString, DatabaseOwner & _
    ObjectQualifier & "GetFolders", GetNull(PortalID), -1, FolderPath), _
    IDataReader)
End Function
```

Microsoft Data Access Application Block

Listing 7-8 shows a reference to the SqlHelper class. This class is part of the Microsoft Data Access Application Block. DotNetNuke uses the Data Access Application Block to improve performance and reduce the amount of custom code required for data access. The Data Access Application Block is a .NET component that works with ADO.NET to call stored procedures and execute SQL commands on Microsoft SQL Server.

Data Layer

The data layer provides data to the data access layer. The data store used in the data layer must be supported by the implementation of the Data Provider API to fulfill the data requests.

Because the DotNetNuke Data Provider model is so extensible, several Data Providers are available. These include both core-released Data Providers and providers released by third-party developers including Microsoft SQL Server, Microsoft Access, mySQL, and Oracle providers. The core DotNetNuke release provides a Microsoft SQL Server implementation of the Data Provider API.

Installation Scripts

Along with the implementation of the API is a collection of scripts that create the database in the data layer during the installation process. These scripts collectively create the database tables, stored procedures, and data necessary to run DotNetNuke. The installation scripts are run only during a new installation and are run from the DotNetNuke.Services.Upgrade.Upgrade.InstallDNN method. Following are the scripts:

- ❑ **DotNetNuke.SetUp.SqlDataProvider:** This script prepares the database for the installation by dropping some key tables.

- ❑ **DotNetNuke.Schema.SqlDataProvider:** This script installs the tables and stored procedures.

- ❑ **DotNetNuke.Data.SqlDataProvider:** This script fills the tables with data.

Upgrade Scripts

For subsequent upgrades performed after the initial installation, a collection of scripts are run that modify the schema or data during the upgrade process. These scripts are run from the DotNetNuke.Services .Upgrade.Upgrade.UpgradeDNN method. There is one script per baseline version of DotNetNuke. A baseline version is a working version of DotNetNuke that represents some internal milestone. For instance, after the core team integrates a major new feature, such as the Member Role provider, the code is tested, compiled, and zipped up for distribution among the core team. This doesn't necessarily mean there is one script per released version of DotNetNuke because behind the scenes we may have several baseline versions before a formal public release.

The file naming convention includes the version of the script followed by the "SqlDataProvider" extension. The extension must be the same name as found in the DefaultProvider attribute of the Data Provider's configuration settings in the web.config file. For example, the filename for the upgrade script for upgrading from baseline version 3.0.11 to 3.0.12 is 03.00.12.SqlDataProvider.

When the DotNetNuke application is upgraded to another version, these scripts will be executed in logical order according to the version number. Only the scripts with a version number that is less than or equal to the value of the constant DotNetNuke.Common.Globals.glbAppVersion will be run. This constant is defined in the /components/Shared/Globals.vb file.

Script Syntax

These scripts are written in SQL; however, two non-SQL tags are used in the scripts that are important to understand. These tags are {databaseOwner} and {objectQualifier}. Both of these tags represent a programmatically replaceable element of the script. Earlier in this chapter, Listing 7-1 showed that the configuration settings for the Microsoft SQL Server Data Provider implementation include two XML attributes named databaseOwner and objectQualifier. The databaseOwner attribute defines the database owner to append to data objects in the scripts. The objectQualifier attribute defines a string to prefix the data objects within the scripts.

As an example, take a look at how we create the GetSearchSettings stored procedure in the 03.00.04.SqlDataProvider script (see Listing 7-9).

Listing 7-9: A SqlDataProvider Upgrade Script

```
CREATE PROCEDURE {databaseOwner}{objectQualifier}GetSearchSettings
    @ModuleID int
AS
SELECT    tm.ModuleID,
          settings.SettingName,
          settings.SettingValue
FROM      {objectQualifier}Tabs searchTabs INNER JOIN
          {objectQualifier}TabModules searchTabModules
                ON searchTabs.TabID = searchTabModules.TabID INNER JOIN
          {objectQualifier}Portals p
                ON searchTabs.PortalID = p.PortalID INNER JOIN
          {objectQualifier}Tabs t
                ON p.PortalID = t.PortalID INNER JOIN
          {objectQualifier}TabModules tm
                ON t.TabID = tm.TabID INNER JOIN
```

```
              {objectQualifier}ModuleSettings settings
                     ON searchTabModules.ModuleID = settings.ModuleID
      WHERE   searchTabs.TabName = N'Search Admin'
      AND     tm.ModuleID = @ModuleID
      GO
```

In Listing 7-9, the code looks like SQL with the addition of these two non-SQL tags. The first line, shown below, will create a new stored procedure. It will be created in the context of the databaseOwner defined in web.config and the name of the stored procedure will be prefixed with the objectQualifier value from wcb.config.

```
CREATE PROCEDURE {databaseOwner}{objectQualifier}GetSearchSettings
```

If in the web.config settings the databaseOwner is set to "dbo" and the objectQualifier is set to "DNN," the preceding line would be programmatically converted to

```
CREATE PROCEDURE dbo.DNN_GetSearchSettings
```

The objectQualifier attribute is useful when you want to maintain multiple instances of DotNetNuke in the same database. For instance, you could have a single web server with 10 DotNetNuke installations on it, each using the same database. But you wouldn't want these 10 installations using the same data tables. The objectQualifier adds the flexibility for you to store data from multiple DotNetNuke installations in the same database.

Security Model

Until DotNetNuke 3.0, the portal only offered a single security solution; the forms-based security that was included with the core release. The forms-based security worked well, but it limited the ability to implement DotNetNuke in way that tightly integrates with other security mechanisms. Although Windows authentication was never supported by the core, enhancements by third-party developers are available that allow Windows authentication to be used in versions prior to DotNetNuke 3.0.

Before diving into the details of how the Membership/Roles API works in DotNetNuke 3.0, it is important to understand how security works in ASP.NET 2.0. This will help you understand the challenges we faced in implementing the API, which will help you understand the finer details of how security works in DotNetNuke today.

Security in ASP.NET 2.0

In ASP.NET 1.x, the native authentication and authorization services relied on external data stores or configuration in the web.config file. For example, in ASP.NET 1.1 an application can provide forms-based authentication. This requires the developer to create a login form and associated controls to acquire, validate, and manage user credentials. Once authenticated, authorization was provided through XML configurations in the web.config file.

In ASP.NET 2.0, the introduction of several new security enhancements expands on these services in three distinct ways:

❑ **Login & User Controls:** A new suite of login and user controls provide plenty of functionality out of the box, which reduces the need for each application to provide its own login and user controls. For instance, it is easy to generate a set of pages for registering a new user, allowing an existing user to log in, and even handle forgotten passwords by simply placing the appropriate controls on a page and setting a few properties.

❑ **User Management:** ASP.NET 2.0 provides a new configuration interface for each application that allows for easy management of that application. One feature of the configuration interface is the ability to manage security for the application. For instance, you can easily create a new user and a new role, and then add the user to the role all within the ASP.NET 2.0 native configuration interface. As an alternative to the configuration interface, security can be managed by writing a custom management tool to access the same functionality programmatically.

❑ **Membership/Roles Provider:** This new provider is the conduit between the presentation layer (specifically the login/user controls and the configuration interface) and the persistence mechanism. It encapsulates all of the data access code required to manage users and roles.

Together these three components reduce the amount of code that is required to provide authentication and authorization services and persist the data to a data store.

DotNetNuke and ASP.NET 2.0

To build an application that fully supports authentication and authorization in ASP.NET 2.0, the Membership/Roles provider should be integrated into the application. Several benefits exist to using this provider in an application. First, it can reduce the amount of code that is written to bring these services to the application. This is true as long as the business requirements fall within the functionality that the default Membership/Roles provider provides. Second, implementing the Membership/Roles provider can allow other applications to share user and role information with the application. With regard to security, this provides seamless integration between diverse applications.

Because ASP.NET 2.0 was not released at the time of the DotNetNuke 3.0 development cycle, we leveraged a backported version of the Membership/Roles provider created by Microsoft. This backported version conforms to the same API as is found in ASP.NET 2.0, except it will run in ASP.NET 1.1. This has been a great addition to DotNetNuke for many reasons, but one key benefit is that it allows DotNetNuke to conform to several ASP.NET 2.0 specifications even before ASP.NET 2.0 is released.

Security in DotNetNuke 3.0

Security in DotNetNuke 3.0 has been implemented with quite a bit of forward thinking. We have combined the best features of prior versions of DotNetNuke with the features of the ASP.NET 2.0 Membership/Roles Provider. The result is a very extensible security model that aligns DotNetNuke closely with best practice security models that will be in ASP.NET 2.0.

Portals and Applications

DotNetNuke supports running many portals from a single DotNetNuke installation. Each portal has its own users and roles that are not shared with any other portals. A portal is identified by a unique key, the PortalID.

Because the default Membership/Role Provider implementation is a generic solution, it does not natively support the concept of having multiple portals, each with their own users and roles. The default Membership/Role Provider implementation was designed in a way that only supports a single portal site in a DotNetNuke installation. The Membership/Role Provider refers to the DotNetNuke installation as an "application," and without customization that application can only support a single set of users and roles (a single portal instance).

To overcome this limitation, a wrapper was needed for the SQL data providers that were provided with the Membership/Role Providers. This customization allows us to support application virtualization. The end result is that the Membership/Role Providers, as implemented in DotNetNuke, can support multiple applications (multiple portal instances in a single DotNetNuke installation). We mapped PortalID in DotNetNuke to the ApplicationName in the Membership/Role Provider. When a call is made to the Membership/Role Provider, the ApplicationName is switched on-the-fly to match the PortalID of the portal instance.

The custom implementations of the SQL data providers for the Membership/Role Providers can be found in

- $AppRoot\Providers\MembershipProviders\CoreProvider\DataProviders\DNNSQL MembershipProvider

- $AppRoot\Providers\ProfileProviders\CoreProvider\DataProviders\DNNSQLProfileProvider

- $AppRoot\Providers\RoleProviders\CoreProvider\DataProviders\DNNSQLRoleProvider

Data Model for Users and Roles

In order to achieve the full benefit from the Membership/Roles Provider, it is important to recognize that User and Role information can be externalized from DotNetNuke and stored in a data store that is independent of the main data store. For instance, DotNetNuke may use Microsoft SQL Server as its database to store content and system settings, but the Membership/Roles Provider may use Windows authentication, LDAP, or another mechanism to handle authentication and authorization. Because security can be externalized using the Provider Model, it was important to ensure that the implementation of the Membership/Roles Provider didn't customize any code or database tables used by the provider. The data tables used by the provider had to be independent from the other core DotNetNuke tables. We could not enforce referential integrity between DotNetNuke data and the Membership/Roles Provider data, nor could we use cascade deletes or other data-level synchronization methods. In a nutshell, all of the magic had to happen in the business layer.

One challenge we faced in implementing the Membership/Roles Provider was dealing with the fields that DotNetNuke currently supports but the Membership/Roles Provider does not support. Ideally, we would have completely replaced the DotNetNuke authentication/authorization-related tables with the tables used by the Membership/Roles Provider. We could not achieve this goal because the authentication/authorization tables in DotNetNuke were already tied to so many existing and necessary features of the application. For instance, the DotNetNuke "Users" table has a column named "UserID," which is a unique identifier for a user. This UserID is used in nearly all core and third-party modules as well as the core. The most significant problem with UserID was that it doesn't exist in the Membership/Roles Provider. Instead, the Membership/Roles Provider uses the username as the unique key for a user within an application. The challenge was that we needed a way to maintain the UserID to preserve the DotNetNuke functionality that depended on it. This is just one example of an attribute that cannot be handled by the default Membership/Roles Provider provided by Microsoft.

Ultimately, we decided that we would need to maintain satellite tables to support the DotNetNuke attributes that could not be managed by the Membership/Roles Provider. The goal was to maintain enough information in the DotNetNuke tables so that functionality was not lost, and offload whatever data we can to the Membership/Roles Provider tables. The end result is a data model that mirrors the Membership/Roles Provider data tables, as shown in Figure 7-6.

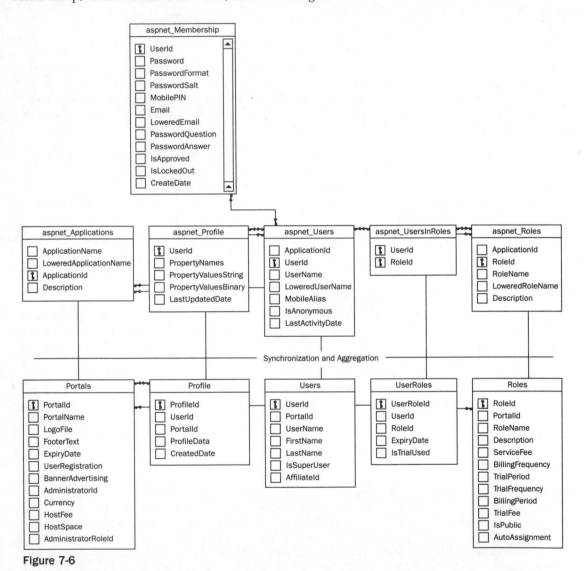

Figure 7-6

Note in Figure 7-6 that none of the tables on top have database relationships to the any of the tables on the bottom. The lines connecting them simply show their relationship in theory, not an actual relationship in the database.

Because the data for portals, profiles, users, and roles is stored in multiple unrelated tables, the business layer is responsible for aggregating the data. For instance, you cannot get a complete representation of a user without collecting data from both the aspnet_Users table (from the Membership/Roles Provider) and the Users table (native DotNetNuke table). Therefore, the business layer is responsible for combining the data from both data structures.

In addition to aggregation, synchronization must also be done to automatically synchronize data between the tables used by the Membership/Roles Provider and the native DotNetNuke tables. Earlier in this chapter you learned that the Membership/Roles Provider supports a wide array of data stores, and in ASP.NET 2.0 the data in those data stores can be managed through a common application configuration utility. If a user is added through this common application configuration utility, the user will not be added to the native DotNetNuke tables. Also, if your Membership/Roles Provider uses an LDAP implementation, for instance, a user could be added to LDAP and the user would not be added to the native DotNetNuke tables. It is for this reason that we need to provide synchronization services between the two data structures.

In DotNetNuke 3.0, the introduction of the Membership/Roles API has brought extensibility to the security framework. We have purposely positioned DotNetNuke 3.0 to implement several ASP.NET 2.0 features so we can convert to ASP.NET 2.0 more quickly and easily. This also provides a great opportunity to learn about some new features found in ASP.NET 2.0 early on.

Namespace Overview

Prior to DotNetNuke 3.0 the namespace overview would have been fairly concise, considering nearly all classes fell under the root DotNetNuke namespace. In DotNetNuke 3.0, we brought structure to the namespace hierarchy by completely reorganizing the namespaces and class locations. Figure 7-7 shows the second-level namespaces that fall under the root "DotNetNuke" namespace, and the list that follows explains each one.

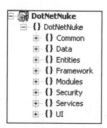

Figure 7-7

❑ **DotNetNuke.Common:** This namespace is used for all classes that are used throughout the entire DotNetNuke application. For example, the global constants that are used throughout the application are found in the DotNetNuke.Common.Globals class.

❑ **DotNetNuke.Data:** This namespace is used for any classes relating to the data access layer. For example, the DataProvider base class for the Data Provider API is in the DotNetNuke.Data namespace.

❑ **DotNetNuke.Entities:** This namespace is used for the classes that represent and manage the five entities that make a portal. They are Host, Portals, Tabs, Users, and Modules. Note that the Modules namespace that falls under DotNetNuke.Entities is home to the functionality behind managing modules. The actual modules themselves have their own second-level namespace defined below (DotNetNuke.Modules).

❑ **DotNetNuke.Framework:** This namespace is home to several base classes and other utilities used by the DotNetNuke application.

❑ **DotNetNuke.Modules:** This namespace is used for organizing portal modules. There is a child namespace in the core named DotNetNuke.Modules.Admin, which is where the classes for all of the core admin modules reside. For instance, the Host Settings module is found in the DotNetNuke.Modules.Admin.Host.HostSettingsModule class.

❑ **DotNetNuke.Security:** This namespace is used for authorization and authentication classes. This includes tab permissions, module permissions, folder permissions, roles, and other portal security classes.

❑ **DotNetNuke.Services:** This namespace is used for any services the core provides for modules. In this namespace the child namespaces for exception management, localization, personalization, search, and several others reside.

❑ **DotNetNuke.UI:** This namespace is used for any user interface classes. For example, the Skin and Container classes are found in DotNetNuke.UI.Skins.Skin and DotNetNuke.UI.Containers .Container, respectively.

Summary

This chapter covered the architecture of the DotNetNuke application. Here are key points to understand about the architecture:

❑ The Provider Model design pattern has enhanced DotNetNuke with greater extensibility without having to make core changes to realize that extensibility.

❑ The use of Custom Business Objects along with the CBO Hydrator has created a foundation for developers to code using best practice standards that allow them to build more maintainable modules and providers that perform well.

❑ The n-tier architecture of the DotNetNuke application provides exceptional layer abstraction and better application maintainability.

❑ The Membership/Role Provider in DotNetNuke has created a very extensible security model that showcases an API that mirrors the API found in ASP.NET 2.0.

❑ The namespace model is organized in a logical hierarchy, making it easy to find the classes used most often.

The next chapter covers the DotNetNuke API to familiarize you with many of the powerful services the DotNetNuke core application provides developers.

8

Core DotNetNuke APIs

Introduction

DotNetNuke provides significant capability straight out of the box. Just install and go. Sometimes, however, you may need to extend the base framework. DotNetNuke provides a variety of integration points: from HTTP Modules to providers to custom modules. In order to fully take advantage of the framework, it is important to understand some of the base services and APIs provided by DotNetNuke.

This chapter examines some of the core services provided by DotNetNuke. These services can be used from within your own code. Since most of the core services are built using the Provider design pattern, it is also possible to swap out the base functionality. If you need your events logged to a custom database or the Windows Event Logs, then just create your own provider.

The second part of this chapter covers several HTTP Modules that are installed with DotNetNuke. These modules provide features like Friendly URLs, Exception Management, and Users Online. Many of the providers installed with DotNetNuke use HTTP Modules to hook into the request processing pipeline. By examining the code used in the core HTTP Modules, you can build your own custom extensions that can be used in DotNetNuke as well as other ASP.NET applications.

The final section examines some of the core interfaces that you can implement in your own modules. These interfaces simplify the process of adding common features to your module, whether it is the module menu, searches, importing and exporting, or even custom upgrade logic. All of these services can be implemented using core interfaces. By using these interfaces in your modules you can provide some of the same features you see in the core DotNetNuke modules with very little coding effort.

Event Logging

The Logging Provider in DotNetNuke provides a very configurable and extensible set of logging services. It is designed to handle a wide array of logging needs including exception logging, event auditing, and security logging. As you may have gathered from its name, the Logging Provider uses the Provider model design pattern. This allows the default XML Logging Provider to be replaced with another logging mechanism without having to make changes to the core code. This section covers the ways you can use the Logging Provider to log events in custom modules.

Before we dive into the details of how to use the Logging Provider API, it is important to understand some concepts and terminology that will be used in this section:

❑ **Log Classification:** There are two different types of log classifications in the Logging Provider. The first is the *event log* classification. This encapsulates all log entries related to some type of event within DotNetNuke. For example, you can configure the Logging Provider to write a log entry when a login attempt fails. This would be considered an event log entry. The second log classification is the *exception* log classification. You can configure the Logging Provider to log exceptions and stack traces when exceptions are thrown within DotNetNuke. These two classifications are distinct only because they have different needs in terms of what type of information they log.

❑ **Log Type:** A *log type* defines the type of event that creates the log entry. For example, an event log type is LOGIN_FAILURE. The Logging Provider can react differently for each log type. You can configure the Logging Provider to enable or disable logging for each of the log types. In the default XML Logging Provider, you can also configure it to log each log type to a different file and optionally send e-mail notifications upon creating new log entries for that log type.

❑ **Log Type Configuration:** The Logging Provider is configured via a module that is accessible from the Log Viewer screen (the Edit Log Configuration module action). This allows you to configure each log type to be handled differently by the Logging Provider.

The API

The Logging Provider functionality lives in the DotNetNuke.Services.Log.EventLog namespace. In this namespace you will find the classes that comprise the Logging Provider API. These are listed in Table 8-1.

Table 8-1: Logging Provider Classes

Class	Description
EventLogController	This class inherits from LogController. It provides the methods necessary to write log entries with the event log classification.
ExceptionLogController	This class inherits from LogController. It provides the methods necessary to write log entries with the exception log classification.
LogController	This class provides the methods that interact with the Logging Provider. It provides the basic methods for adding, deleting, and getting log entries.
LogDetailInfo	This class holds a single key/value pair of information from a log entry.

Class	Description
LoggingProvider	This abstract class provides the bridge to the implementation of the Logging Provider.
LogInfo	This class is a container for the information that goes into a log entry.
LogInfoArray	This holds an array of LogInfo objects.
LogProperties	This holds an array of LogDetailInfo objects.
LogTypeConfigInfo	This class is a container for the configuration data relating to how logs of a specific log type are to be handled.
LogTypeInfo	This class is a container for the log type information.
PurgeLogBuffer	This is a Scheduler task that can be executed regularly if Log Buffering is enabled.
SendLogNotifications	This is a Scheduler task that can be executed regularly if any log type is configured to send e-mail notifications.

The two controller classes, EventLogController and ExceptionLogController, are the two that bring the most functionality to custom modules. Many of the other classes are used in concert with the controllers.

EventLogController

The EventLogController provides the methods necessary to log significant system events. This controller class also defines the EventLogType enumeration that lists each log type that is handled by the EventLogController. The enumerations are shown in Listing 8-1.

Listing 8-1: EventLogController.EventLogType Enumeration

```
Public Enum EventLogType
        USER_CREATED
        USER_DELETED
        LOGIN_SUPERUSER
        LOGIN_SUCCESS
        LOGIN_FAILURE
        CACHE_REFRESHED
        PASSWORD_SENT_SUCCESS
        PASSWORD_SENT_FAILURE
        LOG_NOTIFICATION_FAILURE
        PORTAL_CREATED
        PORTAL_DELETED
        TAB_CREATED
        TAB_UPDATED
        TAB_DELETED
        TAB_SENT_TO_RECYCLE_BIN
        TAB_RESTORED
        USER_ROLE_CREATED
```

(continued)

Listing 8-1: *(continued)*

```
              USER_ROLE_DELETED
              ROLE_CREATED
              ROLE_UPDATED
              ROLE_DELETED
              MODULE_CREATED
              MODULE_UPDATED
              MODULE_DELETED
              MODULE_SENT_TO_RECYCLE_BIN
              MODULE_RESTORED
              SCHEDULER_EVENT_STARTED
              SCHEDULER_EVENT_PROGRESSING
              SCHEDULER_EVENT_COMPLETED
              APPLICATION_START
              APPLICATION_END
              APPLICATION_SHUTTING_DOWN
              SCHEDULER_STARTED
              SCHEDULER_SHUTTING_DOWN
              SCHEDULER_STOPPED
              ADMIN_ALERT
              HOST_ALERT
      End Enum
```

The EventLogController.AddLog() method has several method overloads that allow a developer to log just about any values derived from an object or its properties. Each of the overloaded EventLogController.AddLog() methods are detailed below.

1. To log the property names and values of a Custom Business Object, use the following method:

```
Public Overloads Sub AddLog(ByVal objCBO As Object, ByVal _PortalSettings As _
  PortalSettings, ByVal UserID As Integer, ByVal UserName As String, ByVal _
  objLogType As Services.Log.EventLog.EventLogController.EventLogType)
```

Parameter	Type	Description
objCBO	Object	This is a Custom Business Object.
_PortalSettings	PortalSettings	This is the current PortalSettings object.
UserID	Integer	This is the UserID of the authenticated user of the request.
UserName	String	This is the UserName of the authenticated user of the request.
objLogType	EventLogType	This is the event log type.

2. To add a log entry that has no custom properties, use the following method. This is useful if you simply need to log that an event has occurred, but you have no requirement to log any further details about the event.

```
Public Overloads Sub AddLog(ByVal _PortalSettings As PortalSettings, ByVal UserID _
As Integer, ByVal objLogType As _
Services.Log.EventLog.EventLogController.EventLogType)
```

Parameter	Type	Description
_PortalSettings	PortalSettings	This is the current PortalSettings object.
UserID	Integer	This is the UserID of the authenticated user of the request.
objLogType	EventLogType	This is the event log type.

3. To add a log entry that has a single property name and value, use the following method.

```
Public Overloads Sub AddLog(ByVal PropertyName As String, ByVal PropertyValue As _
String, ByVal _PortalSettings As PortalSettings, ByVal UserID As Integer, ByVal _
objLogType As Services.Log.EventLog.EventLogController.EventLogType)
```

Parameter	Type	Description
PropertyName	String	This is the name of the property to log.
PropertyValue	String	This is the value of the property to log.
_PortalSettings	PortalSettings	This is the current PortalSettings object.
UserID	Integer	This is the UserID of the authenticated user of the request.
objLogType	EventLogType	This is the event log type.

4. To add a log entry that has a single property name and value and the LogType is not defined in a core enumeration, use the following method. This is useful for custom modules that define their own log types.

```
Public Overloads Sub AddLog(ByVal PropertyName As String, ByVal PropertyValue As _
String, ByVal _PortalSettings As PortalSettings, ByVal UserID As Integer, ByVal _
LogType As String)
```

Parameter	Type	Description
PropertyName	String	This is the name of the property to log.
PropertyValue	String	This is the value of the property to log.
_PortalSettings	PortalSettings	This is the current PortalSettings object.
UserID	Integer	This is the UserID of the authenticated user of the request.
LogType	String	This is the event log type string.

5. To add a log entry that has multiple property names and values, use the following method. To use this method you must send into it a LogProperties object that is comprised of a collection of LogDetailInfo objects.

```
Public Overloads Sub AddLog(ByVal objProperties As LogProperties, ByVal _
_PortalSettings As PortalSettings, ByVal UserID As Integer, ByVal LogTypeKey As _
String, ByVal BypassBuffering As Boolean)
```

Parameter	Type	Description
objProperties	LogProperties	This is a collection of LogDetailInfo objects.
_PortalSettings	PortalSettings	This is the current PortalSettings object.
UserID	Integer	This is the UserID of the authenticated user of the request.
LogTypeKey	String	This is the event log type.
BypassBuffering	Boolean	Specifies whether to write directly to the log (true) or to use log buffering (false) if log buffering is enabled.

Two of the most used overloaded methods for EventLogController.AddLog() are discussed in the following section. To exemplify the flexibility of this method, Listing 8-2 shows an example of how you can send in a Custom Business Object and automatically log its property values.

Listing 8-2: EventLogController.AddLog Example

```
Private Sub TestUserInfoLog()
    Dim objUserInfo As New UserInfo
    objUserInfo.FirstName = "John"
    objUserInfo.LastName = "Doe"
    objUserInfo.UserID = 6
    objUserInfo.Username = "jdoe"
    Dim objEventLog As New Services.Log.EventLog.EventLogController
    objEventLog.AddLog(objUserInfo, PortalSettings, UserID, UserInfo.Username, _
        Services.Log.EventLog.EventLogController.EventLogType.USER_CREATED)
End Sub
```

The resulting log entry written by the default XML Logging Provider for this example includes each property name and value in the objUserInfo object as shown in the <properties/> XML element in Listing 8-3.

Listing 8-3: EventLogController.AddLog Log Entry

```
<logs>
     <log LogGUID="92ca39e4-a135-475a-8c0c-7e4949c359b7" LogFileID="b86359bb-
e984-4483-891b-26a2b95bf9bd"
         LogTypeKey="USER_CREATED" LogUserID="-1" LogUserName="" LogPortalID="0"
LogPortalName="DotNetNuke"
         LogCreateDate="2005-02-04T14:33:46.9318672-05:00"
LogCreateDateNum="20050204143346931"
         LogServerName="DNNTEST">
         <properties>
             <property>
                 <name>UserID</name>
                 <value>6</value>
             </property>
             <property>
                 <name>FirstName</name>
                 <value>John</value>
             </property>
```

```
                <property>
                        <name>LastName</name>
                        <value>Doe</value>
                </property>
                <property>
                        <name>UserName</name>
                        <value>jdoe</value>
                </property>
            </properties>
        </log>
</logs>
```

This example logs each of the properties of a Custom Business Object. There are other overloaded EventLogController.AddLog() methods available if you need to log less information, or information that isn't stored in a Custom Business Object. The example in Listing 8-4 shows how you can use the EventLogController.AddLog() method to add a single key/value pair to the log.

Listing 8-4: EventLogController.AddLog Example

```
    Private Sub TestCreateRole()

        Dim objRoleController As New RoleController
        Dim objRoleInfo As New RoleInfo

        'create and add the new role
        objRoleInfo.RoleName = "Newsletter Subscribers"
        objRoleInfo.PortalID = 5
        objRoleController.AddRole(objRoleInfo)

        'log the event
        Dim objEventLog As New Services.Log.EventLog.EventLogController
        objEventLog.AddLog("Role", objRoleInfo.RoleName, PortalSettings, _
        UserId, objEventLog.EventLogType.USER_ROLE_CREATED)

    End Sub
```

In this case, the key Role and the value Newsletter Subscribers will be logged. The resulting log entry written by the default XML Logging Provider for this example is shown in the <properties/> XML element in Listing 8-5.

Listing 8-5: EventLogController.AddLog Log Entry

```
<logs>
      <log LogGUID="2145856a-1e4a-4974-86f6-da1f0ae5dcca" LogFileID="b86359bb-
e984-4483-891b-26a2b95bf9bd"
            LogTypeKey="ROLE_CREATED" LogUserID="1" LogUserName="host"
LogPortalID="0" LogPortalName="DotNetNuke"
            LogCreateDate="2005-02-04T22:00:22.0413424-05:00"
LogCreateDateNum="20050204220022041"
            LogServerName="DNNTEST">
            <properties>
                    <property>
                        <name>RoleName</name>
```

Listing 8-5: *(continued)*

```
                        <value>Newsletter Subscribers</value>
                </property>
        </properties>
    </log>
</logs>
```

ExceptionLogController

The ExceptionLogController exposes the methods necessary for adding information about exceptions to the log. This controller class also defines the ExceptionLogType enumeration. Some examples of ExceptionLogTypes defined in the enumeration are GENERAL_EXCEPTION, MODULE_LOAD_ EXCEPTION, and PAGE_LOAD_EXCEPTION. By defining different log types for exceptions, the configuration of the Logging Provider can treat each exception log type differently with regards to how and if the exceptions get logged.

We will cover exceptions in more detail in the next section. For now, we will focus on how to log the exceptions. The ExceptionLogController.AddLog() method has three overloaded methods that allow you to pass in various types of exceptions. The first method allows you to send in a System.Exception or any exception that inherits System.Exception, as shown in Listing 8-6.

Listing 8-6: ExceptionLogController.AddLog Example

```
Public Sub test()
    Try
        If 1 = 1 Then
            Throw New Exception("Oh no, an exception!")
        End If
    Catch exc As Exception
        Dim objExceptionLog As New Services.Log.EventLog.ExceptionLogController
        objExceptionLog.AddLog(exc)
        'a shortcut to this is simply "LogException(exc)"
    End Try
End Sub
```

In this case, the properties of the System.Exception will be logged along with a collection of properties that are specific to the request. For instance, it will log the filename, line, and column number the exception occurred in if it is available. The resulting log entry written by the default XML Logging Provider for this example is shown in Listing 8-7.

Listing 8-7: ExceptionLogController.AddLog Log Entry

```
<logs>
    <log LogGUID="39c72059-bcd1-42ca-8886-002363d1c9dc" LogFileID="6b780a60-
cf46-4588-8a76-75ae9c577277"
        LogTypeKey="GENERAL_EXCEPTION" LogUserID="-1" LogUserName=""
LogPortalID="-1" LogPortalName=""
        LogCreateDate="2005-02-04T23:25:44.6873456-05:00"
LogCreateDateNum="20050204232544687"
        LogServerName="DNNTEST">
        <properties>
            <property>
                <name>AssemblyVersion</name>
                <value>03.00.10</value>
```

```
        </property>
        <property>
                <name>Method</name>
                <value>DotNetNuke.Framework.CDefault.test</value>
        </property>
        <property>
                <name>FileName</name>
                <value>c:\public\dotnetnuke\Default.aspx.vb</value>
        </property>
        <property>
                <name>FileLineNumber</name>
                <value>481</value>
        </property>
        <property>
                <name>FileColumnNumber</name>
                <value>21</value>
        </property>
        <property>
                <name>PortalID</name>
                <value>0</value>
        </property>
        <property>
                <name>PortalName</name>
                <value>DotNetNuke</value>
        </property>
        <property>
                <name>UserID</name>
                <value>-1</value>
        </property>
        <property>
                <name>UserName</name>
                <value />
        </property>
        <property>
                <name>ActiveTabID</name>
                <value>36</value>
        </property>
        <property>
                <name>ActiveTabName</name>
                <value>Home</value>
        </property>
        <property>
                <name>AbsoluteURL</name>
                <value>/DotNetNuke/Default.aspx</value>
        </property>
        <property>
                <name>AbsoluteURLReferrer</name>
                <value />
        </property>
        <property>
                <name>ExceptionGUID</name>
                <value>128455d6-064a-4222-993f-b54fd302e21e</value>
        </property>
        <property>
                <name>DefaultDataProvider</name>
```

(continued)

Listing 8-7: *(continued)*

```
                        <value>DotNetNuke.Data.SqlDataProvider,
DotNetNuke.SqlDataProvider</value>
                </property>
                <property>
                        <name>InnerException</name>
                        <value>Oh no, an exception!</value>
                </property>
                <property>
                        <name>Message</name>
                        <value>Oh no, an exception!</value>
                </property>
                <property>
                        <name>StackTrace</name>
                        <value>   at DotNetNuke.Framework.CDefault.test() in
c:\public\dotnetnuke\Default.aspx.vb:line 481</value>
                </property>
                <property>
                        <name>Source</name>
                        <value>DotNetNuke</value>
                </property>
            </properties>
        </log>
    </logs>
```

Notice that Listing 8-7 does not tell you the portal module that the exception was thrown from. This is because a general exception was thrown (System.Exception). If a ModuleLoadException is thrown, more details about the portal module that throws the exception will be logged. The next section discusses more on the topic of handling exceptions properly in DotNetNuke.

Exception Handling

The exception handling API in DotNetNuke provides a framework for handling exceptions uniformly and gracefully. Exception handling is primarily handled through four methods, most of which have several overloaded methods. Through these four methods, developers can gracefully handle exceptions, log the exception trace and context, and display a user-friendly message to the end user.

The exception handling API lives under the DotNetNuke.Services.Exceptions namespace. Table 8-2 lists the classes that comprise the Exception Handling API.

Table 8-2: Exception Handling Classes

Class	Description
BasePortalException	This class inherits from System.Exception and contains many other properties specific to the portal application.
ErrorContainer	This class generates formatting for the error message that will be displayed in the web browser.

Class	Description
ExceptionInfo	This class stores information from the stack trace.
Exceptions	This class contains most of the methods that are used in custom modules. It contains the methods necessary to process each type of portal exception.
ModuleLoadException	This class inherits from BasePortalException. It is an exception type for exceptions thrown within portal modules.
PageLoadException	This class inherits from BasePortalException. It is an exception type for exceptions thrown within pages.
SchedulerException	This class inherits from BasePortalException. It is an exception type for exceptions thrown within the Scheduling Provider.

The Exceptions Class

Although there are many classes in the exception handling namespace, the primary class that module developers deal with regularly is the Exceptions class. This class contains all of the methods necessary to gracefully handle exceptions in DotNetNuke. The most widely used method for exception handling is DotNetNuke.Services.Exceptions.ProcessModuleLoadException().

ProcessModuleLoadException Method

The ProcessModuleLoadException method serves two primary functions. The first is to log the exceptions that are thrown from within a module to the Logging Provider. The second is to display a friendly error message in place of the module that threw the exception. Note the friendly error message will only be displayed if the host option Use Custom Error Messages is enabled on the Host Settings page (see Chapter 4).

This ProcessModuleLoadException method has seven overloaded methods:

1. To process an exception that occurs in a portal module, use the following method. If the Custom Error Messages option has been enabled in Host Settings, this method will also handle displaying a user-friendly error message to the client browser.

```
Public Sub ProcessModuleLoadException(ByVal ctrlModule As _
Entities.Modules.PortalModuleBase, ByVal exc As Exception)
```

Parameter	Type	Description
ctrlModule	PortalModuleBase	This is the portal module object.
Exc	Exception	This is the exception that was thrown.

2. This method is the same as the previous one, although it provides the ability to suppress the error message from being displayed on the client browser.

```
Public Sub ProcessModuleLoadException(ByVal ctrlModule As _
Entities.Modules.PortalModuleBase, ByVal exc As Exception, ByVal _
DisplayErrorMessage As Boolean)
```

Parameter	Type	Description
ctrlModule	PortalModuleBase	This is the portal module object.
Exc	Exception	This is the exception that was thrown.
DisplayErrorMessage	Boolean	This indicates whether the portal should render an error message to the client browser.

3. This is the same as the previous method; however, it adds the ability to provide a custom friendly message to the client browser.

```
Public Sub ProcessModuleLoadException(ByVal FriendlyMessage As String, ByVal _
ctrlModule As Entities.Modules.PortalModuleBase, ByVal exc As Exception, _
ByVal DisplayErrorMessage As Boolean)
```

Parameter	Type	Description
FriendlyMessage	String	This is a friendly message to display to the client browser.
ctrlModule	PortalModuleBase	This is the portal module object.
Exc	Exception	This is the exception that was thrown.
DisplayErrorMessage	Boolean	This indicates whether the portal should render an error message to the client browser.

4. Use this overloaded method if you are handling exceptions in a control that isn't directly in a portal module. For instance, if your portal module uses a server control, you can use this method to handle exceptions within that server control. It will display a friendly error message if custom error messages are enabled.

```
Public Sub ProcessModuleLoadException(ByVal FriendlyMessage As String, _
ByVal UserCtrl As Control, ByVal exc As Exception)
```

Parameter	Type	Description
FriendlyMessage	String	This is a friendly message to display to the client browser.
UserCtrl	Control	This is the control. It can be anything that inherits from System.Web.UI.Control.
Exc	Exception	This is the exception that was thrown.

5. This is the same as the previous method; however, it adds the ability to specify whether to display an error message to the client browser (the Host Settings option to Use Custom Error Messages takes precedence over this value).

```
Public Sub ProcessModuleLoadException(ByVal FriendlyMessage As String, _
ByVal ctrlModule As Control, ByVal exc As Exception, _
ByVal DisplayErrorMessage As Boolean)
```

Parameter	Type	Description
FriendlyMessage	String	This is a friendly message to display to the client browser.
ctrlModule	Control	This is the control. It can be anything that inherits from System.Web.UI.Control.
Exc	Exception	This is the exception that was thrown.
DisplayErrorMessage	Boolean	This indicates whether the portal should render an error message to the client browser.

6. This is a simple method that has only two parameters. It will display a generic error message to the client browser if custom error messages are enabled.

```
Public Sub ProcessModuleLoadException(ByVal UserCtrl As Control, _
ByVal exc As Exception)
```

Parameter	Type	Description
UserCtrl	Control	This is the control. It can be anything that inherits from System.Web.UI.Control.
Exc	Exception	This is the exception that was thrown.

7. This is the same as the previous method except it provides the ability to suppress the error message that is displayed in the client browser (the Host Settings option to Use Custom Error Messages takes precedence over this value).

```
Public Sub ProcessModuleLoadException(ByVal UserCtrl As Control, _
ByVal exc As Exception, ByVal DisplayErrorMessage As Boolean)
```

Parameter	Type	Description
UserCtrl	Control	This is the control. It can be anything that inherits from System.Web.UI.Control.
Exc	Exception	This is the exception that was thrown.
DisplayErrorMessage	Boolean	This indicates whether the portal should render an error message to the client browser.

ProcessPageLoadException Method

Similar to the ProcessModuleLoadException method, the ProcessPageLoadException method serves two primary functions. The first is to log the exceptions thrown from outside of a module to the Logging Provider. The second is to display a friendly error message on the page. Note the friendly error message will only be displayed if the host option Use Custom Error Messages is enabled on the Host Settings page (see Chapter 5).

This ProcessPageLoadException method has two overloaded methods that are detailed below.

1. To process an exception that occurs in an ASPX file or in logic outside of a portal module, use the following overloaded method. If the Use Custom Error Messages option has been enabled in Host Settings, this method will also handle displaying a user-friendly error message to the client browser.

```
Public Sub ProcessPageLoadException(ByVal exc As Exception)
```

Parameter	Type	Description
Exc	Exception	This is the exception that was thrown.

2. This is the same as the previous method; however, you must send in the URL parameter to redirect the request after logging the exception.

```
Public Sub ProcessPageLoadException(ByVal exc As Exception, _
ByVal URL As String)
```

Parameter	Type	Description
Exc	Exception	This is the exception that was thrown.
URL	String	This is the URL to redirect the request to.

LogException Method

The LogException method is used for adding exceptions to the log. It does not handle displaying any type of friendly message to the user. Instead, it simply logs the error without notifying the client browser of a problem. This method has four overloaded methods that are detailed below.

1. To log an exception thrown from a module, use the following overloaded method.

```
Public Sub LogException(ByVal exc As ModuleLoadException)
```

Parameter	Type	Description
Exc	ModuleLoadException	This is the exception that was thrown.

2. To log an exception thrown from a page or other logic outside of a module, use the following overloaded method.

```
Public Sub LogException(ByVal exc As PageLoadException)
```

Parameter	Type	Description
Exc	PageLoadException	This is the exception that was thrown.

3. To log an exception thrown from within a Scheduling Provider Task, use the following over-loaded method.

```
Public Sub LogException(ByVal exc As SchedulerException)
```

Parameter	Type	Description
Exc	SchedulerException	This is the exception that was thrown.

4. If you need to log an exception of another type, use the following overloaded method.

```
Public Sub LogException(ByVal exc As Exception)
```

Parameter	Type	Description
Exc	Exception	This is the exception that was thrown.

ProcessSchedulerException Method

The ProcessSchedulerException method is used to log exceptions thrown from within a scheduled task. This method simply logs the error.

To log an exception thrown from a scheduled task, use the following overloaded method.

```
Public Sub LogException(ByVal exc As ModuleLoadException)
```

Parameter	Type	Description
Exc	ModuleLoadException	This is the exception that was thrown.

The exception handling API abstracts developers from the complexity of logging exceptions and presenting error messages gracefully. It provides several powerful methods that handle all of the logic involved in working with the Logging Provider and the presentation layer. The next section covers the various interfaces that module developers can take advantage of to bring more core features to life in their modules.

Localization

The localization API in DotNetNuke provides developers with an interface for performing multilingual translations in custom portal modules. As of the writing of this book, DotNetNuke includes only static localization features. In other words, only text labels and other static strings are localized by the core. Localization of any dynamic content in a module is the responsibility of the module developer.

Locales

A locale is the combination of a country code and a language code. For the sake of accurate translations, it is important to use both a country code and a language code to perform localization. Many languages are spoken in more than one country, and dialects may differ from country to country. For instance, speaking French in Canada is different from speaking French in France. A locale accounts for this differentiation. DotNetNuke supports four types of locales:

❑ **System Locale:** This is the locale (en-US) that DotNetNuke is natively coded to. This locale is a system locale and cannot be changed.

❑ **Default Portal Locale:** This is the portal's default locale that is specified in the Site Settings screen (see Chapter 5). This locale will be automatically selected for any users who have not yet defined their default locale.

❑ **User Selected Locale:** This is the locale that a user selects from the Registration or User Account page.

❑ **Custom Locale:** A custom locale allows for customized translations to be defined for each portal. The localization framework manages this by appending the PortalID onto the locale. For instance, if Portal 2 has configured custom German translations, the custom locale for de-DE for Portal 2 is de-DE.Portal-2.

Resource Files

To align closely to the ASP.NET 2.0 localization implementation, DotNetNuke uses the Windows Resource Files (RESX) format to store translations. This file format uses XML tags to store key/value pairs of string values. In the root App_Resources directory, there is a file named Template.resx. Developers often use this file as a starting place to create their resource files.

The format of the data elements of a resource file looks like the following. This is an example of the Data Provider: form field on the Host Settings page.

```
 . . .
       <data name="plDataProvider.Text">
             <value>Data Provider:</value>
       </data>
       <data name="plDataProvider.Help">
             <value>The provider name which is identified as the default data
provider in the web.config file</value>
       </data>
 . . .
```

Each name attribute is referred to as a *resource* key. Notice each of the two resource keys has an extension. DotNetNuke uses a number of extensions, which help to identify translations more easily.

❑ **.Text:** Used for the text properties of controls (default if not included in resource key)

❑ **.Help:** Used for help text

❑ **.Header:** Used for the headertext properties of DataGrid columns

❑ **.EditText:** Used for the edittext properties of DataGrids

❑ **.ErrorMessage:** Used for the ErrorMessage property of Validator controls

There are three types of static translations in DotNetNuke. They are Application Resources, Local Resources, and Global Resources. Each of these types of static translations is defined in the following sections.

Application Resources

These translations are shared throughout many controls in DotNetNuke. This is the storage area for generic translations. For instance, to localize the words True and False, you would store the translations in the Application Resources files. Other examples of Application Resources are Yes, No, Submit, and Continue.

Application Resources are stored in the App_GlobalResources directory, which is directly under the DotNetNuke root installation directory. The filename for the system locale (en-US) for Application Resources is SharedResources.resx. The file naming convention for other locales is SharedResources .[locale].resx. For instance, the German Application Resource file is named SharedResources.de-DE.resx.

Local Resources

These translations are unique to a user control. For instance, to localize the Announcements module's user control, you would store the translations in a Local Resource file that lives in a child directory beneath the Announcements module's directory.

> *If the Announcements module has static translations, which are generic in nature (such as True and False), the translations should be gathered from Application Resources.*

Local Resource files are stored in a directory named App_LocalResources. Each directory that contains localized user controls must have a directory named App_LocalResources. The filename for the System Locale follows this naming convention:

```
[control_directory]/App_LocalResources/[user_control_file_name].resx.
```

For instance, for the en-US locale, the resource file for the Announcements module would be

```
Announcements/App_LocalResources/Announcements.ascx.resx.
```

The filename for other locales follows this naming convention:

```
[control_directory]/App_LocalResources/[control_files_name].[locale].resx.
```

Global Resources

These translations are for localizing strings from components that do not have Local Resource files, and are not necessarily shared translations. Therefore they do not fit in the first two categories. Because all Local Resources are associated with a user control or a page, there is no place to store translations for components. For this reason, we added this third category for resource files. An example of Global Resource usage is in the component admin/Containers/ActionBase.vb, which needs to localize the word Help in the module action lists.

Global Resources are stored in the same directory as Application Resources (/App_Resources). The filename for the system default locale is /App_Resources/GlobalResources.resx. For locales other than the system default, the naming convention is

```
/App_Resources/GlobalResources.[locale].resx
```

The API

The primary focus of this section is on the DotNetNuke.Services.Localization.Localization class. This class provides the methods necessary for localizing strings, as shown in Table 8-3.

Table 8-3: Localization Methods

Method	Description
AddLocale	This is used for adding a locale to the list of supported locales in the App_GlobalResources/Locales.xml file.
GetHelpUrl	This is used to replace the string [LANGUAGE] in a Help URL with the user's locale (or the portal's default locale if the user has not specified a default locale).
GetResourceFile	The returns the path and filename of the resource file for a specified control.
GetString	This returns the localized string based on the resource key specified.
GetSupportedLocales	This returns the list locales from the App_GlobalResources/Locales.xml file.
GetSystemMessage	This localizes a string and also replaces system tokens with personalized strings.
GetTimeZones	This returns a key/value pair collection of time zones.
LoadCultureDropDownList	This will fill a DropDownList control with the supported cultures.
LoadTimeZoneDropDownList	This will fill a DropDownList control with the list of time zones.
LocalizeDataGrid	This will localize the headers in a DataGrid control.
LocalizeRole	This localizes the three system roles.

The GetString Method

Of the methods in Table 8-3, the most widely used is the GetString method. The GetString method performs localization based on the resource key passed into it. The GetString method has four overloaded methods as detailed below.

1. To localize a string value that has a translation in an Application Resource file, use the following method. The resource file to be used will be automatically selected based on the currently active locale. This will automatically use the currently active PortalSettings object to derive the portal's default locale.

```
Public Shared Function GetString(ByVal name As String) As String
```

Parameter	Type	Description
Name	String	This is the string to be localized.

2. This is identical to the previous method, except you can send in a PortalSettings object to derive the portal's default locale.

```
Public Shared Function GetString(ByVal name As String, ByVal objPortalSettings _
As PortalSettings) As String
```

Parameter	Type	Description
Name	String	This is the string to be translated.
objPortalSettings	PortalSettings	This is the PortalSettings object for the current context.

3. To localize a string value that has a translation in a Local Resource file, use the following method. This method accepts an incoming parameter (ResourceFileRoot) from which the resource file to use is derived. This will automatically use the currently active PortalSettings object to derive the portal's default locale.

```
Public Shared Function GetString(ByVal name As String, ByVal ResourceFileRoot _
As String) As String
```

Parameter	Type	Description
Name	String	This is the string to be translated.
ResourceFileRoot	String	This is the value of a module's LocalResourceFile property. It is used to derive the resource file to be used for the translation.

4. This method allows you to specify the key name to translate, and both the resource file and portal settings to use for the translation.

```
Public Shared Function GetString(ByVal name As String, ByVal ResourceFileRoot _
As String, ByVal objPortalSettings As PortalSettings) As String
```

Parameter	Type	Description
Name	String	This is the string to be translated.
ResourceFileRoot	String	This is the value of a module's LocalResourceFile property. It is used to derive the resource file to be used for the translation.
objPortalSettings	PortalSettings	This is the PortalSettings object for the current context.

The GetSystemMessage Method

This method is used throughout the core code to produce localized and personalized strings. For example, it is used frequently to send e-mail to registered users. The user registration page calls the GetSystemMessage method to localize the content of the e-mail that gets sent to the user. The e-mail that gets sent to the user contains personalized content, too. Therefore, rather than concatenating several dozen strings using the GetString method and wrapping them around personalized data, the GetSystemMessage method takes care of all of this with just one call.

This section first covers the overloads for the GetSystemMessage method, and then discusses the user registration example.

1. Use this method if you need to localize and personalize a string when the personalization can be derived from either the objPortal or objUser properties. By using this method, the translation must be stored in the Application Resource file.

```
Public Shared Function GetSystemMessage(ByVal objPortal As PortalSettings, _
ByVal MessageName As String, ByVal objUser As UserInfo) As String
```

Parameter	Type	Description
ObjPortal	PortalSettings	This is the PortalSettings object for the current context. It is used to derive any personalized content within the localized system message string.
MessageName	String	This is the resource key used to get the localized system message from the resource file.
ObjUser	UserInfo	This is the UserInfo object to derive any personalized content within the localized system message string.

2. Use this method if you need to localize and personalize a string when the personalization can be derived from either the objPortal or objUser properties. In this method you must specify the resource file to retrieve the translation from.

```
Public Shared Function GetSystemMessage(ByVal objPortal As PortalSettings, _
ByVal MessageName As String, ByVal objUser As UserInfo, ByVal ResourceFile _
As String) As String
```

Parameter	Type	Description
ObjPortal	PortalSettings	This is the PortalSettings object for the current context. It is used to derive any personalized content within the localized system message string.
MessageName	String	This is the resource key used to get the localized system message from the resource file.
ObjUser	UserInfo	This is the UserInfo object to derive any personalized content within the localized system message string.
ResourceFile	String	This is the resource file that the localized system message is stored in. It is usually the value of the module's Local ResourceFile property.

3. This method is the similar to the previous method; however, you can specify an ArrayList of strings that can be used in the personalization of the localized string.

```
Public Shared Function GetSystemMessage(ByVal objPortal As PortalSettings, _
ByVal MessageName As String, ByVal objUser As UserInfo, ByVal ResourceFile As _
String, ByVal Custom As ArrayList) As String
```

Parameter	Type	Description
ObjPortal	PortalSettings	This is the PortalSettings object for the current context. It is used to derive any personalized content within the localized system message string.
MessageName	String	This is the resource key used to get the localized system message from the resource file.
ObjUser	UserInfo	This is the UserInfo object to derive any personalized content within the localized system message string.
ResourceFile	String	This is the resource file that the localized system message is stored in. It is usually the value of the module's LocalResourceFile property.
Custom	ArrayList	This is a collection of strings that can be used for personalizing the system message.

4. Use this method if you need to localize and personalize a string when the personalization can be derived from the objPortal property values. Also, you must specify the resource file to use for the translation.

```
Public Shared Function GetSystemMessage(ByVal objPortal As PortalSettings, _
ByVal MessageName As String, ByVal ResourceFile As String) As String
```

Parameter	Type	Description
ObjPortal	PortalSettings	This is the PortalSettings object for the current context. It is used to derive any personalized content within the localized system message string.
MessageName	String	This is the resource key used to get the localized system message from the resource file.
ResourceFile	String	This is the resource file that the localized system message is stored in.

5. Use this method if you need to localize and personalize a string when the personalization can be derived from the objPortal object's properties and the Custom ArrayList collection items. Also, you must specify the resource file to use for the translation.

```
Public Shared Function GetSystemMessage(ByVal objPortal As PortalSettings, _
ByVal MessageName As String, ByVal ResourceFile As String, ByVal Custom As _
ArrayList) As String
```

Parameter	Type	Description
ObjPortal	PortalSettings	This is the PortalSettings object for the current context. It is used to derive any personalized content within the localized system message string.
MessageName	String	This is the resource key used to get the localized system message from the resource file.
ResourceFile	String	This is the resource file that the localized system message is stored in.
Custom	ArrayList	This is a collection of strings that can be used for personalizing the system message.

When using the GetSystemMessage method, you can specify several *system tokens* in the localized string. These tokens are used as keys to render property values from either the UserInfo or PortalSettings objects. The following is an example of this:

```
DotNetNuke.Services.Localization.Localization.GetSystemMessage(PortalSettings, _
"EMAIL_USER_REGISTRATION_PRIVATE_BODY", objNewUser, Me.LocalResourceFile)
```

This code calls the GetSystemMessage method to localize and personalize the body of an e-mail message that is sent to a newly registered user. This code is found in the Admin/Security/Register.ascx portal module. The MessageName parameter value is EMAIL_USER_REGISTRATION_PRIVATE_BODY. This is the resource key to lookup the system message in the resource file. The resource key and associated translation from the resource file /Admin/Security/App_LocalResources/Register.ascx.resx is shown in Listing 8-8.

Listing 8-8: System Message Resource Example

```
<data name="EMAIL_USER_REGISTRATION_PRIVATE_BODY.Text">
    <value>
        Dear [User:FullName],

Thank you for registering at the [Portal:PortalName] portal website. Please read
the following information carefully and be sure to save this message in a safe
location for future reference.

Portal Website Address: [Portal:URL]
Username: [Membership:UserName]
Password: [Membership:Password]

Your account details will be reviewed by the portal Administrator and you will
receive a notification upon account activation.

Thank you, we appreciate your support...

[Portal:PortalName]

    </value>
</data>
```

The GetSystemMessage method will first localize the string within the <value> XML node. Then it will iterate through the system tokens (enclosed in brackets), replacing the tokens with the appropriate property values. For instance, in Listing 8-8 you can see the token [User:FullName]. This will be replaced with the FullName property value of the User object. In this case, the User object is the objUser object passed into the GetSystemMessage method. Listing 8-9 shows the system message has been personalized and localized with the en-US locale.

Listing 8-9: System Message Rendered Example

```
Dear John Doe,

Thank you for registering at the DotNetNuke portal website. Please read the
following information carefully and be sure to save this message in a safe location
for future reference.

Portal Website Address: http://test.dotnetnuke.com
Username: jdoe1234
Password: pwdjdoe1234

Your account details will be reviewed by the portal Administrator and you will
receive a notification upon account activation.

Thank you, we appreciate your support...

DotNetNuke
```

Scheduler

The Scheduler in DotNetNuke is a mechanism that allows developers to schedule tasks to run at defined intervals. It is implemented using the Provider pattern; therefore, it can easily be replaced without modifying core code. Creating a scheduled task is a fairly simple process that we will cover in this section. First, it is important to understand which types of tasks are suitable for the Scheduler.

Since the Scheduler is run under the context of the web application, it is prone to the same types of application recycles as a web application. In a web-hosting environment, it is a common practice to conserve resources by recycling the worker process for a site periodically. When this happens, the Scheduler stops running. Therefore, it is important to understand that the tasks run by the Scheduler do not run 24 hours a day, 7 days a week. Instead, the tasks are executed according to a defined schedule, but they can only be triggered when the worker process is alive. For this reason, you cannot specify that a task should run every night at midnight. It is not possible in the web environment to meet this type of use case. Instead, you can specify how often a task is run by defining the execution frequency for each task. The execution frequency is defined as every x minutes/hours/days.

To create a scheduled task, you must create a class that inherits from DotNetNuke.Services.Scheduling .SchedulerClient. This class must provide a constructor and a DoWork method. An example of a scheduled task is shown in Listing 8-10. This sample scheduled task will move all event log files to a folder named with the current date. By configuring this scheduled task to run once per day, the log files will be automatically archived daily, which keeps the log file sizes manageable.

Listing 8-10: Scheduled Task Example

```
Public Class ArchiveEventLog
    Inherits DotNetNuke.Services.Scheduling.SchedulerClient
    Public Sub New(ByVal objScheduleHistoryItem As _
        DotNetNuke.Services.Scheduling.ScheduleHistoryItem)
        MyBase.new()
        Me.ScheduleHistoryItem = objScheduleHistoryItem      'REQUIRED
    End Sub
    Public Overrides Sub DoWork()
        Try
            'notification that the event is progressing
            'this is optional
            Me.Progressing()      'OPTIONAL
            'get the directory that logs are written to
            Dim LogDirectory As String
            LogDirectory = Common.Globals.HostMapPath + "Logs\"

            'create a folder with today's date
            Dim FolderName As String
            FolderName = LogDirectory + Now.Month.ToString + "-" + _
                Now.Day.ToString + "-" + Now.Year.ToString + "\"
            If Not IO.Directory.Exists(FolderName) Then
                IO.Directory.CreateDirectory(FolderName)
            End If

            'get the files in the log directory
            Dim s As String()
```

```
            s = IO.Directory.GetFiles(LogDirectory)
            'loop through the files
            Dim i As Integer
            For i = 0 To s.Length - 1
                Dim OldFileInfo As New IO.FileInfo(s(i))
                'move all files to the new folder except the file
                'used to store pending log notifications
                If OldFileInfo.Name <> _
                    "PendingLogNotifications.xml.resources" Then
                    Dim NewFileName As String
                    NewFileName = FolderName + OldFileInfo.Name
                    'check to see if the new file already exists
                    If IO.File.Exists(NewFileName) Then
                        Dim errMessage As String
                        errMessage = "An error occurred archiving " + _
                            "log file to " + _
                            NewFileName + ".  The file already exists."
                        LogException(New _
                            BasePortalException(errMessage))
                    Else
                        IO.File.Move(OldFileInfo.FullName, NewFileName)
                        Me.ScheduleHistoryItem.AddLogNote("Moved " + _
                            OldFileInfo.FullName + _
                                " to " + FolderName + _
                                OldFileInfo.Name + ".")        'OPTIONAL
                    End If
                End If
            Next

            Me.ScheduleHistoryItem.Succeeded = True     'REQUIRED

        Catch exc As Exception     'REQUIRED

            Me.ScheduleHistoryItem.Succeeded = False     'REQUIRED

            Me.ScheduleHistoryItem.AddLogNote(String.Format( _
                "Archiving log files failed.", _
                exc.ToString))     'OPTIONAL

            'notification that we have errored
            Me.Errored(exc)     'REQUIRED

            'log the exception
            LogException(exc)     'OPTIONAL
        End Try
    End Sub
End Class
```

Once the class has been compiled into the bin directory, the task can be scheduled from the Scheduling module under the Host tab (see Chapter 6 for details). It is important to include each of the lines of code in Listing 8-7 that is labeled required. These collectively ensure both the exception handling and schedule management are handled uniformly throughout all scheduled tasks.

HTTPModules

ASP.NET provides a number of options for extending the path that data takes between client and server (known as the HTTP Pipeline). A popular method to extend the pipeline is through the use of custom components known as *HTTP Modules*. An HTTP module allows you to add pre- and post-processing to each HTTP Request coming into your application.

DotNetNuke implements a number of HTTP Modules to extend the pipeline. These modules include features such as URL Rewriting, Exception Management, Users Online, Profile, Anonymous Identification, Role Management, DotNetNuke Membership, and Personalization. This section discusses each in turn.

Originally, a lot of the previously mentioned HTTP Modules were implemented inside the core application (global.asax.vb). There were a number of reasons why the functionally was moved to HTTP Modules:

1. Administrators can optionally enable/disable an HTTP module.
2. Developers can replace or modify HTTP Modules without altering the core application.
3. Provides templates for extending the HTTP Pipeline.

HTTP Modules 101

Before we explore each HTTP module within DotNetNuke, let's further examine the concepts of HTTP modules so you'll know when and where to implement them. To understand how HTTP modules work, it's necessary to understand the HTTP Pipeline and how ASP.NET processes incoming requests. Figure 8-1 shows the HTTP Pipeline.

When a request is first made, it passes through a number of stages before it is actually handled by your application. The first participant in the pipeline is Microsoft Internet Information Server (IIS); its job is to route ASP.NET requests to the ASP.NET runtime. Once an ASPX file is requested (or any other ASP.NET file), IIS will forward the request to the ASP.NET runtime (via an ISAPI extension).

Now that the request has been received by ASP.NET, it must pass through an instance of HttpApplication. The HttpApplication object handles application-wide methods, data, and events. It is also responsible for pushing the request through one or more HTTP module objects. The ASP.NET runtime determines which modules to load by examining the configuration files located at either machine level (machine.config) or application level (web.config). Listing 8-11 shows the HTTP modules configuration section of DotNetNuke.

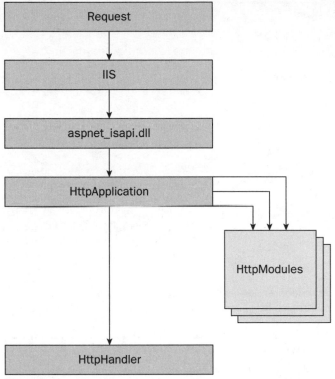

Figure 8-1

Listing 8-11: HTTP Modules Configuration Section

```
<httpModules>
 <add name="UrlRewrite" type="DotNetNuke.HttpModules.UrlRewriteModule,
                          DotNetNuke.HttpModules.UrlRewrite" />

 <add name="Exception" type="DotNetNuke.HttpModules.ExceptionModule,
                          DotNetNuke.HttpModules.Exception" />

 <add name="UsersOnline" type="DotNetNuke.HttpModules.UsersOnlineModule,
                          DotNetNuke.HttpModules.UsersOnline" />

 <add name="Profile" type="Microsoft.ScalableHosting.Profile.ProfileModule,
                          MemberRole,
                          Version=1.0.0.0,
                          Culture=neutral,
                          PublicKeyToken=b7c773fb104e7562" />

 <add name="AnonymousIdentification"
      type="Microsoft.ScalableHosting.Security.AnonymousIdentificationModule,
          MemberRole,
          Version=1.0.0.0,
```

(continued)

Listing 8-11: *(continued)*

```
            Culture=neutral,
            PublicKeyToken=b7c773fb104e7562" />

<add name="RoleManager"
    type="Microsoft.ScalableHosting.Security.RoleManagerModule,
          MemberRole,
          Version=1.0.0.0,
          Culture=neutral,
          PublicKeyToken=b7c773fb104e7562" />

<add name="DNNMembership" type="DotNetNuke.HttpModules.DNNMembershipModule,
                            DotNetNuke.HttpModules.DNNMembership" />

<add name="Personalization" type="DotNetNuke.HttpModules.PersonalizationModule,
                            DotNetNuke.HttpModules.Personalization" />

</httpModules>
```

To invoke each HTTP module, the Init method of each module is invoked. At the end of each request, the dispose method is invoked to allow each HTTP module to clean up its resources. In fact, the two methods mentioned form the interface (IHttpModule) each module must implement. Listing 8-12 shows the IHttpModule interface.

Listing 8-12: The IHttpModule Interface Implemented By Each HTTP Module

```
Public Interface IHttpModule
    Sub Init(ByVal context As HttpApplication)
    Sub Dispose()
End Interface
```

During the Init event, each module may subscribe to a number of events raised by the HttpApplication object. Table 8-4 shows the events that are raised before the application executes. The events are listed in the order in which they occur.

Table 8-4: HTTP Module Events (before application executes)	
Event	**Description**
BeginRequest	Signals a new request; guaranteed to be raised on each request.
AuthenticateRequest	Signals that the request is ready to be authenticated; used by the Security module.
AuthorizeRequest	Signals that the request is ready to be authorized; used by the Security module.
ResolveRequestCache	Used by the Output Cache module to short-circuit the processing of requests that have been cached.
AcquireRequestState	Signals that per-request state should be obtained.
PreRequestHandler Execute	Signals that the request handler is about to execute. This is the last event you can participate in before the HTTP handler for this request is called.

Table 8-5 shows the events that are raised after an application has returned. The events are listed in the order in which they occur.

Table 8-5: HTTP Module Events (after application has returned)

Event	Description
PostRequest HandlerExecute	Signals that the HTTP handler has completed processing the request.
ReleaseRequestState	Signals that the request state should be stored because the application is finished with the request.
UpdateRequestCache	Signals that code processing is complete and the file is ready to be added to the ASP.NET cache.
EndRequest	Signals that all processing has finished for the request. This is the last event called when the application ends.

In addition, there are three per-request events that can be raised in a nondeterministic order. They appear in Table 8-6.

Table 8-6: HTTP Module Events (nondeterministic)

Event	Description
PreSendRequest Headers	Signals that HTTP headers are about to be sent to the client. This provides an opportunity to add, remove, or modify the headers before they are sent.
PreSendRequest Content	Signals that content is about to be sent to the client. This provides an opportunity to modify the content before it is sent.
Error	Signals an unhandled exception.

After the request has been pushed through the HTTP modules configured for your application, the HTTP handler responsible for the requested file's extension (.ASPX) handles the processing of that file. If you are familiar with ASP.NET development, you'll be familiar with the handler for an ASPX page, that is, System.Web.UI.Page. The HTTP handler then handles the life cycle of the page-level request raising events such as Page_Init, Page_Load, and so on.

DotNetNuke HTTP Modules

As stated earlier, DotNetNuke (like ASP.NET) comes with a number of HTTP modules. These modules allow developers to customize the HTTP Pipeline to provide additional functionality on each request. This section investigates each HTTP module provided, and discusses its purpose and possibilities for extension.

URL Rewriter

The URL rewriter is an HTTP module that provides a mechanism for mapping virtual resource names to physical resource names at runtime. In other words, provide a URL that is friendly. The term "friendly" has two aspects; we solved one with the default implementation, but not the other. Instead we provided an extensible architecture to allow you to implement the second at a possible cost of performance.

The first aspect of the term friendly is to make the URL search engine friendly. The main requirement of the enhancement is most search engines ignore URL parameters. Since DotNetNuke relies on URL parameters to navigate to portal tabs, the current application is not search engine friendly. In order to effectively index your site we need a parameter-less mechanism for constructing URLs that search engines will process.

If you browse to a DotNetNuke site that is version 3.0 or greater, you may notice different URLs from earlier versions. Traditionally, a DotNetNuke URL may look something like the following:

```
http://www.dotnetnuke.com/default.aspx?tabid=622
```

With friendly URLs enabled you might see the preceding URL like so:

```
http://www.dotnetnuke.com/RoadMap/Friendly URLs/tabid/622/default.aspx
```

Earlier, we explored the HTTP Pipeline and the events that are raised during the processing of a request. Our URL rewriter is invoked during this process and can optionally subscribe to application-wide events. The particular event we are interested in for this module is the BeginRequest event. This event allows us to modify the URL before the Page HTTP handler is invoked and make it believe the URL requested was that of the old non-friendly format.

The transformation process occurs through the use of regular expressions defined in SiteUrls.config in the root of your DotNetNuke installation. This file contains a number of expressions to LookFor and a corresponding URL to SendTo. Listing 8-13 shows the default SiteUrls.config.

Listing 8-13: SiteUrls.config

```xml
<?xml version="1.0" encoding="utf-8" ?>
<RewriterConfig>
<Rules>
    <RewriterRule>
        <LookFor>.*/TabId/(\d+)(.*)/Logoff.aspx</LookFor>
        <SendTo>~/Admin/Security/Logoff.aspx?tabid=$1</SendTo>
    </RewriterRule>
    <RewriterRule>
        <LookFor>.*/TabId/(\d+)(.*)/rss.aspx</LookFor>
        <SendTo>~/rss.aspx?TabId=$1</SendTo>
    </RewriterRule>
    <RewriterRule>
        <LookFor>.*/TabId/(\d+)(.*)</LookFor>
        <SendTo>~/Default.aspx?TabId=$1</SendTo>
    </RewriterRule>
</Rules>
</RewriterConfig>
```

The rules defined in this configuration file cover the default login and logoff page. You could potentially add any number of additional rules, and even hardcode some extra rules in there. For example, if you wanted to hardcode a link such as http://www.dotnetnuke.com/FriendlyUrl.aspx and have it map to another URL elsewhere, your entry might look like Listing 8-14.

Listing 8-14: SiteUrls.config with Modified Rule

```xml
<?xml version="1.0" encoding="utf-8" ?>
<RewriterConfig>
<Rules>
        <RewriterRule>
                <LookFor>.*/FriendlyUrl.aspx</LookFor>
                <SendTo>~/default.aspx?tabid=622</SendTo>
        </RewriterRule>
        <RewriterRule>
                <LookFor>.*/TabId/(\d+)(.*)/Logoff.aspx</LookFor>
                <SendTo>~/Admin/Security/Logoff.aspx?tabid=$1</SendTo>
        </RewriterRule>
        <RewriterRule>
                <LookFor>.*/TabId/(\d+)(.*)/rss.aspx</LookFor>
                <SendTo>~/rss.aspx?TabId=$1</SendTo>
        </RewriterRule>
        <RewriterRule>
                <LookFor>.*/TabId/(\d+)(.*)</LookFor>
                <SendTo>~/Default.aspx?TabId=$1</SendTo>
        </RewriterRule>
</Rules>
</RewriterConfig>
```

The preceding URL scheme is an excellent implementation for your own applications as well, particularly those with fixed pages. Unfortunately DotNetNuke has potentially any number of pages, so we had to add some functionality that would transform any number of query string parameters.

Let's now examine the default scheme for URL rewriting. You can see from the friendly URL shown earlier (http://www.dotnetnuke.com/RoadMap/Friendly URLs/tabid/622/default.aspx) that we have achieved our requirement, that is, the URL would have no parameters. Examining the URL, we can work something out about the default scheme.

❑   **http://www.dotnetnuke.com/:** The site URL.

❑   **RoadMap/Friendly URLs/:** The breadcrumb path back to the home page.

❑   **tabid/622:** The query string from the original URL transformed (?tabid=622).

The advantage of this scheme is that it requires no database lookups for the transformation, just raw regular expression processing that is typically quite fast.

Earlier in this chapter, we mentioned that there were two aspects of friendly URLs; so far we have only discussed the first (Search Engine Friendly). The second aspect can sometimes impact performance and is known as human friendly URLs.

A URL that is human friendly is easily remembered by the human or able to be worked out. For example, if I had a login to DotNetNuke.com and I wanted to visit the profile page without navigating to it, I might expect the URL to be

```
http://www.dotnetnuke.com/profile/smcculloch.aspx
```

The preceding URL could easily be remembered, but would require additional processing on the request for two reasons:

❑ The URL contains no TabID. We would have to lookup the TabID for the profile page for that portal.

❑ The URL contains no UserID. We would have to perform a lookup on smcculloch to find the corresponding UserID.

For these reasons, this approach was not chosen but is still possible.

So far, we've only explained how incoming requests are interpreted but not how outgoing links are transformed into the friendly URL scheme. A number of options were explored on how to transform the outgoing links, but the best option was to implement a provider-based component that would transform a given link into the chosen scheme. Figure 8-2 shows the URL rewriter architecture.

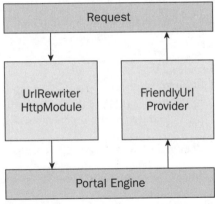

Figure 8-2

Luckily, DotNetNuke had used two shortcut methods already for building links within the application (NavigateUrl and EditUrl). It was relatively simple to place a call to the provider from each of these methods, effectively upgrading the site to the new URL format instantly.

This approach also lightly coupled the HTTP module and the provider together. For this reason you can find them in the same assembly (DotNetNuke.HttpModules.UrlRewrite.dll).

You can see from the architecture that it is quite plausible for you to write your own URL rewriting scheme. If it was more important for your site to have human friendly URLs, you could write a scheme by writing a new provider to format outgoing URLs, and a new HTTP module to interpret the incoming requests.

Writing a new provider involves providing new implementations of the methods in the base class of the FriendlyUrlProvider. Listing 8-15 shows these methods.

Listing 8-15: Friendly URL Provider Methods

```
        Public MustOverride Function FriendlyUrl(ByVal objtab as TabInfo, ByVal
path As String) As String
        Public MustOverride Function FriendlyUrl(ByVal objtab as TabInfo, ByVal
path As String, ByVal pageName As String) As String
        Public MustOverride Function FriendlyUrl(ByVal objtab as TabInfo, ByVal
path As String, ByVal pageName As String, ByVal settings As PortalSettings) As
String
        Public MustOverride Function FriendlyUrl(ByVal objtab as TabInfo, ByVal
path As String, ByVal pageName As String, ByVal portalAlias As String) As String
```

As you can see, there are only four methods to implement so that you can write our URLs in your desired format. The most important part will be to come up with a scheme and to find an efficient and reliable way of interpretation by your HTTP module. Once you have written your provider, you can add an additional entry in the providers section of web.config as shown in Listing 8-16. Make sure to set the defaultProvider attribute.

Listing 8-16: Friendly URL Provider Configuration

```
<friendlyUrl defaultProvider="CustomFriendlyUrl">
      <providers>
            <clear />
            <add name="DNNFriendlyUrl"
                  type="DotNetNuke.Services.Url.FriendlyUrl.DNNFriendlyUrlProvider,
DotNetNuke.HttpModules.UrlRewrite" />
            <add name="CustomFriendlyUrl"
                  type="CompanyName.FriendlyUrlProvider,
CompanyName.FriendlyUrlProvider" />
      </providers>
</friendlyUrl>
```

Exception Management

The exception management HTTP module subscribes to the error event raised by the HttpApplication object. Any time an error occurs within DotNetNuke, the error event is called. During the processing of this event the last error to have occurred is captured and sent to the exception logging class. This class then calls the Logging Provider that handles the writing of that exception to a data store (the default is XML).

Users Online

Users Online was implemented during version 2 of DotNetNuke. It allows other modules to interrogate the applications' data store for information regarding who is online, both expressed as registered users or anonymous users. Previously it had been a custom add-on and was session based. Before the addition of the functionality to the core (like many add-ons incorporated into the core), research was undertaken to investigate the best way to not only handle registered users, but anonymous users.

The module subscribes to the AuthorizeRequest event. This event is the first chance an HTTP module has to examine details about the user performing the request. The HTTP module examines the request and determines whether the user is anonymous or authenticated, then proceeds to store the request in cache. Anonymous users are also given a temporary cookie so they are not counted twice in the future. A scheduled job from the Scheduler executes every minute on a background thread pulling the relevant details out of cache and updating them in the database; it will also clear up any old records. The records are stored within two tables, AnonymousUsers and UsersOnline.

This HTTP module is a good module to disable (comment out of config) if you do not need this information within your portal. Alternatively you can just disable it in Host Settings.

DNNMembership

The DNNMembership HTTP module performs tasks around the security of a user. It stores role information about a user in an HTTP cookie to save requesting the same information again and performs security checks for users switching portals.

There is no real need to extend this module because it is critical to DotNetNuke's operation.

Personalization

The personalization HTTP module is very similar to the Microsoft-provided Profile HTTP module, and in fact, was based on the same concept, just integrated much earlier. It loads a user's personalized information into a serialized XML object at the beginning of the request, and saves it at the end of the request.

If you are interested in storing personalized information about a user, see the personalization classes under /Components/Personalization/.

Module Interfaces

Modules represent a discrete set of functionality that can extend the portal framework. In past versions of DotNetNuke, module interactions with the portal were primarily limited to making method calls into the core portal APIs. While this one-way interaction provides some ability to utilize portal services and methods within the module, it limits the ability of the portal to provide more advanced services.

In order to provide two-way interactions with modules, the portal needs to have a mechanism to make method calls into the module. There are several distinct mechanisms for allowing a program to call methods on an arbitrary set of code, where the module code is unknown at the time the portal is being developed. Three of these "calling" mechanisms are used within DotNetNuke:

- ❑ Inheritance
- ❑ Delegates
- ❑ Interfaces

As discussed previously, every module inherits from the PortalModuleBase class (located in the components/module directory). This base class provides a common set of methods and properties that can be used by the module as well as the portal to control the behavior of each module instance. Because the module must inherit from this class, the portal has a set of known methods that it can use to control the module. The portal could extend the base class to add additional methods to handle new services. One downside to this approach is that there is not an easy mechanism for determining whether a subclass implements custom logic for a specific method or property. Because of this restriction, inheritance is generally limited to providing services that are needed or required for every subclass.

A second method for interacting with the modules involves the use of delegates. A delegate is essentially a pointer to a method that has a specific set of parameters and return type. Delegates are useful when a service can be implemented with a single method call and are the underlying mechanism behind VB.NET's event handling. DotNetNuke uses delegates to implement callback methods for the Module Action menu action event. Although delegates are very useful in some situations, they are more difficult to implement and understand than alternative methods.

The third calling mechanism used by DotNetNuke is the use of interfaces. An interface defines a set of methods, events, and properties without providing any implementation details for these elements. Any class that implements an interface is then responsible for providing the specific logic for each method, event, and property defined in the interface. Interfaces are especially useful for defining optional services that a module may implement. The portal is able to detect if a class implements a specific interface and is then able to call any of the methods, events, or properties defined in the interface.

DotNetNuke 3.0 significantly extends its use of module interfaces. This section examines the six main interfaces that are intended for use by modules:

- ❑ IActionable
- ❑ IPortable
- ❑ IUpgradable
- ❑ IModuleCommunicator
- ❑ IModuleListener
- ❑ ISearchable

IActionable

Every module has a menu that contains several possible action items for activities like editing module settings, module movement, and viewing help. These menu items are called Module Actions. The module menu can be extended with your own custom actions. When your module inherits from the PortalModuleBase class, it receives a default set of actions. These actions are defined by the portal to handle common editing functions. Your module can extend these actions by implementing the IActionable interface.

Interface

As shown in Listing 8-17, the IActionable interface consists of a single method that returns a collection of module actions. The ModuleActions property is used when DotNetNuke renders the module.

Listing 8-17: IActionable Interface Definition

```
Namespace DotNetNuke.Entities.Modules
  Public Interface IActionable
    ReadOnly Property ModuleActions() As Actions.ModuleActionCollection
  End Interface
End Namespace
```

Listing 8-18 shows an example usage as implemented in the Announcements module. Let's break this down. The first two lines tell the compiler that this method implements the ModuleAction method of the IActionable interface. This is a read-only method and therefore we only need to provide a getter function. The first step is to create a new collection to hold our custom actions. Then we use the collection's Add method to create a new action item in our collection. Finally we return our new collection.

Listing 8-18: IActionable.ModuleActions Example

```
Public ReadOnly Property ModuleActions() As ModuleActionCollection _
   Implements IActionable.ModuleActions
   Get
     Dim Actions As New ModuleActionCollection

     Actions.Add(GetNextActionID, _
              Localization.GetString(ModuleActionType.AddContent, _
                                LocalResourceFile), _
              ModuleActionType.AddContent, _
              "", _
              "", _
              EditUrl(), _
              False, _
              Security.SecurityAccessLevel.Edit, _
              True, _
              False)

     Return Actions
   End Get
End Property
```

This is a simple example that demonstrates the basic steps to follow for your own custom module menus. DotNetNuke provides extensive control over each module action.

ModuleAction API

To take full advantage of the power provided by module actions and the IActionable interface, we need to examine the classes, properties, and methods that make up the ModuleAction API.

Table 8-7 lists the classes that comprise the ModuleAction API.

Table 8-7: Module Action Classes

Class	Description
ModuleAction	A module action is used to define a specific function for a given module. Each module can define one or more actions that the portal will present to the user. Each module container can define the skin object used to render the module actions.
ModuleActionType	The ModuleActionType class defines a set of constants used for distinguishing common action types.
ModuleActionCollection	This is a collection of Module Actions.

ModuleActionEvent Listener	This class is used for holding callback information when a module registers for Action events.
ActionEventArgs	The ActionEventArgs class is used for passing data during the click event that is fired when a module action is selected by the user.
ActionEventHandler	The ActionEventHandler is a delegate that defines the method signature required for responding to the Action event.
ActionBase	The ActionBase class is used for creating ModuleAction skin objects. The core framework includes three different implementations: SolPart Actions.ascx, DropDownActions.ascx, and LinkActions.ascx.

The ModuleAction class is the heart of the API. Tables 8-8 and 8-9 show the properties and methods available in the ModuleAction class. Each menu item in the Module Action menu is represented by a single ModuleAction instance.

Table 8-8: ModuleAction Properties

Property Name	Property Type	Description
Actions	ModuleAction Collection	The Module Action API supports hierarchical menu structures. Every skin object that inherits from ActionBase may choose how to render the menu based on the ability to support hierarchical items. For example the default SolpartActions skin object supports sub-menus, while the DropDownActions skin object only supports a flat menu structure.
Id	Integer	Every module action for a given module instance must contain a unique Id. The PortalModuleBase class defines the GetNextActionId method, which can be used to generate unique module action IDs.
CommandName	String	The CommandName property is used to distinguish which Module Action triggered an action event. DotNetNuke includes 19 standard ModuleActionTypes that provide access to standard functionality. Custom module actions can use their own string to identify commands recognized by the module.
Command Argument	String	CommandArguments are used to provide additional information during action event processing. For example, the DotNetNuke core uses the CommandArgument to pass the ModuleID for common commands like Delete-Module.Action.
Title	String	The Title property sets the text that is displayed in the Module Action menu.

Table continued on following page

Property Name	Property Type	Description
Icon	String	This is the name of the Icon file to use for the Module Action item.
Url	String	When set, the URL property allows a menu item to redirect the user to another web page.
ClientScript	String	The Javascript that will be run during the menuClick event in the browser. If the ClientScript property is present then it is called prior to the postback occurring. If the ClientScript returns false, then the postback is canceled.
UseAction Event	Boolean	The UseActionEvent causes the portal to raise an ActionEvent on the server and notify any registered event listeners. If UseActionEvent is false, then the portal will handle the event, but will not raise the event back to any event listeners. The following Command-Names will prevent the ActionEvent from firing: *ModuleHelp, OnlineHelp, ModuleSettings, DeleteModule, PrintModule, ClearCache, MovePane, MoveTop, MoveUp, MoveDown* and *MoveBottom*.
Secure	SecurityAccess Level	The Secure property determines the required security level of the user. If the current user does not have the necessary permissions, then the Module Action will not be displayed.
Visible	Boolean	If the visible property is set to false, then the Module Action will not be displayed. This property allows you to control the visibility of a Module Action based on custom business logic.
Newwindow	Boolean	The Newwindow property will force an action to open the associated URL in a new window. This property is not used if UseActionEvent is True or if the following CommandNames are used: *ModuleHelp, OnlineHelp, ModuleSettings, PrintModule*.

Table 8-9: ModuleAction Methods

Method Name	Return Type	Description
HasChildren	Boolean	HasChildren returns true if the ModuleAction.Actions property has any items (Actions.Count > 0).

DotNetNuke includes several standard module actions that are provided by the PortalModuleBase class or that are used by several of the core modules. These ModuleActionTypes are shown in Listing 8-19. ModuleActionTypes can also be used to access localized strings for the ModuleAction.Title property. This helps promote a consistent user interface for both core and third-party modules.

Listing 8-19: ModuleActionTypes

```
Public Class ModuleActionType
  Public Const AddContent As String = "AddContent.Action"
  Public Const EditContent As String = "EditContent.Action"
  Public Const ContentOptions As String = "ContentOptions.Action"
  Public Const SyndicateModule As String = "SyndicateModule.Action"
  Public Const ImportModule As String = "ImportModule.Action"
  Public Const ExportModule As String = "ExportModule.Action"
  Public Const OnlineHelp As String = "OnlineHelp.Action"
  Public Const ModuleHelp As String = "ModuleHelp.Action"
  Public Const PrintModule As String = "PrintModule.Action"
  Public Const ModuleSettings As String = "ModuleSettings.Action"
  Public Const DeleteModule As String = "DeleteModule.Action"
  Public Const ClearCache As String = "ClearCache.Action"
  Public Const MoveTop As String = "MoveTop.Action"
  Public Const MoveUp As String = "MoveUp.Action"
  Public Const MoveDown As String = "MoveDown.Action"
  Public Const MoveBottom As String = "MoveBottom.Action"
  Public Const MovePane As String = "MovePane.Action"
  Public Const MoveRoot As String = "MoveRoot.Action"
End Class
```

DotNetNuke provides standard behavior for the following ModuleActionTypes: ModuleHelp, OnlineHelp, ModuleSettings, DeleteModule, PrintModule, ClearCache, MovePane, MoveTop, MoveUp, MoveDown, and MoveBottom. All ModuleActionTypes in this subset will ignore the UseActionEvent and Newwindow properties. The ModuleActionTypes can be further subdivided into three groups:

❑   **Basic Redirection:** The following ModuleActionTypes will perform a simple redirection and cause the user to navigate to the URL identified in the URL property: *ModuleHelp, OnlineHelp, ModuleSettings,* and *PrintModule.*

❑   **Module Movement:** The following ModuleActionTypes will change the order or location of modules on the current page: *MovePane, MoveTop, MoveUp, MoveDown,* and *MoveBottom.*

❑   **Custom Logic:** The following ModuleActionTypes have custom business logic that will use core portal APIs to perform standard module-related actions: *DeleteModule* and *ClearCache.*

DotNetNuke uses a custom collection class when working with Module Actions. The ModuleAction Collection inherits from the .Net System.Collections.CollectionBase class and provides a strongly typed collection class. Using a strongly typed collection minimizes the possibility of typecasting errors that can occur when using generic collection classes like the ArrayList.

Most module developers will only need to worry about creating the ModuleActionCollection in order to implement the IActionable interface. Listing 8-20 shows the two primary methods used for adding ModuleActions to the collection. These methods simplify adding ModuleActions by wrapping the ModuleAction constructor method calls.

Listing 8-20: Key ModuleActionCollection Methods

```
Public Function Add(ByVal ID As Integer, _
    ByVal Title As String, _
    ByVal CmdName As String, _
    Optional ByVal CmdArg As String = "", _
    Optional ByVal Icon As String = "", _
    Optional ByVal Url As String = "", _
    Optional ByVal UseActionEvent As Boolean = False, _
    Optional ByVal Secure As SecurityAccessLevel = SecurityAccessLevel.Anonymous, _
    Optional ByVal Visible As Boolean = True, _
    Optional ByVal NewWindow As Boolean = False) _
    As ModuleAction

Public Function Add(ByVal ID As Integer, _
    ByVal Title As String, _
    ByVal CmdName As String, _
    ByVal CmdArg As String, _
    ByVal Icon As String, _
    ByVal Url As String, _
    ByVal ClientScript As String, _
    ByVal UseActionEvent As Boolean, _
    ByVal Secure As SecurityAccessLevel, _
    ByVal Visible As Boolean, _
    ByVal NewWindow As Boolean) _
    As ModuleAction
```

The first method in Listing 8-20 uses optional parameters that are not supported by C#. This method is likely to be deprecated in future versions in order to simplify support for C# modules and its use is not recommended.

The ModuleAction framework makes it easy to handle simple URL redirection from a module action. Just like the Delete and ClearCache actions provided by the DotNetNuke framework, your module may require the use of custom logic to determine the appropriate action to take when the menu item is clicked. To implement custom logic, the module developer needs to be able to respond to a Menu click event.

In the DotNetNuke architecture, the ModuleAction menu is a child of the module container. The module is also a child of the container. This architecture allows the framework to easily change out the menu implementation; however, it complicates communication between the menu and module. The menu never has a direct reference to the module and the module does not have a direct reference to the menu. This is a classic example of the Mediator design pattern. This pattern is designed to allow two classes without direct references to communicate. Figure 8-3 shows the steps involved to implement this pattern.

Let's examine the steps involved in making this work. During this discussion you will also discover ways you can to extend the framework.

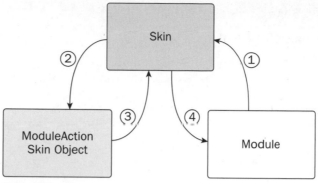

Figure 8-3

Step 1: Register the Event Handler

The first step to implementing the Mediator pattern is to provide a mechanism for the module to register with the portal. The portal will use this information later when it needs to notify the module that a menu item was selected. Handling the click event is strictly optional. Your module may choose to use standard MenuActions, in which case you can skip this step. Because the module does not contain a direct reference to the page on which it is instantiated, you need to provide a registration mechanism.

The Skin class, which acts as our mediator, contains the RegisterModuleActionEvent method, which allows a module to notify the framework of the event handler for the action event (see Listing 8-21). This registration should occur in the module's Page_Load event to ensure that registration occurs before the event could be fired in the Skin class. The code in Listing 8-21 is taken from the HTML module and provides a working example of module-based event registration for the ModuleAction event. While we could have used another interface to define a known method to handle the event, the registration mechanism turns out to be a much more flexible design when implementing a single method.

Listing 8-21: Registering an Event Handler

```
'--------------------------------------------------------------------------------
'-                    Menu Action Handler Registration                          -
'--------------------------------------------------------------------------------
'This finds a reference to the containing skin
Dim ParentSkin As UI.Skins.Skin = UI.Skins.Skin.GetParentSkin(Me)

'We should always have a ParentSkin, but need to make sure
If Not ParentSkin Is Nothing Then

    'Register our EventHandler as a listener on the ParentSkin so that it may
    'tell us when a menu has been clicked.
    ParentSkin.RegisterModuleActionEvent(Me.ModuleId, AddressOf ModuleAction_Click)
End If
'--------------------------------------------------------------------------------
```

Listing 8-22 shows the ModuleAction_Click event handler code from the HTML module.

Listing 8-22: Handling the Event

```
Public Sub ModuleAction_Click(ByVal sender As Object, _
                              ByVal e As Entities.Modules.Actions.ActionEventArgs)

  'We could get much fancier here by declaring each ModuleAction with a
  'Command and then using a Select Case statement to handle the various
  'commands.
  If e.Action.Url.Length > 0 Then
    Response.Redirect(e.Action.Url, True)
  End If

End Sub
```

The DotNetNuke framework uses a delegate (see Listing 8-23) to define the method signature for the event handler. The RegisterModuleActionEvent requires the address of a method with the same signature as the ActionEventHandler delegate.

Listing 8-23: ActionEventHandler Delegate

```
Public Delegate Sub ActionEventHandler(ByVal sender As Object, _
                                       ByVal e As ActionEventArgs)
```

Step 2: Display the Menu

Now that we have a way for the skin (the mediator class) to communicate with the module, we need a mechanism to allow the menu to communicate with the skin as well. This portion of the communication chain is much easier to code. Handling the actual click event and passing it to the skinning class is the responsibility of the ModuleAction rendering code.

Like much of DotNetNuke, the ModuleAction framework supports the use of custom extensions. In this case, we rely on skin objects to handle rendering the module actions. Each ModuleAction skin object inherits from the DotNetNuke.UI.Containers.ActionBase class. The skin class retrieves the module action collection from the module by calling the IActionable.ModuleActions property and passes this collection to the ModuleAction skin object for rendering. The ActionBase class includes the code necessary to merge the standard module actions with the collection provided by the Skin class.

Each skin object includes code in the pre-render event to convert the collection of ModuleActions into an appropriate format for display using an associated server control. In the case of SolPartActions.ascx, the server control is a menu control that is able to fully support all of the features of ModuleActions including submenus and icons. Other skin objects like the DropDownActions.ascx may only support a subset of the module action features (see Table 8-10).

Table 8-10: ModuleAction Skin Objects

Action Skin Object	Menu Separator	Icons	Submenus	Client-Side JavaScript
Actions or SolPartActions	Yes	Yes	Yes	Yes
DropDownActions	Yes	No	No	Yes
LinkActions	No	No	No	No

Step 3: Notify the Portal of a Menu Item Selection

Each skin object handles the click event of the associated server control. This event, as shown in Listing 8-24, calls the ProcessAction method, which is inherited from the ActionBase class. The ProcessAction method is then responsible for handling the event as indicated by the ModuleAction properties. If you create your own ModuleAction skin object, you should follow this same pattern.

Listing 8-24: Click Event Handler

```
Private Sub ctlActions_MenuClick(ByVal ID As String) Handles ctlActions.MenuClick
  Try
    ProcessAction(ID)
  Catch exc As Exception    'Module failed to load
    ProcessModuleLoadException(Me, exc)
  End Try
End Sub
```

Step 4: Notify the Module That a Custom ModuleAction Was Clicked

If the UseActionEvent is set to True, then the ProcessAction method (see Listing 8-25) will call the OnAction method to handle actually raising the event (see Listing 8-26). This might seem like an extra method call when ProcessAction could just raise the event on its own. The purpose of the OnAction method is to provide an opportunity for subclasses to override the default event handling behavior. While not strictly necessary, it is a standard pattern in .NET and is a good example to follow when developing your own event handling code in your applications.

Listing 8-25: ProcessAction Method

```
Public Sub ProcessAction(ByVal ActionID As String)
  If IsNumeric(ActionID) Then
    Dim action As ModuleAction = GetAction(Convert.ToInt32(ActionID))
    Select Case action.CommandName
      Case ModuleActionType.ModuleHelp
        DoAction(action)
      Case ModuleActionType.OnlineHelp
        DoAction(action)
      Case ModuleActionType.ModuleSettings
        DoAction(action)
      Case ModuleActionType.DeleteModule
        Delete(action)
```

(continued)

Listing 8-25: *(continued)*

```
      Case ModuleActionType.PrintModule
        DoAction(action)
      Case ModuleActionType.ClearCache
        ClearCache(action)
      Case ModuleActionType.MovePane
        MoveToPane(action)
      Case ModuleActionType.MoveTop, _
           ModuleActionType.MoveUp, _
           ModuleActionType.MoveDown, _
           ModuleActionType.MoveBottom
        MoveUpDown(action)
      Case Else
        ' custom action
        If action.Url.Length > 0 And action.UseActionEvent = False Then
          DoAction(action)
        Else
          ModuleConfiguration))
        End If
    End Select
  End If
End Sub
```

Listing 8-26: OnAction Method

```
Protected Overridable Sub OnAction(ByVal e As ActionEventArgs)
  RaiseEvent Action(Me, e)
End Sub
```

Because the skin maintains a reference to the ModuleAction skin object, the Skin class is able to handle the Action event raised by the skin object. As shown in Listing 8-27, the Skin class will iterate through the ActionEventListeners to find the associated module event delegate. Once a listener is found, the code invokes the event, which notifies the module that the event has occurred.

Listing 8-27: Skin Class Handles the ActionEvent

```
Public Sub ModuleAction_Click(ByVal sender As Object, ByVal e As ActionEventArgs)
  'Search through the listeners
  Dim Listener As ModuleActionEventListener
  For Each Listener In ActionEventListeners

    'If the associated module has registered a listener
    If e.ModuleConfiguration.ModuleID = Listener.ModuleID Then

      'Invoke the listener to handle the ModuleAction_Click event
      Listener.ActionEvent.Invoke(sender, e)
    End If
  Next
End Sub
```

You are now ready take full advantage of the entire ModuleAction API to create custom menu items for your own modules, handle the associated Action event when the menu item is clicked, and to create your own custom ModuleAction skin objects.

IPortable

DotNetNuke 3.0 provides the ability to import and export modules within the portal. Like many features in DotNetNuke, this feature is implemented using a combination of core code and module-specific logic. The IPortable interface defines the methods required to implement this feature on a module-by-module basis (see Listing 8-28).

Listing 8-28: IPortable Interface Definition

```
Public Interface IPortable
  Function ExportModule(ByVal ModuleID As Integer) As String

  Sub ImportModule(ByVal ModuleID As Integer, _
                   ByVal Content As String, _
                   ByVal Version As String, _
                   ByVal UserID As Integer)
End Interface
```

This interface provides a much needed feature to DotNetNuke and is a pretty straightforward interface to implement. To fully support importing and exporting content, you need to implement the interface in two places within your module.

As modules are being loaded by the portal for rendering a specific page, the module is checked to determine whether it implements the IPortable interface. This check is based on the current module control that is being loaded (remember each module can consist of many user controls). Typically, you will want the portal to add the import and export Module Actions to your primary module control. If the control implements the IPortable interface, DotNetNuke will automatically add the Import Content and Export Content menu items to your Module Action menu (see Figure 8-4). You do not need to supply any logic for the interface methods since we are only using it as a marker interface. See Listing 8-29 for a sample implementation of the ExportModule method. The ImportModule method would contain the same stub implementation.

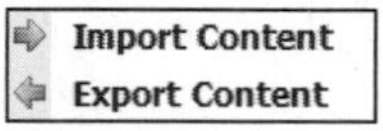

Figure 8-4

A marker interface is used to indicate that a class implements or requires a certain service. A true marker interface does not include any properties or methods. In this case we chose to re-use an existing interface rather than create a new one.

Listing 8-29: ExportModule Stub

```
Public Function ExportModule(ByVal ModuleID As Integer) As String _
  Implements Entities.Modules.IPortable.ExportModule

  'Included as a stub only so that the core knows this module
  ' Implements Entities.Modules.IPortable

End Function
```

Each module should include a controller class that is identified in the BusinessControllerClass property of the portal's ModuleInfo class. This class is identified in the module manifest file discussed in Chapter 14. The controller class is where we will implement many of the interfaces available to modules.

Implementing the IPortable interface requires implementing logic for the ExportModule and ImportModule methods shown in Listing 8-30 and Listing 8-31, respectively. The complexity of the data model for your module will determine the difficulty of implementing these methods. Let's take a look at a simple case as implemented by the HTMLText module.

The ExportModule method is used to serialize the content of the module to an xml string. DotNetNuke will save the serialized string along with the module's FriendlyName and Version. The xml file is saved into the portal directory.

Listing 8-30: ExportModule Stub

```
Public Function ExportModule(ByVal ModuleID As Integer) As String _
    Implements Entities.Modules.IPortable.ExportModule

    Dim strXML As String = ""

    Dim objHtmlText As HtmlTextInfo = GetHtmlText(ModuleID)
    If Not objHtmlText Is Nothing Then
        strXML += "<htmltext>"
        strXML += "<desktophtml>{0}</desktophtml>"
        strXML += "<desktopsummary>{1}</desktopsummary>"
        strXML += "</htmltext>"

        String.Format(strXML, _
                        XMLEncode(objHtmlText.DeskTopHTML), _
                        XMLEncode(objHtmlText.DesktopSummary))
    End If

    Return strXML

End Function
```

The ImportModule method (see Listing 8-31) reverses the process by deserializing the xml string created by the ExportModule method and replacing the content of the specified module. The portal will pass the version information stored during the export process along with the serialized xml string.

Listing 8-31: ImportModule Stub

```
Public Sub ImportModule(ByVal ModuleID As Integer, _
                        ByVal Content As String, _
                        ByVal Version As String, _
                        ByVal UserId As Integer) _
    Implements Entities.Modules.IPortable.ImportModule

    Dim xmlHtmlText As XmlNode = GetContent(Content, "htmltext")

    Dim objText As HtmlTextInfo = New HtmlTextInfo
```

```
    objText.ModuleId = ModuleID
    objText.DeskTopHTML = xmlHtmlText.SelectSingleNode("desktophtml").InnerText
    objText.DesktopSummary = xmlHtmlText.SelectSingleNode("desktopsummary").InnerText
    objText.CreatedByUser = UserId
    AddHtmlText(objText)

End Sub
```

The IPortable interface is a straightforward interface to implement but provides much needed functionality to the DotNetNuke framework. This interface is at the heart of the Templating capability for
DotNetNuke and therefore is definitely an interface that all modules should implement.

IUpgradable

One of DotNetNuke's greatest features is the ability to easily upgrade from one version to the next. The
heart of this capability is the creation of script files that can be run sequentially to modify the database
schema and migrate any existing data to the new version's schema. In later versions DotNetNuke added
a mechanism for also running custom logic during the upgrade process. Unfortunately, this mechanism
was not provided for modules. Therefore, third-party modules were forced to create their own mechanism for handling custom upgrade logic.

This is finally fixed in DotNetNuke 3.0. The IUpgradeable interface (see Listing 8-32) provides a standard
upgrade capability for modules, and uses the same logic as used in the core framework. The interface
includes a single method, UpgradeModule, which allows the module to execute custom business logic
depending on the current version of the module being installed.

Listing 8-32: IUpgradeable Interface

```
Public Interface IUpgradeable
    Function UpgradeModule(ByVal Version As String) As String
End Interface
```

The UpgradeModule method is called once for each script version included with the module. If an earlier version of the module is already installed, then this method is only called for script versions that are
later than the version of the currently installed module.

Inter-Module Communication

DotNetNuke includes the ability for modules to communicate with each other through the Inter-Module
Communication (IMC) framework. Originally the IMC framework allowed a module to pass simple
strings to another module on the same page. This was enhanced in DotNetNuke 2.0 to allow modules to
pass objects rather than simple strings. Additionally, other properties were added that allowed a module
to identify the Sender, the Target, and the Type of message. Let's take a look at the two main interfaces
that provide this functionality to your module.

IModuleCommunicator

The IModuleCommunicator interface defines a single event, ModuleCommunication, for your module
to implement (see Listing 8-33).

Listing 8-33: IModuleCommunicator Interface

```
Public Interface IModuleCommunicator
  Event ModuleCommunication As ModuleCommunicationEventHandler
End Interface
```

To communicate with another module, first implement the IModuleCommunicator interface in your module. You should have an event declaration in your module as shown in Listing 8-34.

Listing 8-34: ModuleCommunication Event Implementation

```
Public Event ModuleCommunication(ByVal sender As Object, _
                            ByVal e As ModuleCommunicationEventArgs) _
                            Implements IModuleCommunicator.ModuleCommunication
```

IModuleListener

Whereas the IModuleCommunicator is used for sending messages, the IModuleListener interface (see Listing 8-35) is used for receiving messages.

Listing 8-35: IModuleListener Interface

```
Public Interface IModuleListener
  Sub OnModuleCommunication(ByVal s As Object, _
                       ByVal e As ModuleCommunicationEventArgs)
End Interface
```

This interface defines a single method, OnModuleCommunication, which is called when an IModuleCommunicator on the same page raises the ModuleCommunication event. What you do in response to this event notification is totally up to you.

DotNetNuke does not filter event messages. Any module that implements the IModuleListener interface will be notified when the event is raised. It is the responsibility of the module to determine whether or not it should take any action.

ISearchable

DotNetNuke 3.0 provides a robust search API for indexing and searching content in your portal. The DotNetNuke search API is broken down into three distinct parts:

1. Core search engine
2. Search data store
3. Search indexer

Like the ModuleAction framework, the search framework also implements a Mediator pattern. When combined with the Provider pattern, this framework provides lots of flexibility. In Figure 8-5 you can see the relationship between these patterns and the three framework elements listed above.

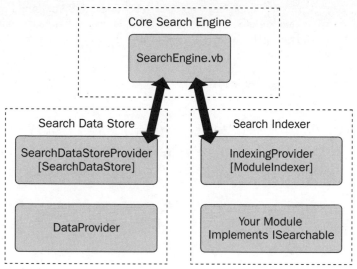

Figure 8-5

The core search engine provides a simple API for calling the IndexProvider and then storing the results using a SearchDataStoreProvider. This API is currently intended for use by the core framework. Future versions of the API will be extended to allow modules greater control over the indexing process.

DotNetNuke includes a default implementation of the SearchDataStoreProvider. The default implementation is meant to provide basic storage functionality, but could be replaced with a more robust search engine. Like other providers, it is anticipated that third-party developers will implement providers for many of the current search engines on the market.

The IndexingProvider provides an interface between the core search engine and each module. DotNetNuke includes a default provider that indexes module content. This provider could be replaced to provide document indexing, web indexing, or even indexing legacy application content stored in another database. If you decide to replace the IndexingProvider, keep in mind that DotNetNuke only allows for the use of a single provider of a given type. This means that if you want to index content from multiple sources, you must implement this as a single provider. Future versions of the framework may be enhanced to overcome this limitation.

When using the ModuleIndexer, you can incorporate a module's content into the search engine data store by implementing the ISearchable interface shown in Listing 8-36.

Listing 8-36: ISearchable Interface

```
Public Interface ISearchable
    Function GetSearchItems(ByVal ModInfo As ModuleInfo) As SearchItemInfoCollection
End Interface
```

This interface is designed to allow almost any content to be indexed. By passing in a reference to the module and returning a collection of SearchItems, the modules are free to map their content to each SearchItem as they see fit. Listing 8-37 shows a sample implementation from the Announcements module included with DotNetNuke.

Listing 8-37: Implementing the Interface

```
Public Function GetSearchItems(ByVal ModInfo As Entities.Modules.ModuleInfo) _
   As Services.Search.SearchItemInfoCollection _
   Implements Services.Search.ISearchable.GetSearchItems
      Dim SearchItemCollection As New SearchItemInfoCollection

      Dim Announcements As ArrayList = GetAnnouncements(ModInfo.ModuleID)

      Dim objAnnouncement As Object
      For Each objAnnouncement In Announcements
        Dim SearchItem As SearchItemInfo
        With CType(objAnnouncement, AnnouncementInfo)

          Dim UserId As Integer
          If IsNumeric(.CreatedByUser) Then
            UserId = Integer.Parse(.CreatedByUser)
          Else
            UserId = 2
          End If
          SearchItem = New SearchItemInfo(ModInfo.ModuleTitle & " - " & .Title, _
                      ApplicationURL(ModInfo.TabID), _
                      .Description, _
                      UserId, _
                      .CreatedDate, _
                      ModInfo.ModuleID, _
                      "Anncmnt" & ModInfo.ModuleID.ToString & "-" & .ItemId, _
                      .Description)
          SearchItemCollection.Add(SearchItem)
        End With
      Next

      Return SearchItemCollection
End Function
```

You can see from the preceding code block we made a call to our Info class for our module, just as we would when we bind to a control within our ascx file, but in this case the results are going to populate the SearchItemInfo, which will populate the DNN index with data from our module.

The key to implementing the interface is figuring out how to map your content to a collection of SearchItemInfo objects. Table 8-11 lists the properties of the SearchItemInfo class.

Table 8-11: SearchItemInfo Properties

Property	Description
SearchItemId	This is an ID that is assigned by the search engine and is used when deleting items from the data store.
Title	The Title is a string that is used when displaying search results.
Description	The Description is a summary of the content and is used when displaying search results.
Author	The content author.
PubDate	This is a date that allows the search engine to determine the age of the content.
ModuleId	The ID of the module whose content is being indexed.
SearchKey	This is a unique key that can be used to identify each specific search item for this module.
Content	This is the specific content that will be searched. The default search data store does not search on any words that are not in the content property.
GUID	The GUID is another unique identifier that is used when syndicating content in the portal.
ImageFileId	The ImageFileID is an optional property that is used for identifying image files that accompany a search item.
HitCount	The HitCount is maintained by the search engine, and is used for identifying the number of times that a search item is returned in a search.

Now that the index is populated with data, users of your portal will be able to search your module's information from a unified interface within DNN.

Summary

This chapter examined many of the core APIs that provide the true power behind DotNetNuke. By leveraging common APIs, you can extend the portal in almost any direction. Replace core functions or just add a custom module; the core APIs are what makes it all possible. Now that you know how to use most of the core functions, the next several chapters examine how to create your own custom modules to really take advantage of this power.

Beginning Module Development

This chapter begins the tour of module development in DotNetNuke. As you have read, DotNetNuke provides a large amount of functionality right out of the box, but we also realize that each one is going to have separate business requirements that DotNetNuke may not meet. Fortunately, DotNetNuke provides developers and third-party independent software vendors (ISVs) to extend the core framework by developing modules.

This chapter focuses on the architecture of one of those specific modules, namely, the Events module. Chapters 10 through 12 cover various other aspects of module development. This chapter starts out with setting up DotNetNuke to interface with your module development in Visual Studio .NET 2003. In addition to configuring DotNetNuke to interface with the development, it also discusses some issues when configuring your development environment.

Planning Your Module Project

Of course to succeed in any project, you should plan out that project before you start writing even one line of code. You're going to have to ask yourself or project team a few questions before beginning your application development.

Can the development effort justify the savings that your application will provide?

Many factors may come into play: skills of in-house staff, costs associated with obtaining the skills, and many others that you will have to account for. This leads into the next question — as with any project, you may be confronted with the choice of developing in-house or outsourcing your project.

Can the module be purchased from a third party?

DotNetNuke has grown in popularity over the past couple of years, and the outlook is continued growth. More independent software vendors are developing modules, so more than likely there is no need to develop a module to accomplish a specific task; you can purchase it for very little cost. As of this writing, more than 250 modules are currently available for sale, and many more are available as a free download.

Is training required for developers?

Module development does require some additional skills. DotNetNuke module development is done using the standard tools you would use to do any ASP.NET development, but knowing how to take advantage of the interfaces available will require some insight into the inner workings of the framework. Many resources are available for learning about DotNetNuke (in addition to this book you're reading) if you want to investigate further.

Should you hire an outside resource to do the development?

Training becomes less of an issue when you have your development done by an outside resource. DotNetNuke's popularity has increased at such a phenomenal rate that many solution providers are out there specializing in module development.

What infrastructure issues are there?

How many developers are going to be working on the same code base? The more developers working on the same code, the more there will be a need for source control. Scalability may also be something to consider. In addition, if you have to access resources over the Web, you'll need to read some of the application settings configured at a host level in DotNetNuke.

Do we need to develop multiple data providers for the module?

What database are you going to use for the backend? DotNetNuke supports a Provider Model that enables developers to abstract out the physical database interaction, allowing the actual DotNetNuke core and module logic to be separate from the database logic. DotNetNuke supports SQL Server out of the box, but a provider can be developed for basically any database backend. How many physical databases you need to support will determine how many providers you will need to develop. Refer to Chapter 7 on DotNetNuke architecture to learn more about abstraction and the Provider Model. Module development closely mirrors the DotNetNuke architecture, and you should create a provider for each platform you wish to support. If you're going to distribute your module on various DotNetNuke installs with different databases like SQL Server, Oracle, or MySQL, then you will need to develop a provider to support those individual databases.

Do we need to support different versions of DotNetNuke?

DotNetNuke is becoming a mature product with several versions released. There have been many major architectural changes going from version 1.x to 2.x and to 3.x. If your module needs to be available on these various versions of DotNetNuke, you will need to determine this and manage the various code bases to accommodate all the required versions.

What resources are needed for ongoing support of the module?

This may not be as much of an issue for modules purchased or developed by an outside party. You may be able to obtain adequate support from the vendor. If you developed in-house you'll need to set aside resources to provide ongoing support of the module.

Of course this list of sample questions is not all-inclusive. You'll have to determine this for your own application.

Ready Your Resources

Now that you have decided to begin module development, you will need to ready your development environment. The entire source and project files are available in the DotNetNuke distribution file that you can download from www.dotnetnuke.com. Just as you installed DotNetNuke on the production server in Chapter 2, you will need to configure a development machine with the source code. Again, this process is the same as it would be for configuring a production machine as in Chapter 2.

Ensure that your development environment is configured with Visual Studio .NET 2003, SQL Server 2000, or MSDE (or your specific data provider). In addition, if you are working with your source files in a location other than the DotNetNuke default (c:/dotnetnuke), you may need to change the solution file (dotnetnuke.sln) and the web information contained within the solution (dotnetnuke.webinfo). By making the changes within these files to point to the location of the virtual directory for your environment, you will ensure that you can open the solution correctly in Visual Studio .NET.

You may want to consider installing Visual Source Safe, or some other source control to ensure integrity of your project source code. Installing Source Safe is beyond the scope of this book, but it is recommended that you use some sort of source control to protect your development.

Another item to note is the publishing process from your development environment to your production environment. Because DotNetNuke is ASP.NET-compiled into several assemblies, the most it takes to publish to production is simply copying the development assemblies, user controls, the associated aspx, and resource files to production. Ensure that you compile as release mode in Visual Studio .NET before placing into production.

In many environments, an extra stage in the development process is added in by placing a sandbox or testing server in between development and production. This testing server should mirror your production environment as closely as possible; you should then install your module to the testing server and test first. Once the business units review the functionality and ensure it is according to specifications, it gets published out to the production servers.

Starting Development

We have covered some topics that will lead you to your development decisions, and it's time to begin developing your module. In this example, you are going to work with the Events module that is included in the DotNetNuke distribution. This chapter and the next three chapters provide an in-depth study of this module and the code to make it work.

Configuring Your Visual Studio .NET Project

DotNetNuke is broken down into several solutions; the primary solution located in the root directory of the distribution file contains all the projects that make up the entire core. This includes any controls, web forms, class files, and any other files required for the core application. With the release of DNN 3, we have changed the solution organization to break them up into more manageable pieces for each specific section of DotNetNuke. For module developers there is the module solution located within the <approot> \Solutions\DotNetNuke.DesktopModules directory. Open the DotNetNuke.DesktopModules.sln file to open the module solution in Visual Studio .NET. You will see a solution containing approximately 30 projects. These projects are the individual modules that make up DotNetNuke.

When you open the solution you should see the project listings shown in Figure 9-1.

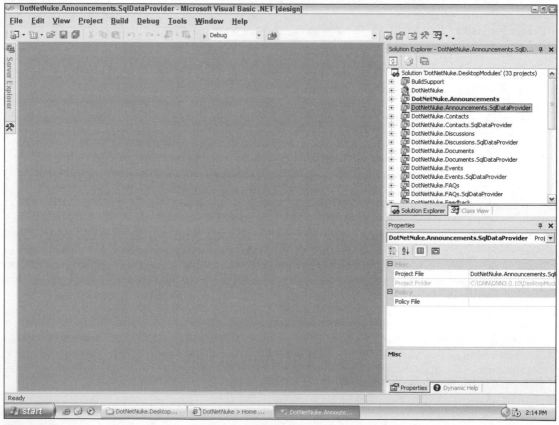

Figure 9-1

Create Your Project

In order to begin module development you will need to create a module project within the DesktopModules solution. Several projects are already included in the solution, and in this example you will be using the Events module. To create your own project, step through the following process:

1. With the Visual Studio .NET DotNetNuke.DesktopModules solution open, right-click the solution at the top of the Solution Explorer. Select Add ⇨ New Project from the context menu. This brings up the Add New Project dialog.

2. Select Class Library from the Templates section, provide a name for your module in the Name text box, and click Browse to pick a location for the project files. For module development select <approot>\DesktopModules\ for the project directory (see Figure 9-2). You should now see your module listed at the bottom of the Solution Explorer.

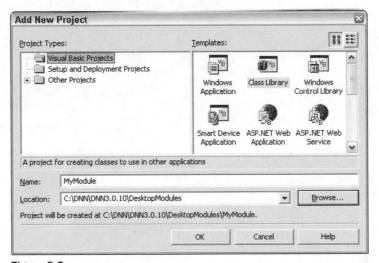

Figure 9-2

3. Notice BuildSupport project within this solution. This project is what helps you to compile your assemblies to the bin directory of the main DotNetNuke project. By compiling to the bin directory of the main DotNetNuke core project, any time you make a change in your development code and compile, those changes will be displayed within your module when you view it within your portal in a web browser. This eliminates the need to copy the dll file into DotNetNuke's bin directory every time you make a change and recompile. You accomplish this by adding a reference to your module project to the BuildSupport project as in Figure 9-3.

4. As you can see in Figure 9-3, a reference is created to each of the module projects in DNN. For the example used in this and the next three chapters, you can see a reference to the Events module — SQLDataProvider (more about this in the next chapter).

Once your module project has been created, you will need to follow the same procedure in order to create your SQLDataProvider project. The only difference for the Data Provider project is the name, which will be ModuleName.SQLDataProvider (depending on your physical provider; if you were using Access, it would be AccessDataProvider). It is generally acceptable to place the Data Provider project in a subdirectory off of your module, so the full path would be <approot>\DesktopModules\Module Name\Providers\DataProviders\SQLDataProvider\. You would then create a directory for each physical database you plan on supporting for your module.

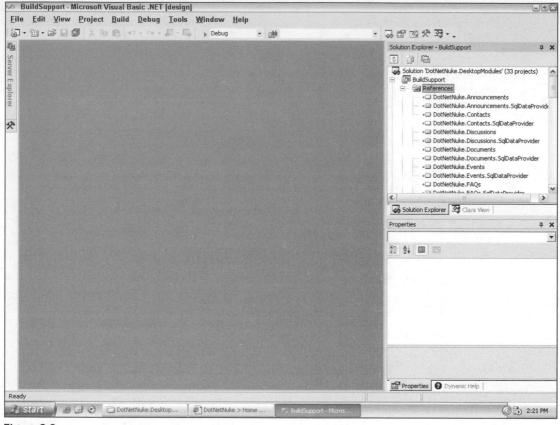

Figure 9-3

Add Controls

Now that your project has been created, you need to add some controls for your users to interface with and some classes for data operations.

There is a limitation with Visual Studio .NET in adding user controls in class projects, user controls (ascx) cannot be added to a class project. In many cases developers will copy an existing ascx control from another module project and then paste it into the newly created project.

For most modules you will need to create three controls:

❑ **View Control:** This is the default view users will see when they first access your module.

❑ **Edit Control:** This is for updating the data contained in the module's tables within the database.

❑ **Settings Control:** This is for specifying unique values for a particular instance of a module.

The Events module example has the Events.ascx (View Control), EditEvents.ascx (Edit Control), and the Settings.ascx (Settings Control).

A member of the DNN Core Team has created templates that you can use to install into your Visual Studio .NET application to ease the process of creating controls, as well as project files. They can be freely downloaded from `http://dnnjungle.vmasanas.net/`. *In addition, you can download Code Smith templates that will reduce the amount of code you will need to write in order to create a data provider for your module.*

Create Your Classes

Now that you have your controls, you also need to create the supporting classes within the module. In most modules you will have three classes contained in your main module project:

- ❑ **DataProvider Class:** This class contains methods that provide your abstraction layer with the database. These methods will be overridden by your data provider class in the Data Provider project (see Chapter 11).

- ❑ **Controller Class:** This class contains the methods for manipulating and obtaining data from the abstraction layer (see Chapter 11).

- ❑ **Info Class:** This class contains properties that define your objects (see Chapter 11).

Contained within the Data Provider project is one class, the DataProvider Class. It contains the actual methods for obtaining and updating the data contained within a specific vendor's database (see Chapter 10).

In the Events module the classes are the DataProvider.vb, EventsController.vb, EventsInfo.vb, and finally the SQLDataProvider.vb in the Data Provider project. We'll get into more detail on what these classes do in subsequent chapters, but for now we just want to cover what files need to be created in order to begin a module development project.

Configuring DotNetNuke to Interface with Your Module

Now that you have your Visual Studio .NET 2003 projects configured, you need to let DotNetNuke know about your module so you can test your development within your portal. DotNetNuke needs to know where your user controls are located in order to display them within the portal. In addition to location, each control type needs to be defined, that is, View, Edit, or Settings. The following section walks through configuring each control located within a module project.

Creating a Module Definition in DotNetNuke

In order to manually configure your modules in DotNetNuke you will need to log in as the host account. The first thing you need to do is navigate to the Module Definitions page in the portal:

1. Select Module Definitions from the Host menu.

2. In the Module Definitions page, select Add New Module Definition from the menu options (see Figure 9-4).

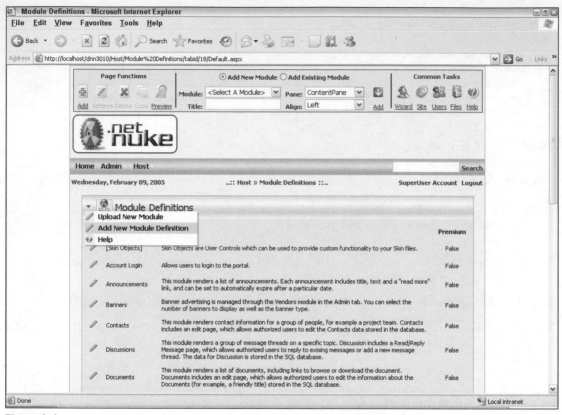

Figure 9-4

3.   Enter in a Name and Description for your module. Select the check box for Premium if this module requires an additional payment in order for each portal admin to use the module.

4.   Click the Update link button. Additional text boxes appear for you to enter in a definition for the Desktop Module (see Figure 9-5).

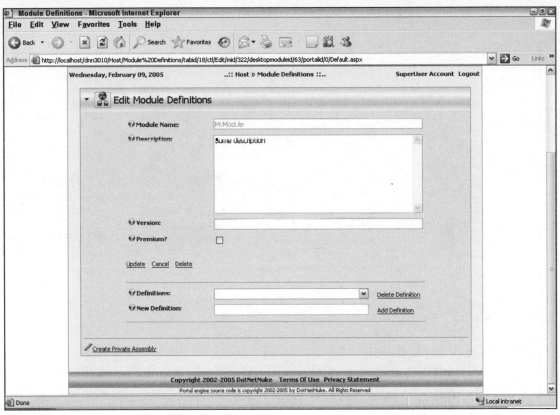

Figure 9-5

5. Provide a name for your module definition. The controls listing will now appear below the Definitions text box (see Figure 9-6).

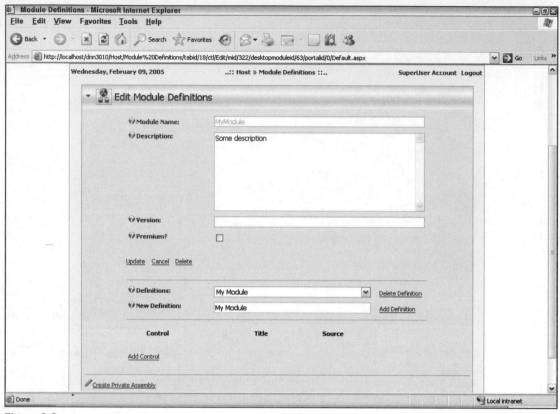

Figure 9-6

6. Here is where you define the location and type of control that you created in Visual Studio .NET 2003. Click the Add Control link button to bring up the Edit Module Control page (see Figure 9-7).

7. Within the Edit Module Control page, you define a key, which you will key off of in your code-behind page. For a default view control you would leave this empty, for an edit control you would use Edit, and for a settings control you would use Settings for your key. Keys are discussed more in Chapter 12, but they provide you with a mechanism to define which control to load at a point in your logic. You can have as many controls as you want within your module; you just need to define a unique key in order to refer to it in your code.

8. Provide a title for your control. This will be displayed within the module container when viewing the control in DotNetNuke.

9. Select a source for the module; this is the actual filename and path to your ascx control located within the DesktopModules directory. DotNetNuke will iterate through the directory structure and find all controls that are located in module projects under the DesktopModules directory. This is why you want to ensure you are creating your projects using the proper directory paths as described earlier in this chapter.

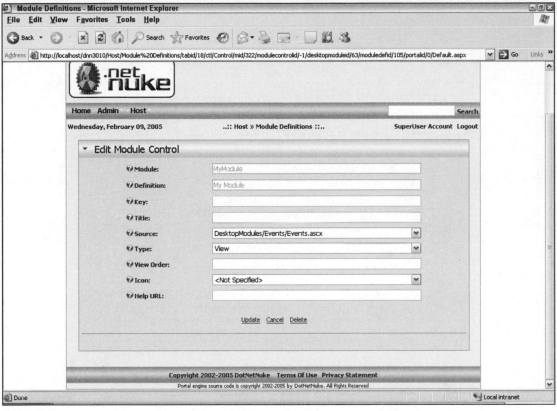

Figure 9-7

10. Select the type of control: Skin Object, Anonymous, View, Edit, Admin, or Host (more on this in Chapter 12).

11. You can enter in an optional View Order for the control.

12. You can select an optional icon to be displayed next to your control. You must first upload the image file to your portal for it to be displayed in the drop-down menu.

13. Finally, there is an option for the Help URL, which allows you to provide online help for your module.

14. Click Update and your control will now be listed. Go through each control that makes up your module project and add a definition. You can see an example of the definition for the Events module in Figure 9-8.

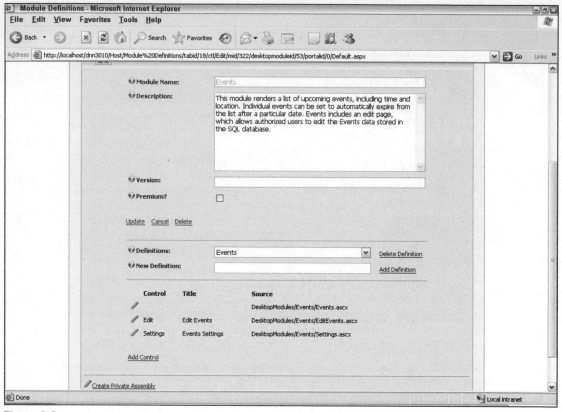

Figure 9-8

Another item you will notice on the Module Definitions screen is the ability to create a private assembly. A private assembly allows you to distribute your module to other portals using an automated setup. This is covered in more detail in Chapter 14.

Once your module is defined, place an instance within a page in your development DotNetNuke. You should see the initial view control after placing the module in the page, enabling you to view and debug your module within a live portal installation. Any changes that you now do and then compile will be instantly seen in this development page.

Summary

This chapter discussed some of the issues you will need to address before you begin any module development project. If, after weighing the options, you decide to develop your own module, you learned how to create your development environment.

The chapter then went on to discuss creating Visual Studio .NET projects and provided an overview of the DesktopModules solution file contained in the DotNetNuke distribution. Once the module project is created, you learned to define in your development DotNetNuke portal how to interface with the controls that make up the module.

The next three chapters cover each layer of module development in detail; these are the Data Provider, Business Logic, and User layers. For the purposes of the example in this book, we will use the Events module located in the DesktopModules solution as a guide for module development.

10

Developing Modules: The Database Layer

Now that you understand the concept of modules and are getting ready to develop your own, this chapter guides you on how to begin development starting with the database layer. As in most application development, you want to build a database structure for your application. This chapter covers some basic database development and how to expose your data to a DotNetNuke module.

Chapter 7 introduced the concept of the Provider Model and how DotNetNuke uses it to abstract the business layer logic from the physical database. In this chapter you develop your modules by modeling the three-tier architecture of DotNetNuke.

The following sections on creating tables and stored procedures review some basic SQL Server development concepts. From there you learn how to expose the stored procedures via a custom Data Provider that you will develop for your module. Extending on the DotNetNuke architecture, you will continue on to develop an abstraction layer for the module to provide a separation from the physical database for your module.

Developing with SQL Server is beyond the scope of this book, but this chapter covers how you expose your database's structure to DotNetNuke. We will cover table structure and stored procedures, but this will be for reference on how the structure relates to your module development.

Again, the Events module is used in the example for this chapter and the next two chapters on module development. The Events module project is located within the DotNetNuke. DesktopModules solution in the Solutions directory contained off of the root of the DotNetNuke distribution package.

Database Design

This section reviews the tables and stored procedures that make up the backend database for the Events module.

The DotNetNuke (DNN) development team wanted a module that could track events, provide a time for the event, and expire the event so it would no longer show after the expiration date was met. In order to accomplish this, we needed to create a database structure to store event information, associate the information with DNN, and then create stored procedures to add, update, and delete event information. In the next couple of sections you learn the structure of the database tables for the module and the stored procedures for performing actions on the data.

For your database manipulation you can use SQL Enterprise Manager, Query Analyzer, or Visual Studio .NET. The examples in this chapter use Visual Studio .NET 2003 for module development and database design. The idea behind this chapter and the next three on module development is to do a comprehensive review of the module structure contained within the DNN distribution that you can review.

As discussed in the DotNetNuke chapter, keep in mind that you are not bound by the underlying physical database. You can use any other database as your backend for module development, and you can develop modules for whatever database your DotNetNuke install is using. We're using SQL Server 2000 throughout the book because DotNetNuke natively supports SQL Server 2000 out of the box. The point of this exercise is to understand the physical database structure and how it applies to the database provider and abstraction layer you will create for your modules.

Database Structure

This section covers the tables used to store the information. Once a table is created you can begin writing stored procedures to manipulate the data. One table is used for storing the event information: the Events table.

Events Table

The Events table stores your event information for the module; it is defined as in Figure 10-1.

The most important field contained within the structure as far as DNN integration goes is the ModuleID field. This field contains an integer value that is assigned by DNN when you create an instance of your module. Any values you store specific to this module instance will key off of the value contained in this field. You will see this as you go through creating the stored procedures. The other fields within the database are specific to the module itself, and all depend on how you structure your application.

The ItemID field is for identifying the primary key of a specific item within your table. The main concept here, however, is to fully integrate and create a unique instance of your module with unique instance items. You will need to specify a ModuleID value that relates to the key provided by DotNetNuke for every module instance. The following list describes each item in the Events table:

❑ **ItemID:** The primary key of the event information within the table.

❑ **ModuleID:** As mentioned, because DNN can contain many instances of a module all with different information, this key consolidates all event information into the one module instance.

- ❑ **Description:** A text description of your event for display.

- ❑ **DateTime:** A date and time for when the event begins.

- ❑ **Title:** The title of the event presented to the user.

- ❑ **ExpireDate:** When the event will no longer be displayed in your portal.

- ❑ **CreatedByUser:** Tracks the ID of the portal user that created the event.

- ❑ **CreatedDate:** When the event was created.

- ❑ **Every:** If this is a recurring event, the period of time the event occurs. This is related to the Period field, which defines the amount of time between events.

- ❑ **Period:** Related to the Every field, this specifies the period between events, that is, days, weeks, months, years.

- ❑ **IconFile:** For displaying an icon next to the event listing within the module.

- ❑ **AltText:** Alternate text to be displayed when hovering your mouse cursor over the icon. This also aids your portal in complying with the Americans with Disabilities Act (ADA) Section 508.

This covers how you're going to store the data that is entered into the module. Next you create the stored procedures necessary for working with the data.

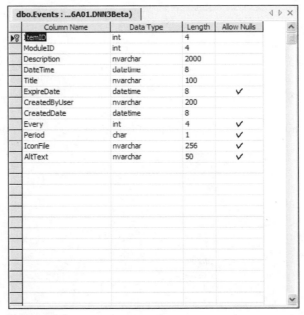

Figure 10-1

AddEvent Stored Procedure

The first stored procedure you're going to create for this module is AddEvent (see Listing 10-1). This procedure used to add an event to the Events table.

Listing 10-1: The AddEvent Stored Procedure for the Events Module

```
ALTER procedure dbo.AddEvent

@ModuleID      int,
@Description   nvarchar(2000),
@DateTime      datetime,
@Title         nvarchar(100),
@ExpireDate    datetime = null,
@UserName      nvarchar(200),
@Every         int,
@Period        char(1),
@IconFile      nvarchar(256),
@AltText       nvarchar(50)

as

insert into Events (
  ModuleID,
  Description,
  DateTime,
  Title,
  ExpireDate,
  CreatedByUser,
  CreatedDate,
  Every,
  Period,
  IconFile,
  AltText
)
values (
  @ModuleID,
  @Description,
  @DateTime,
  @Title,
  @ExpireDate,
  @UserName,
  getdate(),
  @Every,
  @Period,
  @IconFile,
  @AltText
)

select SCOPE_IDENTITY()
```

There is nothing special about this stored procedure — it's a basic insert statement, and it accepts parameters from your database provider for populating the event information. One thing to keep in mind throughout all the stored procedures is that the parameter of ModuleID is always passed when creating a new record that is associated with your module. Later in this book you learn how to obtain the module ID from DotNetNuke and pass it to your stored procedure.

DeleteEvent Stored Procedure

The DeleteEvent stored procedure (see Listing 10-2) is for deleting an event previously added to DotNetNuke.

Listing 10-2: The DeleteEvent Stored Procedure for the Events Module

```
ALTER procedure dbo.DeleteEvent

@ItemId int

as

delete
from    Events
where   ItemId = @ItemId
```

There is no need to pass a parameter value for ModuleID in this procedure. Because you're only concerned about performing a delete operation on the data, you only need to determine the PK of the specific event record.

GetEvent Stored Procedure

The GetEvent stored procedure (see Listing 10-3) is for getting a single event's information.

Listing 10-3: The GetEvent Stored Procedure for the Events Module

```
ALTER procedure dbo.GetEvent

@ItemId    int,
@ModuleId int

as

select Events.ItemId,
          Events.ModuleId,
       Events.Description,
       Events.DateTime,
       Events.Title,
       Events.ExpireDate,
       'CreatedByUser' = Users.FirstName + ' ' + Users.LastName,
       Events.CreatedDate,
       Events.Every,
       Events.Period,
       'IconFile' = case when Files.FileName is null then Events.IconFile else
Files.Folder + Files.FileName end,
```

(continued)

277

Listing 10-3: *(continued)*

```
        Events.AltText
from    Events
left outer join Users on Events.CreatedByUser = Users.UserId
left outer join Files on Events.IconFile = 'fileid=' +
convert(varchar,Files.FileID)
where   ItemId = @ItemId
and     ModuleId = @ModuleId
```

Here, you are passing the ModuleID parameter along with the specific ItemID for the event. This stored procedure is used for obtaining a single event for modification or display.

GetEvents Stored Procedure

The GetEvents stored procedure (see Listing 10-4) is used for obtaining several events for a listing of a specific module instance.

Listing 10-4: The GetEvents Stored Procedure for the Events Module

```
ALTER procedure dbo.GetEvents

@ModuleId int

as

select Events.ItemId,
       Events.ModuleId,
       Events.Description,
       Events.DateTime,
       Events.Title,
       Events.ExpireDate,
       Events.CreatedByUser,
       Events.CreatedDate,
       'IconFile' = case when Files.FileName is null then Events.IconFile else
Files.Folder + Files.FileName end,
       Events.AltText,
       'MaxWIdth' = (select max(WIdth) from Events left outer join Files on
Events.IconFile = 'fileid=' + convert(varchar,Files.FileID) where ModuleId =
@ModuleId and (ExpireDate > getdate() or ExpireDate is null))
from    Events
left outer join Files on Events.IconFile = 'fileid=' +
convert(varchar,Files.FileID)
where   ModuleId = @ModuleId
and     (ExpireDate > getdate() or ExpireDate is null)
order by DateTime
```

The only parameter passed to this stored procedure is the ModuleID value. This will pull all events for one module instance.

GetEventsByDate Stored Procedure

The GetEventsByDate stored procedure (see Listing 10-5) pulls all events within a specified date range for a specific module instance.

Listing 10-5: The GetEventsByDate Stored Procedure for the Events Module

```
ALTER procedure dbo.GetEventsByDate

@ModuleId int,
@StartDate datetime,
@EndDate datetime

as

select Events.ItemId,
       Events.ModuleId,
       Events.Description,
       Events.DateTime,
       Events.Title,
       Events.ExpireDate,
       Events.CreatedByUser,
       Events.CreatedDate,
       Events.Every,
       Events.Period,
       'IconFile' = case when Files.FileName is null then Events.IconFile else
Files.Folder + Files.FileName end,
       Events.AltText
from    Events
left outer join Files on Events.IconFile = 'fileid=' +
convert(varchar,Files.FileID)
where   ModuleId = @ModuleId
and     ( (Period is null and (DateTime >= @StartDate and DateTime <= @EndDate)) or
Period is not null )
order by DateTime
```

UpdateEvent

The final stored procedure for the Events module is the UpdateEvent module (see Listing 10-6). This allows you to update an existing event's information.

Listing 10-6: The UpdateEvent Stored Procedure for the Events Module

```
ALTER procedure dbo.UpdateEvent

@ItemId       int,
@Description  nvarchar(2000),
@DateTime     datetime,
@Title        nvarchar(100),
@ExpireDate   datetime = null,
@UserName     nvarchar(200),
@Every        int,
@Period       char(1),
@IconFile     nvarchar(256),
@AltText      nvarchar(50)

as
```

(continued)

Listing 10-6: *(continued)*

```
update Events
set     Description = @Description,
        DateTime = @DateTime,
        Title = @Title,
        ExpireDate = @ExpireDate,
        CreatedByUser = @UserName,
        CreatedDate = getdate(),
        Every = @Every,
        Period = @Period,
        IconFile = @IconFile,
        AltText = @AltText
where   ItemId = @ItemId
```

That's it for your database procedures. The next section covers how to wrap this up and create your own physical database provider for DotNetNuke.

Database Providers

Module development closely mirrors DotNetNuke architecture. Each module should provide its own abstraction to the underlying database. This enables you to change physical databases without having to change or recompile the underlying code of DotNetNuke and your module. Remember, if you want to support multiple databases with your module, you will need to create a physical provider for each database you want to support. So even if your DotNetNuke implementation is using a provider other than the one included in SQL Support, such as Oracle, for example, you will need to create a provider for your module to support Oracle as well.

The only direct interaction with the previous stored procedures contained in your database will be done in the provider project. In the modules solution of DotNetNuke, you will see that all modules have a corresponding project for a SQL Data Provider. For example, the main module project called `DotNetNuke.Events` is contained in the `DesktopModules` solution; in addition to this project we also have the `DotNetNuke.Events.SQLDataProvider` project. This project contains the class and methods necessary to interact with the stored procedures covered earlier in this chapter. The following sections cover this class and the methods it contains in order to create a provider for this module.

SQLDataProvider Class

The SQLDataProvider class for the Events module, and all modules within the `DotNetNuke.Desktop Modules` solution, closely mirrors the structure of the DotNetNuke core architecture. Therefore, you will see the same methods contained with this project as you would see in the main `DotNetNuke .SQLDataProvider` project included in the solutions directory within the DotNetNuke distribution.

Let's break down the structure of the database provider class for the Events module beginning with Listing 10-7.

Listing 10-7: Importing Namespaces for the Events Module Data Provider Class

```
Imports System
Imports System.Data
Imports System.Data.SqlClient
Imports Microsoft.ApplicationBlocks.Data
```

You can see you import various namespaces into your class for dealing with the database. The `System.Data.SQLClient` is for connecting to the SQL Server database. Since this assembly is for connecting to the physical database, you need to use specific classes for connecting and manipulating the database. The `Microsoft.ApplicationBlocks.Data` provides your assembly, which helps to reduce the code required for calling stored procedures and commands.

You can find more information on Microsoft Application Blocks in the Patterns and Practices section within the MSDN site at `http://msdn.microsoft.com/library/en-us/dnanchor/html/Anch_EntDevAppArchPatPrac.asp.`

You'll notice after importing the namespaces, we then add the namespace DotNetNuke: `Namespace DotNetNuke.Modules.Events`. One thing to take note of here is that we're using a DotNetNuke core module as an example; if you develop your own modules for DotNetNuke, it is recommended practice to create your own unique namespace in the form of `CompanyName.ModuleName` and `CompanyName.ModuleName.SQLDataProvider`. This ensures that your namespace is unique and should not conflict with other third-party modules with a single DotNetNuke portal framework.

From here you have your standard class name, and since you're creating a physical data provider class, you'll also inherit the DataProvider class of DotNetNuke (see Listing 10-8). Each Data Access Layer must implement the methods contained its DataProvider class, which as you'll see later, are overridden for each physical database type.

Listing 10-8: Inheriting the DataProvider Class for the Module

```
Public Class SqlDataProvider
        Inherits DataProvider
```

Each of the following sections of code for the Data Access Layer are broken down by regions. Regions are used in DotNetNuke development in order to organize code and make the code more readable. The first region in the class is the Private Members region (see Listing 10-9). In this region you define the variables for your provider, which is defined within the web.config.

Listing 10-9: The Private Members of the Data Access Layer

```
#Region "Private Members"

    Private Const ProviderType As String = "data"
    Private _providerConfiguration As Framework.Providers.ProviderConfiguration =
Framework.Providers.ProviderConfiguration.GetProviderConfiguration(ProviderType)
    Private _connectionString As String
    Private _providerPath As String
    Private _objectQualifier As String
    Private _databaseOwner As String
#End Region
```

As in the overall DotNetNuke architecture, the code will refer to the provider configuration within the data section of the web.config (see Listing 10-10). In this section you define the values for properties in the SQLDataProvider class.

Listing 10-10: Defining the Default Data Provider in the Web.config

```
<data defaultProvider="SqlDataProvider">
    <providers>
        <clear />
        <add name="SqlDataProvider"
        type="DotNetNuke.Data.SqlDataProvider, DotNetNuke.SqlDataProvider"
        connectionStringName="SiteSqlServer"
        upgradeConnectionString=""
        providerPath="~\Providers\DataProviders\SqlDataProvider\"
        objectQualifier=""
        databaseOwner="dbo" />
    </providers>
</data>
```

Next is the Constructors region, where you read the web.config and then populate the values from the data section to your private members within your class (see Listing 10-11).

Listing 10-11: Constructors Regions in the SQLDataProvider Class of the Events Module

```
#Region "Constructors"

    Public Sub New()
            ' Read the configuration specific information for this provider
            Dim objProvider As Framework.Providers.Provider = _
    CType(_providerConfiguration.Providers(_providerConfiguration.DefaultProvider),
_           Framework.Providers.Provider)
            ' Read the attributes for this provider
            If objProvider.Attributes("connectionStringName") <> "" AndAlso _
System.Configuration.ConfigurationSettings.AppSettings(objProvider.Attributes("conn
ectionStringName")) <> "" Then
                _connectionString =
System.Configuration.ConfigurationSettings.AppSettings(objProvider.Attributes("conn
ectionStringName"))
            Else
```

```
                    _connectionString = objProvider.Attributes("connectionString")
            End If
            _providerPath = objProvider.Attributes("providerPath")

            _objectQualifier = objProvider.Attributes("objectQualifier")
            If _objectQualifier <> "" And _objectQualifier.EndsWith("_") = False
Then
                    _objectQualifier += "_"
            End If

            _databaseOwner = objProvider.Attributes("databaseOwner")
            If _databaseOwner <> "" And _databaseOwner.EndsWith(".") = False Then
                _databaseOwner += "."

            End If

        End Sub

#End Region
```

After populating your private members with values from the web.config, you then expose some public properties for your class (see Listing 10-12). These properties are read-only and contain the values from the web.config.

Listing 10-12: Public Properties, Exposing the Database Connection Information in the SQLDataProvider Class

```
#Region "Properties"

    Public ReadOnly Property ConnectionString() As String
        Get
                Return _connectionString
        End Get
    End Property

    Public ReadOnly Property ProviderPath() As String
        Get
                Return _providerPath
        End Get
    End Property

    Public ReadOnly Property ObjectQualifier() As String
        Get
                Return _objectQualifier
        End Get
    End Property
    Public ReadOnly Property DatabaseOwner() As String
        Get
                Return _databaseOwner
        End Get
    End Property
#End Region
```

Finally, the database operations of your class are contained within the Public Methods region (see Listing 10-13). Remember the stored procedures discussed earlier? Now you're going to expose those procedures to your module so you can do your add, update, and delete operations, as well as obtain the data so it can be displayed in your module.

Listing 10-13: Public Methods within the SQLDataProvider Class

```
#Region "Public Methods"

    Private Function GetNull(ByVal Field As Object) As Object
        Return Common.Utilities.Null.GetNull(Field, DBNull.Value)
    End Function

    Public Overrides Function AddEvent(ByVal ModuleId As Integer, _
            ByVal Description As String, ByVal DateTime As Date, _
            ByVal Title As String, ByVal ExpireDate As Date, _
            ByVal UserName As String, ByVal Every As Integer, _
            ByVal Period As String, ByVal IconFile As String, _
            ByVal AltText As String) As Integer
        Return CType(SqlHelper.ExecuteScalar(ConnectionString, _
            DatabaseOwner & ObjectQualifier & "AddEvent", ModuleId, _
            Description, DateTime, Title, GetNull(ExpireDate), _
            UserName, GetNull(Every), GetNull(Period), _
            GetNull(IconFile), GetNull(AltText)), Integer)
    End Function

    Public Overrides Sub DeleteEvent(ByVal ItemId As Integer)
        SqlHelper.ExecuteNonQuery(ConnectionString, DatabaseOwner & _
            ObjectQualifier & "DeleteEvent", ItemId)
    End Sub

    Public Overrides Function GetEvent(ByVal ItemId As Integer, _
            ByVal ModuleId As Integer) As IDataReader
        Return CType(SqlHelper.ExecuteReader(ConnectionString, _
            DatabaseOwner & ObjectQualifier & "GetEvent", ItemId, _
            ModuleId), IDataReader)
    End Function

    Public Overrides Function GetEvents(ByVal ModuleId As Integer) As _
            IDataReader
        Return CType(SqlHelper.ExecuteReader(ConnectionString, _
            DatabaseOwner & ObjectQualifier & "GetEvents", ModuleId), _
            IDataReader)
    End Function

    Public Overrides Function GetEventsByDate(ByVal ModuleId As Integer, _
            ByVal StartDate As Date, ByVal EndDate As Date) As IDataReader
        Return CType(SqlHelper.ExecuteReader(ConnectionString, _
            DatabaseOwner & ObjectQualifier & "GetEventsByDate", _
            ModuleId, StartDate, EndDate), IDataReader)
    End Function
```

```
        Public Overrides Sub UpdateEvent(ByVal ItemId As Integer, _
            ByVal Description As String, ByVal DateTime As Date, _
            ByVal Title As String, ByVal ExpireDate As Date, _
            ByVal UserName As String, ByVal Every As Integer, _
            ByVal Period As String, ByVal IconFile As String, _
            ByVal AltText As String)
            SqlHelper.ExecuteNonQuery(ConnectionString, DatabaseOwner & _
                ObjectQualifier & "UpdateEvent", ItemId, Description, _
                DateTime, Title, GetNull(ExpireDate), UserName, _
                GetNull(Every), GetNull(Period), GetNull(IconFile), _
                GetNull(AltText))
        End Sub

    #End Region
```

You can see there is a one-to-one relationship within this class, so each method has a corresponding stored procedure within your SQL database. So let's break down a method here and explain what is happening. We'll use the GetEvents method.

Each event is a public method that overrides a corresponding method within the base class (DataProvider), which you inherited in the beginning of the class. So not only do you have a corresponding method in this class for each stored procedure, you also have a corresponding method in the base DataProvider class, which is located in the main module project. The method within the base class is an abstracted method that your module only deals with; this enables you to totally separate the physical database interactions from your module assembly.

Next you'll notice that all parameters that the stored procedure accepts are passed to your methods as well. In addition, you then execute the command and pass the database connection information such as the connection string, database owner account, object qualifier, name of the stored procedure, and the parameters it accepts.

The method then returns an IDataReader (if appropriate, as in SQL select statements) containing the result set from the database using the SQLHelper.ExecuteReader provided by the Microsoft Data Access Application Block you imported at the beginning of the class.

Finally, in order to handle null values returned from the database, DotNetNuke provides the GetNull method. When you create a method for your database, as was done in AddEvent and UpdateEvent in Listing 10-13, you should wrap the parameters with the GetNull method. This will prevent errors from being raised in your Data Provider due to the null values.

That's it for the Data Access Layer. Remember this layer is compiled into its own assembly binary separate from the module's main assembly. By maintaining this separation you can easily plug in providers for other databases. In addition, no recompile to your base class is necessary when changing database operations, or when replacing physical providers.

Data Abstraction

The next part of the module for data operations is the creation of the abstraction class. Remember in the Data Access Layer you created methods that overrode the base class? Well now we need to cover that base class and gain some insight on how you provide an abstraction class for the Events module.

DataProvider Class

You now need to switch over to the main module project (DotNetNuke.Events). In this project we have a class file called DataProvider.vb. This class contains nothing but overridable methods, which you over-rode within your Data Access Layer class in the previous section.

The first thing you'll do within this class is import the necessary namespaces and define your class (see Listing 10-14). You'll notice you use the MustInherit keyword within your class to specify that this class can only be used as a base class, as it is used in the SQLDataProvider class.

Listing 10-14: Creating the Abstraction Class for the Events Module

```
Imports System
Imports DotNetNuke

Namespace DotNetNuke.Modules.Events
    Public MustInherit Class DataProvider
```

Next is the Shared and Static region (see Listing 10-15) within the class. When the class is instantiated you call the CreateProvider method.

Listing 10-15: Shared/Static Methods in the Data Provider Class of the Events Module

```
#Region "Shared/Static Methods"

        ' singleton reference to the instantiated object
        Private Shared objProvider As DataProvider = Nothing

        ' constructor
        Shared Sub New()
            CreateProvider()
        End Sub

        ' dynamically create provider
        Private Shared Sub CreateProvider()
                objProvider = CType(Framework.Reflection.CreateObject("data", _
                "DotNetNuke.Modules.Events", "DotNetNuke.Modules.Events"), _
                DataProvider)
        End Sub

        ' return the provider
        Public Shared Shadows Function Instance() As DataProvider
            Return objProvider
        End Function

#End Region
```

Finally, within the abstraction class you have what provides the abstraction, the abstraction methods (see Listing 10-16). Remember these methods from your SQLDataProvider? Each method contained in this base class has a corresponding method within your Data Access Layer's class. You'll notice each method uses the MustOverride keyword to specify that its method will be overridden by the class inheriting the abstraction class.

Listing 10-16: The Abstraction Methods in the Data Provider Class of the Events Module

```
#Region "Abstract methods"

        Public MustOverride Function AddEvent(ByVal ModuleId As Integer, _
            ByVal Description As String, ByVal DateTime As Date, _
            ByVal Title As String, ByVal ExpireDate As Date, _
            ByVal UserName As String, ByVal Every As Integer, _
            ByVal Period As String, ByVal IconFile As String, _
            ByVal AltText As String) As Integer
        Public MustOverride Sub DeleteEvent(ByVal ItemID As Integer)
        Public MustOverride Function GetEvent(ByVal ItemId As Integer, _
            ByVal ModuleId As Integer) As IDataReader
        Public MustOverride Function GetEvents(ByVal ModuleId As Integer) _
            As IDataReader
        Public MustOverride Function GetEventsByDate(ByVal ModuleId As Integer, _
            ByVal StartDate As Date, ByVal EndDate As Date) As IDataReader
        Public MustOverride Sub UpdateEvent(ByVal ItemId As Integer, _
            ByVal Description As String, ByVal DateTime As Date, _
            ByVal Title As String, ByVal ExpireDate As Date, _
            ByVal UserName As String, ByVal Every As Integer, _
            ByVal Period As String, ByVal IconFile As String, _
            ByVal AltText As String)

#End Region

    End Class

End Namespace
```

Now you should see the separation of the module from the physical database. Module development closely mirrors DotNetNuke architecture; all aspects of the application are totally separated from the underlying physical database.

Summary

This chapter covered the physical database creation all the way to the abstraction class contained in your module project. Here are points to remember when developing your database and data classes for your module:

❑ In addition to a primary key for module records, add a module ID field, because each module instance is assigned a unique module ID by the DotNetNuke framework.

❑ Each stored procedure will have a corresponding method contained within the Data Access Layer.

Chapter 10

❑ Each physical database provider will be created in its own assembly project in the same namespace as the module.

❑ Each abstraction base class will contain duplicate method names in the Data Access Layer that must be overridden.

That's it for the abstraction class. The next chapter covers the Business Logic Layer (BLL), in which you take the data from your database and create objects that you later bind to your user controls for display.

Developing Modules: Business Logic Layer

Previous chapters covered how to create a physical database provider for your module, and how all the methods contained in the provider directly correlate to stored procedures within the database. Once the provider was completed, you created an abstraction class that abstracts the methods contained in the physical database in order to be used by the Business Logic Layer (BLL).

In this chapter, you take the database portion and transform the record set into a collection of objects that is provided by the Business Logic Layer within your module. We will continue with concepts that were introduced in Chapter 7 on the DNN architecture, because module architecture mirrors the architecture provided by DNN.

The idea here is to totally separate the physical database from the module or application logic that you create. Separating the two enables plug-and-play extensibility when you want to change a database provider. Because the provider is abstracted from the actual business logic, you can use the same code, but different data stores, and since they're compiled separately, there is no need to recompile the application in order to change database providers.

We will now continue this provider architecture to the business logic of the application. Here you create a collection of objects with specific properties that will be exposed to your user layer, which is covered in Chapter 12.

Developing the Business Logic Layer

Start by opening the Events module project located in the DotNetNuke.DesktopModules solution in the Solutions directory contained off of the root of the .NET Nuke distribution package. Open the solution in Visual Studio .NET 2003 to view the module projects; specifically, the DotNetNuke.Events module project you were working with in the previous chapter.

As you'll recall, the DataProvider.vb class within this project is the abstraction class, and it contains overridable methods for each method contained in the physical provider class. Now you will take these methods and wrap them with additional classes in order to populate an array of objects with specific properties.

Defining the Properties for the Info Class

This section covers the EventsInfo.vb class contained in the project folder. This class is what describes your objects for the Events module that will be returned from the database.

At the top of the class file, we'll do our imports as in the following code.

```
Imports System
Imports System.Configuration
Imports System.Data
```

Following this we have our namespace. For this example, you'll stay within the DotNetNuke namespace, but if you were creating your own modules separate from DNN, you could use a custom namespace in the form of CompanyName.ModuleName.

```
Namespace DotNetNuke.Modules.Events
```

Listing 11-1 shows the Private Members region at the top of the class. Here you define private variables and their types. These variables will be used to store the values for each property for your class.

Listing 11-1: The Private Members Region of the EventInfo Class

```
Public Class EventInfo

#Region "Private Members"

    Private _ItemId As Integer
    Private _ModuleId As Integer
    Private _Description As String
    Private _DateTime As Date
    Private _Title As String
    Private _ExpireDate As Date
    Private _CreatedByUser As String
    Private _CreatedDate As Date
    Private _Every As Integer
    Private _Period As String
    Private _IconFile As String
    Private _AltText As String
    Private _MaxWidth As Integer

#End Region
```

Below the Private Members region is the Constructors region (see Listing 11-2). In object-oriented programming, the constructor is a special method for this class that must be present in order for the object to be instantiated; in the Events module with VB.NET it is New. If you needed to write special initialization code for the EventInfo class, you would do so here in order to ensure the code is executed.

Listing 11-2: The Constructors for the EventInfo Class

```
#Region "Constructors"

    Public Sub New()
    End Sub

#End Region
```

Next are the public properties of the EventInfo class, which are used to define your object (see Listing 11-3). For example, an event has an ItemID, ModuleID, Description, and other properties. These correspond to the fields contained within the database for this module (see Chapter 10).

Listing 11-3: The Public Properties for the EventInfo Class

```
#Region "Properties"

    Public Property ItemId() As Integer
      Get
        Return _TtemId
      End Get
      Set(ByVal Value As Integer)
        _ItemId = Value
      End Set
    End Property

    Public Property ModuleId() As Integer
      Get
        Return _ModuleId
      End Get
      Set(ByVal Value As Integer)
        _ModuleId = Value
      End Set
    End Property

    Public Property Description() As String
      Get
        Return _Description
      End Get
      Set(ByVal Value As String)
        _Description = Value
      End Set
    End Property

    Public Property DateTime() As Date
      Get
        Return _DateTime
      End Get
      Set(ByVal Value As Date)
        _DateTime = Value
      End Set
    End Property
```

(continued)

Listing 11-3: *(continued)*

```
    Public Property Title() As String
      Get
        Return _Title
      End Get
      Set(ByVal Value As String)
        _Title = Value
      End Set
    End Property

    Public Property ExpireDate() As Date
      Get
        Return _ExpireDate
      End Get
      Set(ByVal Value As Date)
        _ExpireDate = Value
      End Set
    End Property

    Public Property CreatedByUser() As String
      Get
        Return _CreatedByUser
      End Get
      Set(ByVal Value As String)
        _CreatedByUser = Value
      End Set
    End Property

    Public Property CreatedDate() As Date
      Get
        Return _CreatedDate
      End Get
      Set(ByVal Value As Date)
        _CreatedDate = Value
      End Set
    End Property

    Public Property Every() As Integer
      Get
        Return _Every
      End Get
      Set(ByVal Value As Integer)
        _Every = Value
      End Set
    End Property

    Public Property Period() As String
      Get
        Return _Period
      End Get
      Set(ByVal Value As String)
        _Period = Value
      End Set
    End Property
```

```
      Public Property IconFile() As String
        Get
          Return _IconFile
        End Get
        Set(ByVal Value As String)
          _IconFile = Value
        End Set
      End Property

      Public Property AltText() As String
        Get
          Return _AltText
        End Get
        Set(ByVal Value As String)
          _AltText = Value
        End Set
      End Property

      Public Property MaxWidth() As Integer
        Get
          Return _MaxWidth
        End Get
        Set(ByVal Value As Integer)
          _MaxWidth = Value
        End Set
      End Property

  #End Region

  End Class


End Namespace
```

Notice that each property you expose for your object corresponds to a field name within the Events table in DotNetNuke.

Creating Objects Using the Controller Class

Now that you have the properties defined for your objects, you need to populate the objects with values from your database. This object population begins with the Controller class. In this case the controller is contained in the EventsController.vb class file in the module project. Let's open up this file and review its contents.

Again, at the top of the file are the library imports:

```
Imports DotNetNuke.Services.Search
Imports System
Imports System.Configuration
Imports System.Data
Imports System.XML
```

Following this you again have to specify your namespace:

```
Namespace DotNetNuke.Modules.Events
```

Next, you implement a couple of interfaces after you define your class (see Listing 11-4). In this module you implement the Entities.Modules.ISearchable and Entities.Modules.IPortable. These are two interfaces that provide your module with the ability to tie into the search mechanism and the ability to export data from your module and import it into another instance of your module on another page within the portal. We'll cover these interfaces in more detail later in this chapter.

Listing 11-4: Defining the Controller Class for the Events Module

```
Public Class EventController
    Implements Entities.Modules.ISearchable
    Implements Entities.Modules.IPortable
```

Listing 11-5 shows the public methods within the Controller class that are used to populate an ArrayList of objects from the record set received from your abstraction class.

Listing 11-5: Public Methods of the EventsController Class

```
#Region "Public Methods"

    Public Sub AddEvent(ByVal objEvent As EventInfo) _
        DataProvider.Instance().AddEvent(objEvent.ModuleId, _
        objEvent.Description, objEvent.DateTime, objEvent.Title, _
        objEvent.ExpireDate, objEvent.CreatedByUser, objEvent.Every, _
        objEvent.Period, objEvent.IconFile, objEvent.AltText)
    End Sub

    Public Sub DeleteEvent(ByVal ItemID As Integer)
        DataProvider.Instance().DeleteEvent(ItemID)
    End Sub

    Public Function GetEvent(ByVal ItemId As Integer, _
        ByVal ModuleId As Integer) As EventInfo
        Return CType(CBO.FillObject(DataProvider.Instance().GetEvent(ItemId, _
        ModuleId), GetType(EventInfo)), EventInfo)
    End Function

    Public Function GetEvents(ByVal ModuleId As Integer, _
        ByVal StartDate As Date, ByVal EndDate As Date) As ArrayList
        If (Not Common.Utilities.Null.IsNull(StartDate)) And _
        (Not Common.Utilities.Null.IsNull(EndDate)) Then
            Return _
            CBO.FillCollection(DataProvider.Instance().GetEventsByDate(ModuleId, _
            StartDate, EndDate), GetType(EventInfo))
        Else
            Return _
            CBO.FillCollection(DataProvider.Instance().GetEvents(ModuleId), _
            GetType(EventInfo))
        End If
    End Function
```

```
        Public Sub UpdateEvent(ByVal objEvent As EventInfo)
            DataProvider.Instance().UpdateEvent(objEvent.ItemId, _
                objEvent.Description, objEvent.DateTime, objEvent.Title, _
                objEvent.ExpireDate, objEvent.CreatedByUser, objEvent.Every, _
                objEvent.Period, objEvent.IconFile, objEvent.AltText)
        End Sub

    #End Region
```

In Listing 11-5, notice that each method — AddEvent, DeleteEvent, GetEvent, GetEvents, and UpdateEvent — are all methods in the Data Abstraction class (DataProvider.vb) in the Events module project of the solution. Each method creates an instance of the DataProvider class, and calls its corresponding event. Recall from Chapter 10 that each method in the abstraction class (DataProvider.vb in the Events module project) also has a corresponding method in the physical provider (SQLDataProvider project) as a wrapper to the stored procedures contained in the SQL Server database. Each method accepts a value that corresponds to values passed to parameters contained in the stored procedure. For example, the DeleteEvent stored procedure contains a parameter of ItemID for specifying the primary key of the event contained in the Events table. As such, the sub DeleteEvent in the Controller class accepts an ItemID of type integer.

Custom Business Object Help Class

As an item of note here, DotNetNuke provides the Custom Business Object (CBO) helper class. The class file is located in the <webroot>\Components\Shared\CBO.vb class file.

This class provides several methods, but for our area of concern we want to focus on two: the FillObject, which creates an object with one item as in the case with the GetEvents method in Listing 11-5, and the FillCollection method, which creates an ArrayList of objects from matching records returned from the database.

Optional Interfaces for the Events Module Controller Class

The last code region in the EventsController class is the Optional Interfaces region. Contained in this region are methods for interacting with the ISearchable and IPortable interfaces provided by DotNetNuke. You do not have to use these methods, but it is recommended in order to provide a fully functional module that is capable of exposing all the features of DotNetNuke.

ISearchable

Listing 11-6 defines properties of the individual events from your module to be placed in the search catalog of the DotNetNuke index.

Listing 11-6: Defining Search Items of the Module for DotNetNuke Search

```
    Public Function GetSearchItems(ByVal ModInfo As Entities.Modules.ModuleInfo) As _
                Services.Search.SearchItemInfoCollection Implements _
                Entities.Modules.ISearchable.GetSearchItems
        Dim SearchItemCollection As New SearchItemInfoCollection
        Dim Events As ArrayList = GetEvents(ModInfo.ModuleID, _
```

(continued)

Listing 11-6: *(continued)*

```
              Convert.ToDateTime(Common.Utilities.Null.NullDate), _
              Convert.ToDateTime(Common.Utilities.Null.NullDate))
    Dim objEvents As Object
    For Each objEvents In Events
        Dim SearchItem As SearchItemInfo
        With CType(objEvents, EventInfo)
            Dim UserId As Integer = Null.NullInteger
            If IsNumeric(.CreatedByUser) Then
                UserId = Integer.Parse(.CreatedByUser)
            End If
            SearchItem = New SearchItemInfo(ModInfo.ModuleTitle & _
                " - " & .Title, .Description, UserId, .CreatedDate, _
                ModInfo.ModuleID, .ItemId.ToString, .Description, "ItemId=" & _
                .ItemId.ToString)
            SearchItemCollection.Add(SearchItem)
        End With
    Next
    Return SearchItemCollection

End Function
```

Listing 11-6 contains a function called GetSearchItems, which will return a type of SearchItemInfoCollection that contains the values from the Events module when you call the GetEvents method. You loop through the events returned from calling GetEvents and create a new object of SearchItem. You then define the properties of the SearchItem by using the SearchItemInfo. You'll pass the values for the object to the SearchItem, which will be populated into the DotNetNuke catalog for searching. If you do not want to make the items searchable in the portal, simply do not implement the interface and include the GetSearchItems function.

This should sound very familiar after getting to this point in the book. Module development closely mirrors the architecture of DotNetNuke. Not only does the core application support abstraction classes and the Provider Model extensively, but you should also duplicate this methodology in your own development. This ensures your development is consistent with other modules contained in DotNetNuke, and also eases the process of upgrading for future versions of DotNetNuke.

Note that the SearchItemInfo class exposes properties for the SearchItem object, similar to the Events class. This structure is consistent throughout the DotNetNuke architecture and in module development as well.

IPortable

Another interface provided by DotNetNuke that the Events module implements is the IPortable interface. This interface provides the module the ability to export the data contained for that module instance to another module instance.

Listing 11-7 looks at how you export data from the module instance.

Listing 11-7: The ExportModule Function for the EventsController Class

```
Public Function ExportModule(ByVal ModuleID As Integer) As _
        String Implements Entities.Modules.IPortable.ExportModule
    Dim strXML As String = ""
```

```
        Dim arrEvents As ArrayList = GetEvents(ModuleID, _
                Convert.ToDateTime(Common.Utilities.Null.NullDate), _
                Convert.ToDateTime(Common.Utilities.Null.NullDate))
        If arrEvents.Count <> 0 Then
            strXML += "<events>"
            Dim objEvent As EventInfo
            For Each objEvent In arrEvents
                strXML += "<event>"
                strXML += "<description>" & XMLEncode(objEvent.Description) & _
                    "</description>"
                strXML += "<datetime>" & XMLEncode(objEvent.DateTime.ToString) & _
                    "</datetime>"
                strXML += "<title>" & XMLEncode(objEvent.Title) & "</title>"
                strXML += "</event>"
            Next
            strXML += "</events>"
        End If
        Return strXML
    End Function
```

Again as in the population of the search catalog, you call the GetEvents method to obtain all events for this particular instance of the module. You then loop through the results and generate an XML string, which will be returned by the function. Later in your user layer you will implement the method that will then be called based on the user action.

Listing 11-8 looks at how you import the data from the previously generated XML string.

Listing 11-8: The ImportModule Function for the EventsController Class

```
Public Sub ImportModule(ByVal ModuleID As Integer, ByVal Content As String, _
        ByVal Version As String, ByVal UserId As Integer) _
        Implements Entities.Modules.IPortable.ImportModule
    Dim xmlEvent As XmlNode
    Dim xmlEvents As XmlNode = GetContent(Content, "events")
    For Each xmlEvent In xmlEvents.SelectNodes("event")
        Dim objEvent As New EventInfo
        objEvent.ModuleId = ModuleID
        objEvent.Description = xmlEvent.Item("description").InnerText
        objEvent.DateTime = Date.Parse(xmlEvent.Item("datetime").InnerText)
        objEvent.Title = xmlEvent.Item("title").InnerText
        objEvent.CreatedByUser = UserId.ToString
        AddEvent(objEvent)
    Next

End Sub
```

As you can see in Listing 11-7, you process the XML that was generated earlier by the ExportModule routine. This time, you call the AddEvent method of the EventController to populate an event for an element in the XML file.

Summary

This chapter completed the process of obtaining data from your database. In Chapter 10 you learned how to write a provider for a physical database, and in this chapter you converted the data to a collection of objects that will get bound to user controls in your modules.

In building your business logic layer for your modules, you can take advantage of two interfaces provided by the DotNetNuke core: IPortable and ISearchable. IPortable provides your modules with the ability to export the data and settings of one module instance over to another module instance within your portal. ISearchable enables your modules to take advantage of the full-text indexing capabilities that are native to DotNetNuke to provide your portal with a search mechanism.

Chapter 12 covers the user interface of the module. You'll take the collections created by the Business Logic Layer and bind them to controls on your module.

12

Developing Modules:
The Presentation Layer

Now you're at a point where you can start making your presentation layer for your desktop module. You have learned how to pull data from the database, provide abstraction, and then transform the data to a collection of objects from your controller class. This chapter provides you with examples on how to display, modify, and work with the various controls that make up your desktop module in DotNetNuke.

The examples in this chapter first illustrate how to make a call to the business object to obtain the information, and then you'll create an edit control to update the data and to specify settings that are specific to the module instance.

From there the chapter moves on to the various user controls and interfaces that you can use to your advantage in your module development.

Module User Interfaces

Chapter 9 introduced you to module structure and how to manually create references to controls in order to define your module. Each module consists of a couple of user controls that enable the user to interface with your application logic. These controls provide a means to view and modify the data contained in the database supporting the module. DotNetNuke provides you with the ability to define these controls, and how to interface them into your application using a Module Definition.

Table 12-1 lists the files that make up a module, their keys (see Chapter 9), and their function. This example continues with the Events module as in previous chapters.

Table 12-1: Module Definitions and Relation to the Events Module

Type	File Name (Events Module)	Key	Description
View	DesktopModules/Events /Events.ascx		This is the control that your users will see on the first request to the module. You can define multiple view controls for your module; the main thing to keep in mind is that the purpose of the view is to allow your data to be displayed.
Edit	DesktopModules/Events /EditEvents.ascx DesktopModules/Events /Settings.ascx	Edit Settings	This control is used to edit information contained in the database. A DesktopModule can consist of several edit controls based on the complexity of the module. Security for edit permissions is normally done at the module level contained within a specific page.
Admin	N/A	N/A	Not used in the Events module example, but this control will be displayed to administrators for a portal.
Anonymous	N/A	N/A	Use this control for an anonymous view of your data for your DesktopModule.
Host	N/A	N/A	For displaying a host-only control for your module.

As you can see from Table 12-1, several controls are available that you can make use of in your development. The defined types are specific to the user role within a portal. For module development, there may be data that you want to allow certain roles to access. For example, if the module manipulates the application settings or file system, you would want to restrict that functionality to the host who has control over the overall application instance. Your module may modify settings configured at a portal level, like the banner ad management system; in this case you could restrict the control to just administrators within a portal.

You can select many different configurations when doing module development. For now, our focus is to continue the Events module development covered in the previous two chapters.

Table 12-1 covered the controls specific to the Events module. The Events module consists of three primary user controls for displaying and manipulating data:

❑   **View Control** (DesktopModules/Events/Events.ascx): Displays the events either in a listing format sorted by event date or in a calendar format.

❑ **Edit Control (**`DesktopModules/Events/EditEvents.ascx`**):** For adding and updating information for each specific event.

❑ **Edit Control (**`DesktopModules/Events/Settings.ascx`**):** For configuring module-specific settings like the display.

The next few sections break down each control, and display data from the collection that was defined in the Business Logic Layer covered in Chapter 11.

View Control

In the Events module the View control is located in the DesktopModules/Events directory and is called Events.ascx. Open the Events project and look at the user interface to see the controls contained within. You'll see two primary controls, one is a datalist control and the other is a calendar control. These two controls provide the module with two different views on the events data based on what is configured via the edit control (we'll discuss this later in this chapter). Listing 12-1 reviews the datalist control from the Events.ascx file.

Listing 12-1: The DataList Control in the Events.ascx Page

```
<asp:datalist id="lstEvents" runat="server" EnableViewState="false" summary="Events
Design Table">
    <itemtemplate>
        <table summary="Events Design Table">
            <tr>
                <td id="colIcon" runat="server" valign="top" align="center"
rowspan="3" width='<%# DataBinder.Eval(Container.DataItem,"MaxWidth") %>'>
                    <asp:Image ID="imgIcon" AlternateText='<%#
DataBinder.Eval(Container.DataItem,"AltText") %>' runat="server" ImageUrl='<%#
FormatImage(DataBinder.Eval(Container.DataItem,"IconFile")) %>' Visible='<%#
FormatImage(DataBinder.Eval(Container.DataItem,"IconFile")) <> "" %>'></asp:Image>
                </td>
                <td>
                    <asp:HyperLink id="editLink" NavigateUrl='<%#
EditURL("ItemID",DataBinder.Eval(Container.DataItem,"ItemID")) %>' Visible="<%#
IsEditable %>" runat="server"><asp:Image id="editLinkImage"
ImageUrl="~/images/edit.gif" Visible="<%# IsEditable %>" AlternateText="Edit"
runat="server" /></asp:HyperLink>
                    <asp:Label ID="lblTitle" Runat="server"
Cssclass="SubHead" text='<%# DataBinder.Eval(Container.DataItem,"Title")
%>'></asp:Label>
                </td>
            </tr>
            <tr>
                <td>
                    <asp:Label ID="lblDateTime" Runat="server"
Cssclass="SubHead" text='<%#
FormatDateTime(DataBinder.Eval(Container.DataItem,"DateTime")) %>'></asp:Label>
                </td>
            </tr>
            <tr>
```

(continued)

Listing 12-1: *(continued)*

```
                        <td>
                            <asp:Label ID="lblDescription" Runat="server"
CssClass="Normal" text='<%# DataBinder.Eval(Container.DataItem,"Description")
%>'></asp:Label>
                        </td>
                    </tr>
            </table>
        </ItemTemplate>
</asp:datalist>
```

You are going to bind the DataList to values from your database that are returned from a stored procedure, and then up to the provider covered in Chapter 10. The field names are MaxWidth, AltText, IconFile, ItemID, Title, DateTime, and Description.

The calendar control contained in the page provides an alternative view for the module (see Listing 12-2).

Listing 12-2: The Calendar Control within the Events.ascx Provides Another View

```
<asp:calendar id="calEvents" runat="server" BorderWidth="1" CssClass="Normal"
SelectionMode="None" summary="Events Calendar Design Table">
 <dayheaderstyle backcolor="#EEEEEE" cssclass="NormalBold"
borderwidth="1"></DayHeaderStyle>
 <daystyle cssclass="Normal" borderwidth="1" verticalalign="Top"></DayStyle>
 <othermonthdaystyle forecolor="#FFFFFF"></OtherMonthDayStyle>
 <titlestyle font-bold="True"></TitleStyle>
 <nextprevstyle cssclass="NormalBold"></NextPrevStyle>
</asp:calendar>
```

View Control Code-Behind Class

Now that you have some controls on the form, you need to bind some data to them for display. Recall from Chapter 11 that you can take data from an abstraction class, which DotNetNuke can then convert to a collection of objects via the Custom Business Object (CBO) helper class (see Chapter 7). Now you need to take the ArrayList of objects and bind them to your controls in the code-behind file Events.ascx.vb, located in the Events project.

At the top of your class you first need to do your name imports, declare your namespace, and define your class:

```
Imports DotNetNuke
Imports System.Web.UI.WebControls

Namespace DotNetNuke.Modules.Events
Public MustInherit Class Events

        Inherits Entities.Modules.PortalModuleBase
```

PortalModuleBase Class

Notice you inherit from the Entities.Modules.PortalModuleBase class. The PortalModuleBase class provides you with the ability to use a large collection of properties and methods within DotNetNuke. The

PortalModuleBase class file is located in the main DotNetNuke project in the <webroot>/Components /Modules/PortalModuleBase.vb file. In addition to inheriting from the UserControl class of ASP.NET, this class is very important to your module development efforts. It provides several important methods and properties for your module (see Table 12-2).

Table 12-2: PortalModuleBase Class Exposed Methods and Properties

Property	Type	Description

IsEditable	Boolean	Can be used as a reference to check and see if the current user has permissions to edit the module. This is defined in the properties for the DesktopModule in DotNetNuke. For example:
		`If IsEditable Then`
		`    txtEditField.Visible = True`
		`End If`

LocalResource File	String	Contains the path value of the resource file that is being used for the module. This allows you to support localization for your modules. This is covered in more detail in Chapter 8.
HelpFile	String	Contains a value to a local path for a text file containing help information.
HelpURL	String	Contains a value for a URL for an external help file for the specific module.
Module Configuration	Module Info	Provides information about a specific module.
PortalId	Integer	The ID of the current portal that the request is for. This is an integer value that is generated by DotNetNuke when a host creates a new portal.
TabId	Integer	The ID of the current page that the request is going to. This is generated by DotNetNuke when an admin creates a new page within the portal.
TabModuleId	Integer	This contains a value of module within a tab. Multiple tab modules can point to the same Module ID, allowing two instances of a module to point to the same date.
ModuleId	Integer	Returns the current ID of a specific module instance. This is an integer value that is generated by DotNetNuke when you add a new instance of a module into a page.
UserInfo	UserInfo	Contains information for the portal users.
UserId	Integer	Returns the ID of the current logged-on user.
PortalAlias	Portal AliasInfo	Contains various information pertaining to the current portal.
PortalSettings	Portal Settings	Contains setting information specific to a portal, such as the admin e-mail.

Table continued on following page

Property	Type	Description

Settings	Hash Table	The Settings hash table is very important to module development, and is probably one of the most common tools you'll use. Consider it analogous to the registry in Windows. You can use the Settings hash to store and retrieve a key/value pair specific to your module instance. For example, to retrieve a value from the settings hash:
		`Dim myVar As String = Settings("mykey").ToString`
		To set a value:
		`Dim objModules As New`
		`    Entities.Modules.ModuleController`
		`objModules.UpdateTabModuleSetting(TabModuleId,`
		`"mykey", myVar)`

Container Control	Control	Provides a container to wrap a module (see Chapter 6 to learn about what a container is).
HasModule Permission	Boolean	Checks permissions for a specific module instance, such as edit and view.

DotNetNuke Optional Interfaces

Right below your class declaration, you implement several interfaces:

```
Implements Entities.Modules.IActionable
Implements Entities.Modules.IPortable
Implements Entities.Modules.ISearchable
```

These interfaces provide you with the ability to tie into the menu control for your module. As covered previously in this book, each module contains a menu with a list of action items. In order to add items to the menus you need to implement the IActionable interface. This is also so with the IPortable interface, which provides an export and import function for the module, and the ISearchable interface, which enables your module to take advantage of the integrated search engine within DotNetNuke (see Chapter 8 on the DNN API for more information on these interfaces).

These interfaces are optional, and at the bottom of the Events.ascx.vb class file, you see a code region with the name "Optional Interfaces." Within this region is the code showing you how to implement these interfaces (see Listing 12-3).

Listing 12-3: Optional Interfaces Region of the Events Module

```
#Region "Optional Interfaces"

        Public ReadOnly Property ModuleActions() As _
                Entities.Modules.Actions.ModuleActionCollection Implements _
                Entities.Modules.IActionable.ModuleActions
            Get
                Dim Actions As New _
                    Entities.Modules.Actions.ModuleActionCollection
```

```
                    Actions.Add(GetNextActionID, _
        Localization.GetString(Entities.Modules.Actions.ModuleActionType.AddContent, _
        LocalResourceFile), Entities.Modules.Actions.ModuleActionType.AddContent, _
        "", "", EditUrl(), False, Security.SecurityAccessLevel.Edit, True, False)
                Return Actions
            End Get
        End Property

        Public Function ExportModule(ByVal ModuleID As Integer) As String _
            Implements Entities.Modules.IPortable.ExportModule
                ' included as a stub only so that the core knows this
                ' module Implements Entities.Modules.IPortable
        End Function

        Public Sub ImportModule(ByVal ModuleID As Integer, _
            ByVal Content As String, ByVal Version As String, ByVal UserId As _
            Integer) Implements Entities.Modules.IPortable.ImportModule
                ' included as a stub only so that the core knows
                ' this module Implements Entities.Modules.IPortable
        End Sub

        Public Function GetSearchItems(ByVal ModInfo As _
            Entities.Modules.ModuleInfo) As _
            Services.Search.SearchItemInfoCollection Implements _
            Entities.Modules.ISearchable.GetSearchItems
                ' included as a stub only so that the core knows this
                ' module Implements Entities.Modules.ISearchable
        End Function

#End Region
```

As you can see in Listing 12-3, the first method is ModuleActions. Here you implement the IActionable interface in order to add items into the menu for the module. You have a collection of menu items, with an accompanying action. In this example you add a menu item using the Actions.Add method. You can see that instead of passing an absolute value for the menu listing, you're using a localized string using the Localization.GetString method. By using the localization interface provided by DotNetNuke (see Chapter 8), you can have menu items displayed in the language of the current user's profile. Because this action is going to be for editing the module, you will pass EditURL as the action property for this item. This will load your Edit control when the user selects this option from the menu. In addition to localization and the control to load properties, there are security parameters to pass as well. By specifying the security type for the item display, you can restrict the functionality to specific roles configured within your portal. In this example, you check for users with edit permissions for the module by passing the value Security.SecurityAccessLevel.Edit.

Below the menu action item method in Listing 12-3 are the methods covered in Chapter 11 for implementing search and import/export functionality for the module. Recall that these methods make a call to the GetEvents method within the BLL class. You then iterate through all the events for this module instance and either load them into the search or generate an XML feed for export. Now, you need to implement a stub for these methods in order for the core to know that the module implements the interfaces. DotNetNuke will then execute the corresponding methods contained in your BLL class.

Code-Behind Regions

Now you need to break your class into several regions. You'll notice DotNetNuke makes use of named regions throughout the code in order to provide some organization to the code, and for better readability. Let's break down the code regions for this specific module. The first of these regions are the Controls and Private Members regions. As in any ASP.NET development, you need to declare your web controls in order to expose the actions, properties, and methods that they contain. In addition, for this specific example there are some private members — an array of events defined and an integer value for the current month (see Listing 12-4).

Listing 12-4: The Controls and Private Members Regions of the Events Module

```
#Region "Controls"
            Protected WithEvents lstEvents As System.Web.UI.WebControls.DataList
            Protected WithEvents calEvents As System.Web.UI.WebControls.Calendar
#End Region

#Region "Private Members"
            Dim arrEvents(31) As String
            Dim intMonth As Integer
#End Region
```

Following these two regions you begin to get into some code that is going to do something. This code is contained in the Private Methods region. Normally, your private methods are going to contain methods that will obtain your data and bind to your controls. In this example there is one method called the GetCalendarEvents subroutine, which accepts a start date and an end date for obtaining information from your database (see Listing 12-5). Chapter 10 covered the various stored procedures for this module, and this method is what calls that process of obtaining a collection from the Business Logic Layer by calling the GetEvents method. With abstraction, the BLL then calls the abstraction layer, which contains a method that is overridden by the physical provider class that calls the SQL stored procedure GetEvents. The stored procedure then returns the fields matching the query to the physical provider, which finally is converted by DotNetNuke's Custom Business Object helper class to a collection of objects you define in the BLL. This collection, or ArrayList, is then bound to the controls that were placed on the page, in this case either a calendar or datalist control.

Listing 12-5: The GetCalendarEvents Method of the Events Module

```
#Region "Private Methods"
    Private Sub GetCalendarEvents(ByVal StartDate As String, ByVal _
      EndDate As String)
      Try
         Dim objEvents As New EventController
            Dim strDayText As String
            Dim datTargetDate As Date
            Dim datDate As Date
            Dim blnDisplay As Boolean
            Array.Clear(arrEvents, 0, 32)
            Dim Arr As ArrayList = objEvents.GetEvents(ModuleId, _
                Convert.ToDateTime(StartDate), _
                        Convert.ToDateTime(EndDate))
            Dim i As Integer
            For i = 0 To Arr.Count - 1
```

```
                Dim objEvent As EventInfo = CType(Arr(i), EventInfo)
                'While dr.Read()
                If objEvent.Period.ToString = "" Then
                    strDayText = "<br>"
                If Not objEvent.IconFile = "" Then
                    strDayText += "<img alt=""" & objEvent.AltText & """ _
                        src=""" & FormatImage(objEvent.IconFile) & """ _
                        border=""0""><br>"
                End If
                If IsEditable Then
                    strDayText += "<a href=""" & _
                        CType(Common.Globals.ApplicationPath, String) & _
                        "/" & glbDefaultPage & "?tabid=" & TabId & _
                        "&mid=" & ModuleId & "&ctl=Edit" & "&ItemID=" & _
                        objEvent.ItemId & "&VisibleDate=" & _
                        calEvents.VisibleDate.ToShortDateString & _
                        """><img alt=""Edit"" src=""" & _
                        CType(Common.Globals.ApplicationPath, String) & _
                        "/images/edit.gif"" border=""0""></a> "
                End If
                strDayText += "<span class=""ItemTitle"">" & _
                    objEvent.Title & "</span>"
                If objEvent.DateTime.ToString("HH:mm") <> "00:00" Then
                    strDayText += "<br><span class=""Normal"">" & _
                        objEvent.DateTime.ToShortTimeString & "</span>"
                End If
                strDayText += "<br><span class=""Normal"">" & _
                    Server.HtmlDecode(objEvent.Description) & "</span>"
                arrEvents(CDate(objEvent.DateTime).Day) += strDayText
Else    ' recurring event
                datTargetDate = CType(objEvent.DateTime, Date)
            datDate = Date.Parse(StartDate)
        While datDate <= Date.Parse(EndDate)
            blnDisplay = False
            Select Case objEvent.Period
                Case CType("D", Char)        ' day
                    If DateDiff(DateInterval.Day, datTargetDate.Date, _
                        datDate) Mod objEvent.Every = 0 Then
                        blnDisplay = True
                    End If
                Case CType("W", Char) ' week
                    If DateAdd(DateInterval.WeekOfYear, _
                        DateDiff(DateInterval.WeekOfYear, _
                        datTargetDate.Date, datDate), _
                        datTargetDate.Date) = datDate Then
                        If DateDiff(DateInterval.WeekOfYear, _
                            datTargetDate.Date, datDate) Mod _
                            objEvent.Every = 0 Then
                            blnDisplay = True
                        End If
                    End If
                Case CType("M", Char)        ' month
```

(continued)

Listing 12-5: *(continued)*

```
                    If DateAdd(DateInterval.Month, _
                        DateDiff(DateInterval.Month, datTargetDate.Date, _
                        datDate), datTargetDate.Date) = datDate Then
                        If DateDiff(DateInterval.Month, _
                            datTargetDate.Date, datDate) Mod _
                            objEvent.Every = 0 Then
                blnDisplay = True
                            End If
                    End If
                Case CType("Y", Char)        ' year
                    If DateAdd(DateInterval.Year, _
                        DateDiff(DateInterval.Year, datTargetDate.Date, _
                        datDate), datTargetDate.Date) = datDate Then
                        If DateDiff(DateInterval.Year, datTargetDate.Date, _
                            datDate) Mod objEvent.Every = 0 Then
                            blnDisplay = True
                        End If
                    End If
            End Select
            If blnDisplay Then
                If datDate < datTargetDate.Date Then
                    blnDisplay = False
                End If
            End If
            If blnDisplay Then
                If Not _
                    Common.Utilities.Null.IsNull(objEvent.ExpireDate) Then
                        If datDate > CType(objEvent.ExpireDate, Date) Then
                            blnDisplay = False
                        End If
                End If
            End If
            If blnDisplay Then
                strDayText = "<br>"
                If Not objEvent.IconFile = "" Then
                    strDayText += "<img alt=""" & objEvent.AltText & """ _
                        src=""" & FormatImage(objEvent.IconFile) & """ _
                        border=""0""><br>"
                End If
                'check to see if the current user has edit permissions
                If IsEditable Then
                    strDayText += "<a href=""" & _
                        CType(Common.Globals.ApplicationPath, String) & _
                        "/" & glbDefaultPage & "?tabid=" & TabId & _
                        "&mid=" & ModuleId & "&ctl=Edit" & "&ItemID=" & _
                        objEvent.ItemId & "&VisibleDate=" & _
                        calEvents.VisibleDate.ToShortDateString & _
                        """><img alt=""Edit"" src=""" & _
                        CType(Common.Globals.ApplicationPath, String) & _
                        "/images/edit.gif"" border=""0""></a> "
                End If
                strDayText += "<span class=""ItemTitle"">" & _
                    objEvent.Title & "</span>"
```

```
                    If objEvent.DateTime.ToString("HH:mm") <> "00:00" Then
                        strDayText += "<br><span class=""Normal"">" & _
                            objEvent.DateTime.ToShortTimeString & "</span>"
                    End If
                    strDayText += "<br><span class=""Normal"">" & _
                        Server.HtmlDecode(objEvent.Description) & "</span>"
                    arrEvents(datDate.Day) += strDayText
                        End If
                    datDate = DateAdd(DateInterval.Day, 1, datDate)
                End While
            End If
        Next
        intMonth = CDate(StartDate).Month
        calEvents.DataBind()
        Catch exc As Exception                    'Module failed to load
        ProcessModuleLoadException(Me, exc)
        End Try
    End Sub

#End Region
```

The majority of the code in Listing 12-5 is specific to what we're doing for displaying the data. In a simple module you would simply bind the result set to a control, like so:

```
Dim objEvents As New EventsController
myDatalist.DataSource = objEvents.GetEvents(ModuleId, _
                        Convert.ToDateTime(StartDate), _
                        Convert.ToDateTime(EndDate))
myDataList.DataBind
```

But since you have some criteria on how you want to display events, you load the result set into an ArrayList, which you then iterate through and format the data for display.

Other items to note in Listing 12-5 include the use of the IsEditable Boolean value to check to see if the user has permissions to edit content for the module. If the value is true, you then display an edit icon to allow the user to edit events that are displayed.

Finally, in the exception catching you'll notice a call to ProcessModuleLoadException. This method is provided by the DotNetNuke framework for error trapping, which is discussed this later in this chapter.

The next region in this example is the Public Methods region. This is where you expose any methods that you want to make available outside of this class. Here you're dealing primarily with formatting methods and calculating the day of the month (see Listing 12-6).

Listing 12-6: Public Methods Contained in the Events Module

```
#Region "Public Methods"
    Public Function FormatDateTime(ByVal DateTime As Date) As String
        Try
            FormatDateTime = DateTime.ToLongDateString
```

(continued)

Listing 12-6: *(continued)*

```
            If DatePart(DateInterval.Hour, DateTime) <> 0 Or _
            DatePart(DateInterval.Minute, DateTime) <> 0 Or _
            DatePart(DateInterval.Second, DateTime) <> 0 Then
            FormatDateTime = FormatDateTime & " at " & _
            DateTime.ToShortTimeString
                End If
            Catch exc As Exception                    'Module failed to load
                ProcessModuleLoadException(Me, exc)
            End Try
        End Function


        Public Function FormatImage(ByVal IconFile As String) As String
            Try
                    If Not IconFile = "" Then
                    FormatImage = PortalSettings.HomeDirectory & IconFile.ToString
                End If
            Catch exc As Exception                    'Module failed to load
                ProcessModuleLoadException(Me, exc)
            End Try
        End Function

    Public Function GetFirstDayofMonth(ByVal datDate As Date) As String
        Try
                Dim datFirstDayofMonth As Date = DateSerial(datDate.Year, _
            datDate.Month, 1)
                Return GetMediumDate(datFirstDayofMonth.ToString)
            Catch exc As Exception                    'Module failed to load
                ProcessModuleLoadException(Me, exc)
            End Try
        End Function


        Public Function GetLastDayofMonth(ByVal datDate As Date) As String
            Try
                Dim intDaysInMonth As Integer = Date.DaysInMonth(datDate.Year, _
            datDate.Month)
                Dim datLastDayofMonth As Date = DateSerial(datDate.Year, _
            datDate.Month, intDaysInMonth)
                Return GetMediumDate(datLastDayofMonth.ToString)
            Catch exc As Exception                    'Module failed to load
                ProcessModuleLoadException(Me, exc)
            End Try
        End Function

#End Region
```

The next region in the code is the Event Handlers section. As you know from ASP.NET programming, events handlers are methods that respond to a certain action, be it an action performed by a user, such as a click event, or a system action such as the page loading. In this Events module example you are concerned with three events. The first is the page load event. The page load in your module is usually where you determine the initial state of your application. For example, you may check to see if the request is a postback, which means the user clicked on a link button or form button to call the module again. Listing 12-7 looks at the code in the Event Handlers section to see how the page load is handled in this module.

Listing 12-7: The Event Handlers Region in the Events Module

```
#Region "Event Handlers"
        Private Sub Page_Load(ByVal sender As System.Object, ByVal e As _
        System.EventArgs) Handles MyBase.Load
            Try
                Dim EventView As String = CType(Settings("eventview"), _
                String)
                If EventView Is Nothing Then
                  EventView = "C"                        ' calendar
                End If

                Dim objEvents As New EventController
            Select Case EventView
                Case "L"                          ' list
                    lstEvents.Visible = True
                    calEvents.Visible = False
                    lstEvents.DataSource = objEvents.GetEvents(ModuleId, _
                     Convert.ToDateTime(Common.Utilities.Null.NullDate), _
                     Convert.ToDateTime(Common.Utilities.Null.NullDate))
                    lstEvents.DataBind()
                Case "C"                          ' calendar
                    lstEvents.Visible = False
                    calEvents.Visible = True
                If Not Page.IsPostBack Then
                        If Not Request.QueryString("VisibleDate") _
                        Is Nothing Then
                          calEvents.VisibleDate = _
                          CType(Request.QueryString("VisibleDate"), _
                          Date)
                        Else
                          calEvents.VisibleDate = Now
                        End If
                    If CType(Settings("eventcalendarcellwidth"), _
                        String) <> "" Then
                        calEvents.Width = _
System.Web.UI.WebControls.Unit.Parse(CType(Settings("eventcalendarcellwidth"), _
                        String) & "px")
                    End If
                    If CType(Settings("eventcalendarcellheight"), _
                        String) <> "" Then
                        calEvents.Height = _
System.Web.UI.WebControls.Unit.Parse(CType(Settings("eventcalendarcellheight"), _
                        String) & "px")
                    End If
                Else
                        If calEvents.VisibleDate = #12:00:00 AM# Then
                          calEvents.VisibleDate = Now
                        End If
                End If

                Dim StartDate As String = _
                GetFirstDayofMonth(calEvents.VisibleDate) & " 00:00"
```

(continued)

Listing 12-7: *(continued)*

```
                Dim EndDate As String = _
                GetLastDayofMonth(calEvents.VisibleDate) & " 23:59"
                GetCalendarEvents(StartDate, EndDate)
            End Select
        Catch exc As Exception                    'Module failed to load
            ProcessModuleLoadException(Me, exc)
        End Try
    End Sub

    Private Sub calEvents_DayRender(ByVal sender As Object, ByVal e As _
        System.Web.UI.WebControls.DayRenderEventArgs) Handles _
        calEvents.DayRender
        Try
            If e.Day.Date.Month = intMonth Then
                Dim ctlLabel As Label = New Label
                ctlLabel.Text = arrEvents(e.Day.Date.Day)
                e.Cell.Controls.Add(ctlLabel)
            End If
        Catch exc As Exception                    'Module failed to load
            ProcessModuleLoadException(Me, exc)
        End Try
    End Sub

    Private Sub calEvents_VisibleMonthChanged(ByVal sender As Object, _
      ByVal e As System.Web.UI.WebControls.MonthChangedEventArgs) Handles _
      calEvents.VisibleMonthChanged
        Try
            Dim StartDate As String = GetFirstDayofMonth(e.NewDate.Date) & _
            " 00:00"
            Dim EndDate As String = GetLastDayofMonth(e.NewDate.Date) & _
            " 23:59"
            GetCalendarEvents(StartDate, EndDate)
        Catch exc As Exception                    'Module failed to load
            ProcessModuleLoadException(Me, exc)
        End Try
    End Sub
#End Region
```

In the Page_Load event, one of the first things you do is check the value contained within the Settings hash. Remember from Table 12-2 that the Settings hash is similar to the Windows registry where you can store key/value pairs. For example, you first check to see the view:

```
Dim EventView As String = CType(Settings("eventview"), String)
```

This is the purpose of the Settings hash — it allows you to have unique values for each module's instance. This provides maximum code reuse to similar functions. In the Events module example, you can specify different displays for events for each instance. This could be applied to any module in order to provide maximum flexibility for your application. You can see throughout this method there are various keys checked for this module to obtain values.

Continuing through Listing 12-7, you can see some of the private methods covered earlier in this chapter are called for displaying of date information. In addition, you also make a call to the EventsController in order to bind to your Datalist. This is based on the value contained within your Settings("eventview") key. If you're in list view, "L," then you will bind to the controller, and call the GetEvents method. Remember just as before, you bring the data from the various layers starting with the physical database provider to the BLL.

```
Dim objEvents As New EventController
::
::
lstEvents.DataSource = objEvents.GetEvents(ModuleId, _
                       Convert.ToDateTime(Common.Utilities.Null.NullDate), _
                       Convert.ToDateTime(Common.Utilities.Null.NullDate))
lstEvents.DataBind()
```

You'll also notice the call to the Common.Utilities.Null.NullDate. This provides you with a null object of the date type to pass to your method in order to return all events rather than just events within a specified range, as you did previously in this chapter.

We covered the basic structure of a view control for a DesktopModule, but there are a couple items we need to deal with in order to complete the module. For instance, several times in the view control's code-behind class we made calls to values contained within a Settings hash. These values are going to be configured within the edit control, which is used for configuring the settings for this specific module instance. The Settings.ascx control was defined in the module definition in DotNetNuke for the Events module (see Chapter 9).

Settings Control

Now you need to create a control that enables you to customize your module. In the Events module, this will set the values contained in the Settings hash table. The keys you create are primarily for defining the display of the module. You set options for defining whether to display events in a list format or a calendar format.

Listing 12-8 reviews the user control for this module. This file is located in the Events project folder called Settings.ascx.

Listing 12-8: The Settings User Control for the Events Module

```
<%@ Control language="vb" CodeBehind="Settings.ascx.vb" AutoEventWireup="false"
Explicit="True" Inherits="DotNetNuke.Modules.Events.Settings" %>
<%@ Register TagPrefix="dnn" TagName="Label" Src="~/controls/LabelControl.ascx" %>
<table cellspacing="0" cellpadding="2" summary="Edit Events Design Table"
border="0">
  <tr>
    <td class="SubHead" width="175"><dnn:label id="plView" runat="server"
controlname="optView" suffix=":"></dnn:label></td>
    <td valign="bottom" width="125">
      <asp:radiobuttonlist id="optView" runat="server" repeatdirection="Horizontal"
cssclass="NormalTextBox">
```

(continued)

Listing 12-8: *(continued)*

```
            <asp:listitem resourcekey="List" value="L">List</asp:listitem>
            <asp:listitem resourcekey="cmdCalendar" value="C">Calendar</asp:listitem>
      </asp:radiobuttonlist>
   </td>
 </tr>
 <tr valign="top">
    <td class="SubHead" width="175"><dnn:label id="plWidth" runat="server"
controlname="txtWidth" suffix=":"></dnn:label></td>
    <td valign="bottom" width="125"><asp:textbox id="txtWidth" runat="server"
cssclass="NormalTextBox" columns="5"></asp:textbox></td>
 </tr>
 <tr valign="top">
    <td class="SubHead" width="175"><dnn:label id="plHeight" runat="server"
controlname="txtHeight" suffix=":"></dnn:label></td>
    <td valign="bottom" width="125"><asp:textbox id="txtHeight" runat="server"
cssclass="NormalTextBox" columns="5"></asp:textbox></td>
 </tr>
</table>
```

You can see the various controls here to display data; most are standard ASP.NET controls. One exception to this is the use of the DNN Label control. By using DotNetNuke intrinsic controls you are able to take advantage of localization within your modules.

In addition to the DNN Label control, you can see how to specify the Settings hash table values for the view type. If you review Listing 12-7 you can see we checked the value of the Settings ("eventview") to determine in the view control how the events would be displayed. In the Settings.ascx control you can see the form field optView, which has options for how to display the events in the module. You read these values in your code-behind page for the Settings.ascx control and then pass the values to the Settings hash, which you then use to check the view for the module.

Settings Control Code-Behind Class

If you look through the code-behind, you'll notice this file is much smaller than the code-behind for the view control because you're primarily concerned with specifying how you want the module to look. Listing 12-9 shows the class imports and the class definition in the Settings.ascx.vb file.

Listing 12-9: Defining the Settings Control for the Events Module

```
Imports DotNetNuke

Namespace DotNetNuke.Modules.Events
     Public MustInherit Class Settings
           Inherits Entities.Modules.ModuleSettingsBase
```

You can see here you inherit the Entities.Modules.ModuleSettingsBase class. This class is provided by DotNetNuke and inherits the PortalModuleBase as discussed earlier (see Table 12-2), but it extends the PortalModuleBase to include some additional properties. The ModuleSettingsBase class provides methods and properties specific to configuring values for the module instance. Table 12-3 reviews what this class provides for your module development.

Table 12-3: ModuleSettingsBase Class

Name	Type	Description
ModuleId	Integer	ID of a specific single Module instance.
TabModuleId	Integer	ID of the module container within a tab. For example, two module instances in two different tabs could point to the same Module ID allowing them to mirror data.
ModuleSettings	Hashtable	Configuration options that affect all instances of a module.
TabModuleSettings	Hashtable	Affects only a specific instance of a module. This allows you to display the same information for a module, but in a different way.

One item to clarify here is the difference between the two module IDs (ModuleID and TabModuleID) and the two hash tables (ModuleSettings and TabModuleSettings). This is provided so you can use the same data in two different module instances. So, for example, if you want to update the event view for all instances of the same type of module, you would do so the following way:

```
Dim objModules As New Entities.Modules.ModuleController
            objModules.UpdateModuleSetting(ModuleId, "eventview", _
            optView.SelectedItem.Value)
```

In Listing 12-10, you update the specific instance using the UpdateTabModuleSettings method. This updates the view of all module containers pointing to the same data for a specific module, which is identified by its Module ID.

Code-Behind Regions

Next in the Settings class the various code sections are broken down into code regions. You'll notice throughout DotNetNuke certain standards are applied for coding conventions. As a module developer you should strive to emulate the DotNetNuke coding style for easier readability and management.

The first and only section in the Settings.ascx.vb file is the Base Method Implementations region (see Listing 12-10). Here you have two methods, one method called LoadSettings to load settings from your hash table, and another method called UpdateSettings to update the settings values in the hash table.

Listing 12-10: The Base Method Implementations of the Events Module Settings.ascx.vb File

```
#Region "Base Method Implementations"
    Public Overrides Sub LoadSettings()
        Try
            If (Page.IsPostBack = False) Then
                If CType(TabModuleSettings("eventview"), String) <> "" Then
optView.Items.FindByValue(CType(TabModuleSettings("eventview"), _
                String)).Selected = True
```

(continued)

Listing 12-10: *(continued)*

```
                    Else
                        optView.SelectedIndex = 1        ' calendar
                    End If
                    txtWidth.Text = _
                     CType(TabModuleSettings("eventcalendarcellwidth"), String)
                    txtHeight.Text = _
                        CType(TabModuleSettings("eventcalendarcellheight"), String)
                End If
            Catch exc As Exception                    'Module failed to load
                ProcessModuleLoadException(Me, exc)
            End Try
        End Sub

        Public Overrides Sub UpdateSettings()
            Try
                Dim objModules As New Entities.Modules.ModuleController
              objModules.UpdateTabModuleSetting(TabModuleId, "eventview", _
                optView.SelectedItem.Value)
                objModules.UpdateTabModuleSetting(TabModuleId, _
                "eventcalendarcellwidth", txtWidth.Text)
                objModules.UpdateTabModuleSetting(TabModuleId, _
                "eventcalendarcellheight", txtHeight.Text)
            Catch exc As Exception                    'Module failed to load
            ProcessModuleLoadException(Me, exc)
            End Try
        End Sub
    #End Region
```

That's all it takes to configure the settings for your module. The next section covers the second edit control for editing events for the module.

Edit Control

Since you're displaying events in your module, you need a way to add and update events in the database in order to display them. Again, as in the view control you're going to make a call to your BLL in order to pass an update or insert SQL command to your physical provider.

Open the EditEvents.ascx control contained in the Events module project to look at the user interface for adding your events data (see Listing 12-11).

Listing 12-11: Registering Controls for the EditEvents.ascx Control

```
<%@ Register TagPrefix="dnn" TagName="Label" Src="~/controls/LabelControl.ascx" %>
<%@ Register TagPrefix="Portal" TagName="URL" Src="~/controls/URLControl.ascx" %>
<%@ Register TagPrefix="Portal" TagName="Audit"
Src="~/controls/ModuleAuditControl.ascx" %>
<%@ Register TagPrefix="dnn" TagName="TextEditor"
Src="~/controls/TextEditor.ascx"%>
<%@ Control language="vb" CodeBehind="EditEvents.ascx.vb" AutoEventWireup="false"
Explicit="True" Inherits="DotNetNuke.Modules.Events.EditEvents" %>
```

You'll notice you're registering several DotNetNuke intrinsic controls. You did this with the label control in your Settings class, but now you're implementing several more in this file. Table 12-4 lists the controls provided by DotNetNuke and explains their purpose.

Table 12-4: DotNetNuke Controls and Their Description

Control	Location	Description
Label Control	\<approot>/controls /LabelControl.ascx	Provided by the DotNetNuke framework, supports features provided by DNN such as multiple languages based on user profile.
URL Control	\<approot>/controls /URLControls.ascx	Additional support for multi-language support of DotNetNuke based on profile.Portal structure, security, and other DNN intrinsic information.
Audit	\<approot>/controls /ModuleAuditControl.ascx	Provides information on who created the information and the creation date.
Text Editor	\<approot>/controls /TextEditor.ascx	Provides both a text-based and WYSIWYG environment for editing text and HTML for your module.
Address	\<approot>/controls /Address.ascx	Provides an address entry form; this is being used in the user registration within DotNetNuke.
Dual List Control	\<approot>/controls /DualListControl.ascx	Provides two lists for passing values from one list to the other. An example of this control is implemented in the security settings for a module or page.
Help	\<approot>/controls /Help.ascx	Provides inline help for your controls. Supports localization.
Section Head Control	\<approot>/controls /SectionHeadControl.ascx	Provides expandable areas for sections of your module. This is implemented throughout Dot-NetNuke.
Skin Control	\<approot>/controls /SkinControl.ascx	A drop-down list of skins installed for a portal. Primarily used in framework applications like under the admin and host menus.
Skin Thumbnail Control	\<approot>/controls /SkinThumbnail Control.ascx	Generates a thumbnail image of the skin. You can view the functionality in the DotNetNuke skins section under the Admin menu.
URL Tracking Control	\<approot>/controls /URLTrackingControl.ascx	Supports localization and click tracking.

As you can see from Table 12-4, DotNetNuke provides several controls, all of which you can use in your own development. Because DotNetNuke is open source, you can easily open any of the pages of code to find an implementation of these controls. This example covers controls specific to this module.

Now that the controls have been registered in the page and your code-behind declared, let's continue on with the rest of the control and remove some of the formatting parameters for readability (see Listing 12-12).

Listing 12-12: The EditEvents.ascx Control

```
<asp:panel id="pnlContent" runat="server">
      <TABLE width="600" summary="Edit Events Design Table">
      <TR vAlign="top">
          <TD>
              <dnn:label id="plTitle" runat="server" controlname="txtTitle"
           suffix=":"></dnn:label></TD>
          <TD width="450">
              <asp:textbox id="txtTitle" runat="server"></asp:textbox>
           <asp:requiredfieldvalidator id="valTitle" runat="server"
           resourcekey="valTitle.ErrorMessage" controltovalidate="txtTitle"
           errormessage="Title Is Required"
           display="Dynamic"></asp:requiredfieldvalidator></TD>
          </TR>
          <TR vAlign="top">
          <TD>
              <dnn:label id="plDescription" runat="server"
           controlname="txtDescription" suffix=":"></dnn:label></TD>
          <TD width="450">
              <dnn:texteditor id="teDescription" runat="server"></dnn:texteditor>
              <asp:requiredfieldvalidator id="valDescription" runat="server"
            resourcekey="valDescription.ErrorMessage"
            controltovalidate="teDescription" errormessage="Description Is
            Required" display="Dynamic"></asp:requiredfieldvalidator></TD>
          </TR>
          <TR vAlign="top">
          <TD>
              <dnn:label id="plImage" runat="server" controlname="cboImage"
           suffix=":"></dnn:label></TD>
          <TD width="450">
              <portal:url id="ctlImage" runat="server" showtabs="False"
           showurls="False" urltype="F" showtrack="False" showlog="False"
           required="False"></portal:url></TD>
          </TR>
          <TR>
          <TD>
              <dnn:label id="plAlt" runat="server" controlname="txtAlt"
           suffix=":"></dnn:label></TD>
          <TD width="450">
              <asp:textbox id="txtAlt" runat="server"></asp:textbox>
              <asp:requiredfieldvalidator id="valAltText" runat="server"
           resourcekey="valAltText.ErrorMessage" controltovalidate="txtAlt"
           errormessage="<br>Alternate Text Is Required"
           display="Dynamic"></asp:requiredfieldvalidator></TD>
          </TR>
          <TR>
          <TD>
              <dnn:label id="plEvery" runat="server" controlname="txtEvery"
           suffix=":"></dnn:label></TD>
```

```
                <TD width="450">
                    <asp:textbox id="txtEvery" runat="server"></asp:textbox> 
                    <LABEL style="DISPLAY: none"
                for="<%=cboPeriod.ClientID%>">Period</LABEL>
                    <asp:dropdownlist id="cboPeriod" runat="server">
                      <asp:listitem value=""></asp:listitem>
                      <asp:listitem resourcekey="Days" value="D">Day(s)</asp:listitem>
                      <asp:listitem resourcekey="Weeks"
value="W">Week(s)</asp:listitem>
                      <asp:listitem resourcekey="Months"
                value="M">Month(s)</asp:listitem>
                      <asp:listitem resourcekey="Years"
value="Y">Year(s)</asp:listitem>
                    </asp:dropdownlist></TD>
            </TR>
            <TR>
              <TD class="SubHead" width="125">
                  <dnn:label id="plStartDate" runat="server"
                controlname="txtStartDate" suffix=":"></dnn:label></TD>
              <TD width="450">
                  <asp:textbox id="txtStartDate" runat="server"
                columns="20"></asp:textbox> 
                  <asp:hyperlink id="cmdStartCalendar" runat="server"
                resourcekey="Calendar">Calendar</asp:hyperlink>
                  <asp:requiredfieldvalidator id="valStartDate" runat="server"
                resourcekey="valStartDate.ErrorMessage"
                  controltovalidate="txtStartDate" errormessage="<br>Start Date Is
                Required" display="Dynamic"></asp:requiredfieldvalidator>
                  <asp:comparevalidator id="valStartDate2" runat="server"
                resourcekey="valStartDate2.ErrorMessage"
                  controltovalidate="txtStartDate" errormessage="<br>Invalid start
                date!" display="Dynamic" type="Date"
                  operator="DataTypeCheck"></asp:comparevalidator></TD>
            </TR>
            <TR>
              <TD class="SubHead" width="125">
                  <dnn:label id="plTime" runat="server" controlname="txtTime"
                  suffix=":"></dnn:label></TD>
              <TD width="450">
                  <asp:textbox id="txtTime" runat="server"></asp:textbox></TD>
            </TR>
            <TR>
              <TD class="SubHead" width="125">
                  <dnn:label id="plExpiryDate" runat="server"
controlname="txtExpiryDate"
                  suffix=":"></dnn:label></TD>
              <TD width="450">
                  <asp:textbox id="txtExpiryDate" runat="server"></asp:textbox> 
                  <asp:hyperlink id="cmdExpiryCalendar" runat="server"
                resourcekey="Calendar">Calendar</asp:hyperlink>
                  <asp:comparevalidator id="valExpiryDate" runat="server"
                resourcekey="valExpiryDate.ErrorMessage"
```

(continued)

Listing 12-12: *(continued)*

```
                controltovalidate="txtExpiryDate" errormessage="<br>Invalid expiry
            date!" display="Dynamic" type="Date"
                operator="DataTypeCheck"></asp:comparevalidator></TD>
        </TR>
    </TABLE>
    <P>
        <asp:linkbutton id="cmdUpdate" runat="server" resourcekey="cmdUpdate"
    text="Update"></asp:linkbutton> 
        <asp:linkbutton id="cmdCancel" runat="server" resourcekey="cmdCancel"
    text="Cancel" causesvalidation="False"></asp:linkbutton> 
        <asp:linkbutton id="cmdDelete" runat="server" resourcekey="cmdDelete"
    text="Delete" causesvalidation="False"></asp:linkbutton></P>
        <portal:audit id="ctlAudit" runat="server"></portal:audit>
</asp:panel>
```

As you can see in Listing 12-12, the EditEvents form consists of several controls. Many are ASP.NET controls, such as the linkbutton, textbox, validators, and others. In addition to the ASP.NET controls there are several of the DotNetNuke controls covered in Table 12-4. The first control you encounter is the DNN Label control:

```
<dnn:label id="plTitle" runat="server" controlname="txtTitle"
suffix=":"></dnn:label>
```

Initially you registered the control, and now it is placed into the form. Later in the code-behind you will fill the text property of the control. Since the label is a DNN control, it performs like any other label because it inherits from the ASP.NET control, but in addition you can associate information with the control, such as multiple languages from a resource file.

Further down the code is the TextEditor control:

```
<dnn:texteditor id="teDescription" runat="server"></dnn:texteditor>
```

By default DotNetNuke uses FreeTextBox, which is a freely available open source control that you can use in your own applications. Since DotNetNuke uses a Provider Model for the TextEditor control, you can easily use any third-party control.

Next in line are controls that were registered using the "portal" prefix. These controls are for tracking activity within the portal. For example, when someone clicks on an event or any item in the portal, you can use these controls to track how many and who clicked on them. Of course in order to track who clicked on an item, users need to be logged on to the portal.

```
<portal:url id="ctlImage" runat="server" showtabs="False" showurls="False"
urltype="F" showtrack="False" showlog="False" required="False"></portal:url>
```

Some of the options allow you to show a log of clicks next to the item, tracking and other information for tracking activity and display of the item. The control also integrates with DNN security allowing you to display navigation of tab structure, but still maintain the security so only those who have permissions for the resource see the information.

Finally at the bottom of the page is an audit control for tracking activity of the module. The portal audit control will provide you with information on who created the information and the created date.

```
<portal:audit id="ctlAudit" runat="server"></portal:audit>
```

Now let's check out the code-behind to see how to work with the data and the controls. For the most part you have dealt with displaying data from the BLL; now that you're going to be adding and updating information, you'll need to pass parameters to your stored procedures in SQL. Refer to Chapters 10 and 11 to see how this all comes together.

Edit Events Code-Behind Class

Now that we covered the front-end control that the user interacts with, let's look at the code-behind file and see how the class is structured. As before, you import the namespaces and define the class:

```
Imports DotNetNuke
Imports System.Web.UI.WebControls

Namespace DotNetNuke.Modules.Events
    Public MustInherit Class EditEvents
            Inherits Entities.Modules.PortalModuleBase
```

You'll notice again you inherit from the PortalModuleBase class as you did in the view control. Since this control is for adding data specific to your application, you'll inherit the PortalModuleBase. Just to be clear on the difference between this control and the Settings control, which inherits from the ModuleSettingsBase class of DotNetNuke, the Settings control is specific to the operation of the module, not the item data that is entered in tables that you create. The Settings data is stored within internal tables native to DotNetNuke, so you need to inherit from the ModuleSettingsBase, which is focused on this task. An Edit control is specific to your application so it inherits from the PortalModuleBase.

Edit Events Code Regions

Again, each section in the class is broken down into code regions for readability and organization. Let's review the regions specific to the EditEvents.ascx.vb file.

The first region is the Controls region, where you declare the controls you have created in your web form in the EditEvents.ascx control (see Listing 12-13).

Listing 12-13: The Controls Region of the EditEvents.ascx.vb File

```
#Region "Controls"

    Protected WithEvents pnlContent As System.Web.UI.WebControls.Panel
    Protected plTitle As UI.UserControls.LabelControl
    Protected WithEvents txtTitle As System.Web.UI.WebControls.TextBox
    Protected WithEvents valTitle As _
        System.Web.UI.WebControls.RequiredFieldValidator
    Protected plDescription As UI.UserControls.LabelControl
    Protected WithEvents teDescription As UI.UserControls.TextEditor
    Protected WithEvents valDescription As _
        System.Web.UI.WebControls.RequiredFieldValidator
```

(continued)

Listing 12-13: *(continued)*

```
        Protected plImage As UI.UserControls.LabelControl
        Protected WithEvents ctlImage As UI.UserControls.UrlControl
        Protected plAlt As UI.UserControls.LabelControl
        Protected WithEvents txtAlt As System.Web.UI.WebControls.TextBox
        Protected WithEvents valAltText As _
            System.Web.UI.WebControls.RequiredFieldValidator
        Protected plEvery As UI.UserControls.LabelControl
        Protected WithEvents txtEvery As System.Web.UI.WebControls.TextBox
        Protected WithEvents cboPeriod As System.Web.UI.WebControls.DropDownList
        Protected plStartDate As UI.UserControls.LabelControl
        Protected WithEvents txtStartDate As System.Web.UI.WebControls.TextBox
        Protected WithEvents cmdStartCalendar As _
            System.Web.UI.WebControls.HyperLink
        Protected WithEvents valStartDate As _
            System.Web.UI.WebControls.RequiredFieldValidator
        Protected WithEvents valStartDate2 As _
            System.Web.UI.WebControls.CompareValidator
        Protected plTime As UI.UserControls.LabelControl
        Protected WithEvents txtTime As System.Web.UI.WebControls.TextBox
        Protected plExpiryDate As UI.UserControls.LabelControl
        Protected WithEvents txtExpiryDate As System.Web.UI.WebControls.TextBox
        Protected WithEvents cmdExpiryCalendar As _
            System.Web.UI.WebControls.HyperLink
        Protected WithEvents valExpiryDate As _
            System.Web.UI.WebControls.CompareValidator
        'tasks
        Protected WithEvents cmdUpdate As System.Web.UI.WebControls.LinkButton
        Protected WithEvents cmdCancel As System.Web.UI.WebControls.LinkButton
        Protected WithEvents cmdDelete As System.Web.UI.WebControls.LinkButton
        'footer
        Protected WithEvents ctlAudit As _
            DotNetNuke.UI.UserControls.ModuleAuditControl
    #End Region
```

As you can see from the code listing, most of the controls are ASP.NET controls as covered in Listing 12-12. In addition, you can see where you declare the DotNetNuke controls covered earlier.

The label controls:

```
Protected plTitle As UI.UserControls.LabelControl
Protected plDescription As UI.UserControls.LabelControl
Protected plImage As UI.UserControls.LabelControl
Protected plEvery As UI.UserControls.LabelControl
Protected plTime As UI.UserControls.LabelControl
Protected plExpiryDate As UI.UserControls.LabelControl
```

The URL control:

```
Protected WithEvents ctlImage As UI.UserControls.UrlControl
```

And the audit control:

```
Protected WithEvents ctlAudit As DotNetNuke.UI.UserControls.ModuleAuditControl
```

The next region is the Private Members region for storing an item ID value (see Listing 12-14). Because you're in the module's edit control, you use this to add and update individual items. This variable is used to store the primary key of the individual event contained in the Events table.

Listing 12-14: The Private Members Region of the Edit Control

```
#Region "Private Members"

        Private itemId As Integer = -1

#End Region
```

The next region is the Event Handlers region for dealing with click events and the Page_Load event for the control. We'll start with the Page_Load event first and then describe what is happening in each event for the Edit control of the Events module (see Listing 12-15).

Listing 12-15: The Events Handlers Region of the Edit Control – Page Load Event

```
Private Sub Page_Load(ByVal sender As System.Object, ByVal e As _
    System.EventArgs) Handles MyBase.Load
    Try
         ' Determine ItemId of Events to Update
        If Not (Request.QueryString("ItemId") Is Nothing) Then
            itemId = Int32.Parse(Request.QueryString("ItemId"))
          End If
      'this needs to execute always to the
      'client script code is registered in InvokePopupCal
      cmdStartCalendar.NavigateUrl = _
        CType(Common.Utilities.Calendar.InvokePopupCal(txtStartDate), String)
      cmdExpiryCalendar.NavigateUrl = _
        CType(Common.Utilities.Calendar.InvokePopupCal(txtExpiryDate), String)
      ' If the page is being requested the first time, determine if an
      ' event itemId value is specified, and if so populate page
      ' contents with the event details
      If Page.IsPostBack = False Then
          cmdDelete.Attributes.Add("onClick", "javascript:return confirm('" & _
            Localization.GetString("DeleteItem") & "');")
          If Not Common.Utilities.Null.IsNull(itemId) Then
              ' Obtain a single row of event information
              Dim objEvents As New EventController
              Dim objEvent As EventInfo = objEvents.GetEvent(itemId, ModuleId)
              ' Read first row from database
              If Not objEvent Is Nothing Then
                  txtTitle.Text = objEvent.Title
                  teDescription.Text = objEvent.Description
                  ctlImage.FileFilter = glbImageFileTypes
                  ctlImage.Url = objEvent.IconFile
```

(continued)

Listing 12-15: *(continued)*

```
                    If Not objEvent.IconFile = "" Then
                        valAltText.Visible = False
                    Else
                        valAltText.Visible = True
                    End If
                    txtAlt.Text = objEvent.AltText
                    txtEvery.Text = objEvent.Every.ToString
                    If txtEvery.Text = "1" Then
                        txtEvery.Text = ""
                    End If
                    If objEvent.Period <> "" Then
                        cboPeriod.Items.FindByValue(objEvent.Period).Selected = _
                        True
                    Else
                        cboPeriod.Items(0).Selected = True
                    End If
                    txtStartDate.Text = objEvent.DateTime.ToShortDateString
                    txtTime.Text = objEvent.DateTime.ToShortTimeString
                    If objEvent.DateTime.ToString("HH:mm") = "00:00" Then
                        txtTime.Text = ""
                    End If
                    If Not Common.Utilities.Null.IsNull(objEvent.ExpireDate) Then
                        txtExpiryDate.Text = objEvent.ExpireDate.ToShortDateString
                    Else
                        txtExpiryDate.Text = ""
                    End If
                    ctlAudit.CreatedByUser = objEvent.CreatedByUser
                    ctlAudit.CreatedDate = objEvent.CreatedDate.ToString
                Else  ' security violation attempt to
                      ' access item not related to this Module
                    Response.Redirect(NavigateURL(), True)
                End If
            Else
                cmdDelete.Visible = False
                ctlAudit.Visible = False
                valAltText.Visible = False
            End If
        End If
    Catch exc As Exception    'Module failed to load
        ProcessModuleLoadException(Me, exc)
    End Try
End Sub
```

The first thing the Page_Load event does is to check the query string to determine if you're working with an existing item in the events table or if this is a new item.

Further down you check for a null value by using the Common.Utilities.Null.IsNull method and passing it the itemID value. If the event ID is not null, you then instantiate the EventsController class and execute the GetEvent method. Remember, this GetEvent method is contained in the Business Logic Layer, which then executes a call to the abstraction class, and eventually the physical provider that executes the corresponding stored procedure within the SQL database.

```
Dim objEvents As New EventController
Dim objEvent As EventInfo = objEvents.GetEvent(itemId, ModuleId)
```

Here you pass not only the itemID value to the stored procedure, but when you add a record you also add a value for ModuleID. Remember, the ModuleID is being provided by the PortalModuleBase, which exposes the current module instance's ID to your class. The ID is a unique identifier provided by DotNetNuke that is generated each time a module is placed in the page. This ID provides the developer with a means to reuse modules, but have unique data for each instance.

Further down in the Page_Load event you can see another DotNetNuke-specific item, and that is where you populate your audit control with the information on the user creating the new event item:

```
ctlAudit.CreatedByUser = objEvent.CreatedByUser
ctlAudit.CreatedDate = objEvent.CreatedDate.ToString
```

This provides tracking internally so you can see who performed what action in your module. All these controls are totally optional for you to use in your module development.

Now let's move on to button action events. Listing 12-16 contains click events for cmdCancel, cmdDelete, and cmdUpdate link buttons.

Listing 12-16: Handling Linkbutton Events in the EditEvents Class

```
Private Sub cmdCancel_Click(ByVal sender As Object, ByVal e As EventArgs) _
    Handles cmdCancel.Click
    Try
        Response.Redirect(NavigateURL(), True)
    Catch exc As Exception    'Module failed to load
        ProcessModuleLoadException(Me, exc)
    End Try
End Sub

Private Sub cmdDelete_Click(ByVal sender As Object, ByVal e As EventArgs) _
    Handles cmdDelete.Click
    Try
        Dim objEvents As New EventController
        objEvents.DeleteEvent(itemId)
        objEvents = Nothing
        ' Redirect back to the portal home page
        Response.Redirect(NavigateURL(), True)
    Catch exc As Exception    'Module failed to load
        ProcessModuleLoadException(Me, exc)
    End Try
End Sub

Private Sub cmdUpdate_Click(ByVal sender As Object, ByVal e As EventArgs) _
    Handles cmdUpdate.Click
    Try
        Dim strDateTime As String
        ' Only Update if the Entered Data is Valid
        If Page.IsValid = True Then
```

(continued)

Listing 12-16: *(continued)*

```
                    strDateTime = txtStartDate.Text
                    If txtTime.Text <> "" Then
                        strDateTime += " " & txtTime.Text
                    End If
                    Dim objEvent As New EventInfo
                    objEvent.ItemId = itemId
                    objEvent.ModuleId = ModuleId
                    objEvent.CreatedByUser = UserInfo.UserID.ToString
                    objEvent.Description = teDescription.Text
                    objEvent.DateTime = Convert.ToDateTime(strDateTime)
                    objEvent.Title = txtTitle.Text
                    If txtEvery.Text <> "" Then
                        objEvent.Every = Convert.ToInt32(txtEvery.Text)
                    Else
                        objEvent.Every = 1
                    End If
                    objEvent.Period = cboPeriod.SelectedItem.Value
                    objEvent.IconFile = ctlImage.Url
                    objEvent.AltText = txtAlt.Text
                    If txtExpiryDate.Text <> "" Then
                        objEvent.ExpireDate = Convert.ToDateTime(txtExpiryDate.Text)
                    End If
                    ' Create an instance of the Event DB component
                    Dim objEvents As New EventController
                    If Common.Utilities.Null.IsNull(itemId) Then
                        ' Add the event within the Events table
                        objEvents.AddEvent(objEvent)
                    Else
                        ' Update the event within the Events table
                        objEvents.UpdateEvent(objEvent)
                    End If
                    objEvents = Nothing
                    ' Redirect back to the portal home page
                    Response.Redirect(NavigateURL(), True)
                End If
        Catch exc As Exception       'Module failed to load
            ProcessModuleLoadException(Me, exc)
        End Try
    End Sub
```

The first event you're handling in Listing 12-16 is the cmdCancel_Click event. Basically all you want to do here is redirect the user back to where they started from, which is the default view of the module. In this case it would be the View control we talked about earlier in the chapter. One thing you'll notice here is the use of NavigateURL, which is a function that returns a string for your module's view page. The NavigateURL function is provided by the DotNetNuke framework to provide navigation through your module logic to load the appropriate controls based on the module's key that you defined when you first configured DotNetNuke to interface with the module (see Chapter 9). Another key feature to the navigation methods provided by DotNetNuke is the support of friendly URLs (which we'll talk about later in this chapter), which eliminates query strings being passed in the URL and uses a directory structure for passing parameters.

The second event is the cmdDelete_Click event. This event captures when the user deletes a specific event from the listing. You make another call to your EventsController, and pass the ID of the event you want deleted so eventually the stored procedure will be called and delete the event. After the event is deleted you then redirect back to the initial view control of the module.

The final event is the cmdUpdate_Click event. This event handler contains a little more code than the previous methods. Initially you create an instance of the EventController class, and populate the properties for an EventInfo object. These values are passed from the user controls contained in the web form on the web control. Once the values are populated you check to see if this is an existing event by looking at the item ID. If it's an existing event you call the UpdateEvent method of the controller class. If you're adding an event you then call the AddEvent method of the EventController class. Finally, you use the NavigateURL function and redirect to the initial view control of the module.

That completes the architectural review of a DotNetNuke module. Chapter 14 covers packaging up a module for easy distribution in other DotNetNuke portals.

DotNetNuke Helper Functions

In the previous code samples you may have noticed several functions provided by the DotNetNuke core framework to ease your module development. These helper functions consist of error handling and URL navigation. This section provides some quick examples on what these functions do and how to utilize them in your own modules. More detail is provided in Chapter 8 on the DotNetNuke API, but we're going to review common methods that were used in the examples in this chapter.

Error Handling

If you've been developing ASP.NET for any length of time, I'm sure you've seen the yellow error dump on a web page when something goes wrong. This isn't a very nice sight for your users to see, and sometimes it displays a little more information about your application than you would like. Sometimes you don't even realize there is a problem. You could write your own error handling routines, but with DotNetNuke you don't have to. The core framework provides module developers with the ability to check a logged-on user's security level, and display an appropriate error based on who is logged on. For example, an administrator can be presented with a little bit more detail about what specifically erred out, and an average user can just be presented with a friendly error informing them that something is wrong. In addition, combined with the Logging Provider in DotNetNuke you can view a log of the errors that occurred within a timeframe. This ensures you can see what has been happening with your portal, and any errors your modules may have raised.

You probably have noticed in this chapter that the code examples call a method called ProcessModuleLoadException. For example:

```
Try
    'some logic
Catch exc As Exception
    ProcessModuleLoadException(Me, exc)
End Try
```

By using this method you raise the error to DotNetNuke built-in error handling. To view any errors, logon as an admin or host level account, and select Admin ⇨ Log Viewer from the menu options available. This brings up the Log Viewer screen. Errors will be presented with a red entry by default. Just double-click on the entry to view the error information.

Navigation URLs

Another item covered in the sample code was the use of the NavigateURL and EditURL functions. These provide two major functions: one is to load the appropriate control based on the key being passed to the function, and the other is the support for friendly URLs in your module. Friendly URLs allow your module to eliminate the need to pass query strings in the URL. By using friendly URLs, you make it easier for spiders to spider your site, and it is an overall easier method to display and remember URLs to various pages in your site. For example, instead of using something like http://www.dotnetnuke.com /default.aspx?tabid=233 to navigate to a page within a portal, friendly URLs would provide you with http://www.dotnetnuke.com/tabid/233/default.aspx as a path to the page. You can find more about the friendly URLs interface in Chapter 8.

Loading the Appropriate Control

NavigateURL provides you with the ability to load the appropriate control. This function is provided by DotNetNuke.Common.Globals.NavigateURL, located within the Globals.vb file in the <approot> /components/shared/ directory in the DotNetNuke solution. This method accepts a TabID, which is the unique identifier of a page in your portal; ControlKey, which is the unique key you defined when you configured your module definition — it identifies which user control to load for the module; and the final parameter (AdditionalParameters), which is for additional parameters. The additional parameters are a string array of the query string parameters you may need to pass in the URL. By using the AdditionalParameters you easily implement friendly URLs for your module because DotNetNuke will convert the string array to a directory structure to be displayed in the URLs.

For example, the following code snippet sets the NavigateURL property of a link button control using the DotNetNuke.Common.Globals.NavigateURL method:

```
hypRegister.NavigateUrl = NavigateURL(PortalSettings.ActiveTab.TabID, "Edit", _
    "mid=" & objModules.GetModuleByDefinition(PortalSettings.PortalId, _
    "User Accounts").ModuleID, "UserId=" & objUserInfo.UserID)
```

You can see how you pass the ID of the currently active page to the URL, and the control you want to load is the control with the Edit key. In addition, you pass several parameters for the control such as the Module ID and current User ID.

EditURL is another function for building navigation for your module, in addition to the features provided by the NavigateURL method, and is provided by the PortalModuleBase. This method does not accept a Tab ID value, because it assumes it is being used for the module instance currently in use. For example, if you list a record set and you want to edit a particular item, you would pass the key of ItemID, and then the value. The EditURL would pass the information to the Edit control:

```
<asp:HyperLink id="editLink" NavigateUrl='<%#
EditURL("ItemID",DataBinder.Eval(Container.DataItem,"ItemID")) %>' Visible="<%#
IsEditable %>" runat="server"><asp:Image id="editLinkImage"
ImageUrl="~/images/edit.gif" Visible="<%# IsEditable %>" AlternateText="Edit"
runat="server" /></asp:HyperLink>
```

In this example, you're listing the events in a view user control and displaying an edit link to the user if he or she has edit permissions using the IsEditable (see Table 12-2) Boolean value.

Summary

This chapter finalized our series on module development and architecture. In Chapter 10 you developed your physical provider class, which provides methods to expose your stored procedures in the database. From there you moved on to creating an abstraction class, and finally exposing the result set of records as a collection of objects from your Business Logic Layer (see Chapter 11).

In this chapter you combined those classes and then bound them to controls in your module controls. Modules consist of several types of controls. The more common ones are the view control, for the first initial view of a module; the settings control, for configuring properties of a module instance; and the edit control, for editing information specific to your business logic for the module application.

Finally, you learned the various helper functions that you can use in your own projects to reduce the amount of custom code.

This should provide you with enough information to begin developing your own module for DotNetNuke. In Chapter 14, you learn how to package up these modules for distribution in other DotNetNuke portals.

13

Skinning DotNetNuke

The ability to skin DotNetNuke was introduced in version 2 of the application and was a much-anticipated addition. The term *skinning* refers to an application's ability to change the look of the design by a setting in the application. This allows for the separation of the application logic from the user interface or object abstraction. As you learned in previous chapters, DotNetNuke utilizes a three-tier object-oriented design approach, with the user interface segmented as its own tier. This is what allows skinning to work and the application to be able to present a unique feel depending on the parameters passed to the page. This chapter looks at the finer points of skinning and provides you with the tools to start building your own skins for DotNetNuke.

DotNetNuke utilizes templates to accomplish this because they allow for the separation of the presentation and layout attributes from the application logic required to display content to the user. We studied various approaches to allow this functionality and have created a solution that will allow both developers and designers independence when implementing DotNetNuke sites. This allows for faster deployment times and, more importantly, reduced expense with getting your portal functional and performing its intended purpose.

The abstraction of the user interface elements from a page can be accomplished using different methodologies. The method chosen includes some degree of parsing to merge the presentation with the business logic. Therefore, defining where, when, and how this parsing will take place becomes critical to the success of the entire solution.

The use of tokens or identifiers in the user interface files to represent dynamic functionality is a popular technique employed in many skinning solutions. DotNetNuke utilizes this approach in its skinning engine solution — as the page is processed the token is replaced to the proper skin object or control for the function the token identifies. This is accomplished when you install the skin into the application, which we will discuss later.

DotNetNuke allows you to create skins using your favorite editor, which gives you as a skin developer a good amount of flexibility — you only need to follow the rules for creating a skin; the tool you use to create it is up to you. You can either create an .ascx or .html skin. The type you create depends upon your choice of editor and the set of rules you choose to follow. Allowing you to create the skins in HTML or ASP.NET was a conscious choice made to allow for the most flexibility with creating these skins and to help bridge the gap between designers and developers. The Core Team realizes there are still many more HTML developers in the world than ASP.NET developers, so allowing skins to be created in HTML allows many more individuals to utilize this functionality of the application without having to learn new skills other than how to place the tokens within your skin design. Now that you have a little history of why the engine was architected, let's look at the finer points of skinning.

File Organization

Skins files must meet certain conditions before they will install into the application. Once the requirements are met you can upload a compressed zip file containing your skin utilizing the built-in File Manager, and the application will convert your files for use as a portal skin. Skins may be applied at several levels within the application; you can define a skin to be host-, portal-, or page-level, depending upon your needs. Once you upload your skin the application will create a directory for the files under the Portals/_default/Skins directory. If you look at the file structure of the application's root you will also notice there is a Containers directory where any containers you create for your skins will be stored. These file directories are mapped to their corresponding skin ID, which uniquely identifies the skin in the application. These settings are stored in the Skins table and allow the application to correctly determine the skin to load at runtime.

Processing Pages and Loading Skins

The application uses a single page to process the functionality of displaying information to the user, Default.aspx. This page is the container for all the controls and skin elements the application needs to effectively serve its purpose of displaying the content to the portal user. You could refer to Default.apsx as a placeholder for the other information because its content is very basic if you view the source of the page from your IDE. It includes a placeholder for the content to be loaded and some error handling for the application. As you can see in Listing 13-1, there is a lot more that will be injected in the page than it would appear from looking at the code for the page.

Listing 13-1: Default.aspx Source Code

```
<%@ Page CodeBehind="Default.aspx.vb" language="vb" AutoEventWireup="false"
Explicit="True" Inherits="DotNetNuke.Framework.CDefault" %>
<%@ Register TagPrefix="dnn" Namespace="DotNetNuke.Common.Controls"
Assembly="DotNetNuke" %>
<!DOCTYPE HTML PUBLIC "-//W3C//DTD HTML 4.0 Transitional//EN">
<HTML>
      <HEAD id="Head">
            <TITLE>
                  <%= Title %>
            </TITLE>
            <%= Comment %>
            <META NAME="DESCRIPTION" CONTENT="<%= Description %>">
            <META NAME="KEYWORDS" CONTENT="<%= KeyWords %>">
            <META NAME="COPYRIGHT" CONTENT="<%= Copyright %>">
```

```
                    <META NAME="GENERATOR" CONTENT="<%= Generator %>">
                    <META NAME="AUTHOR" CONTENT="<%= Author %>">
                    <META NAME="RESOURCE-TYPE" CONTENT="DOCUMENT">
                    <META NAME="DISTRIBUTION" CONTENT="GLOBAL">
                    <META NAME="ROBOTS" CONTENT="INDEX, FOLLOW">
                    <META NAME="REVISIT-AFTER" CONTENT="1 DAYS">
                    <META NAME="RATING" CONTENT="GENERAL">
                    <style id="StylePlaceholder" runat="server"></style>
                    <asp:placeholder id="CSS" runat="server"></asp:placeholder>
                    <asp:placeholder id="FAVICON" runat="server"></asp:placeholder>
                    <script src="<%= Page.ResolveUrl("js/dnncore.js") %>"></script>
          </HEAD>
          <BODY ID="Body" runat="server" ONSCROLL="__dnn_bodyscroll()" BOTTOMMARGIN="0"
LEFTMARGIN="0"
                    TOPMARGIN="0" RIGHTMARGIN="0" MARGINWIDTH="0" MARGINHEIGHT="0">
                    <noscript></noscript>
                    <dnn:Form id="Form" runat="server" ENCTYPE="multipart/form-data"
style="height:100%;>
                              <asp:Label ID="SkinError" Runat="server" CssClass="NormalRed"
Visible="False"></asp:Label>
                              <asp:placeholder id="SkinPlaceHolder" runat="server" />
                              <INPUT ID="ScrollTop" runat="server" NAME="ScrollTop"
TYPE="hidden">
                              <INPUT ID="__dnnVariable" runat="server" NAME="__dnnVariable"
TYPE="hidden">
                    </dnn:Form>
          </BODY>
</HTML>
```

So how does all this work? When a URL is requested and the user enters the application the request is inspected and the proper skin is determined from the database tables. Once the proper skin is identified the user controls are injected based on the definitions in the skin. The logic that allows this functionality is defined in the Admin/Skins/skin.vb file. Listing 13-2 looks at the logic that allows the skin to be determined and loaded.

Listing 13-2: Skin.vb Init_Page Directives

```
Private Sub Page_Init(ByVal sender As System.Object, ByVal e As System.EventArgs)
Handles MyBase.Init
        '
        ' CODEGEN: This call is required by the ASP.NET Web Form Designer.
        '
        InitializeComponent()

        ' set global page settings
        InitializePage()

        ' process the current request
        ManageRequest()

        ' load skin control
        Dim ctlSkin As UserControl
        Dim objSkins As New UI.Skins.SkinController
```

(continued)

Listing 13-2: *(continued)*

```
            ' skin preview
            If (Not Request.QueryString("SkinSrc") Is Nothing) Then
                PortalSettings.ActiveTab.SkinSrc = _
objSkins.FormatSkinSrc(QueryStringDecode(Request.QueryString("SkinSrc")) & ".ascx",
PortalSettings)
                ctlSkin = LoadSkin(PortalSettings.ActiveTab.SkinSrc)
            End If

            ' load assigned skin
            If ctlSkin Is Nothing Then
                If IsAdminControl() = True Or PortalSettings.ActiveTab.IsAdminTab _
Then
                    Dim objSkin As UI.Skins.SkinInfo
                    objSkin = objSkins.GetSkin(SkinInfo.RootSkin, _
PortalSettings.PortalId, SkinType.Admin)
                    If Not objSkin Is Nothing Then
                        PortalSettings.ActiveTab.SkinSrc = _
objSkins.FormatSkinSrc(objSkin.SkinSrc, PortalSettings)
                    Else
                        PortalSettings.ActiveTab.SkinSrc = ""
                    End If
                ElseIf PortalSettings.ActiveTab.SkinSrc <> "" Then
                    PortalSettings.ActiveTab.SkinSrc = _
objSkins.FormatSkinSrc(PortalSettings.ActiveTab.SkinSrc, PortalSettings)
                End If

                If PortalSettings.ActiveTab.SkinSrc <> "" Then
                    ctlSkin = LoadSkin(PortalSettings.ActiveTab.SkinSrc)
                End If
            End If

            ' error loading skin - load default
            If ctlSkin Is Nothing Then
                ' could not load skin control - load default skin
                If IsAdminControl() = True Or PortalSettings.ActiveTab.IsAdminTab _
Then
                    PortalSettings.ActiveTab.SkinSrc = Common.Globals.HostPath & _
SkinInfo.RootSkin & glbDefaultSkinFolder & glbDefaultAdminSkin
                Else
                    PortalSettings.ActiveTab.SkinSrc = Common.Globals.HostPath & _
SkinInfo.RootSkin & glbDefaultSkinFolder & glbDefaultSkin
                End If
                ctlSkin = LoadSkin(PortalSettings.ActiveTab.SkinSrc)
            End If

            ' set skin path
            PortalSettings.ActiveTab.SkinPath = _
objSkins.FormatSkinPath(PortalSettings.ActiveTab.SkinSrc)

            ' set skin id to an explicit short name to reduce page payload and make
it standards compliant
            ctlSkin.ID = "dnn"
```

```
        ' add CSS links
        ManageStyleSheets(False)

        ' add Favicon
        ManageFavicon()

        ' add skin to page
        SkinPlaceHolder.Controls.Add(ctlSkin)

        ' add CSS links
        ManageStyleSheets(True)

    End Sub
```

As you can see in Listing 13-2, you first call the ManageRequest function, which determines the URL of the requesting user and information about who is requesting the resource. This not only allows you to determine the URL of the request, but also allows you to determine whether the user should have access to the page they are requesting. After learning the identity of the user and which resource they are requesting, you can determine the skin you need to use for this request from the database. So you create the new object ctlSkin and determine the skin you need to load for the page. Then you look at the other attributes and load the proper style sheet and Icon, if they are defined, and finally bind the skin user control and attributes to the page the user has requested. This is what allows DotNetNuke to perform dynamic re-allocation of the application's look on the fly. You should note there is a performance hit with these DB calls and allowing the portal to utilize this dynamic skinning solution, as there is with any application that can change its appearance on the fly, but it is one of the killer features DotNetNuke contains and more than worth the additional overhead the process requires.

Packaging Skins and Containers

Now that you understand the process of getting skin bound to the proper page, let's look at the different parts of a skin package. The package is a compilation of the files and definitions you will use to contain the files and tell DotNetNuke to process your skin when you install it into your application instance. A skin or container package can contain the following file types:

- ❑ ***.htm,*.html files:** These files can contain the layout representing how you want the various skin objects to be located in your design. These files will be converted to *.ascx files upon installation to the application.

- ❑ ***.ascx files:** These are skin definition user controls that are precompiled in the format the skinning engine requires.

- ❑ ***.css files:** These files contain the style sheet definitions you will use to define the files in your skin or container.

- ❑ ***.gif, *.jpeg, *.jpg, *.png:** These file extensions are used in support of the graphics files included in your skin.

- ❑ ***.* Other files:** You can use any other resource files in your package, but these must be of an allowed file type in the host allowed file settings on the Host Settings page.

A package can contain multiple skins or containers. This allows you to create complementing skins for a site in one package. Since the layout will allow for various panes that contain the module content at run-time, this is a powerful feature because you may not want the same layout for all pages in a site, but you will probably want common graphics and defined styles throughout the same site. This ability of packaging multiple skins and containers allows you to install all of the skins for a portal in one installation.

A skin package should make use of a manifest file to identify the various files and elements to be included in the skin. Including this file allows you to combine all the files into one package and give the application the needed instructions for processing the skin to your specifications. Although the manifest file adds some overhead to the skin creation process, it does greatly enhance the abilities of the installation process and allows greater control in a single step. We will discuss the finer points of creating manifest files later in this chapter because this is a very important control mechanism for controlling the installation of your skins.

Creating Your Skin

You have two methods for creating your skin. The method you choose will depend upon your comfort level with the technology and your personal preference. Skins can be created using HTML, or if you prefer, you can create *.ascx skins with VS.NET. This allows you to develop your skin in a comfortable environment and provides flexibility while creating skins. If you are more of a designer who has developed traditional web sites in the past, you may prefer creating your skins in HTML using your favorite editor, but if you are more of a programmer type, you may prefer to use ASP.NET code and develop your skin with Visual Studio. Both these methods are basically the same except you will use the tokens when developing in HTML and you will utilize the user controls when creating your skin. Of course the file extension will change depending upon your choice of methods.

At a minimum you will want to develop at least two skins for each package, one to display to your users and another to display the administrative modules discussed in Chapters 4 and 5. The reason for this is that the user content areas will likely need multiple panes to properly lay out the content as your business needs require, but the administrative areas will likely only display a single module per page, so these two layouts will need to be architected differently to adequately serve the purpose of the area.

There are several different steps to creating a skin. The order in which you perform these steps is not important, but we find the following a valid method to get everything accomplished and your skin into production.

To simplify the development of skin files as well as expedite the packaging process later, it is recommended that you use the following organizational folder structure:

```
\Skins
  \SkinName (this is the package you are developing)
    ... (this is where you create the skin package zip files for deployment)
    \containers (this is a static name to identify the container files for the skin package)
      ... (this will contain all resource files related to your containers)
    \skins (this is a static name to identify the skin files for the skin package
      ... (this will contain all resource files related to your skins)
```

This provides an easy structure to develop your skins and you will find this structure also simplifies preparing your package for deployment and installation into your portal. The free-form nature of skinning provides you a level of creative freedom within designing your skins. Designers may wish to create the initial site designs as full graphical images and then slice the images to meet their needs after the concept is mature. One thing to be aware of when creating skins is that you need to include all user interface elements in your design. This includes static elements such as graphics and text, and it should also include active elements such as Login links, a navigation/menu system, and the other skin objects required for DotNetNuke to adequately display your content to your users.

This is where you need to be aware of the technical issues that will arise in terms of how to most effectively divide the graphical elements into the HTML representation you need. HTML layout is very different from free-flow graphics, and the translation from a graphical image to an HTML representation will determine the layout of the final design. Decisions such as what resolution you want to target your site for will need to be made at this stage. If you want the site to remain fixed regardless of resolution of the user's browser or if the design should adapt to the resolution, you should decide these items and make adjustments to your design based on those decisions. Several example skins are included in the download that show the differences between fixed-width skins and full-width skins, so you can see the differences between these two approaches.

Now that you have your design completed, you will need to actually build the skin. As mentioned earlier, you can use any HTML editor, Visual Studio, or if you prefer, even your favorite text editor to build the skin for your design. The one thing to remember is the HTML in your skin must be well formed or the process will fail. This means you must ensure you close any HTML tags you open, including image tags. Image tags do not normally have closing tags so you should include the trailing / after the image content and before you end the tag. Most modern HTML editors will handle the process of ensuring tags are closed for you, but you should still double-check your work to make sure a bug is not introduced into your skin with a missing tag.

This brings us to the location of images and support files to be used in your skin. Normally you will want to include your support files within the same folder as the rest of your skin elements, but this is not a requirement and you can place them in any folder you wish, but care must be taken to ensure the paths will remain valid after the skin upload process. As part of the upload process the skinning engine will add an explicit path to your images for you. This is to help with the performance of your skin during runtime. The skinning image will automatically append a path of /Portals/_default/YourSkinName/ to your image paths you have specified. One thing to watch out for with this when you are building the content for your site is that if these paths change between development and production, your image paths will be incorrect and the image will not show properly.

An example of when this can happen is when you are building a site on your local machine in a virtual directory of `http://localhost/VirtualDirectory` and then you decide to move to production to a location of `http://www.YourDomain.com`. The easiest way to make this move is to back up your local database, then restore it to your production database, ftp your files to your production system, and make the appropriate changes to the Portal Alias and web.config file. But what you will find when you move the site to production is that the image paths will no longer work. If you run into this issue you have two methods to correct it. You can install the skin again, effectively overwriting the original skin, or you can choose to directly edit your skin file and correct the image paths manually. The best thing is to take these types of items into account before you start building a development site and plan accordingly.

Now that you have your design and a good idea of how your skin will be architected, you need to add the skin objects to the proper location in your skin file. This is so DotNetNuke will know where to insert the various content panes, portal elements, and navigation objects. Depending on the method you chose to create your skin, this process will change to meet the method. If you are using ASCX skins, then you will need to specify the @Register and the actual user control tag in your skin. For example, <dnn:Login runat="server" id="dnnlogin"> will insert the login user control in the section of your skin where you specify the control. If you are using HTML skins, then you will simply need to include the token for the accompanying skin element. So for HTML skins you will simply add [Login] in the location you would like the login control to appear and the engine will replace it with the actual control when the skin is parsed during upload. Each of the different skin objects has their own unique functions, and you must understand the use of each to build a functional skin. Table 13-1 lists each of these objects and describes their purpose, as well as provides an example of their use in each of the two methods.

Table 13-1: Skin Objects

Token	Control	Description
[SOLPARTMENU]	< dnn:SolPartMenu runat="server" id="dnnSolPartMenu">	Displays the hierarchical navigation menu (formerly [MENU]).
[LOGIN]	< dnn:Login runat="server" id="dnnLogin">	Dual state control — displays "Login" for anonymous users and "Logout" for authenticated users.
[BANNER]	< dnn:Banner runat="server" id="dnnBanner">	Displays a random banner ad.
[BREADCRUMB]	< dnn:Breadcrumb runat="server" id="dnnBreadcrumb">	Displays the path to the currently selected tab in the form of PageName1 > PageName2 > PageName3.
[COPYRIGHT]	< dnn:Copyright runat="server" id="dnnCopyright">	Displays the copyright notice for the portal.
[CURRENTDATE]	< dnn:CurrentDate runat="server" id="dnnCurrentDate">	Displays the current date.
[DOTNETNUKE]	< dnn:DotNetNuke runat="server" id="dnnDotnetNuke">	Displays the Copyright notice for DotNetNuke (not required).
[HELP]	< dnn:Help runat="server" id="dnnHelp">	Displays a link for Help, which will launch the user's e-mail client and send mail to the portal Administrator.
[HOSTNAME]	< dnn:HostName runat="server" id="dnnHostName">	Displays the Host Title linked to the Host URL.
[LINKS]	< dnn:Links runat="server" id="dnnLinks">	Displays a flat menu of links related to the current tab level and parent node. This is useful for search engine spiders and robots.
[LOGO]	< dnn:Logo runat="server" id="dnnLogo">	Displays the portal logo.

Token	Control	Description
[PRIVACY]	< dnn:Privacy runat="server" id="dnnPrivacy">	Displays a link to the Privacy Information for the portal.
[SIGNIN]	< dnn:Signin runat="server" id="dnnSignin">	Displays the signin control for providing your username and password.
[TERMS]	< dnn:Terms runat="server" id="dnnTerms">	Displays a link to the Terms and Conditions for the portal.
[USER]	< dnn:User runat="server" id="dnnUser">	Dual state control — displays a "Register" link for anonymous users or the user's name for authenticated users.
[CONTENTPANE]	<div runat="server" id="ContentPane">	Injects a placeholder for module content.

These are the skin objects available for use in your skin creation, and there are also some additional objects available for use in the creation of containers. You can place these objects anywhere in your skin and control the placement of the portal elements. We should note that not all these elements are required, but you should choose the elements you need to accomplish your purpose. Each skin must have at least one content pane, and it must be identified as the content pane or the modules will not display correctly.

Quite a few attributes are also available for use in the skin creation process. These attributes will be defined in the skin.xml or the manifest file we mentioned earlier in the chapter. This file is where you will tell DotNetNuke how you want to utilize the various skin objects. For example, you may want your navigation menu to display horizontally in your skin; this setting will be set in the skin.xml file so the engine will know how to properly insert the menu into the skin. Table 13-2 lists the attributes available to you for use in the manifest file for the skin objects.

Table 13-2: Skin Attributes

Token	Attribute	Default	Description
[SOLPARTMENU]	separatecss	true	CSS defined in a style sheet (values: true, false)
	backcolor	#333333	Background color
	forecolor	white	Forecolor of menu item when selected
	highlightcolor	white	Color of top and left border to give a highlight effect
	iconbackground color	#333333	Background color in area where icon is displayed

Table continued on following page

Token	Attribute	Default	Description
	selectedb ordercolor		Color of border surrounding selected menu item
	selectedcolor	#CCCCCC	Background color of menu item when selected
	selectedforecolor	white	Forecolor of menu item when selected
	display	horizontal	Determines how the menu is displayed, horizontal or vertical (values: vertical, horizontal)
	menubarheight	16	Menu bar height in pixels
	menuborderwidth	1	Menu border width in pixels
	menuitemheight	21	Menu item height in pixels
	forcedownlevel	false	Flag to force the downlevel menu to display (values: true, false)
	moveable	false	Flag to determine if menu can be moved (values: true, false)
	iconwidth	0	Width of icon column in pixels
Menueffects	shadowcolor	dimgray	Color of the shadow
	menueffectsmouse outhidedelay	500	Number of milliseconds to wait until menu is hidden on mouse out (0 = disable)
	mouseouthide delay	1	Number of milliseconds to wait until menu is hidden on mouse out (0 = disable)
	menueffectsmouse overdisplay	Highlight	Adjusts effect when mouse moves over menu bar item (values: Outset, Highlight, None)
	menueffects mouseoverexpand	true	Makes menu expand on mouse-over (unlike any menu found within the Windows environment) (values: true, false)
	menueffectsstyle	filter:progid: DXImage Transform .Microsoft .Shadow(color ='DimGray', Direction=135, Strength=3) ;	IE-only property for SubMenu styles and transitions

Token	Attribute	Default	Description
	fontnames	Arial	
	fontsize	12	
	fontbold	false	
	Menueffects shadowstrength	3	Determines how many pixels the shadow extends
	Menueffects menutransition	None	Determines which direction the shadow will fall (values: None, AlphaFade, AlphaFadeBottomRight, Barn, Blinds, Checkerboard, Constant-Wave, Fade, GradientWipe, Inset, Iris, RadialWipe, Random, RandomBars, Slide, Spiral, Stretch, Strips, Wave, Wheel, Zigzag)
	menueffectsmenu transitionlength	0.3	Number of seconds the transition will take
	Menueffects shadowdirection	Lower Right	Determines which direction the shadow will fall (values: None, Top, Upper Right, Right, Lower Right, Bottom, Lower Left, Left, Upper Left)
	menucontainer cssclass	MainMenu_ Menu Container	Menu Container CSS Class
	menubarcssclass	MainMenu_ MenuBar	Menu Bar CSS Class
	menuitemcssclass	MainMenu_ MenuItem	Menu Item CSS Class
	menuiconcssclass	MainMenu_ MenuIcon	Menu Icon CSS Class
	menuitems elcssclass	MainMenu_ MenuItemSel	Menu Item CSS Class for mouse-over
	menubreakcssclass	MainMenu_ MenuBreak	Menu Break CSS Class
	submenucssclass	MainMenu_ SubMenu	SubMenu CSS Class
	menuarrowcssclass	MainMenu_ MenuArrow	Menu Arrow CSS Class
	menuroot arrowcssclass	MainMenu_ MenuRoot Arrow	Menu Root Arrow CSS Class

Table continued on following page

Token	Attribute	Default	Description
	forcefullmenulist	false	Displays the full menu as an indented list of normal hyperlinks (like a sitemap) {true | false}
	useskinpath arrowimages	false	Use arrow images located in the skin and not those in the /images folder {true | false}
	userootbread crumbarrow	true	Use a breadcrumb arrow to identify the root tab that is listed in the breadcrumb ArrayList {true | false}
	usesubmenu breadcrumbarrow	false	Use a breadcrumb arrow to identify the submenu tabs that are listed in the breadcrumb ArrayList {true | false}
	Rootbread crumbarrow		Image used for root-level menu breadcrumb arrows – i.e., file.gif
	submenubread crumbarrow		Image used for submenu menu breadcrumb arrows – i.e., file.gif
	usearrows		Use arrows to indicate child submenus
	downarrow	menu_ down.gif	Arrow image used for downward-facing arrows indicating child submenus
	rightarrow	bread crumb.gif	Arrow image used for right-facing arrows indicating child submenus
	level	Root	Root level of the menu in relationship to the current active tab {Root | Same | Child}
	rootonly	false	Indicator to turn off submenus {true | false}
	rootmenuitem breadcrumb cssclass		CSS class used for root menu items when they are found in the breadcrumb ArrayList
	submenuitem breadcrumb cssclass		CSS Class used for submenu items when they are found in the breadcrumb ArrayList
	Rootmenuitem cssclass		CSS class used for root menu items
	rootmenuitem activecssclass		CSS class used for root menu items when they are the active tab
	submenuitem activecssclass		CSS class used for submenu items when they are the active tab

Token	Attribute	Default	Description
	rootmenuitem selectedcssclass		CSS class used for root menu items when they are moused-over
	submenuitem selectedcssclass		CSS Class used for submenu items when they are moused-over
	separator		The separator between root-level menu items. This can include custom skin images, text, and HTML (i.e., <![CDATA[<img src="file.gif">]]>)
	separatorcssclass		CSS class used for the root-level menu item separator
	Rootmenuitem lefthtml		HTML text added to the beginning of the root menu items
	rootmenuitem righthtml		HTML text added to the end of the root menu items
	Submenuitem lefthtml		HTML text added to the beginning of the submenu items
	Submenuitem righthtml		HTML text added to the end of the submenu items
	tooltip		Tooltips added to the menu items. These come from the tab object properties, which are filled from the tabs table {Name	Title	Description}
	leftseparator		The separator used just before a root-level menu item. A use for this might be a left edge of a tab image, for example.
	rightseparator		The separator used just after a root-level menu item. A use for this might be a right edge of a tab image, for example.
	Leftseparator active		The separator used just before an active root-level menu item
	Rightseparator active		The separator used just before an active root-level menu item
	leftseparator breadcrumb		The separator used just before a root-level menu item found in the breadcrumb ArrayList

Table continued on following page

Token	Attribute	Default	Description
	rightseparator breadcrumb		The separator used just before a root-level menu item found in the breadcrumb ArrayList
	leftseparator cssclass		CSS class used for leftseparator
	rightseparator cssclass		CSS class used for rightseparator
	leftseparator activecssclass		CSS class used for leftseparatoractive
	rightseparator activecssclass		CSS class used for rightseparatoractive
	leftseparatorbread crumbcssclass		CSS class used for leftseparatorbreadcrumb
	rightseparator breadcrumbcssclass		CSS class used for rightseparator-breadcrumb
	menualignment	Left	Alignment of the menu within the menu bar {Left | Center | Right | Justify}
	cleardefaults	false	If true, this value will clear/empty the default color settings of the menu so that they can be left empty and not just overridden with another value
[LOGIN]	Text	Login	The text of the login link
	CssClass	OtherTabs	The style of the login link
	LogoffText	Logoff	The text for the logoff link
[BANNER]	BorderWidth	0	The border width around the banner
[BREADCRUMB]	Separator	bread crumb.gif	The separator between breadcrumb links. This can include custom skin images, text, and HTML (i.e., <![CDATA[<img src="file.gif">]]>)
	CssClass	SelectedTab	The style name of the breadcrumb links
	RootLevel	1	The root level of the breadcrumb links. Valid values include: -1 — show word "Root" and then all breadcrumb tabs 0 — show all breadcrumb tabs n (where n is an integer greater than 0) — skip n breadcrumb tabs before displaying

Token	Attribute	Default	Description
[COPYRIGHT]	CssClass	SelectedTab	The style name of portal copyright link
[CURRENTDATE]	CssClass	SelectedTab	The style name of date text
	DateFormat	MMMM dd, yyyy	The format of the date text
[DOTNETNUKE]	CssClass	Normal	The style name of DotNetNuke portal engine copyright text
[HELP]	CssClass	OtherTabs	The style name of help link
[HOSTNAME]	CssClass	OtherTabs	The style name of Host link (Powered By xxxxxxxxx)
[LINKS]	CssClass	Command Button	The style name of the links
	Separator		The separator between links. This can include custom skin images, text, and HTML (i.e., <![CDATA[<img src="file.gif">]]>).
	Alignment	Horizontal	The links menu style ("Horizontal" or "Vertical")
	Level	Same	Determines the menu level to display ("Same", "Child", "Parent", "Root")
[LOGO]	BorderWidth	0	The border width around the logo
[PRIVACY]	Text	Privacy Statement	The text of the privacy link
	CssClass	OtherTabs	The style name of privacy link
[SIGNIN]			
[TERMS]	Text	Terms of User	The text of the terms link
	CssClass	OtherTabs	The style name of terms link
[USER]	Text	Register	The text of the register/user link
	CssClass	OtherTabs	The style name of register/user link
[CONTENTPANE]	ID	Content Pane	The content pane key identifier to be displayed in the user interface and stored in the database.

As you can see there are quite a few attributes for each skin object. This complicates the process of creating skins a bit, but it is very important that you learn to utilize the attribute functions of each skin object to adequately realize the true power and flexibility of the DotNetNuke skinning engine. You may notice the menu control monopolizes the majority of the available attributes — this shows the flexibility of the menu system DotNetNuke utilizes. We should note one thing here. The menu control is a fluid development control, which means it is constantly receiving revision and this list of attributes may not be complete by the time you are reading this book. Take a look at the menu documents included in the download to ensure you are aware of all the options available to you with this powerful control.

The skinning engine will support multiple instances of the skin objects where you can define multiple menus for your skin or any other instance. You must of course give each instance an unique name, so you could have a menu skin object defined as [MENU] and a second menu defined as [MENU:1]. These are also important for your content areas because it is likely you will want more than one content area for your skin. You must have at least one pane named [ContentPane], but you will likely want other areas to organize your content in so you can use the named instances like we did with the menu, only use the content skin object instead of the menu.

You can also set the attributes for each of your skin objects according to the ones listed in Table 13-2. Each skin object will support the attributes and you can specify them when you define the skin object. For example, in the earlier example of defining your Login control, you could have specified the text for your control such as <dnn:Login runat="server" id="dnnLogin" Text="Signin" />. This example will only work if you are creating ASCX skins. If you are working with HTML skins, you must include the attribute setting in the manifest file.

A skin package may contain a global attributes specified in a file named "skin.xml" (or "container.xml" for containers) that will apply to your skin files. You can also override the global skin attribute specification with a skin-specific attribute specification by providing a "YourSkinFile.xml" file. The Skin Uploader will merge the skin attributes with the HTML presentation file to create an ASCX skin file. Listing 13-3 shows a section of the manifest file where these attributes are set.

Listing 13-3: Skin Attribute Example

```
<Objects>
    <Object>
        <Token>[LOGIN]</Token>
        <Settings>
            <Setting>
                <Name>Text</Name>
                <Value>Signin</Value>
            </Setting>
        </Settings>
    </Object>
</Objects>
```

As you can see, the code in Listing 13-3 accomplishes the same thing as in the ASCX example, but we were able to keep the additional attributes separate from our presentation. This allows for cleaner and easier-to-understand HTML as you are creating HTML skins because the attributes do not congest the HTML code with additional overhead.

We should note there is a one-to-one relationship of skin object definitions in the skin file (that is, [MENU]) with the attribute specification in the skin.xml file. This is also true for all named instances. For example, if you want to include a vertical and horizontal menu in your skin, you can specify [MENU:1] and [MENU:2] named instances in your skin file and then create definitions for each with different attributes in the skin.xml file.

When creating HTML skins and specifying multiple ContentPanes, you will need to specify the "ID" attribute in the attributes file. This will allow DotNetNuke to identify the proper pane to insert your modules into while you are administering the portal. This also gives you the ability to add some friendly descriptive names to the various panes you may require. For example, look at Listing 13-4 and you will see how the ID of the pane is defined in the manifest file. You can define as many nodes of these various pane IDs as required to accomplish your design.

Listing 13-4: Content Pane Attributes

```
<Objects>
     <Object>
          <Token>[CONTENTPANE:1]</Token>
          <Settings>
               <Setting>
                    <Name>ID</Name>
                    <Value>RightPane</Value>
               </Setting>

          </Settings>

     </Object>
</Objects>
```

As you can see you now will have a pane named RightPane that you can use to display content to the user. You could also define a LeftPane or NavigationPane; basically whatever your business rules require you to include in the skin. This shows some of the flexibility this solution provides because you are able to utilize the number of panes necessary to accomplish your design. The solution allows you to create a layout to utilize the application as you need. By utilizing a combination of the code within your skin and the attributes file you can create almost any iteration of a skin design you can imagine.

Since you have an understanding of the way skins are designed, we will now look at building a cascading style sheet for your skin. The CSS file will need to be defined and saved in your skin directory along with your other resource files. DotNetNuke utilizes an external style sheet specification, which allows you to define your styles separate from your skin files, and there are several levels of these files. This means it is not essential for you to create a CSS file for your skin because one of the other files will define the styles for you, but to keep a unique look to your skin design you will want to build a style sheet specific for your skin design. The multiple style sheets in the application are structured in a hierarchal nature, so one style sheet's definitions may override another. There is a distinct priority of the order in which overriding of styles can occur. The cascading order of the style sheets is summarized in the following list with the previous item overriding the next:

❑ **Modules:** The modules style sheet determines the styles that can be used in the individual module.

❑ **Default:** This is the default style sheet for the host-level styles and the styles are defined in default.css.

❑ **Skin:** These are the skin styles you will create and apply to your skin.

❑ **Container:** Each container can contain styles unique to its design.

❑ **Portal:** These are custom styles defined by the Portal Administrator and named portal.css.

You can define your skin's style sheet in one of two ways. You can create a style sheet named skin.css and place it in your skin directory. This file will apply to all skins that may reside in the skin package. You can also name your style sheet with the format of skinname.css and it will apply to the skin file with the same name as the one you define here. You can add any style definitions you need, but at the minimum you should override the default styles with those that complement the design of your skin.

Now that you have the skin created you need to create an image so you will be able to display the skin in the preview gallery. In order to do this you need to create a high-quality image file with a .jpg extension, and it must be named the same as your skin file. For example, if your skin is named mySkin.ascx, then your image file must be named mySkin.jpg. This same concept is also true of container files you may have created as part of your skin design.

The last step in skin creation is to package the skin for deployment. The compressed file must be a *.zip file. You can utilize any number of third-party compression utilities, such as Winzip or Windows XP's built-in utility. One thing to watch out for when zipping your package is to ensure there are no buried folders between your skin files and the first-level compressed folder. This is a common mistake and will cause the upload process to fail.

In many cases you will want to package a complementary set of skin files and container files in one distribution file. In order to do this you need to package your container files in a compressed *.zip file named "containers.zip." Similarly, you must package your skin files in a compressed *.zip file named "skins.zip." Then you need to package these two files into a single *.zip file that is named after your skin. This will allow people to install the full skin package (skins and containers) by uploading a single file through the Skin Uploader.

Container Creation

This section looks at the procedures associated with creating a container for your skin. Containers are basically skin definitions applied at the container level. The process for creating a container is very similar to the process for creating a skin, with the only real difference being the attributes and skin objects available for a container.

One requirement of creating a container is you must include an Actions control so you will be able to administer the module's functions. The Actions control is a mechanism that allows binding of the module functionality to the portal framework. It is essentially the user control the module will require to do the module's intended work. Each module can define its own actions, but generally you will have functions to add and edit the module's content as well as the portal-level functions to move the module between panes and pages and edit the module settings including permissions, title, and so on. These are the minimum actions required, but the module developer can also create additional actions to perform unique functions of the module in question. For a complete description of adding your own actions, please refer to Chapters 9 through 12. The default actions menu utilizes the SolPartActions control, which functions as a pop-up menu when you hover over the edit icon located in the module container. This menu really only works well on the latest browsers and will perform most reliably when using Internet Explorer 6+. There is a downlevel version of the control that will produce a drop-down box when you connect with one of the older browsers that will not support the advanced browser capabilities.

As we've mentioned throughout this chapter, you will want your skins and containers to complement one another and produce a consistent look throughout your design. So it's best to design the skin and containers in conjunction with one another. The process is probably a little easier if you do develop them in conjunction even though they are really separate entities. Now that you have the basics, let's look at an example for a container manifest file. You will recall the manifest is where you define the attributes you want to define for the associated skin objects. To simplify this operation and provide a higher degree of granularity, a concept known as Pane Level skinning is also available. Pane Level skinning can only be configured at design-time when the skin designer constructs the skin. It involves the use of some custom attributes, which can be included in the markup for the pane. The ContainerType, ContainerName, and ContainerSrc attributes can be used to identify a specific container to be used with all modules injected into the pane. In order for this to work correctly, the container must exist in the location specified, otherwise the default container will be displayed. Listing 13-5 demonstrates a basic example of this concept.

Listing 13-5: Pane Level Skinning

```
<Objects>
    <Object>
        <Token>[CONTENTPANE:1]</Token>
        <Settings>
            <Setting>
                <Name>ID</Name>
                <Value>LeftPane</Value>
            </Setting>
            <Setting>
                <Name>ContainerType</Name>
                <Value>G</Value>
            </Setting>
            <Setting>
                <Name>ContainerName</Name>
                <Value>DNN</Value>
            </Setting>
            <Setting>
                <Name>ContainrSrc</Name>
                <Value>standard.ascx</Value>
            </Setting>
        </Settings>
    </Object>
</Objects>
```

As you can see from this example it is possible to define standard containers for each section of the skin's design. You can also set the default container at the portal level, which will apply to any new modules created in the portal. The preceding example makes the process of adding content less time intensive because you will not need to set the container after the module is added to the page.

As you can see, the container functionality in DotNetNuke is just as powerful as the skinning process and distinct looks of your design can be accomplished utilizing this technology. Table 13-3 showcases the skin objects available to you when you are developing your containers.

Table 13-3: Container Skin Objects

Token	Control	Description
[SOLPARTACTIONS]	< dnn:SolPartActions runat= "server" id="dnnSolPart Actions">	Pop-up module actions menu (formerly [ACTIONS])
[DROPDOWNACTIONS]	< dnn:DropDownActions runat="server" id="dnnDrop DownActions">	Simple drop-down combo box for module actions
[LINKACTIONS]	< dnn:LinkActions runat= "server" id="dnnLinkActions">	Links list of module actions
[ICON]	< dnn:Icon runat="server" id="dnnIcon">	Displays the icon related to the module
[TITLE]	< dnn:Title runat="server" id="dnnTitle">	Displays the title of the module
[VISIBILITY]	< dnn:Visibility runat="server" id="dnnVisibility">	Displays an icon representing the minimized or maximized state of a module
[PRINTMODULE]	< dnn:PrintModule runat= "server" id="dnn PrintModule ">	Displays a new window with only the module content displayed
[CONTENTPANE]	<div runat="server" id="ContentPane">	Injects a placeholder for module content

As you can see you have some of the same functions available to your skinning functions, but we have also added a few additional objects, which do not make sense from a page level but become very important on a module level. These are very powerful objects and can really increase the use of your modules and containers, so you should take some time to experiment with the various uses of these skin objects. Table 13-4 covers the associated attributes you can utilize in conjunction with the skin objects for containers.

Table 13-4: Container Skin Object Attributes

Token	Attribute	Default	Description
[SOLPARTACTIONS]			
[DROPDOWNACTIONS]			
[LINKACTIONS]			
[ICON]	BorderWidth	0	The border width around the icon
[TITLE]	CssClass	Head	The style name of title

Token	Attribute	Default	Description
[VISIBILITY]	BorderWidth	0	The border width around the icon
	MinIcon	min.gif	The custom min icon file located in the skin file
	MaxIcon	max.gif	The custom max icon file located in the skin file
[PRINTMODULE]	PrintIcon	print.gif	The custom print icon file located in the skin file
[CONTENTPANE]	ID	Content Pane	The content pane key identifier to be displayed in the user interface and stored in the database

Now that the objects and attributes are defined, let's look at an example container for the DotNetNuke project. Listing 13-6 displays the DNN-Blue container from the default install. You will see this container utilizes the same attributes we have discussed previously.

Listing 13-6: Example Container

```
<TABLE class="containermaster_blue" cellSpacing="0" cellPadding="5" align="center"
border="0">
        <TR>
          <TD class="containerrow1_blue">
            <TABLE width="100%" border="0" cellpadding="0" cellspacing="0">
              <TR>
                <TD valign="middle" nowrap><dnn:ACTIONS runat="server"
id="dnnACTIONS" /></TD>
                <TD valign="middle" nowrap><dnn:ICON runat="server" id="dnnICON"
/></TD>
                <TD valign="middle" width="100%" nowrap> <dnn:TITLE
runat="server" id="dnnTITLE" /></TD>
                <TD valign="middle" width="20" nowrap><dnn:VISIBILITY
runat="server" id="dnnVISIBILITY" /></TD>
              </TR>
            </TABLE>
          </TD>
        </TR>
        <TR>
          <TD id="ContentPane" runat="server" align="center"></TD>
        </TR>
        <TR>
          <TD>
            <HR class="containermaster_blue">
            <TABLE width="100%" border="0" cellpadding="0" cellspacing="0">
              <TR>
                <TD align="left" valign="middle" nowrap><dnn:ACTIONBUTTON1
runat="server" id="dnnACTIONBUTTON1" CommandName="AddContent.Action"
DisplayIcon="True" DisplayLink="True" /></TD>
```

(continued)

Listing 13-6: *(continued)*

```
                <TD align="right" valign="middle" nowrap><dnn:ACTIONBUTTON2
runat="server" id="dnnACTIONBUTTON2" CommandName="SyndicateModule.Action"
DisplayIcon="True" DisplayLink="False" /> <dnn:ACTIONBUTTON3 runat="server"
id="dnnACTIONBUTTON3" CommandName="PrintModule.Action" DisplayIcon="True"
DisplayLink="False" /> <dnn:ACTIONBUTTON4 runat="server" id="dnnACTIONBUTTON4"
CommandName="ModuleSettings.Action" DisplayIcon="True" DisplayLink="False" /></TD>
              </TR>
            </TABLE>
          </TD>
        </TR>
      </TABLE>
      <BR>
```

The example in Listing 13-6 is a simple container that will really help the display and feel of a portal with a blue-colored theme. You may notice we have included an ASCX container option here. If you were going to utilize this container, you would need to add the Register directive for each of the controls we have added.

Summary

This chapter looked at the basics of creating skins with DotNetNuke. Basically the point of all this is if you can design and program in HTML and can follow the few simple rules enforced by the skinning engine, then you can build beautiful designs for your DotNetNuke site. Many examples of both free and commercial skins are available for you to use as references when creating your skins and containers. There are quite a few examples on the DotNetNuke web site and in the solution as well as a multitude of resource sites in the DotNetNuke directory. We urge you to download some of these examples and, coupled with the knowledge contained in this chapter, you will create high-quality skins of your own in no time. If you can imagine it, then you can build it with the DotNetNuke skinning engine. The next chapter shows you how to take your finished skins and containers, as well as the modules you have built as a result of the information in the preceding chapters, and package them for distribution.

14

Distribution

This chapter examines how DotNetNuke add-ons can be distributed and installed. As DotNetNuke has progressed, we have continued to add functionality to allow developers to package and distribute extensions to the DotNetNuke framework. These add-ons allow the administrators and users to customize the portal to suit their particular needs. Add-ons can provide additional functionality or can alter the visual presentation style for the portal. DotNetNuke uses zip files to package and redistribute add-ons. Each add-on type defines the specific files that may be included in the package. These custom add-ons are broken down into three major categories:

1. Code add-ons

   ❑ Modules

   ❑ Skin Objects

   ❑ Providers

2. Skinning add-ons

   ❑ Skins

   ❑ Containers

3. Language add-ons

   ❑ Language Packs

There are many aspects to consider in the distribution of add-ons. As we look at each of these add-on types, we answer the following questions:

❑ What is the format of the manifest or configuration files for the add-on?

❑ How do you package all of the elements that go into a single add-on?

❑ How do you install the add-on?

Code Add-Ons

DotNetNuke provides mechanisms to extend the core portal functionality through the use of code add-ons. These add-ons can be packaged for easy distribution and installation. DotNetNuke supports three types of redistributable code packages: modules, skin objects, and providers. While these are not the only mechanisms available for extending portal functionality, they are the only officially supported mechanism for distributing code add-ons.

Modules

A module, also known as a DotNetNuke Private Assembly (PA), represents a discrete set of application code that is used to extend the functionality of the DotNetNuke portal. A module provides a user interface for managing and displaying custom content in the portal. Unlike the other DotNetNuke code add-ons, skin objects and providers, modules are designed to be easily added to a page by the administrator. Each module may be comprised of one or more ASP.NET user controls and compiled assemblies. Like the main portal application, the module can take advantage of the Data Provider model to package providers for multiple database management systems. In addition to user controls and assemblies, a module may use additional resources including images, xml files, SQL scripts, text files, cascading style sheets, and Resource archives.

Module Manifest File

The module manifest file is an XML file that is included in the module package to delineate the various elements that comprise a module package. The manifest file is organized to allow the portal to easily identify the module files, and to determine the appropriate database entries necessary for the proper functioning of the module. Listing 14-1 shows the basic manifest file format. DotNetNuke recognizes both version 2.0 and version 3.0 manifest files.

Listing 14-1: Module Manifest File Format

```
<?xml version="1.0" encoding="utf-8" ?>
<dotnetnuke version="D.D" type="Module">
  <folders>                              -- Contains one or more folder nodes
    <folder>
      <name />
      <description />
      <version />
      <businesscontrollerclass />        -- V3.0 only
      <resourcefile />
      <modules>                          -- Contains one or more module nodes
        <module>
          <friendlyname />
          <controls>                     -- Contains one or more control nodes
            <control>
              <key />
              <title />
              <src />
              <iconfile />
              <type />
```

```
              <vieworder />
              <helpurl />              -- V3.0 only
              <helpfile />             -- V2.0 only
          </control>
        </controls>
      </module>
    </modules>
    <files>                           -- Contains one or more file nodes
      <file>
        <path />
        <name />
      </file>
    </files>
  </folder>
 </folders>
</dotnetnuke>
```

Let's break this down and examine the individual xml nodes.

The root element is the dotnetnuke node. This node contains two attributes: version and type.

```
<dotnetnuke version="D.D" type="Module">
```

The version attribute takes a numeric value. DotNetNuke supports two versions — "2.0" and "3.0." Version 1.0 modules are no longer supported in DotNetNuke 3.x.

The type attribute must be set to "Module" for both v2 and v3 formats but may contain additional values to distinguish between the different manifest file formats used by skin objects and providers. These two additional formats will be discussed later in this chapter.

The manifest provides a <folders> element for identifying a collection of individual module folders. A folder node represents a single DotNetNuke module. The folder node may contain seven child elements as defined in Table 14-1.

Table 14-1: Folder Elements

Element Name	Description	Required	Versions Supported
Name	The name element defines both the name of the module as well as the name of the directory that DotNetNuke will create in the DesktopModules folder. This folder becomes the root from which all other module files are installed (dll files are a special exception to this rule since they must be installed to the application \bin directory).	Yes	2.0, 3.0
description	The description element is used for creating the module description that is presented to the host when viewing modules on the Module Definitions page.	Yes	2.0, 3.0

Table continued on following page

Element Name	Description	Required	Versions Supported
version	The version element is the version of the module. This element must be in the format XX.XX.XX where X is a digit from 0 to 9. This version number is used to determine which dataprovider scripts to execute. During installation, any script that has a higher version number than the currently installed module version will be executed. If this is the first time the module has been installed, then all script files will be executed. Scripts are executed in the order of their version numbers.	Yes	2.0, 3.0
business controllerclass	The businesscontrollerclass defines the qualified name of the primary business controller in the module. If the IPortable, ISearchable, or IUpgradeable interfaces are implemented by the module, then they must be implemented in this class. This entry uses the format [namespace].[class name], [assembly name]. An example entry would look like `< businesscontrollerclass >DotNetNuke.Modules.Survey.Survey Controller, DotNetNuke.Modules .Survey</ businesscontrollerclass>`.	No	3.0
resourcefile	The resourcefile identifies a zip file that is included in the module package. The resource file may contain any number of files, which will be installed using folder information defined in the resource file. Files placed in the resource file do not need to be delineated in the files collection of the manifest.	No	2.0, 3.0
modules	The modules element defines a collection of modules that are installed in the current folder. These modules will be associated with the Desktop Module defined by the current folder. See Table 14-2 for a description of each module element.	Yes	2.0, 3.0
files	The files element defines a collection of files that are installed in the current folder. See Table 14-4 for a description of each file element.	Yes	2.0, 3.0

Additionally, the folder node contains two collection child elements: Modules and Files, which are described in Tables 14-2, 14-3, and 14-4, respectively.

Table 14-2: Module Elements

Element Name	Description	Required	Versions Supported
friendlyname	The friendlyname element defines the name of the current module. This element is used primarily for display purposes to distinguish between multiple modules in a single Desktop Module.	Yes	2.0, 3.0
controls	The controls element defines a collection of user controls that are installed as part of the current module. These controls may provide different user or administrative screens for this specific module. See Table 14-3 for a description of each control element.	Yes	2.0, 3.0

Table 14-3: Control Elements

Element Name	Description	Required	Versions Supported
Key	The key element is a unique identifier that distinguishes each control in a single module. The primary view control does not use the key element and must not be included in the control definition. The module can use these key values to determine the appropriate screen to display for the current module state. The portal will display this control on the Module Settings screen if the control key is set to "Settings."	No	2.0, 3.0
Title	The title element defines the text displayed in the module title bar for the module edit screen associated with the current control. The title is not used for the primary view control.	No	2.0, 3.0
Src	The src element is the filename of the ASP.NET user control corresponding to the current control definition. The filename includes any path information relative to the current module folder.	Yes	2.0, 3.0
iconfile	The iconfile element defines the icon file to display in the module title bar. The iconfile setting is ignored for the primary view control and a control with a key of "Settings."	No	2.0, 3.0

Table continued on following page

Element Name	Description	Required	Versions Supported
type	The type element defines the security access level required to view the current control. This level is defined as a subset of the SecurityAccessLevel enumeration. Valid values include Anonymous, View, Edit, Admin, Host.	Yes	2.0, 3.0
vieworder	The vieworder element is used to order the controls when they are injected into the admin UI when multiple controls are associated with the module using the same key.	No	2.0, 3.0
helpurl	The helpurl element defines a URL for help information related to the current control.	No	3.0
helpfile	The helpfile element defines a file for help information related to the current control. The file location is relative to the current module folder. This element was deprecated in 3.0 and has been replaced through the use of LocalResources.	No	2.0

Table 14-4: File Elements

Element Name	Description	Required	Versions Supported
path	The path element defines a relative path to the module folder. The file defined by this node will be installed in this folder.	No	2.0, 3.0
name	The name element is the name of the file in the module package. If the file does not exist in the module package, then an error will be logged.	Yes	2.0, 3.0

Listing 14-2 shows the manifest file for the Survey module. The Survey module is included with DotNetNuke as an example of how to build, package, and deploy modules. The module package and source code can be found in the /desktopmodules/survey directory of the standard DotNetNuke installation.

Listing 14-2: Sample Manifest for the Survey Module

```xml
<?xml version="1.0" encoding="utf-8" ?>
<dotnetnuke version="3.0" type="Module">
  <folders>
    <folder>
```

```
<name>Survey</name>
<description>
   Survey allows you to create custom surveys to obtain public feedback
</description>
<version>01.00.00</version>
<businesscontrollerclass>
   DotNetNuke.Modules.Survey.SurveyController, DotNetNuke.Modules.Survey
</businesscontrollerclass>
<resourcefile>SurveyResources.zip</resourcefile>
<modules>
   <module>
      <friendlyname>DotNetNuke.Survey</friendlyname>
      <controls>
         <control>
            <src>Survey.ascx</src>
            <type>View</type>
            <helpurl>http://www.dotnetnuke.com</helpurl>
         </control>
         <control>
            <key>Edit</key>
            <title>Create Survey</title>
            <src>EditSurvey.ascx</src>
            <iconfile>icon_survey_32px.gif</iconfile>
            <type>Edit</type>
            <helpurl>http://www.dotnetnuke.com</helpurl>
         </control>
         <control>
            <key>Settings</key>
            <title>Survey Settings</title>
            <src>Settings.ascx</src>
            <iconfile>icon_survey_32px.gif</iconfile>
            <type>Edit</type>
            <helpurl>http://www.dotnetnuke.com</helpurl>
         </control>
      </controls>
   </module>
</modules>
<files>
   <file>
      <name>Survey.ascx</name>
   </file>
   <file>
      <name>EditSurvey.ascx</name>
   </file>
   <file>
      <name>Settings.ascx</name>
   </file>
   <file>
      <name>DotNetNuke.Modules.Survey.dll</name>
   </file>
   <file>
      <name>DotNetNuke.Modules.Survey.SqlDataProvider.dll</name>
   </file>
```

(continued)

359

Listing 14-2: *(continued)*

```
        <file>
          <name>01.00.00.SqlDataProvider</name>
        </file>
        <file>
          <name>Uninstall.SqlDataProvider</name>
        </file>
      </files>
    </folder>
  </folders>
</dotnetnuke>
```

Packaging Modules

DotNetNuke private assemblies are packaged as zip files. Files included in the package are placed in predetermined directories as defined by the file type and manifest file settings. Any directory information contained in the zip file is ignored. Only files that are specifically delineated in the manifest file will be extracted and saved to the portal directories. Figure 14-1 shows the survey module package that is included with DotNetNuke.

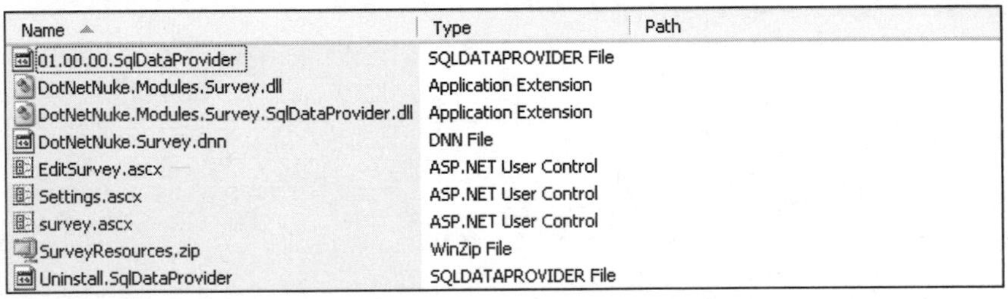

Name ▲	Type	Path
01.00.00.SqlDataProvider	SQLDATAPROVIDER File	
DotNetNuke.Modules.Survey.dll	Application Extension	
DotNetNuke.Modules.Survey.SqlDataProvider.dll	Application Extension	
DotNetNuke.Survey.dnn	DNN File	
EditSurvey.ascx	ASP.NET User Control	
Settings.ascx	ASP.NET User Control	
survey.ascx	ASP.NET User Control	
SurveyResources.zip	WinZip File	
Uninstall.SqlDataProvider	SQLDATAPROVIDER File	

Figure 14-1

Special File Types

DotNetNuke recognizes four specific file types in the private assembly archive. While other file types may be included in the package, DotNetNuke treats these types as special cases. The following list looks at each of these types and how they are handled during installation:

- ❑ **.Dnn file type:** The .dnn file is the manifest file for the Module package. Each package must include a single manifest file that follows the format specified below. The manifest file can use any name, but must have the .dnn file extension. The manifest fully describes each file included in the package and identifies information needed by the portal to create the appropriate module definition entries and install the module files to the appropriate directories required by DotNetNuke. The .dnn file is copied to the module folder defined in the manifest.

- ❑ **.Dll file type:** Dll files are .NET assemblies. In DotNetNuke, these assemblies may represent the compiled module code, a dataprovider assembly, or even an ASP.NET Server Control used in the module. All dll files are installed to the application directory (/bin).

❑ **.Ascx file type:** Ascx files are the visual portion of a user control in ASP.NET. This file defines the layout of the user interface for the specific module. This file will be copied to the module folder and a special entry is made in the DotNetNuke system tables as specified in the manifest file. The Ascx file may represent a single "module control" or may be a constituent control that is used on multiple screens within the module. All module controls should be defined in the manifest, while constituent controls should only appear in the manifest file list.

❑ **Dataprovider script file type:** Dataprovider files contain SQL scripts that define the database-specific code for the module. This file type uses a file extension that follows a standard pattern .[DataProviderType]DataProvider, where [DataProviderType] corresponds to the provider type defined in the DotNetNuke web.config file ("Access," "Sql," "Mysql," "Oracle," and so on). New dataproviders may be written by third-party vendors, and in that case new dataprovider script file types will be defined by the vendor. Dataprovider scripts are installed to a subdirectory of the Providers/DataProviders folder. The subdirectory is created with the same name as the dataprovider type (for example, SQLDataProvider files are installed in the providers/dataproviders/sqldataprovider directory).

> Unlike earlier versions DotNetNuke 3.0 only includes a dataprovider for Microsoft SQL Server. The Microsoft Access Provider was removed from the distribution to simplify maintenance of the core framework. Additional providers, including a Microsoft Access Provider, are available from third-party vendors.

Resource File

In addition to the predefined file types, the module package also allows for the inclusion of a resource file. A resource file is a zip file that may contain any file that is not one of the special types defined earlier. Unlike the main module zip file, all directory information in the resource file will be used to determine the appropriate directory in which to place the individual resources. Any directory that is defined will be created relative to the main module directory as defined in the manifest. Files that are placed in the resource file should not be delineated in the manifest file; however, the resource file must be specified in the manifest. Figure 14-2 shows the contents of the SurveyResources.zip defined in the survey module manifest in Listing 14-2.

Name	Type	Path
EditSurvey.ascx.de-DE.resx	.NET Managed Resources File	App_LocalResources\
EditSurvey.ascx.resx	.NET Managed Resources File	App_LocalResources\
icon_survey_32px.gif	GIF Image	
module.css	Cascading Style Sheet Document	
red.gif	GIF Image	
Settings.ascx.de-DE.resx	.NET Managed Resources File	App_LocalResources\
Settings.ascx.resx	.NET Managed Resources File	App_LocalResources\
Survey.ascx.de-DE.resx	.NET Managed Resources File	App_LocalResources\
Survey.ascx.resx	.NET Managed Resources File	App_LocalResources\

Figure 14-2

Notice that the *.resx files included in the resource file include path information. These files will be installed in the [module folder]/App_LocalResources directory.

Installing Modules

Once you have created a manifest file and properly packaged your module, it is now ready for installation. The use of the zip file format and a well-defined manifest format greatly simplifies module installations over earlier versions of DotNetNuke. Because of the potential security risk, only the Portal Host has permissions to install modules. DotNetNuke supports two distinct methods for installing modules as well as other add-ons: web-based file upload or FTP-based file upload. These two methods differ primarily in the mechanism used for transferring the file to the server. Once DotNetNuke receives the file all processing is the same.

Web-Based File Upload

Follow these four simple steps to install a new module into your portal using the web-based installer.

Step 1

Log in with the Host account and go to the Module Definitions page from the Host menu (see Figure 14-3). Only the Host account is authorized to install modules because modules have full access to the portal including file and database access.

> Modules can pose a security risk since they have unlimited access to the portal. Module code has the same security privileges as the core application. This means that modules could alter key portal tables, manipulate application files, or even gain access to other server resources. Modules should be fully tested in a "safe" environment prior to installation in a production system. In addition, the portal should run in a partial trust environment, which would limit the ability of any module to access restricted resources.

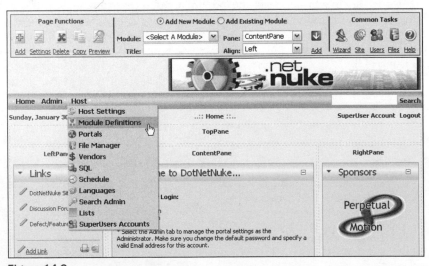

Figure 14-3

Step 2

On the Module Definitions page, select the Upload New Module menu item from the module action menu (see Figure 14-4).

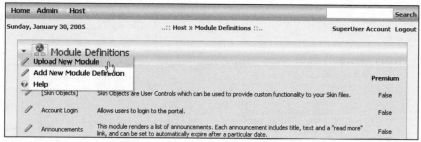

Figure 14-4

Step 3

The File Upload screen provides a simple interface for uploading one or more modules (see Figure 14-5). The File Upload screen provides a common user interface for uploading different add-on types. Browse to the desired module package, click OK on the Browse dialog, and click the Add link on the file upload page. Use the Upload New File link button to finish installing the module.

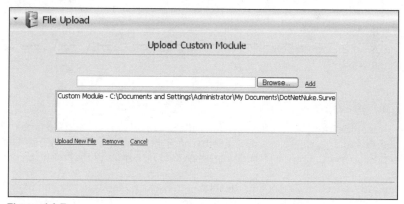

Figure 14-5

Step 4

After installing a new module, you should review the upload logs (see Figure 14-6). Errors will be highlighted in red. If no errors are shown, the module is ready for use in your portal.

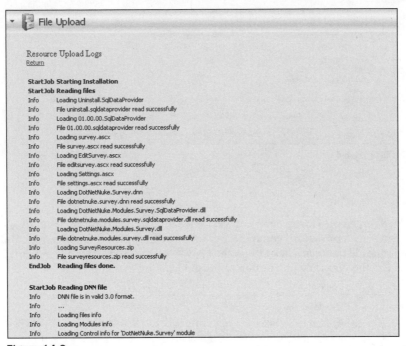

Figure 14-6

FTP-Based installation

DotNetNuke 3.0 includes support for file-based installation of all defined add-on types. The framework includes a scheduled task that runs every minute to check installation folders for new add-ons to install. If you do not need this service, you can disable the scheduled task from the Schedule page in the Host menu.

To install a new module using FTP or any file manager, copy the module into the Install/Module directory of your DotNetNuke installation. When the ResourceInstaller task runs, it will install this module using the standard module installation code. If an error occurs it will be noted in the task history, which is available by selecting the History link for the ResourceInstaller task on the Schedule page (see Figure 14-7).

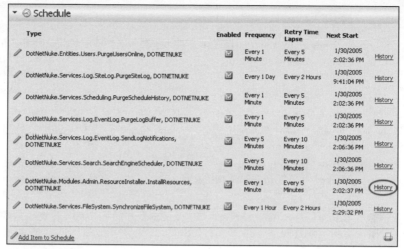

Figure 14-7

Skin Objects

Skins objects, like modules, are active elements designed to programmatically extend the functionality of DotNetNuke. Skin objects are used in skins and containers to produce a dynamic user interface. A number of default skin objects are included with DotNetNuke (see Table 14-5) for common portal functions such as login, status, and navigation.

Table 14-5: Standard Skin Objects

HTML Token	ASCX Control	Usage	Description
[ACTION BUTTON]	< dnn: ActionButton runat="server" id="dnnAction Button">	Container	Displays a list of link buttons that correspond to Action menu items with a specified command name.
[ICON]	< dnn:Icon runat="server" id="dnnIcon">	Container	Displays an icon for the module. If the icon module was not set on the Module Settings page, then no icon is displayed.
[PRINT MODULE]	< dnn: PrintModule runat="server" id="dnnPrintModule">	Container	Displays an image button for printing module contents.
[ACTIONS]	< dnn: Actions runat="server" id="dnnActions">	Container	Displays the module action menu using the Solpart Menu control.

Table continued on following page

HTML Token	ASCX Control	Usage	Description
[SOLPART ACTIONS]	< dnn:SolpartActions runat="server" id="dnnSolpart Actions">	Container	Displays the module action menu using the Solpart Menu control. This is the same as the [ACTIONS] skin object.
[DROPDOWN ACTIONS]	< dnn: DropDownActions runat="server" id="dnnDrop DownActions">	Container	Displays the module action menu items using a dropdownlist.
[LINK ACTIONS]	< dnn: LinkActions runat="server" id="dnnLinkActions">	Container	Displays the module action menu items using a series of link buttons.
[TITLE]	< dnn:Title runat="server" id="dnnTitle">	Container	Displays the module title.
[VISIBILITY]	< dnn:Visibility runat="server" id="dnnVisibility">	Container	Displays the expand/collapse button for hiding or displaying module contents.
[SIGNIN]	< dnn:Signin runat="server" id="dnnSignin">	Skin	Displays the signin control for providing your username and password.
[BANNER]	< dnn:Banner runat="server" id="dnnBanner">	Skin	Displays a random banner ad.
[BREAD CRUMB]	< dnn:Breadcrumb runat="server" id="dnnBreadcrumb">	Skin	Displays the path to the currently selected page in the form of PageName1 > Page-Name2 > PageName3.
[CONTENT PANE]	<div runat="server" id="ContentPane" >	Skin	A placeholder for content modules.
[COPYRIGHT]	< dnn:Copyright runat="server" id="dnnCopyright">	Skin	Displays the copyright notice for the portal.
[CURRENT DATE]	< dnn:CurrentDate runat="server" id="dnnCurrentDate">	Skin	Displays the current date.
[DOTNET NUKE]	< dnn:DotNetNuke runat="server" id="dnnDotNetNuke">	Skin	Displays the Copyright notice for DotNetNuke.
[HELP]	< dnn:Help runat="server" id="dnnHelp">	Skin	Displays a link for Help that will launch the user's e-mail client and send mail to the portal administrator.
[HOSTNAME]	< dnn:HostName runat="server" id="dnnHostName">	Skin	Displays the Host Title linked to the Host URL.

HTML Token	ASCX Control	Usage	Description
[LINKS]	< dnn:Links runat="server" id="dnnLinks">	Skin	Displays a flat menu of links related to the current tab level and parent node. This is useful for search engine spiders and robots.
[LOGIN]	< dnn:Login runat="server" id="dnnLogin">	Skin	Dual state control — displays "Login" for anonymous users and "Logout" for authenticated users.
[LOGO]	< dnn:Logo runat="server" id="dnnLogo">	Skin	Displays the portal logo.
[PRIVACY]	< dnn:Privacy runat="server" id="dnnPrivacy">	Skin	Displays a link to the Privacy Information for the portal.
[SEARCH]	< dnn:Search runat="server" id="dnnSearch">	Skin	Displays a search input box and link button.
[MENU]	< dnn:Menu runat="server" id="dnnMenu">	Skin	Displays the hierarchical navigation menu.
[SOLPART MENU]	< dnn:SolpartMenu runat= "server" id="dnnSolpartMenu">	Skin	Displays the hierarchical navigation menu. This is the same as the [MENU] skin object.
[TERMS]	< dnn:Terms runat="server" id="dnnTerms">	Skin	Displays a link to the Terms and Conditions for the portal.
[TREEVIEW]	< dnn:TreeView runat="server" id="dnnTreeView">	Skin	Displays a tree-based menu of links for the portal pages. The menu can be set to limit the tree to various menu levels.
[USER]	< dnn:User runat="server" id="dnnUser">	Skin	Dual state control — displays a "Register" link for anonymous users or the user's name for authenticated users.

Custom skin objects are packaged and installed using the same processes as custom modules. All of the necessary skin object resource files are combined with a DotNetNuke manifest file (* .dnn) and packaged into a compressed zip file. Follow the installation steps outlined in the "Installing Modules" section earlier in the chapter. The primary difference between modules and skin objects is with the manifest file format.

Skin Object Manifest File

The skin object manifest file format (see Listing 14-3) is derived from version 2 of the module manifest format (shown in Listing 14-1 previously). Changes are highlighted.

Listing 14-3: Skin Object Manifest File Format

```
<?xml version="1.0" encoding="utf-8" ?>
<dotnetnuke version="D.D" type="SkinObject">    -- Changed type value
  <folders>
    <folder>
      <name />
      <description />                            -- Not used
      <version />                                -- Not used
      <resourcefile />
      <modules>
        <module>
          <friendlyname />                       -- Not used
          <controls>
            <control>
              <key />
              <title />
              <src />
              <iconfile />
              <type />                            -- Changed valid values
              <vieworder />
            </control>
          </controls>
        </module>
      </modules>
      <files>
        <file>
          <path />
          <name />
        </file>
      </files>
    </folder>
  </folders>
</dotnetnuke>
```

The type attribute of the root `dotnetnuke` node must be set to "SkinObject." Unlike modules, skin objects ignore the version value. The version must still be a decimal number in the format D.D where D is a single digit.

> While there is no restriction on the actual number, it should be set to "2.0" to prevent conflicts with future versions of the skin object format.

The `description`, `version`, and `friendlyname` elements are no longer used but are still allowed in the manifest file without causing a validation error. The `type` element must be set to "SkinObject."

Providers

Providers are a third mechanism for extending the functionality of the DotNetNuke portal framework. The primary difference between modules, skin objects, and providers is in the usage pattern. Modules provide a mechanism for extending system functionality. No two modules are guaranteed to provide the exact same functionality or implementation. Skin objects follow this same behavior with each skin object being free to implement whatever functionality desired. Providers are unique in that each provider of a given type must implement the exact same functionality. The implementation details may change but the basic functionality (that is, the programming interface) is defined by the portal.

Provider Manifest File

Because providers are a programmatic extension to the portal framework, they use the same packaging and installation mechanism defined for modules. Like skin objects, providers have their own manifest file format (see Listing 14.4), which is derived from the module manifest format.

Listing 14-4: Provider Manifest File Format

```
<?xml version="1.0" encoding="utf-8" ?>
<dotnetnuke version="D.D" type="Provider">  -- Changed type value
  <folder>
    <name />
    <type />
    <files>
      <file>
        <path />
        <name />
      </file>
    </files>
  </folder>
</dotnetnuke>
```

The `type` attribute of the root `dotnetnuke` node must be set to "Provider." Providers follow the same rules as skin objects for the version attribute. Tables 14-6 and 14-7 show the manifest file elements.

Table 14-6: Provider Manifest Folder Elements

Element Name	Description	Required
Name	The name element defines the name of the provider. This name will be used to create the folder in the appropriate provider directory.	Yes
Type	The type element is the provider type. This element may be either "DataProviders" or "LoggingProviders." Additional provider types will be supported in future releases.	Yes
Files	The files element defines a collection of files that are installed in the current folder. See Table 14-7 for a description of each file element.	Yes

Table 14-7: Provider Manifest File Elements

Element Name	Description	Required
Path	The path element defines a relative path to the provider folder.	No
Name	The name element is the name of the file in the provider package. If the file does not exist in the provider package, then an error will be logged.	Yes

Files in the provider package will be installed as

```
[DotNetNuke Root
  Folder]/Providers/[ProviderType]/[FolderName]/[FilePath]/[FileName]
```

Skinning Add-Ons

While code add-ons are designed to extend the functionality of the portal, skinning add-ons are aimed at giving the portal administrator complete control over the visual appearance of the portal. In order to simplify development and maintenance of these skinning packages, no manifest files are required. Instead, skinning packages rely on zip files to package and group the files to be installed in support of a skin. While not utilizing manifest files, skinning packages include support for XML-based configuration files. Configuration files allow the designer to set properties on individual skin elements that are identified inside the skinning source files. These skin elements include all skin objects as well as content panes defined within the skin definition file.

DotNetNuke uses two mechanisms for grouping content in the portal: pages and modules. Skins provide a method for changing the appearance of individual pages, while containers provide this function for each module instance placed on a page. Let's first take a look at how skins are packaged and deployed.

Skins

As discussed in Chapter 13, skins provide the primary method for controlling the appearance of individual portal pages. One of the primary goals for the DotNetNuke skinning solution was to create a simple the process for developing and packaging skins. This process should allow web designers as well as developers to create skins using a variety of tools: from simple HTML editors to complex IDEs like Visual Studio .NET. This separation of form and function is one of the strengths of the DotNetNuke skinning solution.

Packaging Skins

A skin package is comprised of multiple files that constitute a complete skin:

❑ **htm, .html files:** Abstract skin definition files that will be processed by the Skin Uploader to create an .ascx file.

- **.ascx files:** Skin definition user controls that are written in the format required by the skin engine.

- **.css files:** Styles sheets that are related to skins.

- **.gif, .jpg, .jpeg, .png:** Support graphics files.

- **.xml files:** Abstract skin properties files that will be combined with the abstract skin definition files during the upload processing.

- **.zip files:** Skin and container packages that are named according to the parent package.

> You can include any additional files needed by the skin, however these files must be one of the allowable file types defined in the Host File Upload Extensions setting.

A skin package can contain multiple skin files. This allows you to create skins that leverage the same graphics but vary slightly based on layout. Obviously the more skin files you have in a package, the more maintenance will be required when you want to make a general change to the presentation in the future.

When packaging files for the skin, files should be zipped using relative file paths to the skin definition files. When unpacked, all file paths in the definition file will be corrected to point at the new file locations in the portal. Files will be unzipped using the file path information contained in the skin package.

> You should make sure that relative file path information in the zip file matches the relative path information in the skin definition files.

The following example shows two different graphic images from an abstract skin definition file:

```
<IMG src="top_left.gif" height="10" width="10" border="0">
<IMG src="images/top_right.gif" height="10" width="10" border="0">
```

The files should be included in the package as indicated in Figure 14-8.

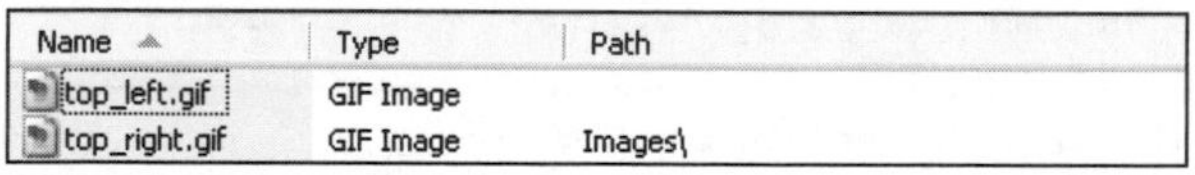

Name	Type	Path
top_left.gif	GIF Image	
top_right.gif	GIF Image	Images\

Figure 14-8

If this snippet was contained in a package called MySkin.zip, the resulting image tags after installation would look this:

```
<IMG src="/Portals/_default/Skins/MySkin/top_left.gif" height="10" width="10"
border="0">
<IMG src="/Portals/_default/Skins/MySkin/images/top_right.gif" height="10"
width="10" border="0">
```

Skin packages may contain files that are applied to all skin definition files in the package or that are specific to an individual skin definition as outlined in Table 14-8. Any properties or styles set in the global file (if present) will be overwritten with the value from the corresponding file that is specific to an individual skin. Graphics and any additional files stored in the skin package are global in scope and may be referenced by any skin definition file included in the package.

Table 14-8: Skin Filenames

File Type	Global Name	Individual Skin Name
Configuration File	Skin.xml	[skin filename].xml
Style Sheet	Skin.css	[skin filename].css

In many cases you will want to package a complementary set of skin files and container files in one distribution file. In order to do this you need to package your container files in a zip file named "containers.zip." Similarly, you must package your skin files in a zip file name "skins.zip." Then you need to package these two files into a single zip file that is named after your skin. This will allow people to install the full skin package (skins and containers) by uploading a single file through the Skin Uploader.

DotNetNuke contains a Skin Gallery for previewing skins installed in the portal. In order for the skin to be viewable in the Skin Gallery, you need to create a high-quality screen shot of your skin. For each skin or container definition file (both html- and ascx-based definitions) you should also have a corresponding screen shot stored with a .jpg file extension (that is, if your skin file is named myskin.html, then your screen shot needs to be named myskin.jpg).

Skin Configuration Files

When creating abstract skin definition files (htm or html files) the designer places tokens in the skin to designate locations for skin objects or content panes. In order to control the behavior and appearance of the skin objects and panes, the author may optionally choose to include one or more configuration files in the skin package. Any public property or field of a skin object or content pane may be set using the configuration file. As noted earlier, the global Skin.xml file property settings will be applied to all skins. If present, these property settings may be overridden by a skin-specific configuration file as well.

The skin configuration file uses a simple format, as shown in Listing 14-5.

Listing 14-5: Skin Configuration File Format

```
<Objects>
  <Object>
    <Token />
    <Settings>
      <Setting>
        <Name />
        <Value />
      </Setting>
    </Settings>
  </Object>
</Objects>
```

Table 14-9 describes the relevant elements from the skin configuration file.

Table 14-9: Configuration File Elements

Element Name	Description
Objects	The Objects element contains one or more Object nodes that provide property settings for the individual skin element.
Token	The Token element defines the skin element to update with the associated settings. This value must match a token that exists in the associated skin definition file(s).
Settings	The Settings element contains one or more Setting nodes that provide the individual name/value pairs for a single skin element property.
Name	The Name element is the name of the skin object property/attribute. If the skin object does not support this attribute, an error may be thrown when the skin is used in the portal.
Value	The Value element is the value to assign to the skin object attribute. If this is an invalid value, then an error may be thrown when the skin is used.

This format allows the author to easily set one or more attributes for each token included in the skin. Each skin object has its own set of supported attributes, as shown in Chapter 13. The Skin Uploader will merge the skin attributes with the HTML presentation file to create an ASCX skin file.

> If you are creating ASCX skins, you will need to specify the attribute directly in your skin file (that is, <dnn:Login runat="server" id="dnnLogin" Text="Signin" />) and no configuration file is necessary.

Please note there is a one-to-one correspondence of skin object declarations in your skin file with the attribute specification in the XML file. This is also true for named instances. For example, if you want to include a vertical and horizontal set of navigation links in your skin, you can specify [LINKS:1] and [LINKS:2] named instances in your skin file and then create definitions for each with different attributes in your XML file.

Listing 14-6 shows a sample configuration file that is used in the PHPDupe skin.

Listing 14-6: Skins Configuration File Format

```
<Objects>
  <Object>
    <Token>[LINKS:1]</Token>
    <Settings>
      <Setting>
        <Name>Separator</Name>
        <Value><![CDATA[  |  ]]></Value>
```

(continued)

Listing 14-6: *(continued)*

```
        </Setting>
        <Setting>
          <Name>Level</Name>
          <Value>Root</Value>
        </Setting>
      </Settings>
    </Object>
    <Object>
      <Token>[LINKS:2]</Token>
      <Settings>
        <Setting>
          <Name>Level</Name>
          <Value>Child</Value>
        </Setting>
        <Setting>
          <Name>Alignment</Name>
          <Value>Vertical</Value>
        </Setting>
        <Setting>
          <Name>Separator</Name>
          <Value><![CDATA[<b><big> &middot;  </big></b>]]></Value>
        </Setting>
      </Settings>
    </Object>
    <Object>
      <Token>[DOTNETNUKE]</Token>
      <Settings>
        <Setting>
          <Name>CssClass</Name>
          <Value>Copyright</Value>
        </Setting>
      </Settings>
    </Object>
  </Objects>
```

When settings are applied to the abstract skin file they are injected in the control tag as attributes and take the form *Name="Value"*. So based on the skin objects defined in Table 14-5 when the preceding configuration file is used, the [DOTNETNUKE] token will be replaced with the following control reference:

```
< dnn:DotNetNuke runat="server" id="dnnDotNetNuke" CssClass="Copyright">
```

Installing Skins

Unlike code add-ons, skins can be installed by both portal administrators as well as hosts. Skins also support web-based file upload or FTP based-file upload.

Web-Based File Upload

Follow these four steps to install a new skin into your portal using the web-based installer. Depending on whether you install the skin from the Admin or the Host menu will determine where the skin files are saved and which portals in a multi-portal site will have access to the skin.

Step 1

Log in with an Admin or Host account. If you are installing a skin for the current portal, go to the Admin/Site Settings menu (see Figure 14-9). Skin files will be stored in the individual portal directory. If multiple portals upload the same skin, then duplicate files will exist in the portal directories.

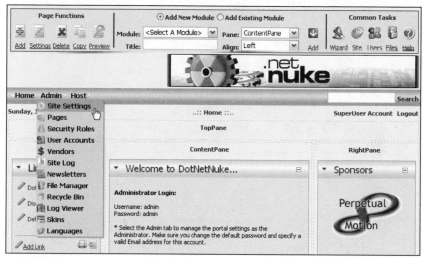

Figure 14-9

If you want all of the portals in a multi-portal installation to have access to the skin, make sure to log in with the Host account and select the Host/Host Settings menu (see Figure 14-10).

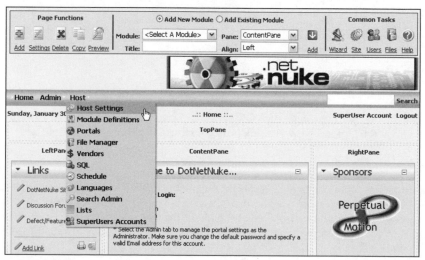

Figure 14-10

Step 2

Figures 14-11 and 14-12 show the key portions of the Portal Settings and Host Settings screens. Select the Upload Skin link to go the File Upload screen.

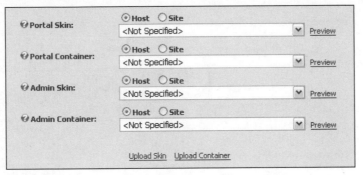

Figure 14-11

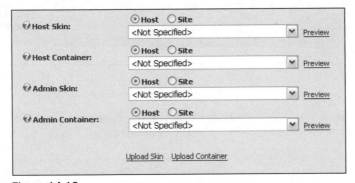

Figure 14-12

Step 3

The File Upload screen provides a simple interface for uploading one or more skins (see Figure 14-13). Browse to the desired skin package, click OK on the Browse dialog, and click the Add link on the File Upload page. Use the Upload New File link button to finish installing the module.

Step 4

After installing a new skin package, you should review the upload logs (see Figure 14-14). Errors will be highlighted in red. If no errors are shown, then the skin is ready for use in your portal. The location of the installation directory will be displayed at the top of the logs. Note that the directory matches the name of the skin package and will only vary based on whether the skin is installed from the Admin menu or the Host menu.

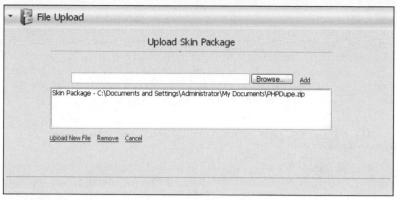

Figure 14-13

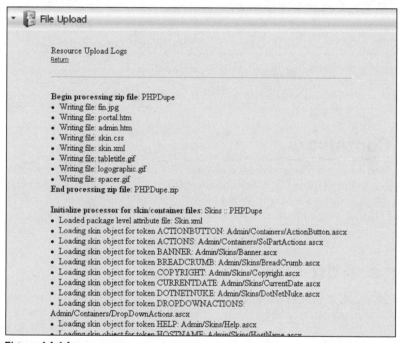

Figure 14-14

FTP-Based Installation

To install a new skin using FTP or any file manager, copy the module into the Install/Skin directory of your DotNetNuke installation. When the ResourceInstaller task runs, it will install this skin using the standard skin installation code. If an error occurs it will be noted in the task history, which is available by selecting the History link for the ResourceInstaller task on the Schedule page (shown in Figure 14-7 previously).

Containers

Containers, like skins, provide the ability to control the appearance of portal. While skins work at the "page" level, containers are designed for wrapping individual modules that appear on the page. Each module on a given page may use any one of the installed containers. Containers follow many of the same packaging and installation processes as skins and differ primarily in the allowable content inside the html or ascx definition files. Let's take a look at these differences.

Packaging Containers

Containers follow all of the same packaging rules as skins. Container packages may contain files that are applied to all container definition files in the package or that are specific to an individual container definition as outlined in Table 14-10. The behavior and purpose of these files is the same as for skins, and only the names of the files are different.

Table 14-10: Container Filenames

File Type	Global Name	Individual Container Name
Configuration File	Container.xml	[container filename].xml
Style Sheet	Container.css	[container filename].css

Installing Containers

Containers follow the same procedures for web- and FTP-based installations. For web-based installations, in Step 2, select the Upload Container link instead of the skin link (shown in Figures 14-11 and 14-12 previously). Containers will be installed in the Portal or Host *containers* directory. To install containers using FTP, place the container package in the Install/Container directory.

Language Add-Ons

DotNetNuke 3.0 added support for multiple languages. The DotNetNuke implementation loosely follows the localization architecture and naming conventions of the upcoming ASP.NET 2.0 framework. DotNetNuke 3.0 only recognizes a single type of language add-on: a Language Pack. This will likely change in future DotNetNuke versions as the Language Pack is split into Core Language Packs and Module Language packs.

Language Packs

The multi-language architecture poses a unique challenge for creating and installing Language Packs due to the number of directories and files involved. Like code add-ons, Language Packs utilize a manifest file to manage the meta-data necessary to get all of the files installed to the correct directory.

Language Pack Manifest File

The Language Pack manifest file follows a very simple format, as shown in Listing 14-7.

Listing 14-7: Language Pack Manifest File Format

```
<?xml version="1.0"?>
<LanguagePack xmlns:xsd="http://www.w3.org/2001/XMLSchema"
xmlns:xsi="http://www.w3.org/2001/XMLSchema-instance" Version="3.0">
  <Culture Code="" DisplayName="" />
  <Files>
    <File FileName="" FileType="" ModuleName="" FilePath=""/>
  </Files>
</LanguagePack>
```

The Language Pack manifest file relies more on the use of attributes, which is a more compact format than using simple elements. Table 14-11 lists the key elements of the manifest file.

Table 14-11: Manifest File Elements

Element Name	Description
LanguagePack	The LanguagePack element is the root element for the manifest file. This element must be created exactly as shown in Listing 14-7. The installation code will validate the file against the listed schemas.
Culture	The Culture element defines the culture information associated with the current Language Pack. The Culture contains two attributes: Code and DisplayName. The Code attribute takes a value corresponding to a valid culture name as defined by the .NET Framework System.Globalization.CultureInfo class. The DisplayName defines the name to display when selecting languages in the portal framework.
Files	The Files element contains one or more File nodes that provide the information necessary to properly install the individual resource file identified by the File node. See Table 14-10 for more information about the individual attributes of the File element.

Each language resource included in the Language Pack must be identified by a corresponding file element in the manifest (see Table 14-12). The files will be saved based on predefined rules depending on the file type.

Table 14-12: Manifest File Elements

Attribute Name	Description	Required
FileName	The FileName attribute defines the name of the physical file. The filename should not include any path information.	Yes

Table continued on following page

Attribute Name	Description	Required
FileType	The FileType attribute defines the type of file identified by this node and is used by the portal to determine the root directory where the file will be installed. The FileType must be one of four values: GlobalResource, AdminResource, ControlResource, or LocalResource. See Table 14-11 for more information on these file types.	Yes
ModuleName	The ModuleName attribute is required for files marked as AdminResource or LocalResource. This value identifies the name of the Admin or DesktopModule that is associated with this file. The ModuleName is the same as the directory name where the module is installed.	No
FilePath	The FilePath attribute defines a path relative to the default resource path. The file path where the file will be saved is: [RootPath]\[ModuleName]\[FilePath]\[ResourceDirectory]. The RootPath and ResourceDirectory values are determined by the file type and are defined in Table 14-11.	No

The FileType attribute will be used to determine the appropriate RootPath and Resource directory (see Table 14-13). The RootPath value corresponds to specific directories defined by DotNetNuke. Admin modules, Controls, and DesktopModules are the only DotNetNuke elements that are permitted to have local language resources. All other elements should use the Global resources. The Resource directory is defined to correspond to ASP.NET 2.0 values and are subject to change before the final ASP.NET 2.0 release.

Table 14-13: FileType Values

FileType	Description	RootPath	Resource Directory
GlobalResource	Shared resources	\	App_GlobalResources
AdminResource	Admin module resources	\admin	App_LocalResources
ControlResource	Control resources	\controls	App_LocalResources
LocalResource	DesktopModule resources	\Desktopmodules	App_LocalResources

To simplify the creation of the manifest file, DotNetNuke includes the ability to generate the Language Pack including the manifest file. Although the manifest file may be hard to maintain by hand, it is a format that lends itself well to automatic generation and is easily read during the installation process. Listing 14-8 shows a partial listing of the generated Deutsch (German) manifest file.

Listing 14-8: German Language Pack Manifest

```xml
<?xml version="1.0"?>
<LanguagePack xmlns:xsd="http://www.w3.org/2001/XMLSchema"
xmlns:xsi="http://www.w3.org/2001/XMLSchema-instance" Version="3.0">
```

```
     <Culture Code="de-DE" DisplayName="Deutsch" />
     <Files>
        <File FileName="GlobalResources.de-DE.resx" FileType="GlobalResource" />
        <File FileName="SharedResources.de-DE.resx" FileType="GlobalResource" />
        <File FileName="TimeZones.de-DE.xml" FileType="GlobalResource" />
        <File FileName="Announcements.ascx.de-DE.resx" FileType="LocalResource"
ModuleName="Announcements" />
        <File FileName="EditAnnouncements.ascx.de-DE.resx" FileType="LocalResource"
ModuleName="Announcements" />

     ...
     ...
     ...
     ...
     ...

        <File FileName="Address.ascx.de-DE.resx" FileType="ControlResource" />
        <File FileName="DualListControl.ascx.de-DE.resx" FileType="ControlResource" />
        ...
        ...
        <File FileName="Classic.ascx.de-DE.resx" FileType="AdminResource"
ModuleName="ControlPanel" />
        <File FileName="IconBar.ascx.de-DE.resx" FileType="AdminResource"
ModuleName="ControlPanel" />
        ...
        ...
     </Files>
</LanguagePack>
```

Packaging Language Packs

A Language Pack includes three different types of files:

❑ **Language Resource File:** A language resource file is a standard .NET resource file that includes a key name and the localized value. A call to the DotNetNuke method GetString(key) returns the value that corresponds to the key.

❑ **Time Zones File:** The TimeZones file includes a list of time zones that are recognized by the DotNetNuke portal.

❑ **Manifest File:** The manifest file identifies the resource files included in the Language Pack.

DotNetNuke includes the ability to generate Language Packs for any of the languages/cultures that are currently installed on your portal. Given the number of files and directories involved in creating a complete Language Pack, the generator is the recommended method for creating Language Packs. Not only does it simplify the creation process, but it also ensures that all necessary files are included and that the manifest file is properly formatted. Follow these simple steps to create a Language Pack.

Step 1

Log in with the Host account and go to the Languages page on the Host menu (see Figure 14-15). Although the Admin account has some ability to edit language resources, they do not have the necessary permissions to Generate or Import Language Packs.

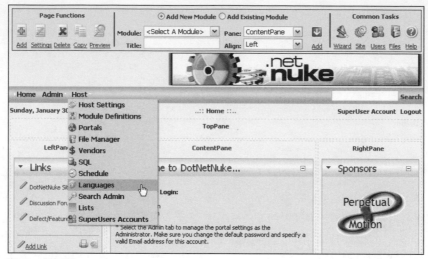

Figure 14-15

Step 2

The Languages screen provides a number of options for adding new Locales/Languages to your portal. If you want to generate a Language Pack for a language that does not show up in the Supported Locales list, you must first add the language to your portal. (See Chapter 4 for more information about adding additional languages.) Select Create Language Pack from the Action menu or from the links at the bottom of the screen as shown in Figure 14-16.

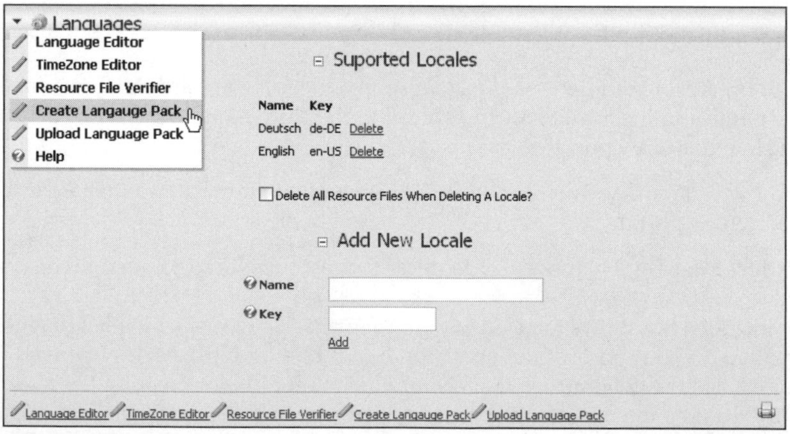

Figure 14-16

Step 3

Select the Locale for which you want to create a Language Pack and then click the Create link (see Figure 14-17).

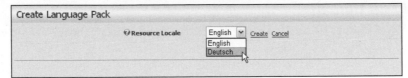

Figure 14-17

Step 4

After the Language Pack has been created, you will be presented with a complete log showing all of the files added to the Language Pack (see Figure 14-18). You should review the logs for errors, which will be highlighted in red. Additionally, the log shows you important information about the directory where the generated Language Pack is stored. The log also provides a link to the File Manager so that you can download the Language Pack from the portal server.

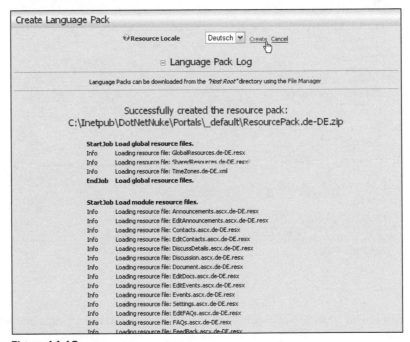

Figure 14-18

Installing Language Packs

Just like code and skinning add-ons, Language Packs also support two installation methods: web-based and FTP-based. Language Packs can include hundreds of files, which must be properly referenced in the manifest file. Any mismatch between the files identified in the manifest and files included in the Language Pack will result in an error. Additionally, the manifest file controls where each resource will be installed. An error in the manifest could result in a resource file being installed into the wrong directory. If the DotNetNuke Language Pack Generator was used to create the Language Pack, the likelihood of errors during installation is significantly reduced.

Web-Based File Upload

Follow these four steps to install a new language into your portal using the web-based installer.

Step 1

Log in with the Host account and go to the Languages page on the Host menu (shown previously in Figure 14-15). Although the Admin account has some ability to edit language resources, it does not have the necessary permissions to Generate or Import Language Packs.

Step 2

The Languages screen provides a number of options for new Locales/Languages. If you want to generate a Language Pack for a language that does not show up in the Supported Locales list, then you must first add the language to your portal. (See Chapter 4 for more information about adding additional languages.) Select Upload Language Pack from the Action menu or from the links at the bottom of the screen (see Figure 14-19).

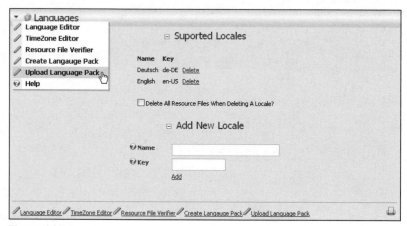

Figure 14-19

Step 3

The File Upload screen appears (see Figure 14-20). Select the file you want to upload and then click the Upload New File link.

Step 4

After the Language Pack has been uploaded, you will be presented with another File Upload screen. This screen displays the complete Resource Upload Logs showing all of the files that have been uploaded (see Figure 14-21). You should review the logs for errors, which will be highlighted in red. Additionally, the log shows you important information about the directory where the generated Language Pack is stored, and the log provides a link to the File Manager so that you can download the Language Pack from the portal server.

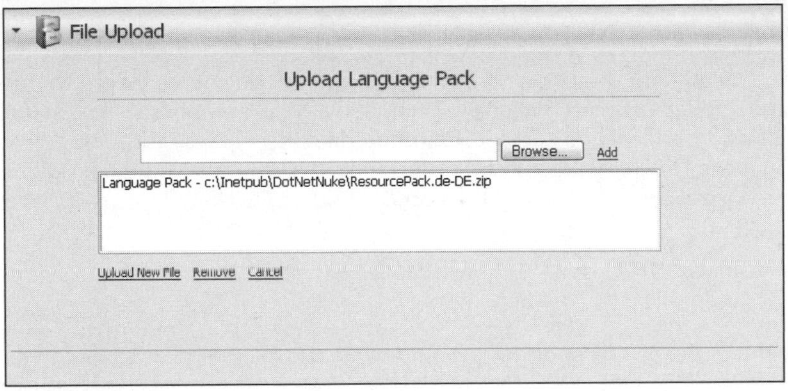

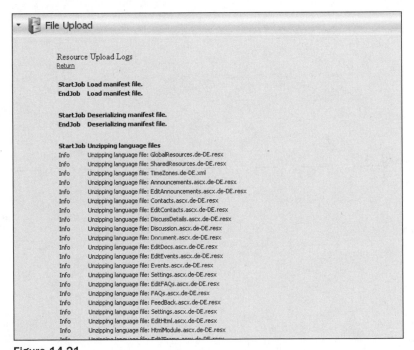

Figure 14-20

Figure 14-21

FTP-Based Installation

To install a new Language Pack using FTP or any file manager, copy the Language Pack into the Install/Language directory of your DotNetNuke installation. When the ResourceInstaller task runs, it will install this Language Pack using the standard skin installation code. If an error occurs it will be noted in the task history, which is available by selecting the History link for the ResourceInstaller task on the Schedule page (shown in Figure 14-7 previously).

Summary

This chapter completes our discussion of DotNetNuke development. We have progressed from administering standard DotNetNuke installations to creating DotNetNuke modules and skins, and finished by documenting the steps needed to package, distribute, and install these add-ons. You are now ready to begin work on using DotNetNuke to build professional web sites that fully take advantage of the power, flexibility, and extensibility provided by the portal.

Resources

The following sections list many helpful resources that bring value to the development or business aspects of using DotNetNuke. A list of great developer tools are shown in Table A-1. Many of these tools are used by the DotNetNuke community and Core Team members. Some of these developer tools are free and others have fees. In Table A-2, several useful custom third-party modules are shown. As of the date of the publication of this book, each of these modules was free.

Table A-1: Developer Tools

Tool	Description
Beyond Compare by Scooter Software `http://www.scootersoftware.com/`	This tool is helpful for comparing files and folders to identify changes in code and to keep directories in synch.
Reflector for .NET by Lutz Roeder `http://www.aisto.com/roeder/dotnet/`	This is a class browser for .NET assemblies. It includes call and called graphs, code viewers for IL, Visual Basic, Delphi, and C#, dependency trees, and more.
Nunit by James W. Newkirk, Michael C. Two, Alexei A. Vorontsov, Philip A. Craig, and Charlie Poole `http://www.nunit.org/`	This is a powerful unit-testing framework for all .NET languages. It is a port of the Unit Java utility.
SQL Compare by Red-Gate `http://www.red-gate.com`	This tool compares the structures of Microsoft SQL Server databases and generates scripts to synchronize the databases objects.

Table continued on following page

Tool	Description
SQL Data Compare by Red-Gate `http://www.red-gate.com`	This tool compares the data in Microsoft SQL Server databases and generates scripts to synchronize the data.
ANTS Profiler by Red-Gate `http://www.red-gate.com`	This is a code and memory profiler for applications writing in any .NET language.
ANTS Load by Red-Gate `http://www.red-gate.com`	This is a tool for load testing web sites and web services.

FileZilla
by Tim Kosse
`http://sourceforge.net/`
`projects/filezilla`
	This is a great open-source FTP client.

CodeSmith
by Eric J. Smith
`http://www.ericjsmith.net/`
`codesmith/`
	This is a powerful freeware template-based code generator. It can generate code for any ASCII-based language including .NET.

CodeSmith Templates for DotNetNuke 3.0 by Vicenç Masanas `http://dnnjungle.vmasanas.net`	This is a great collection of CodeSmith templates that help you create business controllers, business objects, stored procedures, data providers, and SQLDataProvider code very quickly.

FXCop
by Microsoft
`http://www.gotdotnet.com/`
`team/fxcop/`
	This tool analyzes .NET-managed code assemblies to verify that they conform with the Microsoft .NET Framework Design Guidelines.

SnagIt by TechSmith `http://www.techsmith.com/`	This is a great tool for taking screenshots. It can even take screen captures of scrolling windows (like long web pages).
Araxis Merge by Araxis LTD `http://www.araxis.com/`	This is an advanced file comparison and merging tool with integrated folder comparison and synchronization. It allows for two-way or three-way comparisons.
SourceGear Vault by Araxis LTD `http://www.araxis.com/`	Vault is the source control tool used by the Core Team. It is a great source control tool for a distributed development team.
Draco.NET by Chive Software Limited `http://draconet.sourceforge.net/`	This is a Windows service application that facilitates continuous integration. It monitors your source code repository, rebuilds your project, and e-mails the results automatically.

Table A-2: Modules

Module	Description
SQLView by DNN Stuff http://www.dnnstuff.com	This module displays the results from any SQL query in tabular format.
Multi Page Content by BonoSoft http://www.dotnetnuke.dk	This module can show multiple pages of content within a single module. It is helpful for displaying long articles and tutorials in a condensed format.
DnnBB by Bonosoft and Nimo Software http://dnnbb.net/	This is an open-source bulletin board/forum module that is easy to use and easy to install.
SiteMap by Speerio, Inc. http://www.speerio.net	The SiteMap module is ideal for displaying a tree view of your web site. It only displays links to pages the user has access to and also creates a hidden list of hyperlinks for search-engine spiders to crawl.
NewsWire by Speerio, Inc. http://www.speerio.net	This is a complete solution for managing and publishing RSS feed channels. You can publish categorized RSS feed channels that aggregate portal and external content.
PhotoViewer by Speerio, Inc. http://www.speerio.net	This is a photo viewer with a lightbox and integration with photo printing services.
Navigator by Speerio, Inc. http://www.speerio.net	This is a hierarchical HTML content and link organizer for creating categorized documentation and/or link/newsfeed collections.
Das Blog for DNN by Speerio, Inc. http://www.speerio.net	Complete port of the popular Das Blog blogger (http://www.dasblog.net) for DotNetNuke.
PhoneGenie by Inspector IT http://inspectorit.com/iit/	This module allows you to look up names and postal addresses by typing in a phone number to look up.
CSSInclude by DNN Stuff http://www.dnnstuff.com	This module allows you to add a cascading style sheet to a specific tab. This is helpful if you want to override a skin or container's CSS on a specific tab.
Enhanced Feedback by Slalom Services http://www.slalomservices.com	This is a more configurable feedback module that adds some useful features.

Table continued on following page

Module	Description
Private Messages for DotNetNuke 3.0 by Scott McCulloch http://www.smcculloch.net/	This is a messaging module that allows you to send messages to other users of the portal.
Reviews by Vicenç Masanas http://dnnjungle.vmasanas.net	This module can be used to include a list of items on your site and allow users to review them. The item's type can be defined in each module. For any module instance you can define a different set of fields, and configure the properties for posting and approval of reviews and comments.
InfoMap by Vicenç Masanas http://dnnjungle.vmasanas.net	This module can be used to dynamically display information on a picture. It can position user contact lists on a map. InfoMap presents a clickable map with "hot" areas where some information has been entered. Upon clicking in any given area, the list of contacts for this area is displayed.
SimpleDownload by Vicenç Masanas http://dnnjungle.vmasanas.net	This module is like the core Documents module but with a very simple user interface. It just shows a title and an icon for the download. For the rest of the module it's the same as Documents.
TemplatePrint, PagePrint by Vicenç Masanas http://dnnjungle.vmasanas.net	These are skin objects to enhance the printing capabilities of DNN. Let you define skins and containers for the printing.

B

Frequently Asked Questions

The Core Team spends quite a lot of time answering questions in the support forums. Although there is always a wide array of topics in the forums, some questions about DotNetNuke are asked again and again. Each released version of DotNetNuke tends to create a new set of frequently asked questions. The following includes many of the questions that are often asked in the support forums.

Q: What folder permissions are necessary to run DotNetNuke?

A: You need to grant the account that ASP.NET runs as FULL CONTROL over the root folder of DotNetNuke. For further information, see Chapter 2, "Installing DotNetNuke."

Q: Are there any Windows services that tend to interfere with DotNetNuke?

A: The Indexing Service sometimes causes strange errors to surface in ASP.NET. You may see an error that reads something like "Access is denied: SharpZipLib." This is usually fixed by disabling the Indexing Service in the Services management console in Windows.

Q: How can I change the default date format?

A: You can change date format by selecting the locale of the country that matches your date format. For example, if you wanted an Australian date format (DD/MM/YYYY) you would need to select the en-AU language in your portal's site settings.

At the writing of this publication, DotNetNuke currently only has two languages distributed with the core. These are en-US (English-American) and de-DE (Deutsch). So en-AU would not appear in our Site Settings list for selecting a portal's default language.

To create an Australian language, navigate to Host Settings ➪ Languages. In the Add New Locale section type **Australian** for the name, **en-AU** for the key, and click Add. You should see the Australian language appear in the list of defined locales. Because en-AU is an English-based culture, it will use the English locale files, but the Australian date format.

You can now navigate to Admin ➪ Site Settings of the portal and select Advanced ➪ Other Settings, specifying the default language for the portal. You can find a complete list of cultures at http://msdn
.microsoft.com/library/default.asp?url=/library/en-us/cpref/html/frlrfSystem
GlobalizationCultureInfoClassTopic.asp.

Q: What is a portal alias?

A: A portal alias is combination of a domain name and the folder that is entered as the URL to access a portal site. An example of a portal alias is "www.dotnetnuke.com" or even
"www.dotnetnuke.com/myportal." Portal aliases map a URL to a portal site.

Q: What does the error message "Multiple controls with the same ID 'ctr_DD' were found. FindControl requires that controls have unique Ids" mean?

A: This message may be displayed when a portal module's user control (.ascx) file has a syntax error in it. For instance, this error will be displayed when a server-side control doesn't have an end tag.

Q: What does the error message "ERROR: Could not connect to database specified in connectionString for SqlDataProvider" mean?

A: The problem is likely that the connection string has not been set in web.config. Otherwise, the database may not be accessible, possibly due to network connectivity problems or improper database login credentials.

Q: What does the error message "Not associated with a trusted SQL Server connection" mean?

A: If your SQL Server security authentication is set to Windows Only and you try to connect with a SQL Server login, you will see this message. You may see this message if the user specified in the connection string (in web.config) does not have the proper permissions. See Microsoft support article 889615 for more information.

Q: What does the error message "Access to the path "C:\WebSites\DotNetNuke\Portals\0\ portal.css" is denied" mean?

A: This is usually caused by one of two problems. The permissions may not be set correctly on the Portals directory. See Chapter 2 for details. This can also happen when a source control application is open while trying to install DotNetNuke. Try closing the source control application before installing DotNetNuke.

Q: How do I set the default language for all portals?

A: The best way to set the default language for all portals is to make a Site Template and specify the culture in the template. The easiest way is to modify the default template (located at /Portals/_default/ DotNetNuke.Template), or at least create a copy of it and modify the default language tag as follows:

```
<defaultlanguage>en-AU</defaultlanguage>
```

You can now use that template when creating new portals.

Q: Why am I receiving the following error when trying to debug in Visual Studio?
"Error while trying to run project: Unable to start debugging on the web server. The project is not configured to be debugged."

A: This could be caused by one of a few possible issues. First check web.config to make sure you have set "debug" to true in the Compilation node. Also, if you've installed Microsoft's URLScan filter on your machine (or are using win2003 where it is automatically installed), then you will have to edit the urlscan.ini file and add "DEBUG"(case sensitive) into the "[allowverbs]" section. See Microsoft support article 310588 for more details.

URLScan is often installed as part of the larger IIS Lockdown tool. This is an issue with Visual Studio debugging and not a DotNetNuke issue.

C

System Message Tokens

Table C-1: Standard HostSettings Properties

Property Name	Description
ControlPanel	This setting determines whether the new 3.0 Control Panel is displayed or the version 2.0.
Copyright	Display the copyright information in the Page Title. (Y/N)
DemoPeriod	The number of days that a demo portal will be active.
DemoSignup	Allow users to sign up for a demo portal. (Y/N)
DisableUsersOnline	Disable the UsersOnline scheduler tasks. (Y/N)
FileExtensions	List of acceptable file extensions that can be uploaded to the site using any of the file upload mechanisms.
HostCurrency	The default currency used when making payments for Host services.
HostEmail	The e-mail address of the Portal Host.
HostFee	Enter the base fee for site hosting.
HostPortalId	The Id of the default portal.
HostSpace	The amount of file space allowed for an account in megabytes.
HostTitle	The name of the Hosting Account. This name is used throughout the site for identifying the Host.
HostURL	The URL for the Host web site.

Table continued on following page

Property Name	Description
PaymentProcessor	The Payment Processing gateway used for handling payments from client sites.
PerformanceSetting	Determines the optimization level for site performance vs. memory consumption. (1-4)
ProxyPort	The port number of the proxy server.
ProxyServer	The server used for proxying web requests.
SchedulePollingRate	Defines the interval is between scheduled task execution cycles.
SchedulerMode	Setting for determining which method to use for executing scheduled tasks in the Scheduling Provider.
SiteLogBuffer	How many items to hold in the SiteLog before purging the log to disk.
SiteLogHistory	The number of days of activity to keep in the SiteLog.
SiteLogStorage	Identifies storage location for the SiteLog (File or Database).
SkinUpload	Determines whether skins can be uploaded by Portal Administrators.
SMTPAuthentication	The SMTP authentication method: Anonymous, Basic, or NTLM.
SMTPServer	The URL of the SMTP server used for sending e-mail messages.
SMTPUsername	The name of user account used for sending messages.
UseCustomError Messages	Determines whether the portal displays the standard DotNetNuke custom error messages or whether raw ASP.NET errors are shown.
UseFriendlyUrls	Enable or disable the URL rewriter used for implementing FriendlyURLs.
UsersOnlineTime	The length of the user's online buffer in minutes. If a user is inactive for this period of time, they will be marked as offline.

Table C-2: Standard PortalSettings Properties

Property Name	Description
PortalId	The id of the current portal.
PortalName	The name of the current portal. This name is used for branding the portal.
HomeDirectory	The folder name associated with the current portal. The name is a relative path to the portal root directory.
LogoFile	The graphic file used for displaying the Portal Logo.
FooterText	The information displayed in the Copyright skin object.
ExpiryDate	The date that the hosting contract for the portal expires.

Property Name	Description
UserRegistration	Determines whether user registration is required and whether the registration is private (accounts created by the Portal Administrator), public (users can register for their own account and gain immediate access), or verified (users can register their own account but only get access after verification of e-mail address).
BannerAdvertising	Enables or disables use of default banner ads.
Currency	Default currency used for Portal services.
AdministratorId	The ID of the primary Portal Administrator.
Email	E-mail address for the Portal Administrator (this is generally set to a support e-mail address).
HostFee	The monthly charge the portal pays for hosting services.
HostSpace	The maximum amount of disk space allocated to this web site.
AdministratorRoleId	The RoleId of the Administrators role for the portal.
AdministratorRoleName	The RoleName of the Administrators role for the portal.
RegisteredRoleId	The RoleId of the Registered Users role for the portal.
RegisteredRoleName	The RoleName of the Registered Users role for the portal.
Description	Web site description. This information will be included in the meta tags used by search engines.
KeyWords	Specific meta tag keywords.
BackgroundFile	A graphic file used for the portal background.
SiteLogHistory	How many days to keep the SiteLog history for the portal.
AdminTabId	The Page Id of the Admin page (PageId is the DotNetNuke 3 equivalent of TabID). This is the parent page for all Portal Administration pages.
SuperTabId	The Page Id of the Host page. This is the parent page for all Host Administration pages.
SplashTabId	The Page Id to use when no page is specified in the URL.
HomeTabId	The Page Id to use as the portal Home page. If no SplashTabId is designated, the HomeTabId is used.
LoginTabId	The Page Id to use when the user selects the login link. This page should include the Login module.
UserTabId	The Page Id to use when registering users or editing user profiles.
DefaultLanguage	The default locale of the web site. This will determine the language used when anonymous users visit the site.
TimeZoneOffset	The time zone where the web server is located.
Version	The build number for the current portal application.

Table C-3: Standard UserInfo Properties

Property Name	Description
UserID	Unique identifier for a specific portal user.
Username	The logon name of the specific user.
FirstName	The user's first name.
LastName	The user's last name.
FullName	First name and last name with a single space between.
PortalID	The PortalID to which this user belongs.
IsSuperUser	Does the user have "Host" permissions?
AffiliateID	The unique AffiliateID identifying the link used to navigate to the portal. When a user follows an affiliate link and then registers on the portal, the AffiliateID is then associated with the user.

Table C-4: Standard UserMembership Properties

Property Name	Description
Password	The user's password if available.
Email	E-mail address of the user.
Username	The login name of the user.
LastLoginDate	The last date/time the user logged in to the portal.
CreatedDate	The date/time when the user account was created.
Approved	If the user's account has been approved for access to the web site.
LockedOut	If the user's account has been locked due to potential security issues.

Table C-5: Standard UserProfile Properties

Property Name	Description
FirstName	User's first name.
LastName	User's last name.
Street	Street address.
City	City.

Property Name	Description
Region	State, Province, or Region for the user. Primarily used for U.S. and Canada.
PostalCode	The postal code for the user's mailing address.
Country	The country where the user lives.
Unit	The apartment, post office box, or suite for the user's address.
Telephone	Telephone number for the user.
Cell	Mobile phone number.
Fax	Fax number.
Website	A personal or corporate web site for the user.
IM	Instant messenger contact ID.
TimeZone	The user's default time zone. This is used for translating times from the SiteLog.
PreferredLocale	The user's preferred locale. This determines the language used for all static content on the portal.

Index